LORD BYRON'S
JACKAL

LORD BYRON'S JACKAL

THE LIFE OF

Edward John Trelawny

DAVID CRANE

HarperCollins*Publishers*

HarperCollins*Publishers*
77‑85 Fulham Palace Road,
Hammersmith, London W6 8JB

Published by HarperCollins 1998
Copyright © David Crane 1998

David Crane asserts the moral right to be identified as the
author of this work.

1 3 5 7 9 8 6 4 2

ISBN 000 255631 6

Set in PostScript Monotype Bulmer by
Rowland Phototypesetting Ltd, Bury St Edmunds, Suffolk

Printed and bound in Great Britain by
Caledonian International Book Manufacturing Ltd, Glasgow

CONTENTS

v

LIST OF ILLUSTRATIONS

Illustration acknowledgments

Lord Abinger: 24
Brown University Library: 21
National Portrait Gallery, London: 1, 2, 4, 19, 25, 26, 27, 28
V&A Picture Library: 29
© Tate Gallery: 32

LIST OF MAPS

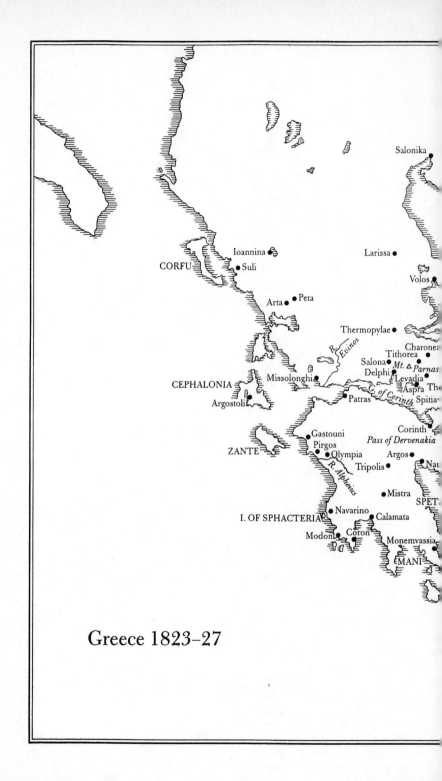

Greece 1823–27

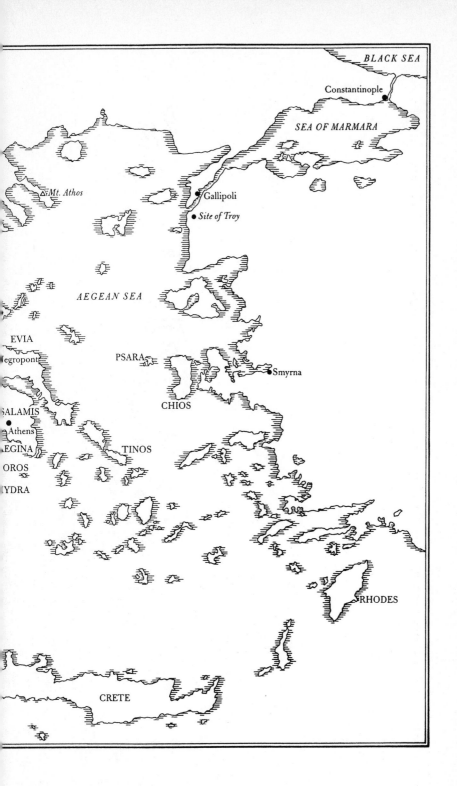

BLACK SEA

Constantinople

SEA OF MARMARA

Mt. Athos

Gallipoli

Site of Troy

AEGEAN SEA

EVIA

egropont

PSARA

Smyrna

CHIOS

SALAMIS

Athens

EGINA

TINOS

OROS

YDRA

RHODES

CRETE

ACKNOWLEDGEMENTS

'Ay, the snake has fascinated you', Byron once warned Trelawny against the influence of the Shelleys. 'I am for making a man of the world of you; they will mould you into a Frankenstein monster.' If ever a man was the product of the imagination it was indeed Edward John Trelawny, so it perhaps requires no apology that the Trelawny I have produced here is in many ways as much a 'monster' as his original, a composite figure stitched together out of all the other and often conflicting Trelawnys that he himself, and a century and more of biographical tradition, have helped create.

A literary biography is inevitably an historical collaboration, a process of synthesis, and it is a pleasure to acknowledge just how much this book owes to the research and judgements of previous authors who have written about Trelawny. In the century after his death there were four full-length biographies of him and numerous memoirs, but anyone writing on Trelawny today will inevitably owe a particular debt to the work of William St Clair, whose pioneering biography is as indispensable reading now as it was when it came out twenty years ago.

I would like to thank Sir John Trelawny for permission to use Joseph Severn's portrait and Lord Abinger for permission to quote from the Abinger Papers. Many people have patiently helped with enquiries, answered letters, suggested and followed up possible leads, or allowed me into houses in which Trelawny once lived and I am very grateful to them all. I would also like to thank Dr Barker-Benfield, the staff of the Bodleian Library, the staff at the British School at Athens for their unfailing kindness over several visits, the staffs of the National Library, Athens, the Gennadios Library, the National Portrait Gallery, the National Army Museum, the Public Record Office, the London Metropolitan Archives, the London Library, the Cornwall Record Office, the West Sussex Record Office, the House of Lords Records Office, the Lambeth Palace Library, and the Beineke Library, Yale. I would also especially like to thank Maria Vakalopoulou for her heroic assistance among the State Archives in Athens. My thanks, too, to Chryssa Alvanou for her help in translating and deciphering some stubbornly difficult documents, to John Ferguson for the photographs of Trelawny's and Shelley's graves, to Alison Munro at the Scots Ancestry Research Society and to the late Mrs Susan Mavrocordato. I am also very grateful to Arabella Pike at HarperCollins.

I would gratefully like to acknowledge the support of the Authors' Foundation, administered by the Society of Authors, whose generous grant made much of the research for this book possible.

Above all, I should like to thank those friends and family who have been force-fed on Trelawny over the last three years, who have read and improved earlier drafts of this book, who have walked over mountains, climbed up into caves and explored cliff-edges that I was reluctant to risk myself. In particular I should like to thank Alan Judd, without whose friendship, enthusiasm and bullying this biography would never have been started let alone finished. One of the happiest memories of working on this book is that of the days spent exploring Trelawny's Parnassus with him and Richard Holmes, for whose criticism and company I am equally grateful. I also enjoyed a memorable time in Greece with my mother and father but I trust they already know that. Adequate thanks to Honor would be impossible and out of place. It is in every way as much her book as it is mine.

NAUPLIA

'What a queer set! What an assemblage of romantic, adventurous, restless, crack-brained young men from the four corners of the world. How much courage and talent is to be found among them; but how much more of pompous vanity, of weak intellect, of mean selfishness, of utter depravity ... Little have Philhellenes done towards raising the reputation of Europeans here!'

Samuel Gridley Howe[1]

ON 6 FEBRUARY 1833 a seventeen-year-old Bavarian prince entered the town of Nauplia as the first king of Modern Greece. Out in the Gulf of Argos the ships of the sponsoring powers rode at anchor in the bright spring sunshine. French, Russian and British bands serenaded each other across the water in an improbable display of amity, while from the batteries on shore salute after salute rolled across the bay in tribute to Christendom's youngest nation.

To the pragmatist and romantic alike there can have been no more fitting place for Otho to begin his reign than here on the Argolic Gulf under the watchful gaze of Europe's navies and Greece's Homeric past. Nothing, it seemed, had been left to chance to guarantee his future. The civilized world had given its blessing and its money. A loan had been provided to buttress his new country through her first years, an indemnity paid to her old Ottoman masters to rescue her from her troubled past.

1

Inside the town Bavarian and French troops stood ready to enforce Europe's choice on a population only too accustomed to dissent, but for the moment the precautions were unnecessary. Mountain Suliotes and island merchants, sailors and Moreot bandits, Peloponnesian peasants and Phanariot politicians waited to greet the young king as their saviour from years of war and chaos. As Otho rode on his white horse through the cheering crowds into the reconquered Turkish town, the peculiar spell of Greece, its unique hold on the nineteenth century as the cradle of Western culture and the champion of Christianity, took on a palpable form that seemed in itself a guarantee of the new order.

For a dozen years this small town on the eastern coast of the Peloponnese, some forty miles south of Corinth, had exercised the same charm over the imaginations of Europe and America. From that moment in 1821 when Bishop Germanos had raised the standard of revolt and called on Greece to throw off four centuries of Ottoman rule Nauplia had been as familiar as any city in Europe. Its news was carried in newspapers from Vienna to Boston, its victories celebrated and its defeats mourned, its dead turned into martyrs, its leaders into the heirs of Demosthenes and Leonidas on a wave of popular enthusiasm which sent money and men to fight for a cause that seemed as much Christendom's as Greece's. 'No other subject has ever excited such a powerful sensation,' one enthusiast could write long after the first flush of excitement had faded,

> The very peasants throughout Switzerland and Germany inquire with anxiety, when their affairs call them to market, what are the last news . . . In France subscriptions have been opened, and money solicited throughout every town, on behalf of a Christian Nation doomed to perish by the sword or by famine. The Duchesses of Albey, Broglio, and De Caze; every Frenchwoman distinguished by rank, riches, talent, or virtue, have divided the different quarters of Paris among them, and traverse on foot every street, and enter into every house, demanding the charity of their inhabitants for a nation of martyrs.[2]

Almost every foreign volunteer swept along by this enthusiasm had passed through the town of Nauplia, many of them to stay for ever, victims of the squalor, disease and factional greed which lay behind the ceremonial glamour of Otho's welcome. Italians, Swiss, Swedes, Scots, Irish and Poles had all come here, national rivalries if not forgotten at least subsumed into a common cause, Germans and French who had fought on opposite sides in the Napoleonic Wars, Americans and English enemies at New Orleans united under the name of 'Philhellene' – friend of Modern Greece, a Greece which Nauplia promised was the true heir to the land of Homer and Thucydides.

The ceremonial entry of Otho was the last great charade in Nauplia's history, the last time that the town would work its illusions on a Europe determined to believe. That place is gone, the walls of its lower town pulled down, the surrounding marshes which once earned its pestilential reputation as the Batavia of Greece drained. Within a year of coming ashore from a British frigate, Otho had moved his capital to Athens and the port that the Venetians had called Napoli di Romania had begun its slow decline into the quaint irrelevance of modern Nauplia.

If you wander now among its steep, narrow streets, or along the waterfront with its view across to the jewel-like island fortress where nineteenth-century Nauplia, with its instinctive dislike for reality, housed its public executioner, there can seem nowhere in Greece that retains so much of its architecture and so little of its history. There is an elegance about even its fortifications that belies their past, that touch of unreality which is Venice's supreme gift to her former possessions. Towards evening, especially, as the sun sinks behind the central mass of the Peloponnese, and the lines of Lassalle's Palamidi citadel almost dissolve into the rock face, it is difficult to believe anything ever disturbed the town's peace. Down in the harbour, near an obelisk commemorating French soldiers, a Hotel Grand Bretagne throws off a confused echo of the excitement of 1824 when a ship carrying English gold made Nauplia a sink for every patriot, idealist, charlatan and scrounger in Greece. In the centre of the old town, where the starving Turkish population once held out for a whole year, their mosque has been turned with an insolence too complete to be accident into a cinema. A little higher up the slope, a bullet mark still pocks the wall where Greece's first president was assassinated. And in that bullet hole, carefully preserved behind glass, we have the quintessential Nauplia–history in aspic, sanitised and mythologized, history reduced to civic statuary and street names, the narrow alleys once notorious for their filth sunk now beneath nothing more oppressive than bougainvillaea, the extravagance, rivalries and violence of its brief years of fame no more intrusive than the wrecks of warships that lie submerged beneath the waters of the gulf.

On a July day in 1841 a group of foreigners gathered in the town's Roman Catholic Church to add their own lie to the great historical deception that modern Nauplia enshrines. The Church of the Metamorphosis is a small domed building, perched alongside the Hotel Byron on a terrace beneath the walls of the upper town, looking out westwards across the bay towards the ruins of Argos and the Frankish citadel of Larissa. At its south east corner the foundations of an old minaret are visible, and inside the sense of space and air still feels closer to the mosque it once was than any Greek church. Above its altar, a copy of a Raphael Holy Family, the gift of Louis Philippe to King Otho, intrudes a fleshily different but no less alien note. Opposite it, framing the door in a sad parody of a triumphal arch, stands the monument that had brought the congregation to the church that day. It was the work of a Frenchman called Thouret, a 'Lt. Colonel' and a 'Chevalier de Plusieurs Ordres' he has signed himself with a gallic swagger. 'A La Memoire Des Philhellènes', it reads across the top, 'Morts pour L'independance, La Grèce, Le Roi, et Leurs Compagnons D'Armes Reconnaissants.' Down the length of its four pillars, inscribed in white on black wood, riddled with mis-spellings, are the names of almost three hundred foreign dead who in the decade before Otho's arrival had come out to fight for Greek independence.

There can be few more forlorn memorials. Sometimes along the Dutch border one comes across a German cemetery from the last war buried deep in a wood, but even those graves with their air of furtive and collective guilt scarcely catch the sad futility that clings

4

to Thouret's monument. There is something about its shabby theatricality that nothing else quite matches, a sense of defeated grandeur and deluded optimism which inadvertently captures the fate of the men it commemorates. 'Hellenes,' it says, 'we were and are with you.' It is not true and it never was. Who, inside or outside Greece, has heard of a single Philhellene other than Byron? How many memorials are there raised by the Greeks themselves in their memory? How, if Greece had deliberately set out to disown their memory, could it have done better than here in Nauplia? – in a town synonymous with Philhellene disillusion, in a converted Turkish mosque given by a German King to the Roman Catholic Church? Could there be any more eloquent or insouciant tribute to the insignificance of these lives than to obliterate their identity in the crude errors and chaotic lettering of their only monument?*

Beneath its hollow rhetoric, however, is that common denominator which links its names with those on the monuments of villages, schools, hospitals or railway stations from the Falklands to Burma, from South Africa to Sevastopol. There is always a sharp poignancy in the way these memorials bring the familiar and strange into such permanent proximity, that lives begun on Welsh farms can end in the mission compound at Rorke's Drift, and nowhere is that more vividly felt than here. Who in 1821 had heard of Missolonghi, Peta, or any of the other battle honours that punctuate the lists of Philhellene dead? What was it that brought William Washington here from America, to die on a British flagship in the harbour at Nauplia, killed by a Greek bullet? Or the nineteen-year-old Heise from Hanover to Peta – only to be beheaded on the field if he was lucky, and if not, forced to carry his comrades' heads back to Arta before being impaled on the grey castellated walls of its Frankish citadel?

'We are all Greeks,'[3] Shelley proclaimed in 1821 with the largesse of a man firmly lodged in Italy, and yet if Washington and Heise might well have made the same claim it is less clear what they would have meant. There are certainly men here who would have echoed the language of Shelley's 'Hellas', homeless refugees from monarchical despotism who would have died to keep the seventeen-year-old scion of the house of Wittelsbach or any other royal line out of

5

Greece. There were men again for whom the war was a crusade, fought with all the polemical and emotional bitterness of religious war. 'I wholly wish,' one volunteer wrote, 'to annihilate, extirpate and destroy those swarms and hordes of people called Turk.'[4] Others fought because they had always fought and knew nothing else. There were young Byronists absorbed in some designer war of their own invention, charlatans attracted by the hope of profit, classicists infatuated with Greece's past, Benthamite reformers, ageing Bonapartists – and then all those there for a dozen different motives, who might just once have known why they came but had long forgotten by the time they died.

'For the most part the scum of their country,' the English volunteer Frank Abney Hastings harshly wrote of them, 'perhaps no crime can be named that might not have been found among the corps called Philhellenes.'[5] This was a verdict, too, which Greek indifference would seem to have endorsed but one need only point to Hastings himself to qualify that judgement.* Or to Number 18 among the Missolonghi dead on the monument, General Normann – the same Normann who had found himself on different sides during the Napoleonic wars, fighting first against, then for, and finally against the French as his native Württemberg changed allegiance. He was in Greece as much to restore his tattered credit in his own eyes as in those of the world. Wounded at Peta, the man who had fought with the Austrians at Austerlitz and with the Grand Army on the retreat from Moscow, died grief-stricken at Missolonghi, finally broken by the last and bitterest disaster of his life.

There are twenty-five dead listed on this monument under Missolonghi; thirty-five under Nauplia; a single name, a man called Coffy, under Mitika; three under Parnassus and so on. In the first and last stages of the war some of these fought and died alongside their comrades, but for most of them these were lonely deaths in a struggle that had no shape and almost no battles, a conflict that wasted lives with a casual and purposeless savagery. There are no decorations after men's names on this monument, no MM's, no Croix de Guerre to suggest their courage or folly was ever recognized; no battalion names – no East Kents, no Artists' Rifles, no Manchester Regiments

– to promise any sense of comradeship. Some of them died of their wounds, some died mad, killed themselves or wasted from diseases. Some were killed by the Turks, others by the Greeks they had come to defend. Lord Charles Murray, a son of the Duke of Atholl, rich, generous and unbalanced, died in Gastoumi with a single dollar in his pocket. The eighteen year old Paul-Marie Bonaparte ran away from the university of Bologna only to shoot himself while cleaning his gun before he had so much as seen action. His corpse was kept for five years in a keg of rum in a Spetses monastery before being laid to rest on the island of Sphacteria.*

One of the more surprising ironies of history that this monument brings out is that if there was a single country that was relatively untouched by the excitement which swept Europe in 1821 it was Greece's friend of popular mythology, Britain. It is true that in Thomas Gordon and Frank Abney Hastings Britain sent two of the wealthiest and most influential of the early Philhellenes, and yet in spite of all the committees formed and the pamphlets written, for a whole gamut of reasons that range from party politics to an oddly modern-looking compassion fatigue, no more than a dozen Britons actually made the journey out to Greece to fight during the first two years of the war.†

In the July of 1823, however, an ill-assorted menagerie of animals and men sailed from Genoa in an ugly, round-bottomed 'tub' on a voyage that would change this for good and hijack for Britain a place in Philhellene history it has never lost.

On board was the greatest of all Philhellenes, Lord Byron, and at his side a figure who embodies more vividly than anyone else the impact for good and ill that Byron had on the generation of Romantics who went to fight for Greek independence. With the exception of Byron he is probably the only English volunteer of whom anyone has heard, and yet for all that he said and wrote of himself in a lifetime of ruthless self-promotion there is scarcely a fact from his birth onwards that biography has not had to prise free of the lies with which he covered his tracks. He called himself one thing when the parish register gives another, claimed the friendship of Keats when he never met him; railed at his poverty with a private income, and boasted of an exotic past as a pirate when he was no more than a failed midshipman with the diluted romance of his family name, a squalid divorce and a musket ball in a knee to show for his first thirty years.

'But tell me, who is this odd fish?' Keats's friend Joseph Severn demanded when he first met him in 1822 and it is a question biographers have been trying to answer ever since.[6] To modern scholarship he is one of the great obstacles to historical truth, a compulsive braggart and liar. To the late Victorians he was the last apostolic link with its Romantic past, the intimate of Byron and Shelley through whom the 'mighty dead' spoke to a smaller and meaner age.[7] To his contemporaries though – more vivid, more imaginatively 'true' than either the Grand Old Man of Millais' portrait or the fraud of modern research – he was the man Severn himself dubbed 'Lord Byron's Jackal';[8] the man known to his friends with an impartiality which perhaps suggests why his name is not among the Philhellene dead, as 'Greek' or 'Turk' Trelawny.

1

THE WOLF CUB

My birth was unpropitious. I came into the world, branded
and denounced as a vagrant; for I was a younger son of a
family, so proud of their antiquity, that even gout and mort-
gaged estates were traced, many generations back, on the genea-
logical tree, as ancient heirlooms of aristocratic origin, and
therefore reverenced. In such a house a younger son was like
the cub of a felon wolf in good King Edgar's days, when a
price was set upon his head.

Trelawny's Adventures of a Younger Son[1]

ONE OF the most depressing assumptions of modern biography is
the belief that the truth of men's or women's lives always lies in the
trivia of their existence. There is often a devotion to the minutiae
of a subject's life that no biographer would dream of expending on
his own, a kind of displaced egotism which produces the biographical equivalent of 'Parnassian' poetry or possession football, an intri-
cate and over burdened account which bears as much relation to
the proper business of biography as chronicle does to history.

The most part of most lives is no more interesting than that of
a cat and as both subject and practitioner of biography no one better
illustrates this fact than Edward John Trelawny. At some stage in
an obscure and embittered youth he seems to have taken stock of
his early years, found them wanting in every detail and invented for
himself a wilder and more glamorous history of rebellion and adventure which he then successfully maintained in conversation and print
for another sixty years.

Of all the silences open to a human being on the subject of himself, Trelawny's is that of a man who knows how little of interest there is to say, and there is an important lesson to be learned from his deception. There are certainly writers like Shelley or Dickens whose creative life is intimately connected with the rhythms and textures of everyday existence, but the 'Trelawny' who still matters, the 'Trelawny' Byron and Shelley could both call friend, is the 'Trelawny' of myth and not dull reality, the romantic hero who sprang fully formed from out of his own fantasies and not the failed midshipman modern scholarship has put in its place.

Edward John Trelawny was born on 13 November 1792, that rich and varied year in the history of English Romanticism, the year which saw the birth not just of two of its greatest leaders in Shelley and John Keble but of its hidden and unsuspected nemesis in the infant shape of the future 'Princess of the Parallelograms' and wife to Lord Byron, Anne Isabella Milbanke. Through both his parents Trelawny was descended from some of the most colourful figures in English and West Country history, and at the end of the eighteenth century the senior branches of his mother's and father's families were still wealthy and important landowners in their native Cornwall. In later years Trelawny usually claimed to have been born in Cornwall himself, but whatever he inherited in terms of character from West Country forebears who fought at Agincourt and against the Armada, the less romantic setting for his own birth was almost certainly his grandfather's house in Soho Square from where, on 29 November, he was baptized John in the parish church of St Mary Le Bone.

The little we know of his early life comes from a work of fiction that the forty-year old Trelawny foisted on a credulous world as 'autobiography' under the title of *Adventures of a Younger Son*. There is no more than a tiny fraction of it that careful examination has left intact as reliable history, but if among all the fantasies with which he embroidered his life there is one subject on which he can be trusted it is that of his parents, as unlovely a couple from all existing evidence as even their son portrayed. His father was a Charles Trelawny, a younger son himself and an impoverished lieutenant-colonel in the Coldstream Guards; his mother was Mary Hawkins, a sister of Sir Christopher Hawkins Bt., of Trewithen, 'a dark masculine woman of three and twenty' with nothing to recommend her but an inheritance.[2] They met at a ball. He was the handsomest man in the room, she apparently the richest catch. In the eyes of the impoverished twenty-nine-year-old officer, wrote their son with that dry economy which characterizes his best prose, 'Rich and beautiful soon became synonymous'.

> He received marked encouragement from the heiress. He saw those he had envied, envying him. Gold was his God, for he had daily experienced those mortifications to which the want of it subjected him; he determined to offer up his heart to the temple of Fortune alone, and waited but an opportunity of displaying his apostacy to love. The struggle with his better feelings was of short duration. He called his conduct prudence and filial obedience – and those are virtues – thus concealing its naked atrocity by a seemly covering. . . . But why dwell on an occurrence so common in the world, the casting away of virtue and beauty for riches, though the devil gives them? He married; found the lady's fortune a great deal less, and the lady a great deal worse than he had anticipated: went to town irritated and disappointed, with the consciousness of having merited his fate; sunk part of his fortune in idle parade to satisfy his wife; and his affairs being embarrassed by the lady's extravagance, he was, at length, compelled to sell out of the army, and retire to economise in the country.[3]

In the history and literature of a century famous for its battles of the generations, it is doubtful whether even Shelley or Samuel Butler pursued their fathers' memory with the same dogged and public hatred that Trelawny showed for his. There is a notorious tale he tells in *Adventures* of what he calls his first childhood 'duel',[4] a mythic battle to the death with his father's pet raven which in its capacity for violence and surrogate vengeance is the archetype of all the real and imagined struggles of his life ahead, of those fights

11

with maddened stallions or the savage encounters with figures in authority who seemed to his adult mind the reincarnations of early tyranny.

> One day I had a little girl for my companion, whom I had enticed from the nursery to go with me to get some fruit clandestinely. We slunk out, and entered the garden unobserved. Just as we were congratulating ourselves under a cherry-tree, up comes the accursed monster of a raven. It was no longer to be endured. He seized hold of the little girl's frock; she was too frightened to scream; I did not hesitate an instant. I told her not to be afraid, and threw myself upon him. He let her go, and attacked me with bill and talon. I got hold of him by the neck, and heavily lifting him up, struck his body against the tree and the ground . . .
>
> His look was now most terrifying: one eye was hanging out of his head, the blood coming from his mouth, his wings flapping the earth in disorder, and with a ragged tail, which I had half plucked by pulling at him during his first execution. He made a horrid struggle for existence, and I was bleeding all over. Now, with the aid of my brother, and as the raven was exhausted by exertion and wounds, we succeeded in gibbeting him again; and then with sticks we cudgelled him to death, beating his head to pieces. After-wards we tied a stone to him, and sunk him in the duck-pond.[5]

Trelawny was five at the time of this incident, but there is no record of where it might have taken place. Judging from *Adventures* and the baptismal records of the successive children born to his increasingly gloomy parents, the Trelawny family lived a peripatetic life during his early years, moving between rented houses in the country, his maternal uncle John Hawkins's seat at Bignor in Sussex and the family house of his grandfather, General Trelawny, at 9 Soho Square. When Trelawny was six his father had taken on the name of Brereton and with it a large fortune. Yet even with this new wealth there seems to have been no thought of an education for Trelawny and he grew up by his own account an intractable and surly boy, unloved and unloving, as large, bony and awkward as his mother and as violent in his moods as his father.

It was one of his father's outbursts of temper that led, when he was about nine or ten, to his being literally frog-marched with his older brother Henry, to a private establishment in Bristol for his first experience of school. It was a bleakly forbidding building, enclosed within high walls and, to a child's eyes, more like a prison. 'He is savage, incorrigible! Sir, he will come to the gallows, if you do not scourge the devil out of him,'[6] was his father's parting injunction to the headmaster. The Reverend Samuel Seyer, incongruously small, dapper and powdered for a man who was a savage disciplinarian even by the standards of the day, eagerly embraced the advice. As a pupil of his, Trelawny later recalled with a nice discrimination, he was caned most hours and flogged most days. It was when he finally turned on his attackers, half-strangling the under master and assaulting Seyer himself, that he was sent home, as ignorant as the day he arrived two years earlier. 'Come, Sir, what have you learnt,' his father demanded of him.

'Learnt!' I ejaculated, speaking in a hesitant voice, for my mind misgave me as to what was to follow.

'Is that the way to address me? Speak out, you dunce! and say, Sir! Do you take me for a foot-boy?' raising his voice to a roar, which utterly drove out of my head what little the school-master had, with incredible toil and punishment, driven into it. 'What have you learnt, you ragamuffin? What do you know?'

'Not much, Sir!'

'What do you know in Latin?'

'Latin, Sir? I don't know Latin, Sir!'

'Not Latin, you idiot! Why, I thought they taught nothing but Latin.'

'Yes, Sir; – cyphering.'

'Well, how far did you proceed in arithmetic?'

'No, Sir! – they taught me cyphering and writing.'

My father looked grave. 'Can you work the rule of three, you dunce?'

'Rule of three, Sir?'

'Do you know subtraction? Come, you blockhead, answer me! Can you tell me, if five are taken from fifteen, how many remain?'

'Five and fifteen, Sir, are – 'counting on my fingers, but missing my thumb, 'are – are – nineteen, Sir!'

'What! you incorrigible fool! – Can you repeat your multiplication table?'

'What table, Sir?'

Then turning to my mother, he said: 'Your son is a downright idiot, Madam, – perhaps knows not his own name. Write your name, you dolt!'

'Write, Sir? I can't write with that pen, Sir; it is not my pen.'

'Then spell your name, you ignorant savage!'

'Spell, Sir?' I was so confounded that I misplaced the vowels. He arose in wrath, overturned the table, and bruised his shins in attempting to kick me, as I dodged him, and rushed out of the room.[7]

As the poet James Michie once remarked, the fact that a man lies most of the time does not mean he lies all of the time, but with Trelawny it is as well to be sceptical. There is no way of knowing whether this exchange, any more than the duel with the raven, actually occurred, and yet what is perhaps more important is that even as a history of Trelawny's inner life *Adventures* needs to be treated with a caution that has not always been shown.

There is an obvious sense in which this same wariness has to be extended to all autobiographies, consciously or unconsciously shaping and selecting material as they inevitably do, but with Trelawny the timing of his *Adventures* makes it of particular relevance. There seems no doubt that the miseries he describes in its pages were real enough, and yet by the time that he came to put them in written form in 1831, the friendships of Byron and Shelley had armed him with a self-dramatizing language of alienation and revolt that enabled him to invest his infant battles with a stature and significance which seem curiously remote from the prosaic reality of childhood unhappiness.

For all that, though, it is clear that the young Trelawny felt and resented these indignities with an unusual intensity. There was an innate physical and mental toughness about him which equipped him for survival in even the most alien of worlds, and yet beneath a hardening carapace of indifference that sense of injustice and emotional betrayal which would fuel his whole life was festering dangerously. On his first night at school, as he lay on a beggarly pallet of a bed, the rush-lights extinguished, he had listened to the snores of his fellow pupils and stifled the sobs that would have betrayed his misery. The child who two years later escaped Seyer's joyless and savage regime would allow no such weakness in his makeup, no vulnerability. Deprived of affection, he had learned the power of brute strength and domination, the virtue of self-reliance. He had become, he says in his richest Romantic strain, 'callous', 'sullen', 'vindictive', 'insensible' and 'indifferent to shame and fear'.[8] 'The spirit in me was gathering strength,' he proudly recalled, 'in despite of every endeavour to destroy it, like a young pine flourishing in the cleft of a bed of granite.'[9]

For a younger son of Trelawny's class and educational inadequacy the options in life were strictly limited, but one of the more intriguing schemes for his future after this failure at school was Oxford and a career in the church. With a boy of thirteen who was still plainly gallows-bound, however, the navy offered a more traditional solution, and soon after leaving Seyer's academy he was taken by his father down to Portsmouth and placed as a gentleman volunteer on the *Superb* under the command of a Captain Keates.

The treatment a volunteer of Trelawny's age could expect in the Royal Navy during the time of the Napoleonic Wars would have varied with the personality of the ship's captain, but even under the

15

most enlightened and humane regime the life in the midshipman's cockpit of a man-of-war was harsh and brutalizing. In the light of his fixed hatred of the service in later life, however, it is interesting that Trelawny's first feelings for his new profession were ones of delight, and he soon had an unforgettable glimpse of the excitement and prize-money which made the wartime navy such a dangerous but attractive option to indigent younger sons. After a few days at sea, his ship crossed with the *Pickle* on its way back from Trafalgar, bringing to the stunned crew of the *Superb* the news of Nelson's victory and death. The next morning they fell in with a part of the triumphant fleet, and Trelawny was transferred first to the *Temeraire* and then across to the stricken *Colossus* for its journey back to Portsmouth.

> We had had a rough passage, being five or six sail of the line in company, some totally, and others partially dismasted. Our ship, having been not only dismasted, but razed by the enemy's shots (that is, the upper deck almost cut away), our passage home was boisterous. The gallant ship, whose lofty canvases, a few days before, had fluttered almost amidst the clouds, as she bore down on the combined fleets ... was crippled, jury-mast, and shattered, a wreck labouring in the trough of the sea, and driven about at the mercy of the wild waves and wind. With infinite toil and peril, amidst the shouts and reverberated hurrahs from successive ships, we passed on, towed into safe moorings at Spithead.
>
> What a scene of joy then took place. From the ship to the shore one might have walked on a bridge of boats, struggling to get alongside. Some, breathless with anxiety, eagerly demanded the fate of brothers, sons, or fathers, which was followed by joyous clasping and wringing of hands, and some returned to the shore, pale, haggard, and heart-stricken. Then came the extortionary Jew, chuckling with ecstacy at the usury he was about to realise from anticipated prize-money, proffering his gold with a niggard's hand, and demanding monstrous security and interest for his monies.

Huge bomboats, filled with fresh provisions, and a circle of boats hung around us, crammed with sailors' wives, children, doxies, thick as locusts. These last poured in so fast, that of the eight thousand said to belong at that period to Portsmouth and Gosport, I hardly think they could have left eight on shore. In a short period they seemed to have achieved what the combined enemies' fleets had vauntingly threatened – to have taken entire possession of the Trafalgar squadron. I remember, the following day, while the ship was dismantling, these scarlet sinners hove out the first thirty-two pound guns; I think there were not less than three or four hundred of them heaving at the capstan.[10]

This passage is memorable enough for that exuberance and energy that made him one of the finest storytellers of the century, yet its real interest lies in the light it throws on an event which must in some way have shaped Trelawny's whole personality and sense of self. Here was an occasion where Trelawny was in a sense there but not really a part, a figure hovering somewhere between participant and spectator at one of the great events of history, an innocently fraudulent beneficiary of the acclaim and excitement which greeted the shattered but victorious *Colossus* on its return to England.

For the rest of his days Trelawny would bitterly regret that he had missed the greatest battle ever fought under sail and the hurrahs of the ships' crews anchored at Spithead lodged deep in his soul. Throughout the whole of his life the instinctive movement of Trelawny's memory would always take him to the centre of great events, cavalierly annexing whole scenes and achievements as if they had been his own, and it was possibly here at Portsmouth, as a romantic and impressionable thirteen-year-old blending invisibly with the men who had won Trafalgar, that he had his first heady taste of that surrogate fame that would be the life blood of his adult existence.

If that is the case, his next years in the navy, from 1806 to 1812, must have been ones of bitter disappointment. By the time that

Trelawny emerged from obscurity onto a public stage he had sunk their memory beneath the piratical fantasies that fill *Adventures*, but in the muster books and logs of Admiralty records his life as a volunteer and then midshipman stretches out from ship to ship in a sobering and unbroken line which leaves no room for romance, ambiguity or fulfilment.*

There is no historical document at once so dry and compelling as a ship's log, nothing that better evokes the routine, discipline and anonymity Trelawny came to hate, but there was another reason, too, for his growing resentment that no mere record could show. 'Who can paint in words what I felt?' he asked of his readers later,

> Imagine me torn from my native country, destined to cross the wide ocean, to a wild region, cut off from every tie, or possibility of communication, transported like a felon as it were, for life, for, at that period, few ships returned under seven or more years. I was torn away, not seeing my mother, or brother, or sisters, or one familiar face; no voice to speak a word of comfort, or to inspire me with the smallest hope that any thing human took an interest in me . . . From that period, my affections, imperceptibly, were alienated from my family and kindred, and sought the love of strangers in the wide world . . .
>
> I could no longer conceal from myself the painful conviction that I was an utter outcast; that my parent had thrust me from his threshold, in the hope that I should not again cross it. My mother's intercessions (if indeed she made any) were unavailing: I was left to shift for myself. The only indication of my father's considering he had still a duty to perform towards me, was in an annual allowance, to which either his conscience or his pride impelled him. Perhaps, having done this, he said, with other good and prudent men, – 'I have provided for my son. If he distinguishes himself, and returns, as a man, high in rank and honour, I can say, – he is my son, and I made him what he is! His daring and fearless character may succeed in the navy.' He left me to

my fate, with as little remorse as he would have ordered a litter of blind puppies to be drowned.[11]

All the evidence suggests, in fact, that his father exerted whatever influence he had in his son's favour. Trelawny's career, however, was proof against help. The account he gave of this time in his *Adventures* is clearly heightened for effect, but his tales of brawls and endless hours of punishment at the masthead are endorsed by his long list of ships as one captain after another rid himself of a recalcitrant midshipman.

From the *Colossus* to the *Puissant*, from the *Puissant* to the *Woolwich* and on to the *Resistance*, the *Royal William*, the *Cornelia* and the *Hecate*; the list stretches out, each change marking another step in Trelawny's disillusionment, another loosening of ties, a fresh confirmation as the surly boy grew into embittered manhood that there was nowhere he belonged.

After his sudden and dramatic baptism of 1805, there was also little action to alleviate the boredom of naval life. In the period immediately after Trafalgar he had gone on two long voyages to the east and South America, but it was not until 1810 – five years and ten ships after going to sea on the *Superb* – that the amphibious assault on the French-held island of Mauritius gave him his first hope of the excitement he craved.

As it turned out, the defendants offered virtually no resistance to the massive force which had been assembled, but the attack on Java in the following year – one of the forgotten classics of British arms – at last brought the nineteen-year-old midshipman into a war that, with only a brief respite, had been going on since the execution of Louis XVI just two months after Trelawny's birth.

The fleets carrying the combined army of native and European troops had sailed from Madras and Calcutta, with the Commander in Chief, General Auchmuty, and the Governor-General, Lord Minto, aboard the HMS *Akbar* on which Trelawny served. After a fraught passage south the invasion force was landed on 4 August 1811 at Chilingching, and marching eastwards through a heavily cultivated landscape of ditches, water tanks and dykes which reminded Minto

19

of a Chinese wallpaper, entered Batavia only to find its defendants withdrawn behind the strongly fortified Lines of Cornelis some six miles to the north.

On 26 August, under the brilliant leadership of Colonel Rollo Gillespie, and supported by naval guns dragged overland and fired by sailors, the lines were stormed and the campaign effectively brought to a conclusion. By that time, however, Trelawny's role in the victory was over. Sometime before the final assault, his gun party had been surprised on the approach to Cornelis, and in the skirmish which followed he received a sabre slash across the face and a musket ball which remained in his leg for over thirty years until it was removed without anaesthetic by an Italian surgeon under the impressed gaze of Robert Browning.

Java was Trelawny's first experience of warfare on any major scale with the navy, and his last. Taken back to the *Akbar*, he soon went down with the cholera that swept through the invasion force, killing more than two hundred sailors. He was lucky to survive, but it marked the end of his career. By the August of 1812 he was back in England, and three years later finally discharged from the navy without a commission, a midshipman *sans* prospects, education or even the halfpay of a lieutenant, one more 'useless Dick Musgrove' left high and dry by the coming of peace.

When Trelawny came to write about his career in the navy, he was again to invest his adolescent anger with all the political and revolutionary radicalism that coloured his schoolday memories. At the age of twenty-three, however, there can have seemed nothing glamorous to him in failure. The knowledge we have of him in these years after he returned from the east is admittedly of a fragmentary and rather special kind, yet the few clues that do survive suggest a far more conventional and vulnerable personality than the man who finally emerged from obscurity to stake his claim as one of the century's most defiant rebels.

The first of these is no more than a footnote, but it is nevertheless interesting that, in these first years of peace, he seems to have gone out of his way to assert his naval credentials. In the confident pomp of his later *Adventures* he might denounce the service as an instrument of arbitrary despotism, and yet, far from rejecting it at the time, he masqueraded in civilian life under the name of 'Lieutenant' Trelawny, a rank to which he had no claim and one the mature Trelawny would have despised.

For a young man of his temperament and background, coming to terms with the blank mediocrity of his prospects, this discreet and venial piece of self-promotion is neither very unusual nor important, but the same years throw up another clue to his personality which is best recorded in his own words.

> The fatal noose was cast around my neck, my proud crest humbled to the dust, the bloody bit thrust into my mouth, my shaggy mane trimmed, my hitherto untrammeled back bent with a weight I could neither endure nor shake off, my light and springy action changed into a painful amble – in short, I was married.[12]

It is as much a truism of biography as it is of fiction that domestic happiness leaves little trace of its presence, and so it is perhaps not surprising that we know what we do of Trelawny's marriage only because and when it failed. His bride, Caroline Addison, was the eighteen-year-old daughter of an East India merchant, a girl of a family 'fully the equal of his own'[13] as he defensively told his uncle John Hawkins, attractive, 'accomplished' and, from the slim evidence of her surviving letters, in love with the tall, handsome midshipman that the ungainly lout of a boy had become.

In spite of the conventional claims he made for his wife's pedigree, the marriage marked another step in Trelawny's alienation from his parents. 'My father was never partial to me,' he later wrote to John Hawkins, touchingly but unsuccessfully eager to preserve some contact with at least part of his family,

> & from the moment of my mariage discarded for ever me, and my hopes, nor has he since either pardoned or even allowed my name to be mentioned in his presence.[14]

The Addison family were clearly as opposed to the union as Trelawny's because with the single exception of the bride's uncle

21

there was nobody from either side at the wedding that followed their brief courtship. They were married on 17 May 1813 in St Mary's Paddington and, after an initial period living in Denham and London, moved first to lodgings in College Street, Bristol, in January 1816, and then in the July of the same year to board with a Captain White and his family at Vue Cottage near Bath.

It was from this house on 31 December 1816, just three and a half years and two daughters after their marriage, that Caroline Trelawny eloped to Southampton with a Thomas Coleman, a Captain in the 98th of Foot. In the immediate shock of betrayal Trelawny spoke and wrote wildly of a duel, but as with everything else in his early life reality lagged dully behind and in the summer of 1817 he began instead a long and public haul through the civil and ecclesiastical courts that only ended with the royal assent to an Act of Parliament permitting his divorce and remarriage in May 1819.

There is something in the very nature of divorce testimony which exposes a side of life that history scarcely notices, and through the evidence of the landladies and servants during these trials we have a squalid picture of a life that must have been the opposite of everything the young Trelawny craved. Even the geography of his betrayal has a sadly ignoble feel to it. His wife's affair with Coleman had begun at their lodgings in Bristol, where the Trelawnys had the first floor, consisting of a drawing room and adjoining bedroom. At the end of March 1816, Captain Coleman, a much older man, arrived, renting a parlour and bedroom on the ground floor beneath. At the hearing in the Consistory Court, the Trelawnys' landlady, Sarah Prout, described her own discovery of what was going on in the house.

> Shortly after Captain Coleman came to lodge in her House, Mrs Trelawny formed an Acquaintance with him unknown to her Husband. Captain Coleman occasionally lent the Deponent (Sarah Prout) Books, but she, having but little time for reading, lent them to Mrs Trelawny, who, as the Deponent afterwards discovered, used to send Margaret Bidder the Servant to Captain Coleman's Apartments to

return or change the Books, and sometimes went herself for
that purpose; and it was by these means, as the Deponent
believed, that the Acquaintance between them first com-
menced. The Deponent further saith that by reason of what
she will hereafter depose, she verily believes that the
Acquaintance between Mrs Trelawny and Captain Coleman
led to a criminal Intimacy between them, and that they were
guilty of many improper Familiarities with each other . . .
One evening . . . the Deponent went out to take a walk, and
returned about eight o'clock in the Evening: Candles were
usually brought and the Window Shutters closed in Captain
Coleman's Parlour before this time, and they were so upon
the present Ocasion, but as the Deponent was waiting for
the Street Door to be opened she observed the Shutters to
be not quite closed, and the Blinds within to be not quite
drawn down; and on then looking through the opening the
Deponent by the light of the Candle saw Mrs Trelawny
reclining on the Sofa on the left Arm of Captain Coleman,
whilst his right Hand was thrust into her Bosom and he was
kissing her. The Deponent, on the street door being opened,
went up Stairs, and almost immediately afterwards heard
Mrs Trelawny go up Stairs from the passage as if she had
just entered the House, and go into her Bed Room as if to
take off her Bonnet after a Walk, Mr Trelawny being, as
the Deponent at that time observed, reading in his own
Room . . . [15]

For all the conventionality of its phrasing, Sarah Prout's testimony
provides a sadly absorbing insight into a world poised between a
Rowlandesque coarseness and an encroaching moral censoriousness.
It is not clear from the evidence how much Trelawny himself suspected, but shortly after Coleman's arrival there had been a row over
a handkerchief which uncannily echoes the *casus belli* in Trelawny's
favourite *Othello*. Another incident followed soon after when
Caroline Trelawny was forced to hide in Coleman's bedroom on
the arrival of some of his fellow officers. Then, one evening at the

beginning of June, Trelawny tried to persuade his wife and landlady to join him at the theatre, one of his favourite activities. Caroline refused and he went on alone. Once he had left the house, Caroline suggested to Mrs Prout that the two of them should go instead to the Circus, 'another place of Theatrical Amusement at Bristol':

The Deponent endeavoured to dissuade her very much from going, and represented the Impropriety of it, in her, Mrs Trelawny's then state of Pregnancy, but she persisted in going, and the Deponent in Consequence agreed to accompany her. They accordingly left home, but had not proceeded far before Mrs Trelawny complained of being very poorly, and requested the Deponent to get someone else to accompany her, saying that she would return home. The Deponent accordingly parted with Mrs Trelawny but followed her home in about a quarter of an Hour afterwards and let herself in with a private Key of her own. She tried the Parlour Door, but found it locked, and then walked out into the Garden behind the House where she observed the Blind of Captain Coleman's Bed Room Window not quite drawn down, and she at the same time observed a Towel lying on the Roof of an adjoining Outhouse, having apparently fallen from Mr and Mrs Trelawny's Bed Room Window. The Deponent's Suspicions having been excited by the Circumstances before deposed of, and by the sudden return home of Mrs Trelawny, she walked out on to the Roof of the said Outhouse which she could very easily do, as if to pick up the Towel, and looked into Captain Coleman's Bed Room, through that part of the Window over which the Blind was not drawn down: It was between eight and nine o'Clock in the Evening, and not quite dark. The Door between the Bed Room and Parlour was also open, and there was light in the latter: the Deponent could therefore distinguish every Object in the Bed Room, and she saith that she then saw Captain Coleman and Mrs Trelawny on the Bed together: Captain Coleman had his Coat and Waistcoat off, his Pantaloons were down, and he was lying upon Mrs Trelawny whose Petticoats were up; and they were then in the Act of Sexual Intercourse with each other. The Deponent remained a Minute or two at the Window, greatly surprised, until she saw Mrs Trelawny get off the Bed, and then she returned into the House, and waited on the Stairs, where in about five minutes she saw Mrs Trelawny come out of the Parlour Door very hastily with her Shoes in her Hand.[16]

Mrs Prout testified that she had confronted Caroline with the evidence of her adultery, and demanded that the Trelawnys should leave. After an initial denial Trelawny's wife had confessed everything, but 'entreated her not to tell her husband of it',

as her, Mrs Trelawny's life depended on it: She also promised most fervently, never to be guilty of such a Crime again, and begged that the Deponent would herself make the Excuse to Mr Trelawny for wishing him to quit his lodgings.[17]

The excuse Mrs Prout came up with was that she needed to paint their rooms, and sometime towards the end of July or the beginning of August the couple moved to new lodgings near Bath owned by a Captain White. Within a short time an unrepentant Caroline was recruiting different members of the White family to collect mail addressed to her under fictitious names at addresses in the town, but if the trial evidence is to be believed, no hint of this seems to have reached Trelawny, who alone among his landladies, servants and his mother-in-law was unaware of his wife's liaison.

Even if Trelawny was ignorant of what was going on, however, relations between him and Caroline had deteriorated beyond repair, and after the birth of their second daughter at Vue Cottage communications between them were bizarrely limited to written requests for interviews. Unable to tolerate this atmosphere any longer, Mrs White finally asked them to leave, fixing 31 December for their departure.

'About four o'Clock in the Afternoon however of that day,' Mrs White testified to the Consistory Court,

> Mrs Trelawny being wanted in the Drawing Room, the Deponent and others of her family went to seek her all over the House but she was not to be found: Captain White and Mr Trelawny then left the House to go different ways in search of her, and the Deponent was afterwards informed by her said husband that he had met with Mrs Trelawny who had acknowledged to him that she had eloped with the Intention of proceeding to Captain Coleman at South-ampton, and pressed him (Captain White) not to prevent her, but that he had conducted her to her Mother in Bath, and left her under her said Mother's protection, without apprizing Mr Trelawny therof.[18]

Trelawny's humiliation was complete, the injury to his pride as the case dragged through the courts public and prolonged. For over two years after her elopement he was forced to live with the sordid details of her betrayal, with the bleak evidence that crumpled sheets and billets doux, towels drying at parlour windows and provincial intimacies made up the sad reality of his waking hours.

The one consolation to emerge from this crisis was the friendship of the White family with whom he and Caroline had boarded, and in particular with the young daughter Augusta. In the wider picture of his life this relationship is of only marginal importance but, in the way their kindness brought out all those feelings that had been stifled in childhood and the navy, it foreshadows the most important ties of his life. From the start the Whites had taken his side against Caroline and when, in the February after her elopement, Captain White, dragged down by debts and depression, killed himself, their friendship was sealed. 'After so dreadful a catastrophe most of your friends would write lamentations at your Father's rash fate,' he wrote to Augusta,

> but as I differ and am not swayed by opinions of other men
> – I shall commence with rejoicing that your unfortunate

Father has at last ended his miseries ... tell your mother
to command me in every way ... If I can be of the most
trivial service command me and I will fly down to my loved
Sisters ... Your mother shall find in me a Son, you a
Brother, and your Brothers a Father.[19]

That last note, so revealing of the emotional vacuum marriage had
done nothing to fill, is repeated in another letter to Augusta, written
from his family house in Soho Square on 1 October 1817. 'With
my trunks,' he wrote,

arrived your affectionate letters My Dear Kind Sister, they
infused new life, into my drooping soul, – ought not such
a friend to counterbalance, all the ills I have endured, –
Your love, and sympathy, soothed my signed soul – and
bid me hope ... O my dearest Sister could you but see my
heart, you would wonder it should be inclosed, in so rough
a form; – my study through life, has been, to hide under
the mask of affected roughness, the tenderest, warmest, and
most affectionate sencibility.[20]

Only a handful of Trelawny's letters survive from this period, and
yet colourful as they are, they need to be treated warily as evidence
of his feelings. The temptations of so sympathetic a correspondent
for a humiliated cuckold are too obvious to need spelling out, but
what is more interesting is the impression his letters give that he
had neither the education nor the vocabulary at this period to express
or even understand the more complex aspects of his personality.

Trelawny was a late and slow developer, and nowhere is this
plainer than in his correspondence. With the mature Trelawny it is
a safe bet that when he writes something he says precisely what he
means to say, but in his early years there is an invariable sense of
a man struggling for a voice and character, of a writer fumbling
towards an identity that he has not yet made his own.

In their very turbulence, however, their romantic theatricality,
their heavy posturing, these letters remain the clearest sign of the
inward transformation that Trelawny underwent during the unhappy

years of navy and married life. There is no doubt that in the best traditions of romantic alienation he went out of his way to exaggerate his loneliness to any woman prepared to listen, but as in childhood the misery was real enough and the overriding consequence of his marriage was to drive Trelawny into an internalized world of the imagination in which he could take refuge from the disappointments of life.

Collaborating in this retreat, shaping and colouring this inner world, were the books on which Trelawny glutted himself during these wilderness years in Bristol and London. If his grammar and spelling are anything to go by, he had left the navy as ignorant and illiterate as the day he entered, but in the first years of peace he set out on a bizarre but heroic course of reading and self-improvement that was to alter his life, immersing himself in the tragedies of Shakespeare and the romances of Scott, in the defiance of Milton's Satan and the violence of Jacobean revenge, in Hope's *Anastasius* and Peacock's *Nightmare Abbey*, in the poetry of Rogers, Cowper, Young, Falconer and Moore, but above all – ten of the fifty odd volumes in his library in 1820 – in the exotic, profligate and dazzling world of Byron's poetry and tales.

The influence of Byron on Trelawny's development is a classic example of the sad paradox that while great art seldom made anyone a better person bad art can be profoundly dangerous. There were certainly aspects of Byron's wonderful mature genius from which Trelawny might well have learned but it was the self-indulgent Byron of *Childe Harold* that lodged in his soul, the gloomily antisocial heroes of the Eastern Tales like Lara or Conrad, mysterious, violent and aristocratic outcasts from a petty world, in whom he found the model, mirror and philosophical justification for his own troubled personality.

It seems almost too pat that also among his books at this time was Volney's *Ruins of Empire*, the work from which Frankenstein's monster, listening at the cottage window, learned all he knew of human society, but it is too potent a symbol of Trelawny's plight to let pass. In old age Trelawny was to become an extraordinarily open-minded and intelligent judge of books, but the failed midshipman who fed off Byron in this way was above all an outcast, an intellectual and emotional outsider incapable of measuring a world of which he was largely ignorant, desperate only to find in his reading some echo or corroboration of his own feelings.

There is nothing rare in men or women shaping their lives by some ideal but as one looks at the influence of Byronic Romanticism on Trelawny during these years it seems doubtful that anyone ever chose so spurious a model. He seems to have been able to read and re-read the great tragedies of Shakespeare, and learn nothing but quotations. Dryden has left no mark. Jane Austen appears never to have been read. Byron, however, filled his imagination, shaped his aspirations and confirmed him in his worst excesses, determined the way he talked and wrote, the way he dressed and behaved, until within a decade it was impossible for contemporaries to know whether he had spawned the Corsair or the Corsair him.

It was under this influence, in the boarding houses of Bristol, Bath and London, that Trelawny now committed himself to that major deception which was ultimately to transform his existence. It is hard to imagine that the idea of actual imposture can have seized hold of him all at once, and yet as the failures became starker his youthful daydreams must have taken on a more urgent and adult significance, edging the innocent escapism of his naval days ever closer to a wholesale denial of a life which had let him down.

It would be another dozen years before the fantasies of these years took on their definitive shape in *Adventures*, but it is still in its pages that we can best trace the genesis of a story that for the next century and more would enjoy the status of history. According to the version of his 'autobiography', Trelawny's ship was in harbour in Bombay when he and a friend called Walter decided to desert, and formed a friendship with a man calling himself De Witt, but whose name turns out to be the equally fictional De Ruyter.* Trelawny's devotion to him was immediate and complete. There was nothing De Ruyter could not do, nothing he did not know, no way either physically or mentally that he was not Trelawny's superior. He was approaching his thirtieth year, could speak most

European languages faultlessly, and all the native dialects from 'the guttural, brute-like grunting of the Malay, the more humanized Hindostanee' to the 'softer and harmonious Persian' with equal ease.[21] In stature he was majestic, 'the slim form of the date-tree' disguising 'the solid strength of the oak'.[22] His forehead was smooth as sculptured marble, his hair dark and abundant, his features well defined, his eyes – the windows to his restless and brilliant soul – as various as a chameleon in their colour.

Shortly after coming under De Ruyter's spell, the incident occurred in this imaginary version of events that ended Trelawny's naval servitude. The two men were playing billiards, when a Scotch lieutenant who had tormented his and Walter's lives entered. He demanded to know when Trelawny was rejoining his ship, which was sailing the next day. At this Trelawny's blood seemed to ignite with fire, and then congeal to ice. He dashed his hat in the man's face, tore off the last insignia of bondage from his own dress, and drew his sword. The lieutenant broke into abject disclaimers of friendship, and begged his pardon. In his rage Trelawny struck him to the ground, kicking and trampling and spitting on him as the creature begged for mercy. 'His screams and protestations,' Trelawny wrote,

> while they increased my contempt, added fuel to my anger, for I was furious that such a pitiful wretch should have lorded it over me so long. I roared out, 'For the wrongs you have done me, I am satisfied. Yet nothing but your currish blood can atone for your atrocities to Walter!'
>
> Having broken my own sword at the onset, I drew his from beneath his prostrate carcass, and should inevitably have despatched him on the spot, had not a stronger hand gripped hold of my arm. It was De Ruyter's; and he said, in a low, quiet voice, 'Come, no killing. Here!' (giving me a broken billiard cue) 'a stick is a fitter weapon to chastise a coward with. Don't rust good steel.'
>
> It was useless to gainsay him, for he had taken the sword out of my hand. I therefor belaboured the rascal: his yells

were dreadful; he was wild with terror, and looked like a maniac. I never ceased till I had broken the butt-end of the cue over him, and till he was motionless.[23]

The young rebel who had suffered under his father's brutality, under the cruelty of the Reverend Seyer, and in the navy, was at last free. The mysterious De Ruyter who had passed himself off in Bombay as a merchant, now revealed himself as a privateer operating under a French flag, an enemy to all tyranny and corruption, and in the seventeen-year-old midshipman recognized his spiritual heir and child.

It was the beginning of a new life, and under the leadership of this man, Trelawny embarked on the imaginary career of adventure, excitement, bloodshed, romance and crime which forms the great bulk of his 'autobiography'. There is no summary of *Adventures* that can possibly do justice to the colour and imaginative profligacy of his fantasies, nothing that can capture either the compelling immediacy of Trelawny's fictional world or the visions of violence and domination with which he took his revenge on Caroline and a world that stolidly refused to come up to expectations. As a lonely and unhappy young midshipman, he had daydreamed with his friend Walter of a life without parents, patrimonies or ties 'amidst the children of nature,'[24] but the dreams now were more sinister. Crazed stallions, Malay peasants, naval officers, ugly old women are all brutally mastered, bullied, beaten, burned, killed or crushed like toads beneath his feet. The vegetation and landscape of the east which so prosaically reminded Lord Minto of a Chinese wallpaper, takes on a vivid almost surrealistic life. Wild animals fill his vision with the same haunting, threatening force that they have in *Othello*. It is wish fulfilment on the grand scale. In De Ruyter the emotional orphan has found a father; in the lovely Zela, shy and beautiful as a faun, devoted to Trelawny until she expires in his arms after a shark attack, the cuckold at last finds the bride he deserves; and in the excitement, colour and violence of his adventures, the un-employed midshipman wins the recognition the Royal Navy had denied him.

31

After the public humiliations of the King's Bench and Consistory Courts, Trelawny was ready to face the world, a Byronic hero with a history and personality to match. In the depths of his imagination he had forged an identity which seemed more vividly true to his sense of self than the reality he had left behind, and if the same might be said of every creative liar, what distinguishes him from a Savage or Baron Corvo is that for the next five years life was to give him what he wanted with an almost Faustian prodigality – years in which invention became a self-fulfilling ordinance, and events danced to the tune of the imagination until fantasy and life pursued each other in an unbreakable circle.

If psychologically he was prepared for a new life, financially, too, he was at last able to expand his horizons. Through all the rows with his father he had continued to draw an allowance of three hundred pounds a year, and while that was scarcely enough to support a family in comfort, for a single man ready to live abroad it opened up possibilities of leisured and gentlemanly self-indulgence. On 19 May 1819, the Royal Assent to his divorce was given, freeing him of those domestic ties which had shackled his turbulent spirit. The seven lean years were over. Caroline, at last, was out of his life, taking their younger daughter, Eliza, with her. The elder child, Julia, had been farmed out to friends of the Whites. He seems to have backtracked too from the brief intensity of his friendship with Augusta, allowing it to mellow into a mutual warmth which lasted throughout their lives.

The disappointment and failures of the navy and marriage, the first-floor parlours and bedrooms, were not just forgotten but buried. Mentally he had toughened and changed, developing out of all recognition from the dull lout his uncle had found him ten years earlier. At the age of twenty-eight he had also physically grown into the role he had created for himself, tall, dark, athletic, immensely strong and handsome. All he needed now was a stage on which to play out his new part. His father had offered to buy him a commission in the army, but for a follower of De Ruyter that was hardly an option. He had talked vaguely for a time of South America as well, of joining either General Wilson or a commune. In the end, however, he settled for the Continent. One of his last addresses in England before leaving was 7 Orange St, the site now of the archives of the National Portrait Gallery. It was a prescient choice of address for a man about to launch himself into the forefront of the nation's consciousness.

2

THE SUN
AND THE GLOW-WORM

'You won't like him.'
Byron to Teresa Guiccioli[1]

IT MUST HAVE BEEN sometime in the autumn of 1819 or the beginning of 1820 that Trelawny finally left England for the Continent, travelling first to Paris where his mother was chaperoning his sisters on a predatory hunt for husbands, and from there to Geneva.

With the poverty of letters from this time it is impossible to be dogmatic about Trelawny's motives but there would have been compelling reasons other than disappointment and money for his decision to live abroad. There appears to have been nothing particular in his choice of Switzerland, but for a man of his burgeoning radicalism the England of Castlereagh and the Peterloo Massacre can have seemed no place to be, a country frozen in the mini ice-age of reaction which gripped post-Napoleonic Europe, a land, in Shelley's savage assault, of,

> An old, mad, blind, despised, and dying king, –
> Princes, the dregs of their dull race, who flow
> Through public scorn, – mud from a muddy spring, –
> Rulers who neither see, nor feel, nor know,
> But leech-like to their feinting country cling,
> Till they drop, blind in blood, without a blow, –[2]

At a time when so many European liberals were seeking refuge in England, there seems something stubbornly wrongheaded in the reverse process, but for Trelawny at least the freedom the Continent offered had more to do with the texture of life than any considered set of principles. Like so many men of his nation and class nineteenth-century Europe represented above all else a continuation of the eighteenth century 'by other means', an opportunity – heterosexual, homosexual, financial, social or whatever – to pursue a style of life which inflation and the looming threat of 'Victorian' morality was endangering at home.

It was an opportunity he embraced with relief and gusto, but amidst the shooting, hunting and fishing that signalled a re-absorption into his own class, a meeting occurred that was to change the direction of his life for good. A family friend of the Trelawnys from the West Country, Sir John Aubyn, kept a generous if irregular open house at his villa just outside Geneva, and it was in this motley expatriate world that Trelawny first met Edward Williams, an Indian army officer living in Switzerland as a married man with the wife of a fellow officer, and Thomas Medwin, the cousin of Percy Bysshe Shelley.

The friendship of Williams, at least, was one that Trelawny treasured all his life, but more important, it was through these two men that he now found himself drawn into the Italian orbit of Byron and Shelley. There is no way of being sure when he first came across the name or work of a poet who, in 1820, was known mainly for his atheism, but Trelawny's account invests the occasion with a significance that is poetically if not literally true. The scene is set in Lausanne in 1820, during a conversation with a bookseller-friend, who would translate passages of Schiller, Kant or Goethe for an ex-midshipman still painfully conscious of his lack of education. The story forms the opening scene of his *Records of Shelley, Byron, and the Author* and among the apocrypha of his early life it holds a special place.

One morning I saw my friend sitting under the acacias on the terrace in front of the house in which Gibbon had lived, and where he wrote the *Decline and Fall*. He said, 'I am trying to sharpen my wits in this pungent air which gave such a keen edge to the great historian, so that I may fathom this book. Your modern poets, Byron, Scott, and Moore, I can read and understand as I walk along, but I have got hold of a book by one that makes me stop to take breath and think.' It was Shelley's 'Queen Mab'. As I had never heard that name or title, I asked how he got the volume. 'With a lot of new books in English, which I took in exchange for old French ones. Not knowing the names of the authors, I might not have looked into them, had not a pampered, prying priest smelt this one in my lumber-room, and after a brief glance at the notes, exploded in wrath, shouting out, 'Infidel, jacobin, leveller: nothing can stop this spread of blasphemy but the stake and the faggot; the world is retrograding into accursed heathenism and universal anarchy!' When the priest had departed, I took up the small book he had thrown down, saying, 'Surely there must be something here worth tasting.' You know the proverb, 'No person throws a stone at a tree that does not bear fruit.'

'Priests do not', I answered; 'so I, too, must have a bite of the forbidden fruit.'[3]*

Set alongside the impact of Byron on Trelawny, the influence of Shelley's poetry seems virtually negligible, but this, in stylized form, is still one of the key moments of his life. A few days after this exchange he was breakfasting at a hotel in Lausanne, when a chance conversation with an Englishman on a walking holiday with two women gave him his first opportunity to test this new enthusiasm. It was only after their party had broken up that Trelawny learned that the 'self-confident and dogmatic' stranger was Wordsworth, but chasing him down again he 'asked him abruptly what he thought of Shelley as a poet.

'Nothing,' he replied, as abruptly.
'Seeing my surprise, he added, 'A poet who has not

produced a good poem before he is twenty five, we may conclude cannot, and never will do so.'

'The Cenci!' I said eagerly.

'Won't do,' he replied, shaking his head, as he got into the carriage: a rough-coated Scotch terrier followed him.

'This hairy fellow is our flea-trap,' he shouted out as they started off . . .

I did not then know that the full-fledged author never reads the writings of his contemporaries, except to cut them up in a review – that being a work of love. In after years, Shelley being dead, Wordsworth confessed this fact; he was then induced to read some of Shelley's poems, and admitted that Shelley was the greatest master of harmonious verse in our modern literature.[4]

It says a lot for Trelawny's critical judgement that, almost alone and untaught, he could have discovered Shelley for himself, but there must also have been more personal and less literary factors that helped quicken his new interest. For a man who saw himself in the self-dramatizing terms he so habitually used, the exiled poet would have offered a mirror to his own miserable experience, and if Shelley was merely the 'glow-worm' to Byron's 'sun', then that can only have made him appear more accessible. The arrival of Medwin meant too that the chance of meeting him was something that had probably been discussed from the earliest days in Switzerland, but the unlamented death of Trelawny's father in 1820 put any thoughts of Italy back by at least a year. Travelling in his own carriage through Chalon-sur-Saône, where he left Edward and Jane Williams to winter in genteel poverty, he continued on to England with his financial hopes high only to discover that he was no better off than he had been before. The old uncertainty of the allowance, the galling necessity of tempering hatred with self-interest, was gone, but there was to be no more money. He had been left £10,000 in 3% gilt-edged stocks which gave him an income of £300 a year.

The evidence for Trelawny's movements during these months is as sketchy as for any time of his life, but it is likely that arriving in

England at the end of 1820 he found himself in no hurry to leave, staying at his mother's new London home in Berners Street before returning to the Continent in the May or June of 1821.

It is at this moment as one begins to attempt to chart his steps, however, that it becomes obvious just how futile an exercise it is, and just how far at this point a traditional sense of 'biographical' time must give way to what could be called 'Trelawny' time. Because to any observer totting up the weeks and months spent shooting and hunting during these years a picture emerges of a life hopelessly and terminally adrift, and yet for Trelawny himself this same time seems to have been crushed into a series of defining highlights that obliterate all else, secular epiphanies which, in the great drama he made of his life, assert a pattern of significance – of destiny – that biography can do nothing but follow.

Throughout his life there would be an almost Marvellian fierceness in the way Trelawny would seize his opportunities and in 1820 this destiny seemed to him to lead nowhere but Italy. Through the summer of 1821 he hunted and fished with an old naval friend Daniel Roberts in the Swiss mountains, but beneath the seemingly aimless wanderings the real business of his life was already taking shape. In April 1821, Edward Williams had written to him from Pisa, where he and Jane were living after a bleak winter of '*soupe maigre, bouilli*, sour wine, and solitary confinement' at Chalon-sur-Saône.[5] He was, he told Trelawny, already an intimate of Shelley. They were planning a summer's boating together, 'adventuring' among the rivers and canals of that part of Italy. 'Shelley', he wrote, tantalizingly

> is certainly a man of most astonishing genius in appearance, extraordinarily young, of manners mild and amiable, but withal full of life and fun. His wonderful command of language, and the ease with which he speaks on what are generally considered abstruse subjects, are striking; in short, his ordinary conversation is akin to poetry, for he sees things in the most singular and pleasing lights; if he wrote as he talked, he would be popular enough. Lord Byron and others

think him by far the most imaginative poet of the day. The style of his lordship's letters to him is quite that of a pupil, such as asking his opinion, and demanding his advice on certain points, &. I must tell you, that the idea of the tragedy of 'Manfred', and many of the philosophical, or rather metaphysical, notions interwoven in the composition of the fourth Canto of 'Childe Harold', are of his suggestion; but this, of course, is between ourselves.[6]

Trelawny printed this letter in his history of this period of his life, the *Records of Shelley, Byron and the Author*. Back to back with it, as if the intervening eight months had simply not existed, comes a second letter from Williams, written in the following December and giving the momentous news of Byron's arrival.

My Dear Trelawny,

Why, how is this? I will swear that yesterday was Christmas Day, for I celebrated it at a splendid feast given by Lord Byron to what I call his Pistol Club – i.e. to Shelley, Medwin, a Mr Taaffe, and myself, and was scarcely awake from the vision of it when your letter was put into my hands, dated 1st of January, 1822. Time flies fast enough, but you, in the rapidity of your motions, contrive to outwing the old fellow ... Lord Byron is the very spirit of the place – that is, to those few to whom, like Mohannah, he has lifted his veil. When you asked me in your last letter if it was probable to become at all intimate with him, I replied in a manner which I considered it most prudent to do, from motives which are best explained when I see you. Now, however, I know him a great deal better, and I think I may safely say that point will rest entirely with yourself. The eccentricities of an assumed character, which a total retirement from the world almost rendered a natural one, are daily wearing off. He sees none of the numerous English who are here, excepting those I have named. And of this I am selfishly glad, for one sees nothing of a man in mixed societies. It is difficult to move him, he says, when he is once fixed, but he seems bent upon joining our party at Spezzia next summer.

I shall reserve all that I have to say about the boat until
we meet at the select committee, which is intended to be
held on that subject when you arrive here. Have a boat we
must, and if we can get Roberts to build her, so much the
better . . . [7]

With the entry of Byron into Shelley's world Trelawny's twin deities
were in place. Even before Williams's second letter, however, he
was already making ready for Italy. He had shipped his guns and
dogs to Leghorn in preparation for a winter's hunting in the Mar-
emma, but with this news of bigger game on the banks of the Arno,
the woodcock were now going to have to wait their turn.

Travelling south from Geneva with his friend Roberts, shooting,
fishing and sketching as they went, Trelawny finally reached Pisa
in the January of 1822 to take up his place among the circle that
had formed around Shelley. Since the early spring of 1818 when
they left England for the last time, Shelley and his tribe of dependents
had been wandering across the Continent, moving restlessly from
one Italian town to another, from Milan to Bagni di Lucca, Venice,
Naples, Rome, Leghorn, Florence, and then, in the January of 1820,
to Pisa, his penultimate resting place in that 'Paradise of exiles –
the retreat of Pariahs' as he called nineteenth-century Italy.[8]

At the beginning of 1822, when Trelawny first joined them,
Shelley and his wife Mary were living above Edward and Jane
Williams in the Tre Palazzi di Chiesa at the eastern end of the
Lung'Arno, diagonally across the river from the Palazzo Lanfranchi
which Byron had taken the previous November. Anxious to be with
them as quickly as he could, Trelawny had left Roberts at Genoa
and hurried on alone. He arrived late, and after putting up his
horse at an inn and dining, hastened to the Tre Palazzi to renew
acquaintances with the Williamses and to meet Shelley. He was
greeted by his old friends in 'their earnest cordial manner', and the
three were deep in conversation,

when I was rather put out by observing in the passage near the open door, opposite to where I sat, a pair of glittering eyes steadily fixed on mine; it was too dark to make out whom they belonged to. With the acuteness of a woman, Mrs Williams's eyes followed the direction of mine, and going to the doorway, she laughingly said.

'Come in, Shelley, it's only our friend Tre just arrived.'

Swiftly gliding in, blushing like a girl, a tall thin stripling held out both his hands; and although I could hardly believe as I looked at his flushed, feminine, and artless face that it could be the Poet, I returned his warm pressure. After the ordinary greetings he sat down and listened. I was silent from astonishment: was it possible this mild-looking beardless boy could be the veritable monster at war with all the world? – excommunicated by the Fathers of the Church, deprived of his civil rights by the fiat of a grim Lord Chancellor, discarded by every member of his family, and denounced by the rival sages of our literature as the founder of a Satanic school? I could not believe it; it must be a hoax.[9]

This account was published in his *Records* almost sixty years after, at a time when Trelawny was established beyond challenge as the last and greatest of Byron's and Shelley's friends, and yet even if much of its ease is of a later date, he clearly slid into the world that revolved around the two poets as if he had known no other. Within twenty-four hours of this first sight of Shelley he was playing billiards with Byron at the Palazzo Lanfranchi, coolly holding his own in conversation (and there is no more conversationally demanding a game than billiards), the acolyte an immediate familiar, a welcome addition to the daily shooting parties and drama plans and as interesting an object to his new friends as they were to him.

Indeed, when Trelawny first burst upon Byron's Pisan world that January, launching himself from nowhere with the same fanfare of lies that fill his *Adventures*, it seemed to them that here at last was the Byronic hero made flesh. Here was a Conrad with a Gulnare in every port, a Lara who had exhausted all human emotion, who had murdered and pillaged, whored and sinned; had loved only to cremate his Zela's corpse on the edge of a Javan bay; betrayed and been betrayed, deserted from the Royal Navy, fought beside his pirate-hero De Ruyter, and all, as Mary Shelley noted with that fine lack of irony that is her hallmark, 'between the age of thirteen and twenty.'[10]

Appropriately, in fact, it is to the author of *Frankenstein* that we owe the first sustained description of Trelawny that we have. The arrival of this exotic figure among their small circle was important enough to warrant a long entry in her journal, and a month later she was still sufficiently intrigued to write to an old friend, Mary Gisborne, of her *giovane stravagante*. He was, she said

> a kind of half Arab Englishman – whose life has been as changeful as that of Anastasius & who recounts the adventures of his youth as eloquently and well as the imagined Greek – he is clever – for his moral qualities I am yet in the dark – he is a strange web which I am endeavouring to unravel – I would fain learn if generosity is united to impetuousness – Nobility of spirit to his assumption of singularity & independence – he is six feet high – raven black hair which curls thickly & shortly like a More – dark, grey – expressive eyes – overhanging brows, upturned lips & a smile which expresses good nature & kindheartedness – his shoulders are high like an Orientalist – his voice is monotonous yet emphatic & his language as he relates the events of his life energetic & simple – whether the tale be one of blood & horror or irresistable comedy. His company is delightful for he excites me to think and if any evil shade the intercourse that time will tell.[11]

It seems fitting in a sense that we have no painting or description of Trelawny before this time, that we have to wait until he was the 'finished article' strutting the public stage to know in any detail what he might have looked like. There are moments when one feels that some glimpse of a younger and more vulnerable Trelawny might help 'explain' him in some way, but there is no image which even half suggests the ghost of another self – either of the boy who cried himself to sleep that first night at school, or the man who sat through Sarah Prout's testimony in the divorce courts. By 1822, cuckold and boy were both gone, hidden behind the mask that so intrigued Mary Shelley, that stares out still from portrait after portrait done over the next fifty years – the eyes aggressive, challenging, the nose aquiline, the lines already set into the obdurate mould Millais caught in old age: the face, as Mary Shelley suggests, of Thomas Hope's *Anastasius*, the one romantic outcast that Byron wept that he had not himself created.

It has always been baffling that Trelawny could have got away with his tales and fantasies among the Pisan Circle, but at a more mundane level it is scarcely less astonishing to find the daughter of Godwin and Mary Wollstonecraft still thinking and writing of an uneducated midshipman in these terms after almost a month of his company.

But if charm, singularity and good-looks were possibly enough to provoke her fascination with him, something more than a lazy and tolerant male camaraderie is needed to explain away the confidence with which he adjusted to the sophisticated literary and political interests of Byron and Shelley.

The admirers of the two poets have traditionally agreed on very little but if there is one thing that does unite them it is a comforting belief that Trelawny was only a marginal figure in their Pisan Circle. The principal reason for this is a natural and proper reaction to the inflated claims he made for himself in his later memoirs, and yet even when one has discounted his exaggerations it is still clear that there was a genuine warmth in their welcome that reflects as well on him as it does on them.

There was a kindness about Shelley and an aristocratic carelessness about Byron which must have smoothed any awkwardness, but in such a circle Trelawny would have had to earn his place with his conversation or simply disappear. In old age the force and vitality of his talk left an indelible impression on all who met him, and even at thirty he was obviously a brilliant and charismatic story-teller with the power to interest men whose lives in many ways had been more circumscribed than his own.

Trelawny's strength and skills, his shooting, his boxing and sailing were all valued currencies in Byron's world and yet the explanation of his success that often goes forgotten is the simple fact that he was a man of real if unformed talent. In terms of sophistication and learning he might well have been out of his depth in this alien literary world, but if one takes out Byron and Shelley and that strange fluke of a novel, *Frankenstein*, was there anything produced by the Pisan Circle that could remotely compare with the books Trelawny would go on to write?

Williams, Medwin, Taafe, Mrs. Mason, Claire Clairmont, even Leigh Hunt? – the truth is that Trelawny wrote at least one book and probably two that were beyond the compass of any of them. There is certainly nothing in his letters from this period to suggest he had yet found the voice to match his abilities, but there must have been an inner conviction of power that rubbed off on others, a strong and even savage faith in his own singularity that enabled him to brazen out his adopted role in a world whose very lifeblood was the imagination. It is again as if all those years of misery that seem so arid and sterile from the outside had been nothing of the sort, but rather an essential apprenticeship in romantic alienation, a training in disaffection whilst the inner man, fed on little more than the poetry of Byron and Shelley, shaped for himself a destiny he was ready to seize the moment it was offered him.

Not even Trelawny, though, in the drawn-out loneliness of his life at sea or the humiliations of the divorce courts, could have anticipated that destiny would bring him to Italy in time to play his part in English Romanticism's *Götterdämmerung*. Neither, during his first weeks, was there any hint of the dramas that lay ahead. Through the early months of 1822, the sexual and political tensions that were always part of their Pisan world were stirring ominously beneath the surface, and yet in the very ordinariness of Edward Williams's journal for this same time one glimpses in its last, leisurely days a world that feels as if it might have gone on for ever.

At the end of March their peace was threatened by an unpleasant and absurdly inflated incident with a sergeant major called Masi, a degrading brawl that ended in Masi's wounding and ultimately Byron's exit from Pisa. Some of the details of this incident are still obscure but it began when the party of Byron and Shelley, returning from shooting practice, took umbrage at a dragoon who galloped through their ranks on the road into Pisa. When the English gave chase there was a scuffle beneath the city gate that left Shelley on the ground and a Captain Hay wounded, but it was only when an unknown member of Byron's household subsequently stabbed Masi outside the Palazzo Lanfranchi that the incident threatened serious consequences.

After one fraught night through which he was not expected to live, Masi recovered from his wound. But anti-English feeling ran high in the city, and even before the Gambas, the family of Byron's mistress Teresa Guiccioli, were expelled and Byron went with them, Shelley and Mary had determined to quit Pisa.

The final calamity, when it came, however, sprang from a different direction with all the suddenness and violence of the Mediterranean storm that caused it. From long before Trelawny's appearance there had been excited talk in Shelley's circle of boats and boating expeditions, and when Trelawny arrived in January 1822 he immediately assumed, as the ex-naval man among them, a leading role in their schemes. In his journal for 15 January, Williams noted that Trelawny had brought them a model for an American schooner, and that they had settled to have a 30-foot boat built along its lines. Within days an order was placed through Daniel Roberts for this boat, together with a larger vessel that Trelawny was to skipper himself for Byron. Then, on 5 February, Trelawny wrote to Roberts again with his last, fateful instructions, dangerously reducing the original specifications for Shelley's boat by almost half.

> Dear Roberts,
>   In haste to save the Post – I have only time to tell you, that you are to consider *this letter as definitive*, and to *cancel every other regarding the Boats.*

First, then, continue the one that you are at work upon for Lord B. She is to have *Iron Keel*, copper *fastenings* and *bottom* – the Cabin to be as *high* and *roomy* as possible, no *expense* to be *spared* to make her a complete BEAUTY! We should like to have four guns, one . . . as *large* as you think *safe* – to make a devil of a noise!– fitted with locks – the swivels of brass! – I suppose from one to three pounders.

Now as to our Boat, we have from considerations abandoned the one we wrote about. But in her lieu – will you lay us down a small beautiful one of about 17 or 18 feet? To be a thorough *Varment* at *pulling* and *sailing*! Single handed oars, say four or six; and we think, if you differ not, three luggs and a jib – *backing ones*![12]

It is given to few men to kill two major poets, but the friend to whom Byron turned for his doctors and Shelley for his boat has claims to be considered one of the seminal influences on nineteenth-century literature. It was not until the middle of May that the *Don Juan* as she was named was finally delivered to Shelley at Lerici, but even then there were further sacrifices of stability to elegance to be made, additions of a false stern and prow to accentuate her lines, and a new set of riggings which gave her, to Williams's eye, all the glamour and prestige of a 50-ton vessel.

Fast, graceful and spirited as she was, the *Don Juan* was certainly no craft to survive the approaching storm into which, with Shelley, Edward Williams and the boat-boy Charles Vivian on board, she disappeared off Leghorn on 8 July 1822. Trelawny had initially intended to accompany them on their journey back to Lerici in Byron's *Bolivar*, but at the last was delayed by the port authorities. Sullenly and reluctantly, he refurled the *Bolivar*'s sails, and watched the *Don Juan*'s progress through his spy-glass. The sea had the smoothness and colour of lead, but to the south-west black storm-clouds were massing dangerously. The devil, he was told by his Genoese mate, was brewing mischief. On shore, an anxious Daniel Roberts took a telescope to the top of the lighthouse, straining to get one last view of the boat before it vanished into the thickening mist.

Sometime after six the storm broke with a sudden and spectacular violence. The captain of an Italian vessel which had made it back to the safety of the harbour reported sighting the *Don Juan* in mountainous seas. He had offered to take its crew aboard, but a voice had cried back 'No'. A sailor called across for them to reef their sails at least, but when Williams was seen trying to lower them Shelley had seized an arm, angrily determined to stop him.[13]*

It was the last time the *Don Juan* was seen. Over the next ten days, while Mary and Jane waited in agony and Trelawny tirelessly patrolled the coast, pieces of wreckage followed by the bodies of Vivian, Williams and Shelley were washed ashore. Shelley's corpse was found on the beach at Viareggio. After so long in the water the face was gone but Trelawny was able to identify him by the clothes and a copy of Keats's poems still folded back in his jacket pocket. The body was buried where it lay in a shallow grave of quicklime, and Trelawny hurried to the Casa Magni on the Gulf of Spezia, the summer house where the Shelleys and Williamses had been living since the end of April. Over fifty years later he returned to the memory in a passage honed by time and repetition.

> I had ridden fast, to prevent any ruder messenger from bursting in on them. As I stood on the threshold of the house, the bearer, or rather confirmer, of news which would rack every fibre of their quivering frames to the utmost, I paused, and looking at the sea, my memory reverted to our joyous parting only a few days before.
>
> The two families, then, had all been on the veranda, overhanging a sea so clear and calm that every star was reflected on the water, as if it had been a mirror; the young mothers singing some merry tune, with the accompaniment of a guitar. Shelley's shrill laugh – I heard it still – rang in my ears, with Williams' friendly hale, the general *buona notte* of all the joyous party, and the earnest entreaty to me to return as soon as possible, and not forget the commissions they had given me.
>
> My reverie was broken by a shriek from the nurse

Caterina, as, crossing the hall she saw me in the doorway. After asking her a few questions, I went up the stairs, and, unannounced, entered the room. I neither spoke, nor did they question me. Mrs Shelley's large grey eyes were fixed on my face. I turned away. Unable to bear this horrid silence, with a convulsive effort she exclaimed –

'Is there no hope?'

I did not answer, but left the room, and sent the servant with the children to them. The next day I prevailed on them to return to Pisa. The misery of that night and the journey the next day, and of many days and nights that followed, I can neither describe nor forget.[14]

There were quarantine laws to meet before the bodies of Shelley or Williams could be touched, but the man who claimed to have cremated his eastern bride was more than up to the challenge of a proper funeral. Mary Shelley had at first wanted her husband buried alongside their son in the Protestant cemetery in Rome, but in the end more exotic council prevailed. On 14 August, the body of Williams was finally exhumed and cremated in a macabre dress rehearsal for what was to follow. The next morning, with Byron and the newly arrived Leigh Hunt present, it was Shelley's turn in a scene which in all its gruesome detail has etched itself onto the Romantic imagination.

> The lonely and grand scenery that surrounded us so exactly harmonized with Shelley's genius, that I could imagine his spirit soaring over us. The sea, with the islands of Gorgona, Capraja, and Elba, was before us; old battlemented watch-towers stretched along the coast, backed by the marble-crested Appenines glistening in the sun, picturesque from their diversified outlines, and not a human dwelling was in sight. As I thought of the delight Shelley felt in such scenes of loneliness and grandeur whilst living, I thought we were no better than a herd of wolves or a pack of wild dogs, in tearing out his battered and naked body from the pure yellow sand that lay so lightly over it, to drag him back to the light

of day; but the dead have no voice, nor had I power to check the sacrilege – the work went on silently in the deep and unresisting sand, not a word was spoken, for the Italians have a touch of sentiment, and their feelings are easily excited into sympathy. Byron was silent and thoughtful. We were startled and drawn together by a dull hollow sound that followed the blow of a mattock; the iron had struck a skull, and the body was soon uncovered. Lime had been strewn on it; this or decomposition had the effect of staining it of a dark and ghastly indigo colour. Byron asked me to preserve the skull for him; but remembering that he had formerly used one as a drinking-cup, I was determined Shelley should not be so profaned. The limbs did not separate from the trunk, as in the case of Williams's body, so that the corpse was removed entire into the furnace . . . After the fire was well kindled we repeated the ceremony of the previous day; and more wine was poured over Shelley's dead body than he had consumed during his life. This with the oil and salt made the yellow flames glisten and quiver. The heat from the sun and fire was so intense that the atmosphere was tremulous and wavy. The corpse fell open and the heart was laid bare. The frontal bone of the skull, where it had been struck with the mattock, fell off; and, as the back of the head rested on the red-hot bottom bars of the furnace, the brains literally seethed, bubbled, and boiled as in a cauldron, for a very long time.

Byron could not face this scene, he withdrew to the beach and swam off to the 'Bolivar'. Leigh Hunt remained in the carriage. The fire was so fierce as to produce a white heat on the iron, and to reduce its contents to grey ashes. The only portions that were not consumed were some fragments of bones, the jaw, and the skull; but what surprised us all was that the heart remained entire. In snatching this relic from the fiery furnace, my hand was severely burnt; and had anyone seen me do the act I should have been put into quarantine.[15]

In the long years ahead, Shelley's funeral would come to seem the making of Trelawny, the beginning of his public ministry as high priest and interpreter of English Romanticism. During the short time that he had known Shelley and Byron he had certainly become an integral part of their Pisan world, but the truth is that it was his role at their deaths and not the friendship of a few brief months which gave him his apostolic authority over a generation infatuated with their memory.

In account after account over the next sixty years he would return to this summer of 1822 with ever new details, peddling scraps of history or bone with equal relish. Yet if his long-term strategy became one of ruthless self-promotion, in the short term Shelley's death brought out a streak of selfless and generous kindness his earlier life had stifled. In the bleak and wearing months after the *Don Juan* went down, Trelawny almost single-handedly sustained the grieving widows, giving them not just unstinted emotional support but practical and financial help that earned their deep and genuine gratitude. 'His whole conduct during his last stay here has impressed us all with an affectionate regard, and a perfect faith in the unalienable goodness of his heart,'[16] Mary Shelley wrote to Jane Williams from Florence on 23 July 1823, shortly before her own departure for England where Jane had already gone. 'It went to my heart to borrow the sum from him necessary to make up my journey,' she wrote again only a week later, 'but he behaved with so much quick generosity, that one was almost glad to put him to the proof, and witness the excellence of his heart.'[17]

Through the desolate winter of 1822–3 Trelawny came closer to Mary than at any time in their long relationship, but it was with another of Shelley's circle that he formed during this time what is possibly the most enduring, if impenetrable, friendship of his life.

A curious compound of apparent opposites, of selfishness and generosity, common sense and fatuous silliness, of shrewd judgement and uncontrollable passion, of clinging dependence and brave and dogged self-sufficiency, Claire Clairmont is at once the most touching and exasperating member of Shelley's and Byron's world. She had been born in the spring of 1798 as the illegitimate child of a woman who went under the name of 'Mrs Clairmont', and at the age of three was taken with her brother Charles to Somers Town in London, where in the same year their mother met and married the widower of Mary Wollstonecraft, the great radical and political philosopher, William Godwin.

From the earliest age, Claire thus found herself in one of the most free-thinking and politically conscious households in England, the step-daughter of a famous writer and step-sister to another in the future Mary Shelley. As a child, too, she was raised and educated with the same care that was expended on the boys of the family, and she grew up with all the principles and beliefs that lay at the core of the Godwin ménage, as exuberantly and unapologetically a child of the revolutionary age as if she had indeed been Godwin and Mary Wollstonecraft's natural daughter.

When Claire was fourteen her half-sister, Mary, fell in love with the young poet and disciple of Godwin, Percy Bysshe Shelley. Shelley was already a married man when he first met Mary, but two years later the couple eloped to France and took Claire with them, walking, riding and slumming their way across the French country-side until poverty and Mary's pregnancy brought them back to England and reality.

It is hard to imagine what the sixteen-year-old girl thought she was doing with Mary and Shelley in France at this time, but if her teasing and subversive presence in their lives is still one of the unresolved mysteries of biography, there was odder yet to come. Within two years of their triangular elopement and still only seventeen, she eclipsed Mary's conquest of Shelley with a married poet of her own, throwing herself at Lord Byron with a reckless and infatuated passion that his indolent and self-indulgent nature was unable to resist. 'An utter stranger takes the liberty of addressing you,' she wrote to him above the assumed name of E. Trefusis.

It may seem a strange assertion, but it is none the less true that I place my happiness in your hands ... If a woman, whose reputation as yet remained unstained, if without either guardian or husband to control, she should throw herself on your mercy, if with a beating heart she should confess the love she has borne you many years ... could you betray her, or would you be silent as the grave?[18]

If a whole life can ever be said to hinge on a single action or judgement, then Claire Clairmont's unprovoked assault on Byron in the March of 1816 is it. In the wake of the scandalous collapse of his marriage Byron was certainly ready for a brief and loveless affair, but to Claire it was the most important moment of her life, a moment at once of complete fulfilment and self-destructive folly which she was to regret for sixty bitter years.

Had the affair ended there and then, however, Claire Clairmont's history might well have been very different, but in that same summer of 1816, a mixture of her persistence and Byron's weakness saw it revived on the shores of Lake Leman and in January 1817 she gave birth to his daughter. The following March the baby was christened Clara Allegra Byron, but other than giving the child his name the father was unmoved. Boredom with Claire had long turned to an uncharacteristically implacable dislike of what he called her 'Bedlam behaviour', and even when the following year he agreed to assume responsibility for his daughter, it was an arrangement from which the mother was ruthlessly excluded.

It was this unstable, passionate and generous woman, with a past and pedigree to match – the step-daughter of Godwin, the sister-in-law of Shelley and the ex-mistress of Byron – with whom Trelawny now fell violently in love. Claire was still only twenty-three when they first met at the house of the Williamses in February 1822, a gifted linguist and musician, dark haired, clever and attractive enough – whatever the evidence of Amelia Curran's Rome portrait – to have inspired at least one brilliantly shallow lyric of homage from Byron.

In her journal Claire recorded this first meeting without comment, and yet even had she felt any reciprocal interest at this time, the sudden death from typhoid of her daughter Allegra in the convent where Byron had placed her was soon to eclipse all else. In the immediate aftermath of the news Claire seems to have behaved with a dignity and calm that surprised everyone, but the silence of her journal over the next five months is an eloquent measure of a grief which only grew with the years.

It was a grief, too, which no one around could ignore, an event about which no one could remain neutral, and Allegra's death marks the first major split in the Pisan Circle that had gathered around Byron and Shelley, the first bitter issue over which those battle lines were drawn that were to hold their partisan shape way beyond the deaths of the main protagonists.

At a time of such drama and tension it is difficult to see Trelawny remaining indifferent, but there is no clue to the way his relationship with Claire developed until in a sense it was all over. In the wake of Allegra's and Shelley's deaths his kindness must have brought her closer in the same way it did Mary and Jane, and yet as Claire prepared over the summer of 1822 to leave Italy there is nothing in any surviving correspondence that could possibly suggest a crisis in their friendship, and still less the torrent of passionate letters from Trelawny that followed her into her long exile as a governess.

That crisis is cryptically marked in her journal. The last prosaic entry had been for 13 April, just six days before Allegra's death. It resumes again on Friday 6 September 1822, with a simple note of the date and nothing else. Three years later, however, while Claire was living on the country estate of her employers at Islavsk, outside Moscow, another entry gives some hint of what that date had meant to her. 'Tuesday August 25th. Septr. 6th.' she recorded, using both calendars

> Lovely weather. I think a great deal of past times to-day and
> above all of this day three years. but the sentiments of that
> time are most likely long ago, vanished into air. This is life.
> So live to nothing but toil and trouble – all its sweets are
> like the day whose anniversary this is – more transitory than
> a shade – yet it had been otherwise if Inwalert had been

different and I might have been as happy as I am now wretched.[19]

In Trelawny's letters over the autumn and winter of 1822–3, however, the crackling fallout of that day in September has left a less ambiguous trace. It is impossible to say with any certainty what happened when they met for the last time on the banks of the Arno, but the bond that it established and its devastating impact on Trelawny are beyond question. Over the next months he sent letter after letter to Claire in Vienna, violent and tender, demanding and conciliatory, histrionic and emotionally truthful by turn. 'A gnarled tree may bear good fruit,' he gnomically declared from the back of his horse in one undated letter soon after, 'and a harsh nature may find good council . . .'

> let us be firm and staunch friends we both want friends – you have lost in Shelley one worthy to be called so – I cannot fill his place – as who can – but you will not find me altogether unworthy the office. Linked thus together we may defy the fate that separates us for a time – with united hearts – what can separate us . . . In solitude silence or absence I think of your words – and can even make sacrifices to reason . . . [20]

The last six lines of this letter have been scratched out by Claire, but enough of Trelawny's correspondence remains uncensored to underline the Byronic tenor of his courtship. You 'tortured me almost into convulsions,' he told her in a letter written from Pisa when he realized she was irreparably lost to him, 'have left me fetid, morbid, and broken hearted.'

> Why have you thus plunged me into excruciating misery by deserting him that would – but bleed on in silence my heart – let not the cold and heartless mock thee with their triumphs.[21]

'Your weak impress of Love was a figure Trenched in ice; which with an hour's heat dissolved to water!' he complained on 4 October,

you! you! torture me Claire, your cold, cruel heartless letter
has driven me mad – it is ungenerous under the mask of
love – to enact the part of a demon . . . you have had my
heart, and gathered, and gathered my crudest, idlest most
entangled surmises . . . I am hurt to the very soul. I am
shamed and sick to death to be thus trampled on & despised,
my heart is bruised . . . much as endurance has hardened
me, I must give you the consolation of knowing – that you
have inflicted on me an incurable wound which is festering
& inflaming my blood.[22]

'I have used no false colours,' he again told her with more emotional
than literal truth, 'no hypocrisy – enacted no part.'

I have as dispassionately as I could – disclosed my feelings
. . . I loved you the first day, – nay before I saw you, – you
loathed and heaped on me contumely and neglect till we were
about to separate – Clare I love you and do what you will – I
shall remain deeply interested for you. I think you are right in
withdrawing your fate from mine – my nature has been perverted by neglect and disappointment in those I loved – my
disposition is unamiable. I am sullen, savage, suspicious &
discontented – I can't help it – you have sealed me so.[23]

Somewhere behind the grief, the mortification and the posturing at
Claire's abandonment, however, Trelawny probably knew, as he
suggests here, that she was right to keep their two lives apart. There
seems no need to question the intensity of his feelings for her, and
yet it is difficult to resist the sense that it was her history as much
as herself that attracted him, or that his love was something that
could flourish more easily *in absentia*.

This was something Claire, despite her genuine and lasting fondness for him, also recognized. 'I admire esteem and love him;' she
wrote to Mary Shelley eight years later, when experience had damped
down those passions that had ruined her life,

some excellent qualities he possesses in a degree that is
unsurpassed but then it is exactly in another direction from

the centre of my impetus. He likes a turbid and troubled
life; I a quiet one; he is full of fine feelings and has no
principles; I am full of fine principles but never had a feeling
(in my life). He receives (every) all his impressions through
his heart; I through my head. *Che vuol? Le moyen de se
rencontrer* when one is bound for the North Pole and the
other for the South.[24]

It is characteristic of Trelawny that at the same time as he was
berating Claire for her inconstancy, he was consoling himself with
other affairs, but without her or the circle that had gathered round
Shelley and Mary, his life threatened to lapse back into the brainless
rhythms of former days. On 22 November, he wrote half-heartedly
to her of his plans. Byron's boat, the *Bolivar*, which he had skip-
pered, was laid up, but he had thoughts of shooting with Roberts
and then sailing among the islands in the spring in the salvaged
Don Juan. It was, he told her 'a weary and wretched existence
without ties,' his life little more than 'dying piecemeal'.[25]

Almost in spite of himself, however, there was a buoyancy about
Trelawny that would always assert itself, and in Shelley's death, too,
he still had unfinished business. In January 1823, Shelley's ashes
had been deposited in the Protestant Cemetery at Rome, but when
Trelawny visited the place in the spring he found them in a public
grave, 'mingled in a heap with five or six common vagabonds'.[26]

His distress at this indignity was certainly genuine, and yet a
letter of Keats's friend, Joseph Severn – complaining of Trelawny's
cavalier attitude to a memorial design Severn had done for the tomb
– underlines just how far down the road to recovery he had come:

> There is a mad chap come here – whose name is Trelawny.
> I do not know what to make of him, further than his queer,
> and, I was near saying, shabby behaviour to me. He comes
> on the friend of Shelley, great, glowing, and rich in romance.
> Of course I showed all my paint-pot politeness to him, to
> the very brim ... I made the drawing, which cost us some
> trouble, yet after expressing the greatest liking for it, this
> pair of Mustachios has shirked off from it, without giving

us the yea or no – without even the why or wherefore. – I was sorry at this most on Mr Gotts account, but I ought to have seen that this Lord Byron's jackal was rather weak in all the points I could judge, though strong enough in stiletto's. We have not had any open rupture, nor shall we, for I have no doubt that this 'cockney corsair' fancies he has greatly obliged us by all this trouble we have had. But tell me who is this odd fish? They talk of him here as a camelion who went mad on reading Ld. Byron's 'Corsair'.[27]

With the help of Severn, Trelawny had Shelley's ashes disinterred and reburied in a 'beautiful and lonely plot'[28] near the pyramid of Caius Cestius. He added an inscription from *The Tempest* to Leigh Hunt's simple 'Cor Cordium', and planted the grave with 'six young cypresses and four laurels'.[29] In a gesture which, in 1823, must have had more to do with a clinging sense of identification than inspired prescience, he then had his own grave dug next to that of Shelley – 'so that when I die,' as he reported back to Mary in a burst of necrophiliac chumminess,

> there is only to lift up the coverlet and role me into its – you may lie on the other side or I will share my narrow bed with you if you like.[30]

But if Shelley was gone Byron was still left, and for all the talk of death and world-weariness, the sniff of celebrity Trelawny had enjoyed in Pisa had been too intoxicating for him to face oblivion now with any equanimity. Throughout his life Trelawny would always ride the shifting thermals of their literary fame with effortless ease, but in truth it had always been the 'sun' rather than the 'glow-worm' that had warmed his youthful imagination into life, and it was to Byron now that he turned in search of a new role.

He was fortunate, too, in his timing, as events in both his and Byron's lives now freed them from the chains of their Italian idleness.

Trelawny was still writing long letters to Claire, but the first intensity of his attachment had cooled to something more honest, more in keeping with what they both wanted and needed of their friendship. In a letter written to her from Rome in April 1823, he told her that she had misunderstood his meaning, that he had never intended her staying with him. The following month he was more explicit. 'Now to proceed to your most urgent questions, which I have hitherto avoided,' he wrote in reply to a lost letter:

> As to my fortune – my income is reduced to about £500 a year – the woman I married having bankrupted me in fortune as well as happiness. If I outlive two or three relations – I shall, however, retrieve in some measure my fortunes – so you see, dear Clare how thoughtless and vain was my idea of our living together: as Keats says
>
> > 'Love in a hut, with water and a crust,
> > Is – Love, forgive us! cinders, ashes, dust;'
>
> Poverty and difficulties have not – or ever will – teach me prudence or make me like Michael Cassio a great Arithmetician – all my calculations go to the devil – in anything that appeals to my heart – and this kind of prodigality has kept me in troubled water all my days: as to my habits – no Hermit's simpler – my expenses are within even the limits of my beggarly means – but who can have gone through such varieties of life as I have – and not have formed a variety of ties with the poor and unfortunate; – I am so shackled with these that I do not think I have even a right to form a connection which would affect them – what abject slaves are us poor of fortune – enough of this hateful topic.
>
> It is a source of great pleasure to me, your friendship – to be beloved – and Love – under whatever circumstances – is still happiness – the void in my affections is filled up – and though separate – I have lost that despairing dreary feeling of loneliness – I look forward with something of hope.
>
> I am anxious to get to sea. Write to me here – and let

me know your address – I do not like to importune you
about writing. There are some pleasant women here, which
induces me to go more into society than usual . . . .

Dear, I am not in the vein for writing –
Your unalterably
Attached
Edward.
May 15 1823
Florence[31]

At the time of this letter Trelawny probably had nothing fixed in
mind when he spoke of the sea, but over the next months the
unspoken possibility of joining Byron on an expedition took on a
solid form. From the very start of their acquaintance there had
always been desultory talk of travel in one direction or another, and
when the idea of fighting for Greek independence suddenly became
more than talk in the early summer of 1823, Trelawny was ready
to join the crusade. 'I wish Lord Byron was as sincere in his wish
of going to Greece – as I am,' he confided to Mary Shelley,

every one seems to think it a fit theatre for him . . . at all
events tell him how willingly I will embark in the cause –
and stake my all on the cast of the die – Liberty or nothing.[32]

By the early summer of 1823 Greece had been at war with Ottoman
Turkey for just over two years, drawing men from all over Europe
and America to a country that had long held a special place in the
Western imagination. From the day in March 1751 when James
Stuart and Nicholas Revett landed at the port of Athens to make
the first accurate drawings of its ruins, travellers, painters, scholars,
dilettanti, soldiers and architects had all made their way out to
Greece, sketching and plundering its sites, charting its battlefields
and searching the modern Greek's physiognomy for some trace of its
ancient lineaments, some link between the Greece which languished

under Turkish rule and the land that had produced the poetry of Homer and the sculpture of the Acropolis.

It was in 1809 that the twenty-one-year-old Byron had first followed in this tradition, travelling with his long-suffering Cambridge friend John Cam Hobhouse through Ali Pasha's Albania to Delphi, Athens, and on to Smyrna, Ephesus and Constantinople. In the years before this 'pilgrimage', Byron had gained a minor reputation in England as an aristocratic poetaster and satirist, but it was with the verses of 'Childe Harold', published on his return, that he not only made his own name but cast this old Philhellenism into the form that was to galvanize Romantic Europe into action.

Oh, thou, Parnassus! whom I now survey,
Not in the phrensy of a dreamer's eye,
Not in the fabled landscape of a lay,
But soaring snow-clad through thy native sky,
In the wild pomp of mountain majesty!
What marvel if I thus essay to sing?
The humblest of the pilgrims passing by
Would gladly woo thine Echoes with his string,
Though from thy heights no more one Muse will wave her wing.

Fair Greece! sad relic of departed worth!
Immortal, though no more; though fallen, great!
Who now shall lead thy scatter'd children forth,
And long accustom'd bondage uncreate?
Not such thy sons who whilome did await,
The hopeless warriors of a willing doom,
In bleak Thermopylae's sepulchral strait –
Oh! who that gallant spirit shall resume,
Leap from Eurotas' banks, and call thee from the tomb?

Where'er we tread 'tis haunted, holy ground;
No earth of thine is lost in vulgar mould,
But one vast realm of wonder spreads around,
And all the Muse's tales seem truly told,
Till the sense aches with gazing to behold
The scenes our earliest dreams have dwelt upon;

Each hill and dale, each deepening glen and wold
Defies the power which crush'd thy temples gone:
Age shakes Athena's tower, but spares gray Marathon.[33]

There is not an idea here that was new – not an idea of any sort it could be argued – but faced with verses of this power it is as idle to think of Byron as a product of Philhellenism as it is to see Shakespeare as a mere child of the Elizabethan Renaissance. The excitement and sentiments displayed were certainly no more Byron's invention than was the 'Byronic hero', and yet in 'Childe Harold' and his Eastern Tales he succeeded in setting the stamp of his personality on a whole movement, giving it a new and popular currency and charting the emotional and topographical map-references from which Philhellenism has never tried to escape.

It is not simply that there is no figure in Philhellene history to compare with Byron, there is no second to him. What we are looking at in the verses of 'Childe Harold' or 'Don Juan' is some kind of literary take-over, at a whole disparate, woolly and amorphous movement captured and vitalized by the specific genius of one man. Before Byron, it is safe to say, for all its seriousness, its achievements, its intelligence, there was no folly of which western Philhellenism was incapable: after Byron, for all its romantic froth, there was nothing to which it would not aspire.

> The mountains look on Marathon –
> And Marathon looks on the sea;
> And musing there an hour alone,
> I dream'd that Greece might still be free;[34]

The history of the Philhellene movement is so impossible to imagine without Byron that it always comes as a surprise to remember that for almost three years of the war his involvement remained no more than this 'dream'. On the outbreak of rebellion in 1821, he had returned to the theme of Greek freedom with some of the most famous lyrics in 'Don Juan' and, again, in the following year, there had been some desultory talk of volunteering, but his letters for this period – for the years that Trelawny knew him – are the letters of a man submerged in a life of literary and social affairs that left little room for Greece. It was a life full of gossip and flirtations, of boats, business and his mistress, Teresa Guiccioli, of Italian politics and proof-reading, of arguments about Pope and the deaths of Shelley and Keats, of Leigh Hunt's financial affairs and repulsive children, of rows with his publisher Murray and over Allegra, of Lady Byron and his half-sister Augusta – a life at once so full and empty as to be much like any other except that it was lived out by Byron. In 1823 Byron could as easily have gone to Spain as Greece; or Naples, or South America, or a South Sea Island, or nowhere at all. Chance, pique, sloth, lust, avarice, good nature and pride might still have disposed of him in any of a dozen ways that summer: only myth pushes him towards Greece with a confidence that will brook no dissent.

Given how much was at stake there is something alarming in the precariousness of this historical process, in its casual and arbitrary shedding of options until all that was left was the brittle chain of events that in 1823 lead Byron from Italy to Missolonghi. During the months that Trelawny chafed impatiently at his irresolution, the London Greek Committee had done all it could to flatter and cajole Byron into a proper sense of his destiny, and yet it remains as hard to define what it was that finally stirred him to action as it is for the most obscure volunteer whose name is alongside his on that Nauplia monument.

It is tempting to think, in fact, that there is no one about whom so much was said and written and about whom we know so little as the figure on whom Trelawny and all Philhellene Europe waited that summer. A generation before Byron, Boswell's Johnson had been the object of the same obsessive interest to his circle, but between the two men something had happened – some permanent and vulgarizing shift in the popular conception of the artist – that the Byron myth both lived off and fed.

The minutiae of Johnson's life seemed of value to Boswell because, with the instinct of genius, he knew that they revealed the inner man. With Byron the details were all that mattered, valuable by a simple process of association, the raw material of an indiscriminate and insatiable curiosity which set the pattern for all future fame.

Nobody it seems, at this time, met Byron without recording their impressions. Nothing, either, was too small to be saved for posterity. We know then the state of the Cheshire cheese he ate and the manufacturer of his ale, the colour and trimming of his jacket, the style of his helmet and every last detail of the bizarre retinue of servants, horses and dogs that he collected in preparation for war: what remains a mystery is the lonely process by which he came to terms with the realities of his commitment to the Greek cause.

It is more than likely that he did not know himself. Certainly his letters – flippant, self-deprecating, brilliant, but ultimately elusive – give nothing away. Byron was far too intelligent to indulge in the inflated expectations of so many Philhellenes, only too aware of Greek attitudes and of his own limitations. He had enjoyed and suffered far too much fame to need to find it in Greece. He was thirty-six years old, though sixty in spirit, as he had been claiming on and off since 1816. He was, since the collapse of his disastrous marriage seven years earlier, an exile. He was a poet writing the greatest poetry of his life, but conscious too of a world of action that held an irresistible fascination. He was an aristocrat alert to his status, and a liberal conscious of his moral duties. He was, above all, half reluctantly, indolently, but inescapably, the repository of the expectations of an age he had done so much to shape – expectations which carried with them a burden that took on all the heaviness of fate: 'Dear T.,' he finally wrote to Trelawny in June: 'you may have heard that I am going to Greece. Why do you not come with me?... they all say that I can be of use in Greece. I do not know how, nor do they; but at all events let us go.'[35]

It was the letter for which Trelawny had been waiting – for months certainly, possibly all his life. On 26 June, he wrote to his old friend Daniel Roberts from Florence.

> Dear Roberts,
>   Your letter I have received and one from Lord Byron. I shall start for Leghorn to-morrow, but must stop there some days to collect together the things necessary for my expedition. What do you advise me to do? My present

intention is to go with as few things as *possible*, my little horse, a servant, and two very small saddle portmanteaus, a sword and pistols, but not my Manton gun, a military frock undress coat and one for superfluity, 18 shirts, &c. I have with me a Negro servant, who speaks English – a smattering of French and Italian, understands horses and cooking, a willing though not a very bright fellow. He will go anywhere or do anything he can, nevertheless if you think the other more desirable, I will change – and my black has been in the afterguard of a man of war. What think you?

I have kept all the dogs for you, only tell me if you wish to have all three. But perhaps you will accompany us. All I can say is, if you go, I will share what I have freely with you – I need not add with what pleasure! . . . How can one spend a year so pleasantly as travelling in Greece, and with an agreeable party?[36]

The next day, on the road to Leghorn, there was a more difficult letter to write.

Dearest Clare,

What is it that causes this long and trying silence? – I am fevered with anxiety – of the cause – day after day I have suffered the tormenting pains of disappointment – tis two months nearly since I have heard. What is the cause, sweet Clare? – how have I newly offended – that I am to be thus tortured? –

How shall I tell you, dearest, or do you know it – that – that – I am actually now on my road – to Embark for Greece? – and that I am to accompany a man that you disesteem? ['Disesteem' to one of the century's great haters!] – forgive me – extend to me your utmost stretch of toleration – and remember that you have in some degree driven me to this course – forced me into an active and perilous life – to get rid of the pain and weariness of my lonely existence; – had you been with me – or here – but how can I live or rather exist as I have been for some time? – My ardent love of freedom spurs me on to assist in the struggle for freedom. When was there so glorious a banner flying as that unfurled in Greece? – who would not fight under it? – I have long contemplated this – but – I was deterred by the fear that an unknown stranger without money &. would be ill received. – I now go under better auspices – L.B. is one of the Greek Committee; he takes out arms, ammunition, money, and protection to them – when once there I can shift for myself – and shall see what is to be done![37]

The implied urgency in Trelawny's letters, their sense of bustle and importance, was for once justified. Now that Byron had made up his mind, he moved quickly. The *Bolivar* was sold, and his Italian affairs brought into order. He had engaged a vessel, the *Hercules*, he told Trelawny, and would be sailing from Genoa. 'I need not say,' he added, 'that I shall like your company of all things,' – a tribute he was movingly to repeat in a last footnote to Trelawny in a letter written only days before his death.[38]

Travelling on horseback from Florence to Lerici, where he wandered again through the desolate rooms of Shelley's Casa Magni, Trelawny reached Byron at the Casa Saluzzi, near Albaro. The next day he saw the *Hercules* for the first time. To the sailor and romantic in him it was a grave disappointment. To Byron, however, less in need of exotic props than his disciple, the collier-built tub – 'roundbottomed, and bluff bowed, and of course, a dull sailor'[39] – had one estimable advantage. 'They say', he told Trelawny, 'I have got her on very easy terms ... We must make the best of it,' he added with ominous vagueness. 'I will pay her off in the Ionian Islands, and stop there until I see my way.'[40]

On 13 July 1823, horses and men were loaded on board the *Hercules*, and Trelawny's long wait came to an end. Ahead of him lay a life he had so far only dreamed of, but he was ready. The war out in Greece might have been no more than 'theatre' to him, yet if there was anyone mentally or emotionally equipped to play his role in the coming drama, anyone who had already imaginatively made the part his own, then it was Trelawny.

Over the last eighteen months too, he had grown into his role, grown in confidence, in conviction, in plausibility. At the beginning of 1822 Byron had announced Trelawny's arrival to Teresa Guiccioli with a cool and ironic amusement: by the summer of 1823 he had become an essential companion.

And now, too, as the *Hercules* ploughed through heavy waters on the first stage of its journey south, all the landmarks that had bound Trelawny to the Pisan Circle slipped past in slow review as if to seal this pact: Genoa, where the *Don Juan* had been built for Shelley to Trelawny's design – 'the treacherous bark which proved his coffin,'[41] as he bitterly described it to Claire Clairmont; St Terenzo, with the Casa Magni, Shelley's last house, set low on the sea's edge against a dark backdrop of wooded cliffs; Viareggio where he and Byron had swum after Williams's cremation until Byron was sick with exhaustion; Pisa where they had first met at the Palazzo Lanfranchi, and finally Leghorn, from where almost exactly a year earlier, Shelley, Edward Williams and the eighteen-year-old Charles Vivian – one of Romanticism's forgotten casualties – had set out on their last voyage.

It was on the fifth day out of Genoa, and only after a storm had driven them back into port, that the *Hercules* finally made Leghorn. Byron had business ashore, and some last letters to write – a three-line note to Teresa Guiccioli, assuring her of his love, and a rather more fulsome declaration of homage to Goethe, 'the undisputed Sovereign of European literature'.[42] On 23 July they were ready to sail again, and took on board two dubious Greeks and a young Scotsman, Hamilton Browne, who had served in the Ionian Isles. Browne was rowed out to the ship by a friend, the son of the Reverend Jackson who had famously poisoned himself during the Irish troubles to thwart justice. Byron recognized the name and was quick with his sympathy. 'His lordship's mode of address,' Browne wrote of this first meeting, 'was peculiarly fascinating and insinuating – "au premier abord" it was next to impossible for a stranger to refrain from liking him.'[43]

Byron, however, was going to need more than charm to survive the months ahead as their brief stop in Leghorn underlined. While the *Hercules* was still in the roads, he wrote a final letter to Bowring, the Secretary of the London Greek Committee to which he had been elected, striking in it a note that can be heard again and again in his subsequent letters from Greece. 'I find the Greeks here somewhat divided amongst themselves', he reported,

> I have spoken to them about the delay of intelligence for the Committee's regulation – and they have promised to be more punctual. The Archbishop is at Pisa – but has sent me several letters etc. for Greece. – What they most seem to want or desire is – Money – Money – Money . . . As the Committee has not favoured me with any specific instructions as to any line of conduct they might think it well for me to pursue – I of course have to suppose that I am left to my own discretion. If at any future period – I can be useful – I am willing to be so as heretofore. –[44]

The punctuation of Byron's letters invariably gives a strong sense of rapidity and urgency of thought, an immediacy that makes him one of the great letter writers in the language, and yet curiously here it only serves to reinforce a sense of uncertainty and drift. It is a feeling that seems mirrored in the mood on the *Hercules* as each day put his Italian life farther behind him. There is an air of unreality about this journey, as if the *Hercules* and its passengers were somehow suspended between the contending demands of past and future, divorced from both in the calm seas that blessed the next weeks of their passage. It is hard to believe that, for all his clear-eyed and tolerant realism about the Greeks, Byron had any real sense of what lay ahead. The memory of Shelley's corpse on the beach could quicken his natural fatalism into something like panic at the thought of pain but even this was a passing mood. As Trelawny later recalled, he had never travelled on ship with a better companion. The weather, after they left Leghorn, was beautiful and the *Hercules* seldom out of sight of land. Elba, the recent scene of Napoleon's first exile, was passed off the starboard bow with suitable moralizings. At the mouth of the Tiber the ship's company strained in vain for a glimpse of the city where Trelawny had buried Shelley's ashes and prepared his own grave. During the day Byron and Trelawny would box and swim together, measure their waistlines or practise on the poop with pistols, shooting the protruding heads off ducks suspended in cages from the mainyard. At night Byron might read from Swift or sit and watch Stromboli shrouded in smoke and promise another canto of 'Childe Harold'.

And yet Byron, if he ever had been, was no longer the 'Childe' and in that simple truth lay a world of future misunderstandings. One of the most moving aspects of his last year is the way his letters and actions reveal a gradual firming of purpose, a steady discarding of the conceits and fripperies of his Italian existence, a unifying of personality, an alignment at last of intelligence and sensibility – a growth into a human greatness which mirrors the development of his literary talents from the emotional and psychological crudity of 'Childe Harold' into the mature genius of 'Don Juan'.

For anyone interested in poetry it is in that last masterpiece that the real Byron is to be found, but it was not the Byron that Trelawny had come to Italy in search of. Even before the *Hercules* had left Leghorn he was airing his reservations in letters to Roberts and Claire, but the fact is that his unease in Byron's company was as long as their friendship itself. Eighteen months earlier, in January 1822, Trelawny had come looking for Childe Harold and found instead a middle-aged and worldly realist. He had come to worship and found a deity cynically sceptical of his own cult. 'I had come prepared to see a solemn mystery,' he wrote of their first meeting in the Palazzo Lanfranchi, 'and so far as I could judge from the first act it seemed to me very like a solemn farce.'[45]

One of the great truisms of Romantic history is that Byron was never 'Byronic' enough for his admirers but this failure to live up to expectations seems to have constituted a more personal betrayal for Trelawny than it did for other acolytes. In trying to explain this there is a danger of ignoring the vast intellectual gap which separated the two men, yet nevertheless something is needed to account for the resentment which, even as they set off together, he was stoking up against Byron. Partly, of course, it was the bitterness of the disappointed disciple, but there was something more than that, something which Romantic myth and twentieth-century psychology in their different ways both demand to be recognized – the rage of the creature scorned in the language of one, of childhood rejection in the more prosaic terminology of the other.

The moment words are put to it they seem overblown and lame by turns but it is impossible to ignore the evidence of a lifetime's anger. No iconoclast ever had such a capacity for hero-worship as Trelawny and, of the long string of real or imagined figures who filled the emotional vacuum of a loveless childhood, Byron was the earliest and the greatest. In among the fantasies that Trelawny published as his *Adventures*, there is a description of his first meeting with the mythical De Ruyter, the imagined archetype and amalgam of all Trelawny's heroes. It gives a vivid insight into what he had sought in Byron when he first came to Italy. 'He became my model,' he wrote,

> The height of my ambition was to imitate him, even in his defects. My emulation was awakened. For the first time I was impressed with the superiority of a human being. To keep an equality with him was unattainable. In every trifling action he evinced a manner so offhand, free, and noble, that it looked as if it sprung new and fresh from his own individuality; and everything else shrunk into an apish imitation.[46]

This kind of hero, however, was not a role that the thirty-five-year old Byron, with his anxieties over his weight or the thickness of his wrists, had either the inclination or temperament to fill. The helmets and uniforms in his luggage are reminders that, even in his last year, the exhibitionist in him was never entirely stilled, but the irony and self-mockery with which he treated himself in his poetry was now equally, if humorously, turned on his 'corsair'. Trelawny, he memorably remarked, could not tell the truth even to save himself. In another variant on this he suggested that they might yet make a gentleman of him if they could only get him to tell the truth and wash his hands.

For a man who was probably only too familiar with Trelawny's battle against his father's pet raven, this was a dangerously cavalier attitude to take to the child of his poetic imagination. 'The Creator', as Claire had warned Byron in her first letter to him before they met, 'ought not to destroy his Creature.'[47] For a man, also, who in Pisan lore had been responsible for the death of Claire's Allegra, this was doubly true. Byron was too careless, however, to see the trouble he was laying down. On board the *Hercules* a mixture of his own tolerance and Trelawny's presumption kept relationships cordial, but it was a deceptive calm. 'Lord B. and myself are extraordinarily thick,' Trelawny wrote edgily to his friend Roberts in a letter from Leghorn.

> We are inseparable. But mind, this does not flatter me. He has known me long enough to know the sacrifices I make in devoting myself to serve him. This is new to him, who is surrounded by mercenaries. I am no expense to him, fight my own way, lay in my own stock, etc . . . Lord B. indeed does everything as far as I wish him.'[48]

It was a sad delusion but it was enough to preserve the peace of the voyage. At the toe of Italy the *Hercules* turned east, through the Messina Straits and towards Greece. Their first destination was the port of Argostoli on Cephalonia, one of the Ionian Isles under British control. As they passed through the untroubled waters between Scylla and Charybdis, Byron complained of the tameness of life. His boredom was premature. His and Trelawny's lives were moving to their distinct but inseparable crises. 'Where', Byron had mused at Leghorn, 'shall we be in a year?' It afterwards seemed to Pietro Gamba, Teresa Guiccoli's brother, 'a melancholy foreboding; for on the same day of the same month, in the next year, he was carried to the tomb of his ancestors.'[49] On 2 August 1823, the *Hercules* entered the approaches to Argostoli. Byron had just nine months to live: Trelawny, nearly sixty years to vent his feelings against the man who had first created and then wearied of him.

3

ET IN ARCADIA EGO

'And without ties – wearied and wretched – melancholy and dissatisfied – what was left me here? – I have been dying piecemeal – thin – careworn – and desponding – Such an excitement as this was necessary to rouse me into energy and life – and it has done so – I am all on fire for action – and ready to endure the worst that may befall, seeking nothing but honour.'

Trelawny to Claire Clairmont 22 July 1823[1]

TEN DAYS AFTER THE *Hercules* anchored off the port of Argostoli, a small group from the ship lay picnicking beside the Fountain of Arethusa on the Homeric isle of Ithaca. Beneath them the water from the spring tumbled away into a dark ravine. 'The view,' Hamilton Browne, the young Philhellene who had joined them at Leghorn, recalled ten years later,

> embracing the vast sea-prospect, the Aechirades, the entrance to the Gulf of Corinth, or Lepanto, with the distant purple mountains of Epirus and Aetolia, lifting their lofty peaks into the clouds, was superb; and ascending the hill at the back of the cavern, Santa Maura, the ancient Leucadia, with its dependencies, was distinctly descried, together with Cephalonia, apparently close at hand; Zante, and the coast of the Peloponessus, trending far away to the southeast. A more lovely situation could scarcely be imagined.[2]

*

It would be difficult also to imagine a view more completely at odds with reality. If one could have followed Browne's panoramic sweep across the map of western and southern Greece, only seen it shorn of that seductive allure which distance and classical associations gave it for him – if one could have extended that view further, beyond the ruined city of Tripolis to Nauplia and Argos in the east, and beyond those again as far northwards as Salonica or south to Crete and Cyprus: or, again, if one shortened that perspective, to take in the emaciated figures crowding the little port of Vathi hidden at the picnickers' feet, refugees from the ruins of Patras and the horrors of Chios, then wherever one looked the wasted faces of survivors or the whitening bones which littered the Greek landscape in their thousands would all have told the same story of a war of unimaginable brutality.

The conflict that had so devastated Greece had begun just over two years earlier in the spring of 1821. On 6 March, a Russian general of Greek extraction had crossed the River Pruth from Bessarabia into what is now modern Romania, raised his banner of the phoenix and called on the Christian populations of the Ottoman empire to throw off their oppressors.

Political realism has never been a feature of modern Greek history but, even by the extravagances of the last century and a half, Moldavia was a curious place to start a revolution. For almost four hundred years the Trans-Danubian provinces of Moldavia and Wallachia had suffered the heavy burden of Ottoman rule, and yet at the end of all that time, if there was a single sentiment beyond a hatred of the Turks that might have united its disparate peoples, it was a loathing of the Greek that ran almost as deep. For nearly four centuries Greeks had worked within the Ottoman Empire as assiduously as they had within its Roman predecessor, their women stocking its harems and their children its armies, their merchants, sailors, translators and administrators garnering to themselves those tasks and powers that seemed below Moslem dignity, and their great Constantinople families – the Greeks of the Phanar on the southern shore of the Golden Horn – sending out generation after generation to govern in the Danubian provinces with a greed that comfortably eclipsed that of their masters.*

It was one of the great tragedies of the War of Independence that the melancholy condition of Greece itself meant that its leadership inevitably fell to these Greeks of the Phanar and the scattered communities which made up the world of the Greek diaspora. Since the last, magical flowering of Byzantine culture at Mystra in the fifteenth century the geographical area of Modern Greece had declined into a state of impoverished misery, an almost forgotten backwater of Ottoman Europe, its traditions of freedom wilted to the bandit culture of the mountain klephts and all memory of its unique artistic and political inheritance buried under centuries of oppression.

It was from the West that this memory, so vital and so hazardous to the regeneration of the country, was re-imported into Greece, but it was crucially among the educated communities of the diaspora that the first Greek converts were made. Throughout the eighteenth century, these colonies had grown and prospered in capitals and ports from Marseilles to Calcutta, and as this new pride in their ancient past seeped into their consciousness, western Hellenism underwent a crucial seachange that took it out of the study and into the realm of political ambition.

The result was a volatile and dangerous new faith which owed as much to the trading and cultural links of these colonies with the Phanariot world of Constantinople as it did to the architectural purism of Stuart and Revett. In the journals and paintings of European travellers and scholars, eighteenth-century Philhellenism largely remained an innocuous and literary phenomenon, but as it made its way back to the Greek communities of the Black Sea and southern Russia it became a heady mix of Hellenistic posturing and Byzantine nostalgia, of alien political theory and grandiose ambition that looked to Constantinople – simply but eloquently the '*polis*' – as the centre of a new-born Greece.

With the spread of the ideas and language of revolution after 1789 and the increased trade of the Napoleonic years, these aspirations gained a momentum that not even the Congress of Vienna could halt. By 1820, revolution to most Greeks within and without the Ottoman Empire seemed inevitable. For the previous five years a secret society called the Philike Hetairia had been at work, proselytizing and fund raising within the thriving Greek communities of Europe and Russia, and recruiting among the clergy and leaders of the Peloponnese and Northern Greece.

In 1820, a year of revolution across Europe, with rebellions in Portugal, Spain, Italy, and crucially, Ali Pasha's in Albania, the moment seemed at hand. Through the winter the Apostles of the Philike Hetairia moved through the islands and mainland of Greece, spreading the word from initiate to initiate to prepare for war. Secrecy was virtually abandoned, so certain was everyone of the approaching rebellion, so rightly confident of Turkish indolence. In the Peloponnese, Germanos, the Bishop of Patras, and Petro Bey Mavromichaelis, head of the Maniots in the southern mountains of ancient Sparta, made ready. From the Ionian Isles, the great bandit leader, Theodore Colocotrones, slipped back from exile onto the mainland, drawn by the irresistible lure of patriotism and plunder; and in a town in southern Russia, the committee of merchants who were the sole reality behind the Philike Hetairia's shadowy 'Grand Arch' appointed Alexander Ypsilanti to its supreme command.

Perhaps nothing so typifies the limitations of the Hetairists as that choice, because if Moldavia was an improbable place to begin a Greek revolution then Alexander Ypsilanti was an even more unlikely candidate for leader. A major general in the Russian army and the son of a Moldavian Greek *hospadar* or prince, Ypsilanti seems to have brought little to his task beyond the arrogance of the court and the morals of an autocracy, his single, dubious qualification for command being an arm lost in battle.

Within days of crossing the Pruth and beginning his leisurely march south, the 'steward of the stewards of the August Arch,' as he styled himself in a piece of characteristic masonic flummery, had succeeded only in alienating the Christian population he had come to redeem. By June the revolution in the Danubian provinces was over before it had ever really begun, disowned by the Tsar and riven by jealousies, a casualty of the indecision and moral cowardice of its leader and the sheer fatuity of Greek ambitions.

Ypsilanti's campaign and his own subsequent flight into Austria rank among the most disgraceful episodes of the whole war, and yet while the insurrection had failed in the Danubian provinces, it had taken hold in Greece itself. It had seemed inconceivable to conspirators there that the Philike Hetairia could enter Moldavia without the tacit support of the Tsar, and as they took stock of an Ottoman Empire frustrated from within by the conservatism of its military and religious leadership, threatened on its borders by their Russian co-religionists, its authority in Africa no more than nominal and its forces engaged in a war against its most powerful vassal in Albania, the expectations raised by the Society generated their own self-fulfilling momentum.

'Bliss was it in that dawn to be alive,' Wordsworth had once believed of the French Revolution, and few of Europe's Philhellenes who now saluted the Greek insurrection in the same vein can have had any idea of the forces they had unleashed. For centuries Greek and Turk had lived together in close proximity and when fighting burst out in 1821 it was not between army and army, but between community and community, atrocity met by atrocity and massacre by massacre in a frenzy of racial and religious hatred that convulsed the whole of the Greek world.

Within months of Germanos declaring a Holy War at Ayia Lavra, twenty thousand Turks had disappeared in the Peloponnese, as Monemvassia, Navarino, Tripolis, and eventually Nauplia fell into Greek hands. On the island of Chios, eighteen thousand Greeks were slaughtered in a matter of days. At Athens, Constantinople, Nicosia, Smyrna, Saloniki, on Rhodes and Cos, Greek butchered Turk and Turk Greek until, finally, when ancient hatreds had been glutted, when there were no more Turks to burn, rape, baptize and slaughter in the Peloponnese, and no more Greeks to circumcise and kill on Chios; when two thousand women and children had been stripped and butchered in a pass outside Tripolis, and the eighty-year-old patriarch hanged outside his cathedral in Constantinople, the war settled down into a more conventional shape.*

There are few conflicts before this century which so insistently demand to be remembered in terms of human misery, but if it is these horrors of 1821 that have left their most vivid mark on the national psyches of Greece and Turkey, it was the events of the next year that determined whether revolt would ever blossom into a full-scale war for independence. During the first months of rebellion Ottoman armies had been too busy with Ali Pasha of Ionnanina to deal with a second uprising as well, but with Ali's murder on 5 February 1822 Sultan Mahmoud II, a ruler of slow and inexorable purpose, was at last free to turn his full attention to Greece itself.

The Ottoman plan was simple, and was embarked on with a characteristic confidence that took no account of terrain, season or opposition. From his base at Larissa in northern Greece the overall commander in Roumeli, Khurshid Pasha, sent two armies south-wards down the western and eastern sides of the country, the first towards Misssolonghi and the other under the command of Dramali Pasha across the Isthmus of Corinth and into the Peloponnese and the heartland of the revolt.

With 23,000 men and 60,000 horses, Dramali's army was the greatest to enter Greece in over a hundred years. Sweeping virtually unchallenged across the isthmus in July 1822, the Turks pushed down as far as Argos only to be reduced within a month by disease, privation, incompetence and unripened fruit to a dangerous and humiliating retreat through the unsecured mountain passes south of Corinth.

This retreat of Dramali's weakened army gave the Greeks their greatest opportunity of the war in a terrain for which history, temperament and necessity had left them supremely well equipped. To the disgust of every foreigner reared on western tactics, their irregulars could never be made to stand up to Turkish cavalry in open conflict, but here among the crags and narrow mountain paths of Dervenakia it was another story, with those guerrilla skills honed by generations of brigand *klepht*s coming spectacularly into their own.

With the Ottoman army trapped 'like a herd of bisons'[3] in the narrow passes, flight or defiance equally useless, Dervenakia was less a battle than a massacre. If the Greeks had not been more interested in plunder than killing, the slaughter would have been still worse, but even so five thousand Turks were killed and the

army which had been sent to bring back 'the ashes of the Peloponnese' effectively destroyed. Ravaged by disease and hunger the rem-
nant began their retreat along the southern coast of the Gulf of
Corinth towards Patras, reduced first to horseflesh and then canni-
balism, fighting among themselves over the graves of their comrades,
burying their dead in the mornings only to dig them up again at
night in a gruesome bid to ward off starvation.

Dervenakia gave the Greek army its most decisive victory of the
whole war but just as important in its way was the campaign fought
at the same time in western Greece. The army that had slaughtered
the Turks in the passes of the north-east Peloponnese had fought
under the most experienced of brigand chiefs in Theodore Colocotrones, but the force raised to face the Ottoman threat to Missolonghi
was entrusted to the leadership of a newly arrived Phanariot
aristocrat, Alexander Mavrocordato, a man for all his other talents
without any experience of warfare and little enough of Greece
itself.

The details of the campaign which followed belong properly to
the military history of the rebellion, but the political and psychological impact of Mavrocordato's failure are too important to ignore.
The first task of this force was to relieve the Christian Suliote tribes
of Epirus on the Turkish army's right flank, and with this in mind
Mavrocordato marched north from Missolonghi towards Arta with
an army of a little over two thousand men, including in its ranks
about one hundred Philhellene volunteers who had come out in the
first months of the uprising.

The absurd vanity of many of these Philhellenes and the ingratitude of the Greeks they had come to save had already strained
relations in Mavrocordato's camp, and the first pitched battle they
fought together confirmed the prejudices of both sides. Establishing
his own headquarters at Langada on the eastern shore of the Ambra-
cian Gulf, Mavrocordato pushed his army forward under the command of General Normann, his Chief of Staff. Advancing as far as

Peta, a small village in the low hills to the east of the Turkish held town of Arta, Normann's army prepared to face the enemy in a battle which could lose them everything and win them very little. In the van were their regular troops, comprising the Philhellene corps, and two battalions of Ionian volunteers and Greek soldiers. Behind them, holding the high ground and guarding their right flank, was a force of Greek irregulars led by an old and cynical bandit chief of dubious loyalty, Gogos.

Against the vastly superior force of infantry and cavalry that issued from Arta, the regulars held firm, their discipline and firepower repulsing the first Turkish assault without casualties. For the next two hours the battle seemed still to go their way, but while the Turkish commander, Reshid Pasha, kept up a desultory frontal attack on this force, a large contingent of his Albanian soldiers was marching in a flanking movement to the north in a bid to turn the Greek position.

With a strong body of Greek irregulars commanding the high ground, this should have been impossible, and the first that the Philhellenes knew of their fate was when they saw the Ottoman standard planted on the highest hill behind them. Gogos, in league with the enemy, had fled. The regulars were now hopelessly surrounded. Leading the cavalry himself, Reshid stormed their position, capturing their two pieces of artillery. Only twenty-five of the volunteers managed to force a way at bayonet point through the Turkish lines. The rest, fighting heroically to the end, redeemed every Philhellene folly by their courage, dying where they stood, or more horribly, on the walls of Arta.

The failure of Reshid to follow up his victory by taking Missolonghi limited the short-term significance of this campaign, but the strategic consequences of Peta reverberated dangerously on through the rest of the war. From the first tactless intrusion of Philhellene volunteers there had been an innate prejudice among Greeks against western methods of warfare, and with the contrasting evidence of Peta and Dervenakia at their disposal that breezy sense of superiority which is never far below the surface of the Greek national character hardened into an arrogance that would have fatal consequences.

For the time being, however, the rebellion was safe. With the defeat of Dramali's army in the east and the withdrawal of Reshid in the west, Turkish initiative and energy were exhausted. Their troops still held on to Patras at the western end of the Gulf and to Modon and Coron – the old 'Eyes of Venice' – in the south-west. Up in the north, Greek resistance, isolated and exposed, had all but collapsed. In Attica, though, the former pupil of Ali Pasha, Odysseus Androutses, held Athens. In western Greece the heroism of Missolonghi had saved the town for even greater fame. At sea Ottoman and Greek fleets seemed as bent on avoiding each other as anything else. And in the Peloponnese – or the Morea as it was more usually known – the original heartland of the revolution, the Greeks did what Greeks have always done best when freed of external threat, and turned on one other.

Even through the dangers and triumphs of 1821–2, the divisions among the Greek leaders were never far below the surface, and by the middle of 1823 the country was sliding inexorably towards civil war. To the enthusiastic Philhellenes of Europe and America, it might seem that Greece had found itself the heirs to Demosthenes and Epaminondas, and yet even after a National Constitution and Government were established at Epidaurus on 13 January, with an executive and legislature and all the trappings of modern statehood, real power remained in the hands of local factions bent on turning the rebellion to their own narrow profit.

The politics of revolutionary Greece were so riddled by family and regional loyalties and feuds that no coherent picture is possible, but there were four main factions that dominated this struggle for power: the military *capitani* who won the first battles of the conflict; the great island families, grown powerful on the rich pickings of the Napoleonic War, who controlled the Greek fleets; the landlords or 'primates' of the Morea who had exercised such influence under the Turks; and the educated Phanariots and Greeks of the diaspora who had flooded in at the beginning of the revolution.

The social and economic realities which lay behind these divisions were real enough to hold serious consequences for the future of Greece, but to most foreigners and natives allegiances were more a matter of personalities than politics. In Athens, Odysseus Androutses governed eastern Greece with an Ali Pasha-like selfishness which made him a law to himself, but in western Greece and the Morea all those antagonisms that the successes of 1822 had exposed, the divisions between civilian and military, between constitutionalist and brigand, between Phanariot and native Greek, embodied themselves most vividly in the destructive rivalry of the two men who had presided over disaster and triumph at Peta and Dervenakia, Alexander Mavrocordato and Theodore Colocotrones.

It would be difficult to imagine two leaders more opposed in their backgrounds, aspirations or personalities. A descendant of the great Phanariot families that had governed in the Danubian provinces through the eighteenth century, 'Prince' Alexander Mavrocordato as he was styled, was living in impoverished exile in Italy – and teaching Mary Shelley Greek – when the rebellion broke out in the spring of 1821.

Among the first volunteers to sail from Marseilles to join the cause, Mavrocordato was perhaps its only leader who not only spoke but understood the languages and the 'language' of European diplomacy and Philhellenism. Among the native commanders of the rebellion Colocotrones or Petro Bey might invoke the shade of Epominandas or the principles of the nation state when it suited their purposes, but their Hellenism and liberalism were the thinnest of veneers on a narrow feudalism which had nothing in common with the modern and centralized Greece of which Mavrocordato dreamed at Epidaurus.

It is perhaps perverse to dismiss the career of the first President of Modern Greece as a failure, but because of this fundamental difference of vision Mavrocordato was never as successful a leader as his talents and meteoric rise had seemed to promise. At the first congress of 1821 he had been elected to the Presidency of the Assembly and then the country, and yet even in this moment of triumph, the determination of the old primates and captains to hold on to power guaranteed that while the Constitution might be written in his image Greece would still be run in theirs.

With the military failure of Mavrocordato at Peta any last hope of a stable and powerful central government was dealt a fatal blow, but the fact is that with his western frock coat, spectacles and principles he was always going to be at a disadvantage in a country locked in a ruthless and savage war. To the Greeks who had fought at Tripolis and Dervenakia there was inevitably something alien in his western skills, and it is a sobering fact about the way Greece still sees its revolution that while there is only one statue in the whole country to the most civilized of its leaders, it is difficult to find anywhere – from Tripolis to the old Parliament building in Athens – where the hawk-like features of Theodore Colocotrones do not glower down from under a 'classical' helmet on a nation only too happy to sacrifice political integrity to glamour.*

Avaricious and violent, corrupt, bold, cynical and charismatic, the fifty-year-old Colocotrones was everything as a military leader that the cosmopolitan and haplessly civilian Mavrocordato could never be. 'It would be impossible for a painter or novelist to trace a more romantic delineation of a robber chieftain,' the Philhellene soldier and great historian of the war, Thomas Gordon, wrote of Colocotrones,

> tall and athletic, with a profusion of black hair and expressive features, alternately lighted up with boisterous gaiety, or darkened by bursts of passion: among his soldiers, he seemed born to command, having just the manners and bearing calculated to gain their confidence.[4]

Along with this air of authority, with the physical strength and presence so essential to any klepht leader, went a history to match. Born under a tree in the hills of Messenia on the Easter Monday of 1771, Colocotrones came from a long line of Turk-haters who had slid between policing the mountains as *armatoles* and living off them as bandits in the central Morea.

It was always his proud boast that in four hundred years of occupation his family had never once succumbed to Ottoman rule, and at the age of only fifteen Colocotrones himself fell naturally into the brigand life which had already killed his father and thirty-three of his nearest kin.

After twenty years of indiscriminate banditry against Greek and Turk alike, he was forced into exile in the Ionian Isles, but when the revolution broke out in 1821 he was ready again to resume his old life with a new and expanded brief. Present at the fall of Kalamata in the first days of the uprising, his influence and guerrilla talents soon gained him command of the troops besieging Tripolis, and victory there and at Dervenakia the following year gave him the plunder and prestige to make him the most powerful man in the Morea.

It was a position he exploited entirely for his own ends. He was not interested in the fate or even the idea of a Greece beyond the Peloponnese. To Colocotrones the war was about wealth and power, not about nationhood or any of the other battle cries of Philhellenism. In April 1823 he used the threat of his soldiers to have himself and Petro Bey elected to the Presidency and Vice Presidency, but it was a gesture of contempt for the position Mavrocordato had once held and not an endorsement of the political process. His authority, like his vision, was that of a chieftain, and by the middle of the year the rump of the government that he had usurped had fled from his vengeance to the safety and irrelevance of the islands.

It was this political situation, with the two-year-old nation only weeks from civil war, with feudal warlords in control of their private fiefdoms in the Morea and eastern Greece, with western Greece in chaos, the government in exile and Mavrocordato fled for his life to the island of Hydra, which greeted Byron when he landed at Argostoli.

From on board the *Hercules* he had pointed out the distant coastline of the Morea with all the excitement of a man reliving his youth, but it was not long before the reality that lay behind the shimmering image was brought rudely home. 'The instinct that enables the vulture to detect carrion from far off,' Trelawny wrote of their arrival, 'is surpassed by the marvellous acuteness of the Greeks in scenting money.

> The morning after our arrival a flock of Zuliote refugees alighted on our decks, attracted by Byron's dollars. Lega,

the steward, a thorough miser, coiled himself on the money-chest like a viper. Our sturdy skipper was for driving them overboard with hand-spikes. Byron came on deck in exuberant spirits, pleased with their savage aspect and wild attire, and, as was his wont, promised a great deal more than he should have done.[5]

In the months ahead Byron would have to pay for the caprice that made him take on these Suliots as a bodyguard, but it was the wider chaos of Greece that was soon engrossing his attention. From the moment that he went ashore at Argostoli on 3 September 1823, the struggle among the Greek factions for his money and support began. 'No stranger,' the young Philhellene George Finlay,* who was on Cephalonia at this time, recalled, 'estimated the character of the Greeks more correctly than Lord Byron . . .'

It may, however, be observed that to nobody did the Greeks ever unmask their selfishness and self-deceit so candidly. Almost every distinguished statesman and general sent him letters soliciting his favour, his influence, or his money. Colocotrones invited him to a national assembly at Salamis. Mavrocordato informed him that he would be of no use anywhere but at Hydra, for Mavrocordato was then in that island. Constantine Metaxa who was governor of Meso-longhi, wrote, saying that Greece would be ruined unless Lord Byron visited that fortress. Petrobey used plainer words. He informed Lord Byron that the true way to save Greece was to lend him, the bey, a thousand pounds. With that sum not three hundred but three thousand Spartans would be put in motion to the frontier, and the fall of the Ottoman empire would be certain.[6]

Byron was never one to need much encouragement towards parsimony, but it was not now just his own money that was at stake. After an initial coolness in Britain to the fate of Greece, there were moves afoot in London to raise a Stock Exchange loan on her behalf, and as the sole agent of the London Greek Committee on the spot

Byron had to take this into account. It made him move with a caution that other Philhellenes would have done well to emulate. He was not going to budge a foot farther until he could see his way, he told Trelawny, and to the Greeks he was equally firm. 'And allow me to add once for all,' he addressed their government in a letter,

> I desire the well-being of Greece, and nothing else; I will do all I can to secure it; but I cannot consent, I never will consent that the English public, or English individuals, should be deceived as to the real state of affairs. The rest, gentlemen, depends on you: you have fought gloriously; act honourably towards your fellow-citizens, and towards the world; then it will no more be said, as it has been said for two thousand years, with the Roman historian, that Philopoeman was the last Grecian.[7]

The vigour and propriety of every action of Byron's in these dealings with the Greek parties makes an extraordinary contrast with the indolent rhythms of his Italian life. There were certainly times on Cephalonia when the seeming hopelessness of his task made him wish that he had never come, and yet in spite of all the disappointments the truth is that he had not felt so alive and decisive in years, writing letters and meeting visiting Greeks, arranging or parrying loans, assessing military reports and projects for steam vessels, or playing the strategist with the English Representative and future conqueror of Sind, Colonel Napier.

He was also working to a strict regime preserved in the account of Pietro Gamba, Teresa Guiccioli's brother. He would leave his bedroom at nine, and for the next two hours would deal with his correspondence, with Gamba to help. He would then breakfast on a cup of tea. At noon he would ride until three, and dine on cheese and vegetables. There would then be pistol shooting practice, and after that he would retire to his room until seven, only then emerging to talk until midnight.

There was, too, another aspect of Byron's existence on Cephalonia which is more difficult to quantify but no less important to his emotional well-being. During the long years of exile in Italy there had never been any shortage of English acquaintances in his life, but the common denominator of the Pisa Circle, the tie as it were that bound them all together, was a sense of alienation which made their 'Englishness' a burden rather than a source of any emotional comfort.*

On Cephalonia it was different. Over the first three years of the Greek rebellion there had been a gradual thawing of British attitudes towards the insurgents, but Turkey was still technically an ally and Britain was as cautious in her sympathies for a people in revolt from their rightful sovereign as anywhere in conservative Europe. In the Ionian Isles, governed by that irascible foe of Greece, Sir Thomas Maitland, this caution shaded into downright hostility but Cephalonia was an exception. There, the underlying popular sympathy for the Greeks that ran as a powerful countercurrent to government policy, found eloquent support in the official Representative. Byron had chosen the island in the first place because of Napier's strong Greek sympathies, and in his company or that of the garrison officers who surprised and touched Byron with the warmth of their welcome, he probably felt more entirely at home – more English even – than he had done in the seven years of his exile.

There was, however, little place for Trelawny in all this. Before he left Italy he had managed to half-convince himself that he was only using Byron to get to Greece, but as the 'Childe' moved from on board the *Hercules* into a cottage near Argostoli and settled into his fixed routine, the fears he had confided to Mary Shelley weeks earlier seemed only too justified. 'The Poet's attention', he had written to her with an authentic mix of resentment and pride, 'and professed kindness is boundless; he leaves everything to my discretion';

> if I had confidence in him this would be well, but I now
> only see the black side of it; it will eventually rob me of my
> free agency, by so weaving me in with his fortunes that I
> may have difficulty in separating myself from them.[8]

Even now this would probably not have much mattered, had he been able to feel any sense of importance in the connection. In Italy his feelings for Claire Clairmont had inevitably drawn him into her camp against Byron, and yet so long as he had been in charge of the *Bolivar* or giving orders on the *Hercules* he could at least preserve an illusion of independence that was his own best protection against his meanest instincts.

With their arrival on Cephalonia, however, and the sense of his own waning importance, even that illusory prop to his self-esteem was gone. He could go on competing in those kind of ways that were his sole resort, could shoot, box or swim better than Byron. But Byron now belonged to another and larger world than anything he could imagine, to a world of politics and finance which left him with a galling proof of his own insignificance and that sense of emotional abandonment which shadowed all his deepest relationships.

'Dear Hunt,' he wrote on 2 September, continuing a letter he had begun three weeks earlier: 'You will see a long blank, in which nothing having been done, I had nothing to communicate.'[9] It was a blank Trelawny was ill-equipped to fill. His motives for coming to Greece, his aspirations, had none of Byron's complexity about them, none of his selflessness, and no room now for any of his circumspection. Whatever cloak of Byronic despair he might throw over them in his letters to Claire or Mary, he was there in search of raw excitement and little else.

'When was there so glorious a banner as that unfurled in Greece?' he had asked Claire in his last letter to her from Italy. 'Who would not fight under it?'[10] As the days stretched into weeks on Cephalonia, however, the prospect of fighting was looking increasingly distant. Rumours filtered across the channel that separated them from the Morea of 'battles never fought, prisoners never taken'.[11] There was talk of the islands and the Peloponnese at loggerheads; of the factions on the brink of civil war.

Despite the presence of refugees, though, they were no nearer that conflict than when they first arrived. By the beginning of September, Trelawny had determined to assert his independence and leave, to proceed to the Greek centre of government, he told Hunt, and 'apply to be actively employed'.[12] In a letter to Mary Shelley written four days later on the 6th, he was at once more venomous about his decision and more silkily double-tongued. 'The Noble Poet has been seized with his usual indecision, when just on the brink', he told her, 'and when I would have him, without talking, leap.'

> After being here a month in idleness, we seemed both to have taken our separate determination, his to return to Italy and mine to go forward with a tribe of Zuliotes to join a brother of Marco Bozzaris, at Missolonghi . . . He [Byron] has written nothing more, but will I doubt not. Our intimacy has never been ruffled, but smoother than ever, and I am most anxious in upholding his great name to the world.[13]

That last sentence is revealing. Whatever the private grievances that might emerge in his letters, Trelawny knew where his public credit lay. His plans, so extravagant in their telling here, were more circumscribed, more dependent on Byron than he would ever have confessed to the Pisan women. On 2 September, he was loading his belongings onto a small vessel, waiting for an opportunity to run the Turkish blockade under the cover of dark, and land on the western coast of the Peloponnese. His instructions were to go with Hamilton Browne to the Greek leaders, and acting as Byron's secretaries, deliver letters and report back on the political situation.

On the night of the 6th, they were at last ready to leave. Their farewell was warm. 'As I took leave of him,' Trelawny recalled in his *Records*, 'his last words were, "Let me hear from you often, – come back soon. If things are farcical, they will do for 'Don Juan'; if heroical, you have another canto of 'Childe Harold'."'[14]

It was the last time Trelawny saw Byron. Farewells over, he and Hamilton Browne embarked on a caique for the short journey across to the Peloponnese, beaching the next morning without incident on the scruffy coastline beneath the half-ruined tower of the Pirgos customs house.

In classical times, this north-west corner of the Peloponnese had been celebrated for its prosperity, but the long depredations of

Turkish rule had begun a task that two years of war had now completed. There was only a solitary guard on the customs post to mark their arrival, a 'creature' of Colocotrones living under semi-siege in a sort of hen coop at the top of the tower, reachable only by a ladder which he pulled up at night. It was a necessary precaution. The sole authority he recognized, he told Trelawny, was Colocotrones's, but even his writ had a limited jurisdiction. A few days earlier a party of Turks from Patras had raided the village of Gastoumi a few miles to the north, killing a number of inhabitants and carrying off women and other booty.

Byron's name, however, seemed enough to secure the guard's co-operation and their bags went unsearched. They were treated to a breakfast of fowl and eggs, an execrable sweet wine and raki and then escorted on foot through a landscape of dunes and prickly thorn into Pirgos. That night they spent in the town. Twenty Spanish dollars secured them mules and a guide for the journey on to Tripolis and early the next morning they were ready to start.

In later years when Trelawny looked back to these first hours on Greek soil, reality was adjusted to fall more in line with expectations, and that single guard cowering in his hencoop was replaced by a squad of Moorish mercenaries. If Greece, however, fell short of what was required, Trelawny did not. His whole life had been an imaginative preparation for this, and he was ready. Like some initiate, he had held himself aloof from their hosts, from the sordid reality embodied in the poverty and pinched, emaciated faces of Pirgos. His old clothes were gone too, and he was dressed now in Suliote costume, 'which wonderfully became him', Hamilton Browne admiringly recorded, 'being tall in stature and of a dark complexion, with a fine, commanding physiognomy'.[15] Less than a day's ride ahead of them lay the gentle, wooded hills among which the ancient shrine of Olympia nestled. Beyond those, clearly visible in the distance, and filled for every Philhellene with all the violent glamour of its classical past rose the massive and spectacular heartland of the central Peloponnese.

It was a hard, four-day journey to Tripolis and it was the afternoon of the first day before the two men emerged from a defile onto a long, narrow plain covering the remains of Olympia. Along its southern edge the River Alpheius marked their course, shallow and clear in the late summer, its gravelly bed broken up by little islets as it flowed westwards to its mythical union beneath the waters of the Mediterranean with the nymph Arethusa.

For many volunteers following this same route, the first sight of the river, with all its classical associations, came almost as a guarantee that their crusade had at last begun. To the Moreot peasants who lived on its ravaged banks it was nothing more romantic than the 'Rufea', but to every Philhellene who passed this way it was still stubbornly the 'Alpheius' – the river of Ovid's *Metamorphoses* and Pausanias's travels, the path not just into the central highlands where it has its source but into a Greece that was more real to them than the land they had come to save.

It is one of the paradoxes of 'Philhellenism' that while the word means the love of Modern Greece, as opposed to 'Hellenism' which is concerned with its past, it was precisely that past which had brought most volunteers to the war. It can seem at times, in fact, as if the Greece through which the volunteer travelled was two separate countries, occupying the same physical space and clothed in the same landscape, but as distinct in his mind as the Holy Land and modern Israel to the devout pilgrim, the present only sanctified by its association with a history which was at once inspiration and balm, moral justification and emotional crutch among the horrors of Balkan warfare. 'The dress, the manners, the very ignorance of the people has something in it wild and original,' Lytton Bulwer rhapsodized in a letter home that captures the mental confusions and immaturity of so many Philhellenes at this time.

> We are brought back to our boyhood by the very name of Greece; and every spot in this land reminds us of the days devoted to its classic fables, and the scenes where we were taught them. Methinks I see old Harrow Churchyard, and its venerable yews, under whose shadow I have lain many a summer evening.[16]

And now, as the two men skirted the plain of Olympia, it was this other and older Greece, invisible but potent, that lay quite literally buried around them beneath the silt left by centuries of inundation. Across the river a few piles of ruined brickwork and the odd massive fragment of marble from the temple of Zeus were visible, but six years before the first systematic excavations that was almost all of the ancient site that could be seen.

It is a futile but irresistible exercise to try to balance the profit and loss that stand between contemporary experience and the Greece the Philhellenes knew. There is such a deceptive feeling of immutability about even its ruins that it is easy to forget how different their Greece was, but it is worth remembering that for all the remote beauty of early nineteenth-century Olympia everything that now conjures up its classical past for us, the stadium, the treasuries, the Philippeion, the drinking cup of Pheidias, the inscribed helmet of Miltiades, the victor of Marathon – that supreme symbol of the Greece Philhellenism invoked with such totemic force – still belonged to the future.

There is a genuine poignancy in the image of a great classicist like Colonel Leake standing alone in the middle of what he called 'a beautiful desert',[17] cut off by the mud as much from this future as Olympia's history. With a man of his seriousness it is tempting to feel that he was born a century too soon, and yet for most Philhellenes the name itself was enough, the past all the richer for existing nowhere outside their imaginations, entwined with school-day memories and unfettered by an historical knowledge which Byron only half-jokingly denounced as the enemy of romance. Gladiators could fight here in the fancy where they had never trod in history, crowds bay for blood. 'How striking the contrast between the silence of these fields,' one Philhellene wrote of Olympia,

> now melancholy and deserted, and their jubilee in the old times of Greece! One marvelled in re-peopling the spot, all lonely but for a few travellers on their sorry mules, with the glad assemblage of aspiring thousands; – in listening for the spirit of eloquence in that solitude, and looking on a

desolate waste as the glittering arena of pride, valour, and wisdom.[18]

Here was a vision of Greece which in its dangerous sentimentality was fraught with certain disillusion, but for the moment it found an echo in a landscape as seductive as itself. Ahead of Trelawny and Browne waited the barren uplands and wild gorges of the central Morea, yet as they began their ascent out of the plain of Pisa, crossing and recrossing the Alpheius, they were in the world of myth and classical association which western art has so curiously expropriated for Arcadia.

In 1821, the young English volunteer William Humphreys, feverish and embittered by his first experience of warfare, had invoked the myth of Alpheius on the banks of the Rufea as if somehow he could wash away the contagion of reality in its pure, classical stream. Now, for Trelawny and Browne, the same magic held sway. The crops of maize and wheat which before the war had grown on its banks, were ruined or burned; but pines, and wild olive, groves of oaks and chestnuts, and thickets of vallonia still bore out Pausanias's claims for the Alpheius as the 'greatest of all rivers . . . the most pleasure giving to the sight'.[19]

Gradually, however, as they climbed, the gravitational pull of the past gave way to a more brutal present. Often their path would be scarcely wide enough for their mules, a sheer drop of hundreds of feet awaiting the first false step. On some outcrop of rock, a shepherd would suddenly appear, warily watching them, long gun in hand, his figure etched against a sky in which eagles soared.

On the second day it began to rain in torrents, bringing, even in September, a piercing cold. As night fell and they sought the rough shelter of an overhang they saw the lights of an isolated settlement. Approaching it, they were attacked by a pack of dogs. Trelawny was about to shoot when their owners appeared out of the dark, their faces, caught in the lurid glare of their torches, showing 'the most ferocious and cut-throat countenances' Browne had ever seen.[20]

In his years in the Ionian service stories had reached Hamilton Browne of travellers eaten alive by the dogs of these nomadic northern shepherds and the two men resigned themselves to a long and nervous night. They were refused food but were eventually allowed shelter, making beds out of sacks of maize, while their hosts huddled at a distance around their fire, eyeing Trelawny's weapons and 'jabbering in their own dialect'.[21] The next morning they had ridden some distance when Trelawny discovered a pistol missing. On turning back, they were attacked again by the dogs. From high above them shots rang out as the shepherds swarmed down across the rocks, but they made their escape unharmed, injured in nothing worse than their dignity.

On the fifth day after landing at Pirgos they finally rode out of a narrow cut in the hills to see the towers and curtain walls of the town that only two years earlier had been the Ottoman capital of the Morea. As they made their way through the gate of the ruined city of Tripolis, the debris of its recent history lay on all sides. A few orange trees and the odd evergreen remained of the old seraglio gardens, but everything else was gone, looted and taken back on mules to the Mani, or smashed, burned or razed to the ground in the frenzy of destruction that had followed the town's capture in October 1821.

There is a sense in which the brutalities of the Greek War of Independence all lie beyond imaginative recall, too sickening to be stomached in detail, too numbing to make much sense as statistics. Tripolis, however, seems to belong to another realm again, the ultimate expression of the racial and religious hatred that convulsed the Morea in the first summer of war. It is estimated that in the first weeks after the Greek flag was raised at Ayia Lavra, something like ten thousand Turks were slaughtered across the Peloponnese: in the days that followed the fall of Tripolis that number was to be doubled.

Throughout the long summer of 1821 the siege had dragged itself out in inimitable Greek fashion, heat, disease and starvation doing their grim work within the walls while Maniots bartered in their shadow and the captains negotiated their own private deals with the richer Turks. By the beginning of October it was clear the town could not hold out much longer. From all points of the Morea and even the islands, peasants congregated on the surrounding plain, determined to share in the spoils. Mutterings of discontent grew among the soldiers, conscious of negotiations that threatened their pockets, fearful of being balked of their reward. Then, on 4 October, a curious silence fell over the camp, an air of suppressed anticipation, the calm, as one witness put it, that was precursor of the bloody horrors to come.

All the Philhellene officers had left by this time except a young Frenchman in charge of the Greek artillery called Maxime Raybaud. Too young to do anything more than 'assist' France in her final reverses, as he quaintly put it, Raybaud had been culled from the French army in the cuts of 1820 and, inspired by thoughts of Ancient Sparta and Athens, joined Mavrocordato's ship at Marseilles.

It was on 18 July that a Greek bishop had blessed their ship and Raybaud took his last emotional farewell of France. Less than three months later he watched as the morning sun rose bright above the barren plain on 5 October, burning with an implacable fierceness on a defenceless population about to expiate the crimes of four centuries of oppression. The air, Raybaud remembered, was heavy and dolorous. At nine o'clock a second French officer arrived at his tent, in time for the final rites. Half an hour later they heard a commotion from the direction of the town, and rushing out found that a small party of Greeks had forced the Argos gate, and the flag of independence was flying from a tower. As Raybaud ran into the town he became an impotent witness of Greece's first great triumph of the war.

The streets were thick with unburied corpses, victims of famine and disease that lay putrefying where they had dropped. Soon, however, the stench of the dead mingled with that of fresh blood and fire as the Greeks began a long orgy of looting and revenge. They seemed to Raybaud to be everywhere, killing and mutilating, chasing their victims through the streets, the town's packs of famished and maddened dogs in their wake, ready to tear apart the inhabitants and devour them as they fell. Beauty, age, sex, nothing could stop the attackers. Pregnant women were obscenely mutilated and butchered, children beheaded, dismembered and burned.

Wherever Raybaud went, helpless to interfere, there was the crackle of flames and the crash of masonry. Everywhere too there were the screams of victims, competing with another sound which was to haunt Raybaud's memory – the guttural ululation of the Greek soldier in sight of his victim, and then the change of note as the *ataghan* was plunged in, an inhuman blood cry that was half scream, half laugh, '*le cri de l'homme-tigre, de l'homme devorant l'homme*'.[22]

If the sun beat down in judgement all that day, night brought no relief. The slaughter went on, and with it the search under the October moon for fresh victims, dragged from their hiding places. Mere death, as Raybaud says, was a gift of rare generosity. Some faced it when it came, however, with a curious impassivity, an indifference almost. Others, young women and children, driven by some inexplicable impulse, a symbiotic urge of victim and attacker to bring centuries of religious hatred to a supreme pitch, died goading their killers on to fresh brutalities with insults of 'infidel', 'dog', and 'impure'. Only the discovery of one of the town's Jews could divert a Greek's hatred from his Turkish victims for a moment. Then he might stop even with his dagger raised, postponing the pleasure to assist in the roasting of a Jew, revenge for the indignities Constantinople's Jews had heaped on Patriarch Gregorius's corpse.

No one could end it. An order went out to stop the killing. It was ignored. A second order went out from Colocotrones that there should be no killing within the town's walls, but that too was useless. Not even the dead were safe. Tombs were ransacked, bodies exhumed, fuel to the contagion that was the inevitable aftermath of siege.

Perhaps, though, the worst crime was still to come. After the first attack something between two and three thousand inhabitants, mainly women and children, were taken out and held in the Greek camp at the foot of the hills. On 8 October they were stripped naked, and herded into a narrow gorge just to the west of the town. It was a perfect killing field the attackers had chosen for their business, sealed off at one end so there could be no escape, its grey limestone walls streaked with red as if the rocks themselves bled in sympathy. There are no descriptions of what happened that day, but a week later the Scottish Philhellene and historian, Thomas

Gordon, passed the scene on his way back to the Ionian Isles. He was never able to bring himself to write of it in his great history of the war, but while serving out his quarantine in the lazar house on Cephalonia he told the English doctor – a Doctor Thomson, whose report made its way back through Sir Thomas Maitland to London – what he had seen. The corpses lay where they had been butchered, 'the bodies of pregnant women were ripped open, their bodies dreadfully mangled, their heads struck off and placed on the bodies of dogs, whilst the dogs heads were placed on theirs, and also upon their private parts.'[23]

There are towns and places which seem to remain the same through every change, as if there is some indestructible genius about them, some essence that will reassert itself like a damp mould through every disguise. It is perhaps nothing more than fancy that finds an echo of these horrors among the hills that squat so balefully above the modern town, and yet in the way Tripolis subverts history to the triumphalism of a national myth, we are brought as close as landscape or place can take us to the Greece of 1821.

With the bombast of its civic statuary, with the tyres, rubbish and broken-down trucks that mix with the brittle bones in that nearby gorge, Tripolis is even now a litmus test of sensibility that is not easy to fail and it is a sobering thought that in Trelawny's account it merits only a casual half-line. It is often as worth noting what a man omits of his experience as what he includes, and Trelawny's silence here – so different from Gordon's – seems as eloquent as anything he wrote, an involuntary revelation of the man himself, a sudden glimpse into a moral abyss all the more chilling because he was too blind to try to hide it.

Here was the Greece for which he had come to fight, here on its barren upland plain was the capital of the real Arcadia, where death was not an elegiac inscription in a Poussin painting but a dog's head stuffed on the corpse of a young girl – and Trelawny did not so much as flinch. The atrocities, he told Mary Shelley, were the one guarantee that the war would go on, that there could be no turning back, no peace, no compromise. It is a judgement, even if true, that must still make one pause, one of the first hints we have of just how

profoundly different he was from all those Byronic Romantics who
flooded into Greece during the War of Independence. It was one
thing for Hellenists of an earlier generation like Leake or Clarke to
rise above their disappointment in the modern Greek, to find in his
degeneracy grist to the mill of historical theory, but almost alone
among the Philhellenes who came to fight Trelawny did not recoil
from what he found. For many of them who came out, full of
expectation and ambition, the shock was as much to their vanity as
anything else, but the same can hardly be said of Gordon or Hastings,
of Philhellene-turned-Turcophile David Urquhart, or even of the
young English volunteer, Humphreys – less interesting and so more
representative than the others – who came to hate his Greek companions so much that he prayed for battle 'if only to see some of
these wretches knocked off'.[24]

The mixture of bitterness, disgust, guilt and disappointed expectations captured in Humphreys's journals represents perhaps the
central experience of the Philhellene volunteer and yet not even the
shadow of it seems to have clouded Trelawny's consciousness. One
reason for this was that he had taken over from Byron an unromantic
view of the modern Greek, but whereas Byron's realism was the
index of a mature and tolerant intelligence, Trelawny's was a simple
front for callous indifference. Their ships could refuse to sail, he
again told Mary Shelley, their soldiers desert, their captains could
fight among themselves and hate all foreign volunteers, it would
make no difference to him: 'My lot is decided,' he wrote,

> With all the crimes the Greeks themselves are taxed, with
> treachery, avarice, envy, break of faith, if Greece was hell
> and the Greeks all devils, I would not turn back whilst I
> have free will.[25]

It is during these first weeks after leaving Byron that we first hear
the authentic voice of the mature Trelawny. It is not that he had at
last outgrown the Byronic posturing of his youth, but rather that in
the perfection of the role, in the stripping away of all inessentials
to leave the adventurer in him free for action, he had revealed to
himself a self-sufficiency which up until this point had been no more

than bluff. There is no way of knowing what internal adjustment Trelawny had to make when faced with the horrors of Tripolis, but it was as if the years of Byronic reveries, the fantasies of eastern violence that he had lived out day and night, the memories of his father's pet raven or of the needles stuck into the brains of his captain's chickens on board ship, were all the preparation he needed. 'With meditating that she must die once,' Shakespeare's Brutus declares on Portia's death, 'I have the patience to endure it now.'[26] With the constant imaginative supping of horrors, Trelawny could stare at the real thing with equanimity. He had killed in his stories, and he found that in Greece he could look upon death and brutality with an indifference which was entirely unfeigned.

But the real frustration that faced him was that while the evidence of death lay on every side, the Morea was no longer the theatre of action he craved. Wherever they moved the landscape was scarred by the ravages of the recent war, by burned and deserted villages, or pyramids of heads heaped high in victory monuments. When Hamilton Browne called his narrative of their travels *A Voyage to the Seat of War*, however, he was simply being fanciful. The war had moved on, and the Morea itself was probably no more dangerous for a foreigner than at any other time in the century. Patras in the north-west, Modon and Coron in the south-west were still in Turkish hands, but the only real threat came from the Greek factions as they drifted towards outright conflict. 'I asked him if his house owed its wretched condition to the ravages of the Turks,' the Philhellene Bulwer enquired of one peasant he met on the banks of the Alpheius.

> Turks or Greeks, (sighed the poor man) it is much the same: here comes one of our captains, who if you do not belong to his party, kills you without ceremony; if attached to him, you must show your friendship by giving up your property to gorge his followers: – then, to finish all, comes another, who burns your dwelling over your head, and demolishes every thing, because, forsooth, his enemy plundered you.[27]

It was not long before Trelawny and Browne found themselves at the centre of these factional intrigues. They had scarcely been in

Tripolis an hour before a follower of Mavrocordato found them, but they had no sooner taken up with him than a party of Colocotrones's partisans intercepted them with an 'invitation' backed by a display of ataghans, scimitars and cuirasses which was clearly best accepted. They were conducted through the ruins of the town, past desolate gardens and the remains of miniature kiosks and smashed fountains, destroyed in the siege. Finally they came 'into a noble apartment, richly adorned with arabesques, and with windows of stained glass'.[28] There, crosslegged on an ottoman of crimson velvet and gold, surrounded by armed guards, and looking with his hawkish features like an 'ancient chieftain',[29] sat the heir to Epominandas and much of the wealth of Turkish Tripolis, Theodore Colocotrones.

At the age of fifty-two Colocotrones had lost nothing of the bearing and the presence of a brigand chief and yet even at the height of his success there always seemed an air of brooding dissatisfaction about him, of Milton's Lucifer eternally at war with the world around him. His opening demand of Trelawny and Browne was why had they not visited him first? He loved Britain, he told them, had served with the Greek Battalion raised against the French in the Ionian Isles under Colonel Church, would love to serve under him again – '*credat Judaeus*'[30] is Hamilton Browne's only comment – and looked forward to Church's return. He warned them that no one else was to be trusted, especially the Phanariot party, the source of all intrigue in the Morea. Mavrocordato was 'a cowardly plotter,'[31] he would place backwards on an ass, and drive from the Peloponnese if he appeared again.

It was clear to Browne at least that Colocotrones had no real idea as to whom Byron might be. In their letters to Cephalonia, however, they were more enthusiastic about him than they would later admit. On 13 September, Browne reported back to Byron on the first part of their mission, sycophantically warning his Lordship against the rigours of the route he and Trelawny had followed. More significant was a caution against taking up Mavrocordato's invitation to Hydra. 'From all I have heard of him,' Browne told Byron, he was 'an honourable and estimable man.' He had, though, 'lost the confidence of the people in the Morea . . . we have not once heard his name mentioned with respect, but as one who wished to deliver Greece to a foreign power.'[32]

By way of contrast, Colocotrones was very strong, his military successes at Tripolis and Dervenakia bringing irregulars flocking to his standard. Forage, he added was plentiful, living cheap, 'a harem to be formed on reasonable terms'[33] – or 'maidenheads as plentiful as blackberries' as Trelawny put it.[34]

The following day Trelawny added his own report and prepared to leave on the next stage of their journey. Neither man had seen much hope of any accommodation between Colocotrones and Mavrocordato, but Trelawny repeated Browne's wish that Byron should come in person to do what he could to soothe the different factions. In his absence, however, there were obvious compensations. 'We go on to the Congress at Salamis,' he wrote, 'will attend all its deliberations consequently be enabled to give much useful intelligence to you.'[35]

That same day, or early the next, Colocotrones provided them with horses and a guide, and franked their journey on through Argos and Nauplia to meet the other leaders on the island of Salamis. The story, when they got there, was all too familiarly the same. The only thing anyone was interested in was 'money, money and more money':[36] their only refrain, the duplicity of every rival. 'You only need ask a Greek where he comes from to discover his sentiments', Trelawny complained to Mary Shelley.

> If from the Morea, his God is Colocotroni; if an Athenian, Ulysses; Missolonghi, Marco Bozzaris; nor are they content with this: they will try to convince you that all the others are bad patriots and bad men.[37]

The realities of Greek politics had undermined the resolve of more committed men than Trelawny but in the expansive freedom of his new role his spirits remained unaffected. In letters to Cephalonia and England he aired his views with all the confidence of a fortnight's experience of the country, touting military options or dissecting leaders with a breezy contempt which marched happily with an improbable optimism.* 'I am convinced', he wrote from Hydra – at a time when Greece was only weeks away from civil war,

> if they succeed in getting the loan which the English Com-
> mittee held out hopes of, the freedom of Greece will be
> founded on a firm basis. True there is much difference of
> opinion existing among the people in power here, as well
> as in every country, and some little squabbling for place and
> power, but they are all united against their common enemy,
> and as Hotspur says – 'yet all goes well, yet all hearts are
> united'.[38]

Beneath this buoyancy, however, and the renewed sense of importance, the old wounds and doubts remained. There is no question
that Trelawny enjoyed his role at the heart of Greek politics, but
the further that his journey took him from Lord Byron, the slacker
his ties became with distance, the more intolerable the slightest
obligation seems to have been. He had sailed out to fight, and he
had seen no action; he had grown with his freedom into a transcen-
dent sense of his own capacities and was still, in the eyes of the
world, no more than Byron's 'secretary'.[39] In public Trelawny
remained keen to support what he thought the 'myth' of Byron's
generosity. In private, though, and particularly in letters to Mary
Shelley, at this time his closest and most sympathetic confidante,
this frustration and bitterness came out in a language of vindictive
contempt which was quite new. 'The child repented of his voyage
before leaving Leghorn,' he lied to her.

> Pride and shame have brought him as far as Cephalonia, not
> without much great difficulty. He now, perhaps, is struggling
> against his constitutional malady of avarice. To redeem his
> honour in the meantime he cries out aloud on the manners,
> poverty, ingratitude, and cruelty of the Greeks . . . If [Misso-
> longhi] falls, Athens will be in danger, and thousands of
> throats cut. A few thousand dollars would provide ships to
> relieve it. A portion of it is raised, Lord Byron, or the Child,
> has been applied to, but I fear will do nothing. I would coin

my heart to save this key-stone of Greece; he must be heartless to look on indifferent, which he is to the fate of Greece
and everything else but his golden idols, for gold is his
God.[40]

In the archives of the National Library in Athens there is a copy of
this letter in Mary Shelley's hand, sent on by her to the London
Greek Committee. In it she has faithfully transcribed all Trelawny's
news but cut out the attacks on Byron. Tact? Residual gratitude?
A lingering fascination with her 'Albi'? Or the coterie sense that,
Byron – the 'real' Byron, mean, avaricious, selfish – was in some
way their private property, not to be shared with the public for fear
of destroying the reflected credit of his friendship?

Mary Shelley should, perhaps, be given the benefit of the doubt,
but it is questionable whether Trelawny deserves such generosity.
Nor, now, did he need it. He had, on Salamis, already found what
he was looking for. Escape and fulfilment both pointed him in the
same direction. While Browne prepared to return to Cephalonia
and then London with the Greek deputies appointed to negotiate
the loan, Trelawny laid out his own plans. 'You will be anxious to
hear of my intentions, amongst this hurly-burly state of the nation,'
he wrote to Mary Shelley on 14 October from Hydra:

After having attentively weighed the matter, I have decided
to accompany Ulysses to Negropont, to pass the winter there,
there being excellent sport between Turk and woodcock
shooting. I am to be a kind of aide-de-camp to him, and a
German officer accompanies me. The General gives me as
many men as I choose to command, and I am to be always
with him; my equipments are all ready, two horses, two
Zuliots as servants. I am habited exactly like Ulysses, in red
and gold vest, with sheep-skin capote, gun, pistols, sabre,
& a few dollars or doubloons; my early habits will be
resumed, and nothing new, but dirt and privations, with
mountain sleeping, are a good exchange for the parched
desert, dry locusts, and camels' milk.[41]

It is a revealing letter. Athens, Missolonghi, 'the key-stone of Greece', all the protestations of Philhellene ardour are forgotten. Trelawny had shaken himself free of one hero only to find himself another.

4

ODYSSEUS

Mother, to the Turks I cannot be a slave; that I cannot endure.
I will take my gun and will henceforth be a Klepht; I will dwell
with the wild beast on the hills and the high rocks. The snows
shall be my coverlet and the stones shall be my bed in the
stronghold of the Klephts. I go, but weep not, my mother,
bless me rather, and pray that I may kill many Turks.

Klepht Ballad[1]

AT THE BEGINNING of November 1823 Trelawny crossed back
to the Morea and headed northwards to join Odysseus, his journey
taking him through the same upland passes in which Dramali's
army had perished a little over a year earlier. If the desolation at
Tripolis had left him untouched there was something almost aes-
thetic in his response to the carnage of Dervenakia, an element of
that romantic intensity and artistic detachment that Gericault brought
to his studies of severed heads. The aftermath of massacre seemed
to him 'a perfect picture' of the war, a tableau under the direction
of Death itself. 'Detached from the heaps of the dead,' he memorably
recalled,

> we saw the skeletons of some bold riders who had attempted
> to scale the acclivities, still astride the skeletons of their
> horses, and in the rear, as if in the attempt to back out of
> the fray, the bleached bones of the negroes' hands still
> holding the hair ropes attached to the skulls of their camels
> – death like sleep is a strange posture master.[2]

In the bleak passes of Dervenakia, surrounded by the whitening bones of Dramali's soldiers, Trelawny had at last found the 'Greece' for which he was searching. For over three hundred years of Ottoman rule the crags and gorges of its mountains had formed almost a separate and unconquered kingdom, its palaces the great peaks of Mani and Suli, its traditions and liberties guarded from generation to generation by the brigand ancestors of the men who had fought and won at Dervenakia.

Through the long centuries of Turkish rule the only real freedom that Greece knew was the freedom of these klephts and the Christian militia – or 'armatoles' – whom the Turks in despair had been forced to recruit from among them to police the mountain passes. In the years after the revolution the stories of these bandits became so inextricably linked with national aspirations that it is difficult to reach any balanced judgement of them, but if revisionist history has painted a bleaker picture than romance, 'klephtouria' indisputably gave Greece both its ablest captains and those traditions of liberty and courage without which independence could never have been won.

With all the vices and virtues of the mountain culture from which they sprang, with its ruthlessness and physicality, its narrowness of vision and freedom of movement, its intense loyalties and brutal rivalries, these captains were never going to know what to do with independence when they won it, but win it they did. It was not the Phanariot Mavrocordato or the trained Philhellene who gained the great victories of 1822. It was not a liberal constitution, with its guarantee of religious freedom and its abolition of slavery and torture, that kept Moslem armies at bay. It was not Orthodox Russia or Christian France, Britain or Austria that sustained Greece through its first perilous years. Grim as the thought is, Trelawny was right: it was the men who could butcher women and children in the hills behind Tripolis, or roast Jews within its walls in the name of Orthodox vengeance; the men who could give safe conducts to the Turks of Athens or Navarino and then slaughter them when they surrendered: those same captains and palikars who had littered the pass of Dervenakia with the bones of Dramali's army.

Unembarassed by their venality, unashamed of their cruelty, modern Greece has always known this and among the great heroes of its revolution still is the man in whom this breed reached its unforgiving apotheosis, Trelawny's new master, Odysseus Androutses.

The son of a brigand leader celebrated in the ballads of the time as the pattern of all Christian and Homeric virtues, Odysseus Androutses was born in Prevesa on the mainland opposite Corfu. While he was still only a baby, the Venetian authorities, true to themselves to the last, betrayed his father to the Turks and imprisonment and death in Constantinople. Something of the father's charisma must have clung to the son, however, and as a child he was brought up as a favourite pipe bearer of Ali Pasha, the notorious Albanian chieftain who had raised cruelty to the pitch of art in his lakeside fortress at Ioannina.

As with all the great klephts, stories of his legendary prowess clung to Odysseus's name, of his ability to divine water in the rockiest landscape, or of a childhood race against Ali's swiftest stallion with his own head the price for defeat. 'The race was to be performed on rising ground,' the traveller George Waddington reported from Athens in the February of 1824,

> and the man was to keep pace with the beast till the latter should fall down dead. In case of failure he was to forfeit his head to the indignation of his noble competitor. The Pasha accepted the challenge for his horse, as well as the condition proposed by the challenger, the execution of which he prepared to exact with great fidelity. The animals ran in his presence, – the biped was triumphant, and became from that moment the distinguished favourite of the master.[3]

The magnetism and strength celebrated in stories of this kind were indispensable to any klephtic chief but it was the lessons learnt in the moral sink of Ali's court which marked Odysseus apart. At the age of only eighteen he had been appointed to the Armatolic of Livadia which his father had once held, and over the next twelve years he carved for himself out of Boeotia a virtual fiefdom which he governed with the stark and ruthless efficiency he had witnessed at Ioannina.

Violent, cruel, subtle, ambitious, wary to the point of paranoia, Odysseus was, in Gordon's memorable catalogue, the perfect compound of Arnaut brutality and Greek mendacity. The same might well have been said of any number of *capitani* at this time, of course, but Odysseus's early history had given him a priceless advantage over his rivals, and when rebellion broke out in 1821 his years in Livadia left him better placed than anyone to plunder the rich pickings along the borders of Greek and Turkish territories. Devoid of patriotism, idealism or religion as he was, the conflict to him was not a means to an end, but an end in itself. As with Colocotrones, it was the old life of the klepht given a new dimension, new legitimacy, new horizons. When it was needed he could fight as bravely as any captain, as he had early in the war at Gravia. When it was politic he treated with the Turks, or ambushed their convoys to sell their own grain back to them. When it suited he could sign his letters with a simple and effective dignity, 'The patriot Odysseus'. And when a nervous Government tried to assert its authority over his territory in Eastern Greece he had their delegates eliminated with a ruthlessness that would have done credit to Ali Pasha himself.

To Trelawny, wilfully blind all his life to his new hero's faults and duplicity, Odysseus was everything he was looking for. He was another Shelley, a second Washington or Bolivar, another 'De Ruyter', 'a man incomparably good in all his relations of social and private life. He was ardent, and yet patient,' he wrote of him,

> he was confident in himself, yet modest toward every one; venturing on such enterprises as seemed impossible to accomplish, and accomplishing them before the wonder at the undertaking had subsided. Appearing in different parts of Greece at nearly the same instant, and spreading the report by his emissaries that he was threatening the positions he had perhaps left behind them, his intentions and movements were unknown and unsuspected. Hence with five thousand

men he slew twenty thousand of the enemy, and allowed
them no leisure to fortify cities or throw up entrenchements.[4]

After the disappointments of the Morea it is no surprise to find
Trelawny falling under his sway, and yet the remarkable thing about
Odysseus was that he could exert the same fascination over a very
different sort of Philhellene. One reason for this was that under his
iron rule Athens enjoyed a far greater security than any other part
of Greece, but more important than that was the fact that he could
fill the Philhellene imagination in a way no other leader did, his
history and crimes simply lending an exotic glow to his natural grace
and born genius for command.

Romanticism and 'altitude snobbery' – that perennial prejudice
of the English, the innate preference for the mountain dweller over
the poor peasant of the plain which the nineteenth century raised
to a virtual principle of empire – alike pointed volunteers in his
direction. The wonder of it, the young Humphreys remarked, was
not that Odysseus had vices, but that brought up in Ali's court, he
had any virtues at all. 'Odysseus is in no respect distinguished from
his meanest soldier,' Waddington wrote in probably the fairest and
most balanced portrait we have of him at the time Trelawny first
joined him:

> otherwise than by the symmetry of his form, and the express-
> ive animation of a countenance which, though handsome, is
> far from prepossessing; for an habitual frown, and a keen
> and restless eye, betoken cruelty, suspiciousness, and incon-
> stancy; and those who have derived their opinion of his
> character from the observation of his exterior, and the
> rumour of his most notorious actions, pronounce him to be
> violent, avaricious, vindictive, distrustful, inexorable. Those,
> on the other hand, who believe themselves to have penetrated
> more deeply into his feelings and principles, consider him
> to be under the excessive guidance of policy and interest.
> His passions, (they say) however habitually impetuous, will
> never betray him into any measure of great imprudence,
> while his flexibility will allow him to change with every

change of circumstances; his violence and cruelty will seldom be wanton or excessive, while he possesses the power of assuming what virtues he pleases; so that he is equally capable, for the accomplishment of his purpose, of a very good or a very wicked action. Nor is it doubted that he possesses talents to discern, and firmness to pursue that interest which alone he is imagined to pursue.[5]

The glamour and violence of Odysseus's history would have been enough in themselves to seduce Trelawny but the intense loyalties and antipathies of the klephtic code acted even more strongly on his starved emotions. There had always been in his make-up a craving for recognition and identity that Byron's casual and ironical companionship never gave him, and as Mary Shelley was astute enough to recognize, Odysseus's appeal was as much to Trelawny's warm heart as his imagination.

Perhaps only Claire Clairmont touched his deepest feelings in the way the great male heroes of his life did. It can seem in fact that in some oddly Oedipal displacement even his sexuality was bound up in these friendships, so that the women he fell in love with – or at least imagined himself in love with – were those who might bring him closer to the men he successively put in his father's place. Claire herself was the mother of Byron's child and Trelawny confessed that he loved her before they had even met. Subsequently he would propose, too, to Shelley's widow. In Greece now, as he grew closer to Odysseus, a similar pattern emerged. This time it was Odysseus's half-sister, the thirteen-year-old Tersitza. 'I gather from your last letter,' Mary Shelley quizzed him, with a hint of jealousy in her tone which is nicely apportioned between brother and sister, 'that you think of marrying the sister of your favourite chief – & thus will renounce England – and worse the English for ever.'

'Adieu, dear Trelawny,' she finished her letter, 'take care of yourself, & come and visit us as soon as you can escape the sorceries of Ulysses.'[6] There is something quaintly motherly in the solicitude of her tone here, but Trelawny was in thrall to his new hero in a way Shelley's widow ought to have recognized from Italy. 'According to Trelawny,' Byron's young doctor Julius Millingen wrote, 'Odysseus was the personification of the beau ideal of every manly perfection, mental and bodily.'

> He swore by him and imitated him in the minutest actions. His dress, gait, and address were not only perfectly similar, but he piqued himself even in being as dirty; having as much vermin, and letting them loose from his fingers in the same dignified manner as if sparing a conquered enemy.[7]

For all its comic appeal, however, Millingen's description is a reminder of another and darker side to Trelawny's capacity for hero worship. There was in all his adulations of this kind a sinister element of the incubus about him, an instinct for emulation which shaded imperceptibly into possession, an almost compulsive urge to rise upon the stepping stones of his heroes' stolen lives to a fuller sense of his own identity.

This was true of his friendship with Byron and Shelley, whose lives and imaginations he pillaged for his own, and it was true now with Odysseus. For Trelawny, he represented the culmination of a search for identity which had begun in the violence of childhood rebellion. He had found in the poetry of Byron and Shelley the literary endorsement of his emotional turmoil, a language of revolt which could invest an inchoate rage with all the trappings of libertarian principle or romantic individualism. It was only with Odysseus, however, and in a world which sanctioned all the darker instincts of his personality, which legitimized every fantasy of violence under the specious banner of freedom, that his life finally seemed to fall into the coherent pattern he craved. 'My parents hard usage and abandonment had long gnawed at my heart,' he wrote in *Adventures*,

> till years of absence, in which both body and mind had expanded, taught me that it was the worst of slavery to submit the freedom of either to those who we cannot esteem nor love. The pride of my nature impelled me to shake off

the bondage. I did so. I could not endure the weight of slavery; but I cheerfully put on the heaviest chains the foes of liberty have to impose, – and they are heavy. I walked with an elevated front. Alone I withstood a fate that would have overpowered thousands, often defeated it is true, but even in losing I have still won. In this hard struggle I had little refreshment but from the fountains of my own soul. Had I not clung to myself, the atrocity of others had made me a demon. In the very onset of my freedom, I gained what neither wealth nor rank can purchase – the friendship of the really noble.[8]

From his Hydra letter to Mary Shelley it is clear that Odysseus's impact was immediate and complete, but from the months after he joined him at Athens in November 1823 to the April of 1824 almost no records survive. There is mention in Hastings's journal of a dinner Trelawny gave for the political leaders of Athens in December.[9] From the same source we know that he tried, unsuccessfully, to take Greek lessons. Gossip found its way back to England and a tolerantly unsurprised Mary Shelley of a 'harem' he had bought himself, but that, almost, is all.

For all the paucity of evidence, however, it is obvious that through the winter and early spring of 1823–4 Trelawny was probably as happy as he had ever been, parading at Odysseus's side in Athens or campaigning with him on the island of Euboea. 'Dear Mother', he wrote proudly on 18 February,

> I am enabled to keep twenty-five followers, Albanian soldiers, with whom I have joined the most enterprising of the Greek captains and most powerful – Ulysses. I am much with him, and have done my best during the winter campaign, in which we have besieged Negroponte [Euboea], to make up for the many years of idleness I have led. I am now in my element, and the energy of my youth is reawakened. I have clothed myself in the Albanian costume and sworn to uphold the cause.[10]

It is interesting that he should write to his mother in this way, so different in its patent need for approval to his public tone, but it would seem that there was nothing exaggerated in his claims. In his own later *Recollections* he would be casually dismissive about his activities during these months, but we have both Humphreys's and Finlay's testimony to the success he made of his new military role. He had the strength, physical courage and indifference to hardship to win the confidence of soldiers who had no time for Philhellene poseurs. And he had, too, the complete and unquestioning loyalty a klepht chieftain demanded of his followers. A thousand men like him, Odysseus told Humphreys, and he would take Constantinople.

It was as a loyal follower that he was at Odysseus's side in Athens when a curious incident took place on 1 March. The British ship, the *Hind* was in the Piraeus, and its officers under the command of Lord John Churchill invited Odysseus on board for dinner. Against the advice of his followers, wary of foreigners bearing gifts, Odysseus accepted. With him, as a precaution, he took thirty men. Among them were Trelawny, a Dr Tindall and, probably the greatest of all English Philhellenes after Byron, the brilliant and courageous sailor, Frank Abney Hastings.

The course of events at dinner is unclear, but Hastings says that too much was drunk. A quarrel seems to have developed, and the next thing the *Hind* was moving with its guests still on board. Fearing treachery and kidnap, Odysseus's men sprang to their chief's side on the deck, arms drawn, demanding to be set ashore. Their pleas ignored, Odysseus's lieutenant, the ferocious Ghouras, cut the tiller rope in an attempt to ground the *Hind*. When that failed Odysseus's bodyguard seized the ship's boat and made their escape. 'Thus all Ld J Churchill obtained by this unwarrantable trick,' Hastings indignantly reported, 'was to have this insult placed on the British flag.'[11]

The *Hind*'s log has not survived, there is no mention of this in Admiralty files or Trelawny's letters, but the incident was probably no more than a practical joke. With Britain's reputation in Greece at this time, however, and Odysseus's personality, Churchill was lucky that it did not end in bloodshed. It is impossible to imagine that he could have had any treacherous designs, but Odysseus and his companions remained convinced that this had been an attempt to kidnap him and hand him over to the Turkish authorities at Smyrna.

The wariness this incident reveals was rooted deep in Odysseus's character and upbringing, but when the long-awaited loan was finally floated on the London Stock Exchange at the beginning of 1825, the political map of Greece was changed in ways that would mature suspicion into a fixed paranoia. For the previous three years the only cry a foreigner ever heard from Greeks was for money and more money, and now at last they were to have it, forty thousand pounds in the first instance, followed by further massive and uncontrolled loans as gullibility and greed drove British investors to sink almost three million pounds in the bottomless and venal sink of the Greek Fund.

It would, in fact, be June before the first instalment found its way into the government party's coffers but the day of the war-lord was effectively over. The power of captains like Colocotrones in the Morea or Odysseus in Attica was ultimately based on their ability to maintain their palikars or soldiers, and this sudden influx of English gold meant that a previously bankrupt 'government' now had the financial power to buy off the private armies these fiefdoms depended on.

This would have been bad enough for Odysseus in any circumstances but, when the government party under the nominal leadership of the Hydriot Conduriottes was little more than a rival faction, it spelled disaster. There was indeed a genuine if tenuous line of legitimacy that linked the government in Nauplia with the Constitution of Epidaurus and the first heady days of revolution, and yet by 1824 it was little more than a few island families in league with a handful of chieftains, impotent without money but with it vengefully determined to settle old scores.

Perhaps the only element of the government faction that gave it any intellectual or moral credibility was the support of Mavrocordato and the 'western' party but his long-standing enmity meant simply one more nail in Odysseus's coffin.

It was, however, the arrival in Athens in January 1824 of the man appointed alongside Byron to administer the coming loan that brought home to Odysseus how close his day of reckoning had come. The younger son of the Earl of Harrington, Colonel Leicester Stanhope had spent the greater part of his life in the army, seeing action in India and in the disastrous 1807 campaign in South America before retiring on half-pay to pursue the radical, Benthamite interests that were closest to his heart.

There is possibly no major figure in Philhellene history who has suffered so consistently dismissive a press as this principled, dedicated and ludicrous man. He had first arrived in Cephalonia in the December of 1823, armed only with copies of Bentham's works, plans for Lancastrian schools and that unshakeable faith in the virtues of a free press which was to provide some of the rare comedy of Byron's last, bleak months. 'A zealous disciple of Mr Bentham,' the Philhellene historian Thomas Gordon wrote of him,

> neglecting the present crisis to gaze upon an imaginary future, he turned the question upside down, and began at the wrong end; he did not, perhaps, overrate the importance of education and publicity, but he committed a mistake in point of time. 'We want artillery men, and heavy ordnance,' said the Greeks! the Colonel offered them types and printers. 'The Turks and Egyptians are coming against us with a mighty power!' – 'Model your institutions on those of the United States of America.' – 'We have neither money, ammunition, nor provisions.' – 'Decree the unlimited freedom of the press!' If inclined at first to suspect that he was playing off a mystification upon them, they were acute enough speedily to discover the purity of his enthusiasm, and to humour his day-dreams. So entirely was he wedded to his doctrine, that he hoped in a few months his journals would enlighten

the savage Albanians; that the shepherds and warriors of Roumelia would peruse the works of Bentham, and Constantinople be shaken by his paper battering-ram.[12]

It was Byron's ironic quip that while the poet relied on the sword, the 'typographical colonel' seemed determined to free Greece with the pen, and it would be hard to imagine anyone less likely to fall under Odysseus's sway than this aristocratic and priggish Benthamite. One of the teasing imponderables of the Philhellene story is what Byron would have made of Odysseus had they ever met, but on the face of it at least Stanhope was a far more formidable test of political skills for a bandit chief whose whole life was a refutation of every belief the colonel held dear.

It was a challenge Odysseus met with a cynicism and sheer élan that has the richly comic appeal of imposture on a vast scale. Returning with Trelawny to Athens from his abortive campaign on Euboea, he was ready to meet every demand that philosophical radicalism could make. If Stanhope wanted a museum or schools then Athens should have them. If he wanted a hospital then Odysseus could provide details and figures for a hospital that never existed. If free elections were the colonel's favoured route to a liberated Greece, then Odysseus could be found presiding over meetings which were a tribute to Periclean Athens. 'Yesterday a public meeting took place for the purpose of choosing three persons to serve as magistrates,' Stanhope reported back to London.

> This day another meeting took place for the purpose of choosing three judges. I attended the assembly held in the square opposite the port. Odysseus, with others, was seated on the hustings. Opposite stands an old tree, surrounded with a broad seat, from which the magistrates addressed the people, explained the objects for which they were assembled, and desired them to name their judges. A free debate then took place, it lasted long, became more and more animated, and at last, much difference existing, a ballot was demanded and the judges were chosen.[13]

Here was a charade of a kind only possible under dictatorships and Stanhope fell for it. 'I have been constantly with Odysseus', he wrote to Byron on 6 March:

> He has a very strong mind, a good heart, and is brave as his sword; he is a doing man; he governs with a strong arm, and is the only man in Greece that can preserve order. He puts, however, complete confidence in the people. He is for strong government, for constitutional rights, and for vigorous efforts against the enemy. He professes himself of no faction, neither of Ipsilanti's, nor Colocotronis's, nor of Mavrocordato's; neither of the primates, nor of the Capitani; nor of the foreign king faction. He speaks of them all in the most undisguised manner.[14]

It is characteristic of Stanhope that he can have described Odysseus's position with such clarity and still failed to draw the only valid conclusion. He was right in his claim that Odysseus belonged to no other faction in Greece, but that was simply because the one interest he recognized was his own, the only power structure he understood the iron grip he and his lieutenant, Ghouras, held over Athens.

Through the early spring of 1824, however, as the threat of the loan loomed ever larger, events beyond his borders or control were moving in a direction which would fatally erode that position. At the beginning of January Byron's 'shilly-shallying'[15] on Cephalonia, as Trelawny contemptuously described it, had finally came to an end when he sailed for Missolonghi, once again Mavrocordato's headquarters and power-base in western Greece.

Up until almost the last moment Byron had wavered between Missolonghi and the Morea, and yet it is difficult to think that for a man of his ideals there was really any choice. For all his earlier failures in office Mavrocordato was still the one leader in Greece who saw its future in the way that Byron did, and however temperamentally different the two men were or fragile Mavrocordato's authority, moral and technical legitimacy alike pointed to him as Byron's only proper ally.

Hindsight gives all the manoeuvrings and politicking that followed this decision a curious sense of irrelevance but there is no mistaking their urgency at the time. In Athens Byron's choice was greeted with horror. Through the early years of the rebellion Odysseus had been able to trample over the Phanariot ambitions of Mavrocordato with complete impunity, but with Byron's arrival on the Prince's soil the whole axis of political life shifted westwards in a way that he could no longer ignore. Over the next months, as men, money, stores, equipment and weapons flowed into Missolonghi, Odysseus, with Trelawny's devoted and uncritical support, set out to prise Byron away from Mavrocordato and on to his own territory. Throughout February and March a constant stream of letters and demands went from Athens to Missolonghi, urging Byron's presence in eastern Greece or demanding their share of the London Greek Committee's supplies that had followed him to western Greece. 'Dear Prince', Trelawny wrote to Mavrocordato on 17 February,

> Will you permit me to introduce to you Mr Finley a friend of mine who in conjunction with one of Ulysses officers Capt. Panace is the bearer of a letter from Ulysses to Lord Byron & for other purposes of obtaining supplies if possible, of which we are greatly in want here? May I take the liberty of intreating that you will aid and advice them in the affair which I do not hesitate to request, as I know you act on the broad basis of real patriotism and feel as much interested in the taking of Negropont [Euboea] as Lepanto – as they are of equal importance to the great cause in which you have so nobly devoted yourself & fortunes – [16]

In this interest too, Stanhope – flattered, hoodwinked, deliberately, almost criminally, blind to Odysseus's real character – was a willing tool. 'Odysseus is most anxious to unite the interests of Eastern and Western Greece,' Stanhope faithfully reported in a letter to Byron at Missolonghi, 'for which purpose he is desirous of immediately forming a congress at Salona. He solicits your Lordship's and Mavrocordato's presence.'[17]

Odysseus must have known that Mavrocordato could never accept the invitation but the possibility of unity was a lure that Byron himself could not refuse. At the bottom of the letter Stanhope threw his own weight behind the appeal. 'I implore your Lordship and the President', he wrote, 'as you love Greece and her sacred cause, to attend Salona.'[18] Here was the endorsement Odysseus and Trelawny had schemed for, the reward for all the lectures endured, the demands humoured, the talk of schools and printing presses and horticultural societies. The next day they were back again in Negroponte, secure in the knowledge that Stanhope was theirs. On 15 March, just two months after his first arrival in Athens, a letter from the colonel followed them, underlying just how close their ambitions now ran, how far Benthamite principles could be bent in the interests of 'strong' government.

> At the ensuing congress, I expect to see Odysseus taking the lead in every thing that is just, and proclaiming his sentiments loudly to his country and the world. It is devoutly to be wished that all other chiefs engaged in the congress should co-operate in these measures; but if they have not the virtue to act this nobly I am convinced that your strong mind will take its own bold course – a course that must lead to the downfall of the Turks, to the permanent establishment of the liberties of Greece, and of your power and fame . . . If there be any Greek with a vast mind, and possessing great power, who has the nobleness of soul to pursue the public good, that man will soar above all his contemporaries; he will save his country from Turks and faction, and entail on millions for ages to come the blessings of liberty.[19]

This was a giddy prospect to dangle before the favourite pipebearer of Ali Pasha. By the end of March it looked, too, as if events were bringing it a step closer, as if all the pressure of the early spring and all the letters sent to Missolonghi had at last achieved their object. On 19 March, almost a month after Trelawny's letter to him, Mavrocordato wrote back to Stanhope in Athens, smoothly diplomatic in his protestations:

If the weather had not prevented Mr Finlay's return, you would already have known, that we have decided on coming to meet General Ulysses, as far as Chrysso, or even as Salona. You know better than anybody the difficulties which were to be overcome in order to arrive at this decision; but you are equally persuaded that his Lordship and myself will never let slip an opportunity which holds out the hope of any thing advantageous for the affairs of my country.[20]

On 30 March another of Odysseus's Philhellenes, the young English volunteer Humphreys, arrived back from Missolonghi with confirmation that despite Mavrocordato's fears of kidnap Byron had agreed to the meeting. A last message, touchingly, ended with the postscript of how much Byron was looking forward to seeing Trelawny again. Events now moved quickly forward. Less than three weeks later Stanhope arrived on the border of eastern and western Greece for the congress, his spirits high, and 'everyone breathing the spirit of liberty' he told Bowring in London: 'I reached Salona this morning', he wrote:

> Nothing can exceed the beauty and sublime character of the scenery between the gulf and this place. There the eye embraces at a glance the rude sea, a valley of flowers, a winding stream, and mountains covered with firs and topped with snow.[21]

Here, under the western slopes of Parnassus, was the Greece Byron's poetry had conjured into being for a whole generation of Philhellenes. The one man missing, however, was Byron himself. The next day, on 17 April, Stanhope was writing again to Bowring, nervous now, explaining that he had persuaded Odysseus to despatch Trelawny to Missolonghi to accompany Byron's suite back to the congress.

The same day Trelawny set off with his palikars, keeping to the mountain passes to avoid Turkish cavalry in the plains. With him he carried Stanhope's last letter to Byron.

My Dear Lord Byron,

We are all assembled here with the exception of your Lordship and Monsieur Mavrocordato. I hope you will both join us; indeed after the strong pledges given, the President ought to attend. As for you, you are a sort of Wilberforce, a saint whom all parties are endeavouring to seduce; it's a pity that you are not divisible, that every prefecture might have a fraction of your person. For my own part, I wish to see you fairly out of Missolonghi, because your health will not stand the climate and the constant anxiety to which you are there subjected.

I shall remain here till we receive your and the President's answer; I mean then to go to Egina, Zante, and England. If I can be of any service, you may command my zealous services.

Once more, I implore you to quit Missolonghi, and not to sacrifice your health and perhaps your life in that Bog.

I am ever you most devoted

Leicester Stanhope.[22]

It was perhaps the only sensible advice Stanhope ever gave in Greece, but it was already too late. Two days later, slowed down by the April rains, Trelawny reached the swollen banks of the Evvenus river, still some miles short of Missolonghi. His path crossed with a troop of palikars coming in the opposite direction. For some reason the sight of them filled him with foreboding. 'It was the second after having crossed the first torrent,' he later wrote to Stanhope,

> that I met some soldiers from Missolonghi. I had let them all pass me, ere I had resolution enough to enquire the news from Missolonghi. I then rode back and demanded of a stranger – then I heard nothing more than – Byron is dead.[23]

5

THE DEATH OF BYRON

'You will think me more superstitious than ever (said Byron) when I tell you, that I have a presentiment that I shall die in Greece. I hope it may be in action, for that would be a good finish to a very *triste* existence, and I have a horror of death-bed scenes; but as I have not been famous for my luck in life, most probably I shall not have more in the manner of my death, and that I may draw my last sigh, not on the field of glory, but on the bed of disease.'

Lady Blessington[1]

'I said to a Greek one day 'Byron is dead.' He replied, 'No, never,' then striking his left breast at the same moment his soul rushed into his eyes, 'he will always live here and in the hearts of my countrymen.' When a Greek speaks of Lord B– it is as if he was speaking of some superior deity who had visited them from heaven on an errand of mercy.'

*From a letter of Private Wheeler:
Argostoli, June 10 1824*[2]

No one should have to die in Missolonghi. Perched on the south-western corner of mainland Greece, the town struggles along a shoreline where sea and land seem not so much to meet as simultaneously expire, the distant hills of Aetolia finally petering out in a last few reedy flats that stretch into the shallow waters of a dying lagoon.

Out in the entrance to the Gulf of Corinth only a few miles away, the galleons of the Turkish and Christian fleets fought at Lepanto in

1571 one of the decisive battles of the western world, but the waters here seem too shallow ever to have allowed the approach of history. Now, too, a road carries the traffic past to the north, up towards Arta and Ioannina and eastwards to Nafpactos and Delphi, by-passing Missolonghi altogether, leaving it marooned on the edge of its silent, mosquito-infested basin, geography, economics or strategy equally at a loss to explain its role in the birth of Modern Greece.

It is one of those ironies that Thomas Hardy so much loved – the one anniversary we all miss, he remarked, is the anniversary each year of our own death – that Byron should have passed this way in 1809 without so much as noticing the town that was to kill him. Even as late as the December of 1823 he was still undecided where he should go in Greece, but from the moment he stepped ashore at Missolonghi it is as though his destiny was fulfilled, as if in his gaudy uniform and plumed helmet he had arrived like some sacrificial god-king of ritual to be garlanded and feted by his people and then killed to redeem the land.

There is not a single step on this final journey to his deathbed that hagiography has not set in stone, invested with all the cruel and symbolic meaning of stations on the road to Byron's and English Romanticism's own Calvary: the tumultuous welcome on the water-front; the convulsive fit; the ride in the rain; the bleeding by the doctors, and the final exhausted days, as Byron hovered between consciousness and death, surrounded by some of the most improbable figures ever to preside over one of the great moments of Romantic history while a storm raged prophetically above the town.

There is nothing that can be said about Byron's last days that has not been said a hundred times already yet it always comes as a surprise to remember how short a time he was in Missolonghi. There were so many frustrations and disappointments crammed into that brief space that each day has taken on an epic status, with the weeks seeming to stretch out into endless, barren months, and yet the whole period from the time Stanhope welcomed him to the mainland as Greece's Messiah until his death on Easter Monday was in fact just fifteen weeks.

Those weeks started, too, so full of promise and expectation, that the subsequent failure seems all the starker. From the moment he landed on 5 January 1824 Missolonghi became the focus of foreign and Greek enthusiasm which Odysseus had feared, as English, Scots, Irish, Americans, Germans, Swiss, Belgians, Russians, Swedes, Danes, Hungarians and Italians were drawn there by the magnetism of Byron's fame.

Even men who never got to Missolonghi liked, later, to pretend that they had, that they had been part of this doomed crusade, or that their lives had somehow intersected with his. In family memoirs and reminiscences generation after generation would hand on the legend that an uncle – a great-uncle, a great-great uncle – had been part of the 'Byron Brigade'. Soldiers in the Ionian Isles would say that they had seen the ship that carried his coffin home. In America, Edgar Alan Poe – a fantasist to rival Trelawny – claimed to have set out to join him.

No one who did, either, would ever forget it. Parry,* the drunken old humorist in charge of the weapons factory, Millingen, Byron's young and feckless doctor, Kennedy who had tried to convert him on Cephalonia, Trelawny, Humphreys, Stanhope, Hamilton Browne, Gamba, Finlay all left their memories of Byron's last days. When he talked, they would recall, they heard the voice of 'Don Juan'; when things went awry among the chaos and mud of Missolonghi, they joked nervously of his threats to put them in its next canto, their antics preserved in its stanzas as surely as the Grub Street nonentities of eighteenth-century London had been in the couplets of Pope's *Dunciad*.

The poetry and the fame had brought them, but it was the fascination of his personality that held them. 'Both his character and his conduct presented unceasing contradictions,' wrote Finlay, himself the most Gibbonian of romantics,

> It seemed as if two different souls occupied his body alternately. One was feminine, and full of sympathy; the other masculine, and characterized by clear judgement, and by a rare power of presenting for consideration those facts only which were required for forming a decision. When one

arrived the other departed. In company, his sympathetic soul was his tyrant. Alone, or with a single person, his masculine prudence displayed itself as his friend. No man could then arrange facts, investigate their causes, or examine their consequences with more logical accuracy, or in a more practical spirit. Yet, in his most sagacious moment, the entrance of a third person would derange the order of his ideas, – judgement fled, and sympathy, generally laughing, took its place.[3]

Masculine and feminine, redeemer and conqueror, poet and man of action, in his last months Byron had become all things to all men and in the hopeless and lonely attempt to fulfil that obligation he died. It is possible that his health would have failed him wherever he had gone, but in Missolonghi, as day after day the rain lashed the town and each successive plan foundered on the factionalism and greed endemic to the war, it was almost certain.

As he watched Greek fight with Greek and Greek with Suliote, Suliote with Philhellene and Philhellene with Philhellene, as the promised stores were delayed and attacks abandoned, Byron's patience, spirit and energies slowly gave in, leaving only his integrity intact. That, though, never wavered, even when the last emotional attachment of his life, to a young Greek boy he had taken into his service, met with an indifference which brought cruelly home his sense of ebbing powers. Privately unhappy, he remained robustly, publicly true to himself and those principles which had brought him to Missolonghi, ready to serve or command as necessary – it was 'much the same to him'[4] – in the interest of a united Greece.

It was not just Greece, either, that benefited from his presence. When a Turkish brig ran ashore, he secured the release of the prisoners, adopting a nine-year-old girl with the plan of providing for her. 'Coming to Greece,' he wrote to the English Consul in Prevesa, where he had managed to send twenty-four of the prisoners,

one of my principal objects was to alleviate as much as possible the miseries incident to a warfare so cruel as the present. When the dictates of humanity are in question, I know no difference between Turks and Greeks. It is enough that those who want assistance are men, in order to claim the pity and protection of the meanest pretender to humane feelings.[5]

That is not a voice one often comes across in this war, but it had not long to make itself heard. Even as he made his plans to go to Salona in a bid to unite eastern and western Greece, his time was running out. The first sign came in the middle of February. In the last entry in his journal he recorded the details.

Upon February 15th – (I write on the 17th. of the same month) I had a strong shock of a Convulsive description but whether Epileptic – Paralytic – or Apoplectic is not yet decided by the two medical men who attend me – or whether it be of some other nature (if such there be) it was very painful and had it lasted a moment longer must have extinguished my mortality – if I can judge by sensations. – I was speechless with the features much distorted – but not foaming at the mouth – they say – and my struggles so violent that several persons – two of whom – Mr Parry the Engineer – and my Servant Tita the Chasseur are very strong men – could not hold me – it lasted about ten minutes – and came on immediately after drinking a tumbler of Cider mixed with cold water . . .

With regard to the presumed cause of this attack – as far as I know there might be several – the state of the place and of the weather permits little exercise at present; – I have been violently agitated with more than one passion recently – and a good deal occupied politically as well as privately – and amidst conflicting parties – politics – and (as far as regards public matters) circumstances; – I have also been in an anxious state with regard to things which may be only interesting to my own private feelings – and perhaps not uniformly so temperate as I may generally affirm that I was wont to be – how far any or all of these may have acted on the mind or body of One who had already undergone many previous changes of place and passion during a life of thirty six years I cannot tell . . . [6]

Within days of the attack Byron was assuring his friends of his recovery, but the complex medley of private and public concerns, of emotional, physical and mental anxieties which lie behind that final paragraph were taking a toll he recognized. Three weeks earlier, on 22 January 1824, he had articulated them in a poem that in its sad and lonely inadequacy makes the courage and firmness of his public face seem all the more heroic.

'T is time this heart should be unmoved,
Since others it hath ceased to move;
Yet, though I cannot be beloved,
Still let me love!

My days are in the yellow leaf;
The flowers and fruits of love are gone;
The worm, the Canker, and the grief
Are mine alone!

The fire that on my bosom preys
Is lone as some volcanic isle;
No torch is kindled at its blaze –
A funeral pile.

. . . .

But 't is not thus – and 't is not here –
Such thoughts should shake my soul, nor now,
Where glory decks the hero's bier,
Or binds his brow.

. . . .

Tread these reviving passions down,
Unworthy manhood! – unto thee
Indifferent should the smile or frown
Of beauty be.

If thou regrett'st thy youth, *why live?*
The land of honourable death
Is here: up to the field, and give
Away thy breath!

Seek out – less often sought than found –
A soldier's grave, for thee the best;
Then look around, and choose thy ground,
And take thy rest.[7]

Byron was not to be allowed even this. His wry prophecy to Lady Blessington was to be unerringly accurate. On 19 March he wrote to Stanhope, announcing his intention of meeting Odysseus and Trelawny at Salona. The weather and the flooded rivers, however, delayed his start, and on 9 April he went out riding, was soaked in the rain, and came down the next day with fever.

After years of alternate diet and excess, and still weak from the doctors' leeches applied to combat his fit, he was in no state to resist. Over the next days his condition worsened, his nerves shaken, his head dizzy, and pains in his stomach. It was on 17 April that the doctors for the first time feared for the life their repeated bleedings had done so much to shorten. The next day, Easter Sunday, the town itself seemed to hold its breath, the traditional volleys of rifle fire to greet Christ's resurrection silenced as a sense of imminent loss sank in. 'Die I must,' Byron, in between fits of delirium, told Millingen.

> I feel it. Its loss I do not lament; for to terminate my weari-some existence I came to Greece. My wealth, my abilities, I devoted to her cause. – Well: there is my life to her.[8]

At about six o'clock the next evening Greece finally took that too. 'I saw my master open his eyes and then shut them,' his servant Fletcher remembered, 'but without showing any symptoms of pain, or moving hand or foot. "Oh! my God!" I exclaimed, "I fear his lordship is gone." The doctors then felt his pulse, and said, "You are right – he is gone."'[9]

'Lord Byron accomplished nothing at Missolonghi except his own suicide,' Harold Nicolson once memorably declared, 'but by that single act of heroism he secured the liberation of Greece.'[10] There has always been such a compelling desire to find some kind of meaning in Byron's death that this graceful accommodation between the demands of piety and realism has come to stand as something like his epitaph. It is impossible of course to put any other certainty in its place, but before Nicolson's verdict is accepted as the last word it should at least be remembered that this was not how it looked in 1824. The *feu de joie* that broke from the blockading Turkish fleet at the news was perhaps the most spontaneous proof of this but it was left to Mavrocordato to put it in its bleakest terms. 'Nobody knows,' he lamented with prophetic accuracy,

> except perhaps myself, the loss Greece has suffered. Her safety even depended on his continuing existence. His presence here has checked intrigues which will now have uncontrolled sway. By his aid, alone, have I been able to preserve Missolonghi; and now I know, that every assistance I derived from him will be taken away.[11]

If it is perhaps no surprise that Greek gratitude or English guilt have preferred the consolations of myth to Mavrocordato's despair, it seems more curious that history should have colluded in its growth. There are perhaps other explanations for this phenomenon but the reasons lie at heart in that modern disbelief in the individual, in a profound scepticism that Byron or any other outsider could have imposed his personality on the chaos and factionalism of Greek politics. It is certainly true, too, that his last months at Missolonghi offer little room for hope, and yet in this casual sacrifice of man to symbol an important fact of the Greek war is lost, a genuine distinction buried under an unhistorical sense of familiarity.

The Balkans now, and the Balkans which formed part of the Ottoman Empire are not the same place. The Balkans of the 1990s, for all the similarities, the political and ethnic violence, the religious hatreds and fierce tribalism are at least half constrained by laws which in 1824 had no sanction. In 1824, when Byron died, there were still 'answers' there that are no longer internationally acceptable; in 1824, with genocide not just a possibility but an accomplished fact, victory in Greece was there to be seized. It was not a matter of diplomacy or international pressure, no longer a cause in need of martyrs to stir the conscience of liberal Europe. It was a matter for a Napier or Hastings, as Byron would tell anyone ready to listen, a question of ships and guns, and above all of money – the money through which Byron alone, had he made it to Salona, might have been able to reach the warring factions. If he had only lived another fifteen days, even Gordon, the soberest of historians, was driven to exclaim, if he could have just held on until Blaquiere's arrival with the first consignment of the loan! 'The Loan,' Napier wrote, spelling out its importance to Bowring, just days after Byron's death but still weeks before its news reached him in London:

> The old Story, Money, Money, Money, and I have no hesita-
> tion in saying that were I in Greece with the full command
> of the 40,000 l. which Blaquiere has taken I would form an
> army and be in possession of Salonica within four months
> from the day I landed . . . and Give the Greeks Constanti-
> nople in less than two months after.[12]

Napier's was no idle boast, and it is this tantalizing sense of what might still have been as much as the tragic waste of the years ahead that makes the antics of the different factions in the weeks before and after Byron's death so shameful. It is clearly an absurd anachronism to judge the Greek captains by standards that have no bearing on their lives, but the same weary relativism cannot be applied to the volunteers who had gravitated towards Byron and Missolonghi without obscuring the issues that now split their ranks. By what right were they in Greece? Under whose authority did men like Finlay, Humphreys or Stanhope act? To whom did they owe loyalty? What was it, as Parry demanded, that distinguished them from common buccaneers or prevented the Philhellene committing murder every time he pulled a trigger?

If these would have seemed irrelevant questions to Trelawny they would not have seemed so to Byron. He had never been under any illusion about his role in the Greek revolution, or that his technical and moral legitimacy flowed from his relations with a central authority and it is impossible to understand the bitterness of Mavrocordato's supporters in the weeks that followed unless this is remembered. The divisions that split the brigade which Byron had gathered around him were not simply those between faction and faction: they were between legitimacy – however tenuous a thing that had become – and opposition; between the future and the past: between the united but yet unborn Greece for which Byron had died and the feudal anarchy of Odysseus or Colocotrones.

This, however, was still in the future. The 'Captain Trelawny' who arrived in Missolonghi on either 24 or 25 April, flush with the importance of his role over the last few months, was in no mood to recognize any authority, least of all Mavrocordato's. A growing sense of power is evident in the surviving letters of these next weeks, an exultant and dangerous conviction that he had at last come into his own. 'I am transformed from the listless being you knew me to one of all energy and fire,' he wrote to Mary Shelley from Missolonghi only days after his arrival. 'Not content with the Camp, I must needs be a great diplomatist. I am again, dear Mary, in my element, and playing no second part in Greece.'[13]

An element of self-aggrandizement had always co-existed with his hero-worship of course, but it was only with Byron's death that its complex and unstable pathology at last showed itself in full. Trelawny could never forgive Byron the maturity, the irony, the self-knowledge that made his own life seem nothing more than the small change of another's imagination and he now took his revenge with a blend of condescension and vitriol he was to keep up for over fifty years. There was a public show of sorrow for the benefit of a town in mourning, but behind the routine encomiums and proprietorial jostlings for place he rapidly set about redefining his relationship with 'the greatest man in the world'. 'With all his weaknesses, you know I loved him,'[14] he wrote to Mary Shelley in the immediate aftermath of death, and perhaps even half-believed it himself. Within a short time, however, Byron had become the 'paltry tool of the weak, imbecile, cowardly being calling himself Prince

Mavrocordato'.[15] 'Five months he dozed away at Cephalonia in the old way,' he told her in a letter that in its only printed version has been carefully doctored, the worst of Trelawny's charges in this, the autograph version, silently omitted.

> and five months he drawled away in the most pusillanimous and disgusting acts at that miserable mud-bank Missolonghi ... he fell victim to an excess of unnatural acts having previously disordered himself by a fit of unusual hard-drinking – By the Gods! the lies that are said in his praises urges one to speak the truth ... I now feel my face burn with shame that so weak and ignoble a soul could so long have influenced me. It is a degrading reflection, and ever will be. I wish he had lived a little longer, that he might have witnessed how I would have soared above him here, how I would have triumphed over his mean spirit.[16]

In a life punctuated by shabby betrayals and coarse boasts these letters of Trelawny to the dispirited rump of the Pisa Circle still stand out. There are letters to Jane Williams, to Mary Shelley, to Claire Clairmont and in all of them the message is the same. Byron was nothing, did nothing, achieved nothing; he was a drifter, a sybarite, better dead – better for himself, better for Greece. 'But he is dead,' he triumphantly crowed;[17] 'I am playing a first part here,' he told Claire Clairmont. 'Byron, who was mine as well as your evil genius, has ceased to be.'[18]

If Trelawny meant by that that he had at last escaped from Byron he could not have been more wrong. Before the *Florida* had left a grieving Missolonghi with Byron's body, the news was preceding it across Europe, leaving its indelible trail in the letters, diaries and newspapers of the time. '*Lord Noel Byron est mourru dans mes bras,*' the Swiss Philhellene Meyer, an old sparring partner in the battle of the 'press' against the 'sword', had jubilantly reported to Stanhope,

in his excitement misdating his letter two days before the actual
end;

*étrange affaire que l'homme qui toujours parlait contre le
sens de ma gazette devait mourrir dans mes bras . . . mais
grâce á Dieu, j'ai vaincu. Byron est mort!*[19]

From Corfu to Boston, from Salona to Calcutta, from Pushkin's
Caucasus to Goethe's Weimar, in the letters of men as diverse as
Lord Guilford and Private Wheeler, in diplomatic correspondence
and secret service transcripts or carved in sandstone, the message
was the same. On the banks of the Hoogly river an East India
Company memsahib heard prayers for his soul rise from the small
Greek chapel. In Russia, where she was working as a governess,
the news reached an unrelenting Claire Clairmont, unmoved and
disbelieving that he had murmured her name on his deathbed. 'This
then was the coming event that cast its shadow on my last night's
miserable thoughts,' Mary Shelley wrote in her mawkish prose on
15 May: 'Byron had become one of the people of the grave.'[20] 'I
was told it all at once in a room full of people,' Jane Welsh wrote
to Carlyle,

My God if they had said that the sun or the moon had gone
out of the heavens it could not have struck me with the idea
of a more awful and dreary blank in the creation than the
words Byron is dead.[21]

'Poor Byron! Alas poor Byron!' Carlyle replied.

The news of his death came down upon my heart like a
mass of lead; and yet, the thought of it sends a painful twinge
thr' all my being, as if I had lost a brother! O God! That
so many souls of mud and clay should fill up their base
existence to its utmost bound, and this, the noblest spirit in
Europe, should sink before half his course was run! Late so
full of fire, and generous passion, and proud purposes, and
now forever dumb and cold! Poor Byron . . . we shall hear
his voice no more: I dreamed of seeing him and knowing
him; but the curtain of everlasting night has hid him from

our eyes. We shall go to him, he shall not return to us. Adieu my dear Jane! There is a blank in your heart, and a blank in mine, since this man passed away.[22]

There has always been a good dose of sexual and physical prurience in England's fascination with Byron, but however mixed the motives by the time his coffin was landed by rowing boat at Westminster steps on 10 July 1824 London was in no mood to let his name die.

For the next two days the body lay in state at Sir Edward Knatch-bull's home in Great George Street. At eleven o'clock on the morning of the 12th, with the Abbey bells tolling and a vast crowd lining the streets, the funeral cortege began its slow journey north to the family vault in Hucknall church in Nottinghamshire. The route of the procession took Byron's corpse along Parliament Street and up Whitehall, past the top of Oxford Street into the Tottenham Court Road. At the toll gate in Frederick's Place the long train of carriages turned back, leaving only the hearse and a second vehicle containing Byron's heart to continue with the chief mourners. Behind them, a silent crowd followed on foot. At her window in Kentish Town, Shelley's widow watched with Jane Williams as the cortege passed by. 'He could hardly be called a friend,' she wrote of it to Trelawny,

> but connected with him in a thousand ways, admiring his talents & with all his faults feeling affection for him, it went to my heart when the other day the herse that contained his lifeless form, a form of beauty which in life I often delighted to behold, passed my window going up Highgate Hill on his last journey to the last seat of his ancestors.[23]

That night Byron's body rested at Welwyn. The second day the journey continued on to Highdan Ferrars. The third took him as far as Oakham and late in the afternoon of the 15th the cortege reached Nottingham. A room had been prepared for its reception at the Blackmoor's Head. Through the night the coffin lay on trestles, surrounded by wax candles and guarded by constables, as thousands filed past.

The next morning, with a silent crowd cramming every window

and rooftop, Byron's hearse, adorned with sable plumes, and pulled by six black and plumed horses set off on the last eight miles to Hucknall. Four and a half hours later, with the church draped in black, an escutcheon bearing the family arms and motto '*Crede Byron*' hanging beneath the pulpit, and the minute bell tolling, the body and urn were at last brought in and placed in the aisle. A part of the Anglican burial service was read, and then the coffin and urn were slowly lowered into the family vault, watched to the last possible moment by Byron's friends and lifelong companions. 'The poor black servant never took his eyes from the coffin,' reported *The Times*,

> and bent his body that they should follow it to the last glimpse, which its gorgeous reflection still cast from the gloomy abyss of the tomb to which it was consigned. The Italian servant seemed as if he were a stranger and friendless; and the valet (Fletcher), from his late master's childhood his attendant, was so overpowered as the coffin was lowering into the vault, that he was obliged to draw back from the chief mourners, among whom the domestics unconsciously mixed, in pressing forward to take a final glance, and to support himself against a pew in an agony of grief.[24]

Penetrate the conventions of nineteenth-century mourning, and the most striking aspect of every account of Byron's funeral is the sheer breadth of sympathy that greeted his loss. There was of course nothing new in the cult of personality that surrounded Byron's name, but with his death it took on a new impetus, a richer and more democratic resonance, a universality which reflected something more than the prurient curiosity of London society. The carriages of the Dukes of Sussex and Bedford, the Marquises of Lonsdale and Tavistock might have accompanied the coffin on its first stage, but it was not the nobility who followed in their thousands to Hucknall church. It was parents with their grown-up daughters, American seamen docked at Liverpool, the officers of an infantry battalion, clerks and mechanics who would sign the visitors' book in the months to come. It was an unknown Greek on Cephalonia who told

Private Wheeler that Byron would live for ever in his heart, some nameless stranger Hobhouse found on the *Florida*, cutting off a relic of the linen pall that covered the coffin. Among the London mourners following the hearse, a solitary sailor is picked out in Parry's account, 'an honest looking tar' who had been with Byron sixteen years earlier in the Greek isles. In Hucknall church it is Fletcher who grasps at a bench, overcome by grief; Byron's black servant who is caught for all time, his body arched to catch a final glimpse as the coffin is lowered into the vault.

It does not matter how often the details of Byron's fame are rehearsed, the evidence of his grip on the imagination of a whole age never loses its startling impact. In an obvious sense of course the men who fought in Greece are hardly representative of the wider world, but it is impossible to read a letter, journal or essay without coming up against the proof of Byron's power. Twenty years earlier, Jane Austen had written of the unconscious presence of Shakespeare in the speech of every Englishman, but has any writer created a language that liberated sensibility, which extended the capacity of ordinary people to see and feel in the way Byron did? Soldiers, sailors, medical students, classicists, gentlemen travellers, ships' chaplains, ardent romantics or drunken cynics, it does not matter where one turns, the proof is there. When *The Times* casts round for the right sentiment, it is 'Childe Harold' that provides it. When Humphreys stares up at the near impregnable fortress of Acrocorinth, 'he much wished to make the assault to realise Lord Byron's beautiful poem'.[25] Men walk where Byron had walked, look at what Byron looked at, see things with his eyes, describe things with his language, respond to a world that, quite simply, he has called into being for them.

Against this, against the evidence of everything that was said and done in both England and Greece, there is something almost comic in Trelawny's belief that death had at last freed him from Byron's hold. Perhaps at some level he actually thought this, but while there can be no doubting his capacity for self-delusion, it co-existed with a streak of calculation that invariably served him well. He could say what he liked in letters to Claire Clairmont, there was no abuse of

Byron the mother of Allegra would not lap up; but at the same time as he slandered him in private he moved in public to assume the role of Byron's closest friend and heir. 'With all his faults I loved him truly,' he wrote to Stanhope on the 28th,

> He is connected with every event of the most interesting years of my wandering life – his every day companion – we lived in ship – boats and in house, together, we had no secrets – no reserve, and though we often differed in opinion, never quarrelled.[26]

Within hours of arriving in Missolonghi he had taken command of Byron's household, going through his papers, organizing, interviewing and interfering, reinventing the deathbed scene he had missed, grafting his own personality onto the Byronic myth in a way which foreshadowed the long-term strategy of the years ahead.

'It was the 24th or 25th of April when I arrived,' he recalled nearly forty years later, in a superb passage which represents the final distillation of everything he wanted believed of that April in Missolonghi. It is a companion piece to his cremation of Shelley, wonderfully vivid in the same way but even more wayward in its inventions – inventive in its detail, in its emotions, in its description of Byron's lameness, inventive even more stunningly in the strong likelihood that the scene never occurred:*

> I waded through the streets, between wind and water, to the house he had lived in; it was detached, and on the margin of the shallow slimy sea waters. For three months this house had been besieged, day and night, like a bank that has a run on it. Now that death had closed the door, it was as silent as a cemetery. No one was within the house but Fletcher, of which I was glad. As if he knew my wishes, he led me up a narrow stair into a small room, with nothing in it but a coffin standing on trestles. No word was spoken by either of us; he withdrew the black pall and the white shroud, and there lay the embalmed body of the Pilgrim – more beautiful in death than in life. The contraction of the

muscles and skin had effaced every line that time or passion had ever traced in it; few marble busts could have matched its stainless white, the harmony of its proportions, and perfect finish; yet he had been dissatisfied with that body, and longed to cast its slough . . . I asked Fletcher to bring me a glass of water. On his leaving the room, to confirm or remove my doubts as to the exact cause of his lameness, I uncovered the Pilgrim's feet, and was answered – the great mystery was solved. Both his feet were clubbed, and his legs withered to the knee – the form and features of an Apollo, with the feet of a sylvan satyr.[27]

And it was not simply within Byron's household that Trelawny moved to assert his authority, but on the wider political stage. Two months before Byron's death the munitions sent out by the London Greek Committee had finally arrived, and Trelawny now turned his attention to prising away from Missolonghi at least a share of the weapons left under the care of William Parry. The legality of this was doubtful, the folly of it with Missolonghi on the brink of a second siege unquestionable. Trelawny however cared for neither. Part credulous dupe, part fellow conspirator, he pressed Odysseus's claims to the artillery. 'The sheet anchor of Greece – is Odysseus – I think,' he wrote to Leicester Stanhope, as vulnerable now to the flattering consequence Trelawny gave him as he had earlier been to Odysseus.

> I am serving the cause of liberty in my attachment to him – I love noble men. I have no selfish stake in view all my feelings are now concentrated on the attainment of this – the greatest and noblest game that is now playing in the world – the liberation of Greece.[28]

The guns were wasted, too, in Missolonghi, Trelawny insisted. No English would stay there, and no brute of a Greek in the town was interested in anything but money. 'Hodges and Gill will not stay here', he told him. 'All the English wish to be off. Do, my dear Sir, take some prompt and decisive steps . . . Divide the artillery brigade in two, for it is, in force, two brigades.'[29]

Behind this appeal lies the feverish activity and lobbying that can still be followed among the papers of the London Greek Committee and Leicester Stanhope. There is a feeling of immediacy about primary sources that has to be guarded against, a temptation to give the written document an imaginative weight out of proportion to its real value; Trelawny's letters from this period, however, preserve his character in ways that no printed transcript could adequately suggest.

From his earliest days in Italy many of Byron's idiosyncrasies had found their way into Trelawny's epistolary style, but it is only in these weeks after his mentor's death that his letters cut loose of all convention, with language, grammar and even handwriting – quite serviceable earlier – all swept up in the intoxication of power and borne along on a torrent of violence and abuse.

His hand is at times virtually illegible, his language savage and unrestrained. 'Let such beings as those who conceive this', he wrote to Stanhope of the plan to bury Byron's body in the Ionian Isles,

> rot like rats in the obscene holes & corners in which they die – who are only distinguished from such vermin – by their shape and form which obliges naturalists to clap them for distinction sake – with the human race.[30]

Arbiter, kingmaker, statesman and soldier, it seemed to Trelawny in these last days of April that he alone had the energy and vision to take control of events. Everyone else in Missolonghi was a block-head, or a crook. 'I am at the fountain head of procrastination', he again told Stanhope,

> The pestilential fever of these torpid waters seems to have infected everything: the atmosphere is as dense as a Novem-ber in London, and it is infected by reptiles; everything is transacted, not under the rose, but under the mud; imbecile councils, – intriguing people – greedy soldiers, and factious

captains, are the beings I have to deal with in this Ionian sand (or rather slime) isthmus.[31]

There was nobody who escaped either his patronage or scorn, but it was to the 'paltry Jew' Mavrocordato with his frockcoat and spectacles that his behaviour became most bizzarely wayward. Throughout the last week of April and the beginning of May Trelawny intrigued against him among the captains and Philhellenes in Missolonghi, undermining his influence and prising away men, money and arms. 'I have just learned,' Mavrocordato wrote,

> that Mr Trelawny is quite enraged against me, perhaps on account of the brigade. I laugh at his rage. This conduct, on the part of these gentlemen, is well worthy of the love of liberty of which they wish to make their boast. Can there be a more cruel despotism than that of a foreigner, who, without any right whatever, wishes to command, without the least regard to the existing laws? My God! Does the first comer think then that he can tread us under his feet, or are we thought capable of being led by the nose by the first intriguer? Have we shaken off the Ottoman yoke, only to fall beneath another?[32]

Even Mavrocordato's letters were not safe. 'Before I begin', he indignantly complained to that busiest of Philhellenes Edward Blaquiere, back in Greece again with the first instalment of the loan,

> I can not help informing you of an occurrence that has certainly vexed me exceedingly. It is, that your countryman Mr Trelawny having met the courier on the road, stopped him, asked him whether he had any letters and on being answered that he had despatches for the Governor General of Western Greece, Mr T. insisted on his giving them up immediately & proceeded to break open the seals on pretence of ascertaining whether there were any letter for himself inside.[33]

Trelawny's behaviour, Blaquiere told Stanhope, was the constant talk of Missolonghi. The faction he had drummed up threatened to

destroy whatever credibility Britain still had in Greek eyes. 'If suf-
fered to proceed in their late & present system of cabal and intrigues,'
Blaquiere remonstrated impotently in a letter to the London Greek
Committee,

> they will not only disgrace their country *sans retour*, but do
> a great deal of mischief to the most sublime and sacred cause
> that ever occupied the hopes and fears of mankind. You are
> well acquainted with Mr Trelawny, who indeed I believe
> considers you as his most particular friend. I heard several
> things at Missolonghi that convinced me such a person was
> not most likely to increase our popularity in Greece ...
> Aware of the gross and scurrilous system of calumny and
> abuse which Mr T has practised against Mavrocordato ever
> since the first days of his arrival in Greece, and knowing
> that he is the bosom friend of Mr Ulysses, I shall be surprised
> at nothing he does: it would also be the height of gullibility,
> were I for one instant to imagine, that Mr T does not traduce
> and abuse me to all his correspondents all over the world.
> He would belie his character and former history if he did
> not. Now, as it is of infinite importance to keep the committee
> fully informed of everything, I have particularly to request
> that you will place every letter of Mr T's in which my name
> appears on the table, to be read aloud to all and in silence
> by each member, if they feel so disposed.[34]

Blaquiere's protests were too late. Less than three weeks after reach-
ing Missolonghi Trelawny had what he wanted. A letter from Stanhope arrived for one of the mechanics called Hodges, authorizing
him to 'deliver over to Captain Trelawney's charge one howitzer
and three three-pounders, with cartridges and everything complete
for field service.'[35]

It was the 'typographical colonel's' final disservice to Greece. A
peremptory recall had already arrived from Horse Guards, summon-

ing him back to army duties in the name of the King. In London his family and friends exchanged worried letters, nervous of what any public disgrace might do to his old father. 'Lord Tavistock told me this morning, that there was imminent danger of his being struck off the list,' Hobhouse reported to the committee,

> and if that happened it might go hard and mean to break Lord Harrington's heart – we have had calamity enough in that country already & I trust that you will write immediately to recommend Stanhope's return.[36]

It is a strange reflection on the London Greek Committee that Greece could be weighed in the scales with old Lord Harrington's heart and found wanting. There was, though, no need for their anxiety. The prospect of losing his half-pay had been quite enough to persuade the colonel. The republican bowed down to royal demand, the democrat to the expectations of his caste, the idealist to economic realities and Missolonghi was abandoned to the mess his interfering had done so much to sustain. In spite of the protests of Parry and Mavrocordato, in spite of all the claims of common sense and legality, the guns were handed over to the one man in Greece most likely to turn them on his own countrymen.

The inconsequentiality of most Philhellene activity defuses anger but the feckless irresponsibility of Stanhope and Trelawny in stripping Missolonghi of its defences at this critical moment is of a different scale. Years later, in one of those moods of honesty that sometimes took him, Trelawny wrote of a lifetime of bitterly regretted follies and vanity. It would be some consolation to think that he had Missolonghi in mind. From another letter to John Hunt, however, written in the April of 1826, it seems that his memory was as selective on this subject as most others. 'We are sunk in gloom and despair' he wrote of the town,

> Its heroic defence for five years, insulated, unaided, and alone, standing in opposition against a mighty Empire – a paltry fishing town, floating on a mud-bank, – inhabited by petty traffickers, – banked in with mud – defended by a few

useless cannon – has kept for five years a succession of
immense armies in check – and stood as an advanced bulwark
in defence of its country! – But man is not omnipotent –
heroes are not immortal – and the heroic bosoms that for
years have stood the bulwark of their country are now cold
as the heroes of Marathon and Thermopylae.[37]

It was these same heroes Trelawny in the May of 1824 abandoned
to their fate. At some point during the middle of the month he left
Missolonghi with his guns and artillerymen and headed eastwards
towards Parnassus.

Only the prolonged and desperate courage of Missolonghi's
inhabitants delayed the consequence of this, but almost two years
to the month later, 9000 starving survivors of the siege broke out
of the town in the harrowing nocturnal exodus of 22 April 1826.
Just days before the end, Meyer, Byron's old adversary, wrote a
last, eloquent letter, describing the town's plight in its last hours.

> We are reduced to feed upon the most disgusting animals
> – we are suffering horribly with hunger and thirst. Sickness
> adds much to the calamities which overwhelm us . . . In the
> name of all our brave men . . . I announce to you the resol-
> ution, sworn to before Heaven, to defend, foot by foot, the
> land of Missolonghi, and to bury ourselves, without listening
> to any capitulation, under the ruins of this city. We are
> drawing near our final hour. History will render us justice
> – posterity will weep over our misfortunes. I am proud to
> think the blood of a Swiss, of a child of William Tell, is
> about to mingle with that of the heroes of Greece.[38]

Within days seven thousand of those heroes had been slaughtered
or captured in the surrounding hills. Those who were too old or
sick to attempt the escape, locked themselves into cellars and blew
the magazines. And as they died – the Greek historian Tricoupi
imagined – the old heroes of Greece, arrayed in their panoplies,
bathed in the light of their immortal glory, rose up from their tombs

to receive into their ranks those who had perished to make the name of Greece live once more.

The ashes of those defendants lie under a tumulus in a mass grave, in the Garden of Heroes just inside the town's walls. The Suliote, Marco Botsaris – the Leonidas of the revolution – is there too, alongside the statue raised among the cypresses in 1881 above a casket containing some uncertain part of Byron's body. Beside one of the paths is the grave of Meyer, that unlikely child of William Tell and Jeremy Bentham. He was the last of a long list of Philhellenes to die of wounds, fever or by their own hands in the defence of Missolonghi. Bettier, Beck, Beck, Brumbacher . . . the monument in Nauplia records their names. 'This, though horrible, is a fitting consummation to a man determined to be free,' Trelawny told Hunt, 'and death is freedom.'[39] For himself, though, he had a very different sort of freedom in mind.

6

PARNASSUS

Odysseus. Now, Trelawny, look before thee. Dost thou discern
the cleft there?
Trelawny. Distinctly.
Odysseus. There is the mansion of thy entertainment!
Trelawny. There is no path to it.
Odysseus. For enemies none; for friends one rough and
dangerous.

Landor: Imaginary Conversations.[1]

THERE CAN BE NO landscape in Greece that so vividly preserves
the magic it held for the nineteenth-century Philhellene as the
country around Parnassus. From high above the ruins of ancient
Delphi it can seem as if not just Greece but all Greek history is
there, the underlying logic of its wars and divisions laid out below
in the unyielding realities of the terrain.

From the distant mountains of Sparta in the south to Thermopylae
in the north, from the scene of Lepanto in the west to the battlefields
of Plataea and Charoneia to the east, this was the country and these
were the names that above all fired the Philhellene imagination.

'Where'er we tread 'tis haunted, holy ground,' Byron had written
in 'Childe Harold' and it was this world that for the next fifteen
months Trelawny made his own. It is as difficult as ever to be sure
how much the great drum-roll of Greek history really meant to him,
but if this sacred past was never the moral or emotional support it
was to other volunteers there was no one so alive to the theatre of
its landscape.

From the moment, nine months earlier, that he had cast off his old clothes for Suliote dress he had been searching for a backdrop like this. There is a portrait of him by Seymour Kirkup which shows Trelawny as he liked to see himself at this time, his tall figure framed against the entrance of a mountain cave, gun in hand, engraved ataghans jutting out from a red sash at his waist, turban falling with a casual grace over one shoulder, moustaches curling *à la klepht*, the eyes not so much averted from the viewer as sublimely unaware of his presence — the self-absorbed and self-fulfilled hero of Byronic romance in his natural habitat.

The cave pictured in Kirkup's painting is set high in a cliff on the north-east face of Mt Parnassus, a hard hour's climb above the village of Tithorea at the entrance of the Velitza gorge. 'When the Muses deserted Parnassus,' Trelawny wrote of this new domain, 'the Klephtes ... took possession of their haunts'[2] and in at least one sense they are still theirs. Relics of an immemorially older world still survive here but it is a statue of Trelawny's chief, Odysseus Androutses, that dominates the valley. It stands, without any incongruity in the Greek mind, next to the village church on a small belvedere high above the rocky bed of the Kakoreme, or 'evil stream'.* It is a powerful rather than a handsome head, heavily moustached, long hair falling over the shoulders, closer in its deliberate idealization to Trelawny's 'Bolivar' than to the historical pupil of Ali Pasha. From under a brow creased in concentration he stares out across the fertile plains he once controlled towards the distant island of Euboea and the Aegean.

Behind him is the gorge which Odysseus first fortified in 1823, and if there is anywhere on the vast expanse of Parnassus that still retains its primitive magic it is here on its northern slopes, in the great gash which cuts into the mountainside beneath the cloud-covered peaks eight thousand feet above. From just below the 'Wolf's Head' summit which crowns the whole Parnassan range, the waters of the Velitza Gorge drop giddily away, carving their path through remote forests of pine and barren scree, the winter spates which earned the Kakoreme its name sculpting and gouging out a deep ravine before bottoming out and sweeping in a final wide curve around the great bluff on which ancient and modern Tithorea stand.*

In the autumn of 1824 a party of a dozen palikars picked their way across this boulder-strewn river-bed and began the last steep climb towards the massive limestone cliff that closes in the true left of the Velitza Gorge.

At their head, dressed in the ubiquitous Albanian costume of the romantic Philhellene, was the young English volunteer, W. H. Humphreys. The son of a captain in the Royal Artillery and one of the first cadets at Sandhurst, William Humphreys had initially come out to Greece after the collapse of revolution in Italy in the summer of 1821, a victim in about equal measure of Byron's poetry and his own failure to gain a commission in the British Army.

Like so many others who fit that pattern, the young Humphreys seems cruelly of less interest in himself than as an example of a certain kind of volunteer. At first glance he might pass with his daggers and turban for Trelawny's double, and yet there was a softness and priggishness about him which signals a different type altogether – the mental softness of Romanticism in decay, the self-righteousness of a man with one foot as firmly planted in Dr Arnold's Rugby as Byron had his good foot in the eighteenth century.

The horrors of warfare had already driven Humphreys out of Greece once by this time, but as he emerged now from the dry bed of the Kakoreme and began the long zig-zag climb through a land-scape of rocky outcrops and stunted trees towards the distant lime-stone wall of the gorge, the romantic in him might have been forgiven for thinking that here at least reality was in terminal retreat. Half way up on a plateau, almost hidden by a circle of ancient oaks once sacred to Apollo, stood a small stone church. Beyond that, as the climb steepened, a straggling encampment of huts and shelters came into view that seemed to Humphreys to have sprung straight from the pages of Walter Scott. At the highest point of the camp, flush against the perpendicular wall, stood a long, low guardhouse. Directly above it, lashed and bolted to the rock along the natural line of a fissure, a series of connecting iron ladders snaked their way up the sheer face. A hundred feet up, was 'an immense vaulted

aperture, receding deep in the rock'. 'I mounted the three flights of
ladders,' he later wrote, in a description in which romance fights
for air beneath a clutter of nineteenth-century domesticity, 'and on
entering was welcomed,

> in this far, wild, and almost inaccessible dwelling, in my
> native tongue, by Trelawny, and a Mr Gill, an English
> engineer who was making several improvements in the fort-
> ress. The high vault perfectly admitted the light and sun,
> though, as the sun passed to the west, the overarching rock
> above threw its long shadow over the mountain some time
> before sunset, spreading a dusky stillness over surrounding
> objects, and heightening the effects of the wild scenery. In
> the interior of the cave were several houses, that of the
> chieftain, Ulysses, forming a part of the battlements on a
> line with the perpendicular height, while deeper and higher
> up in the cave (the inequality of the ground forming stages,
> one above another), were the dwellings of his wife and sister,
> who, after the Turkish custom, were kept in perfect seclu-
> sion, his mother only appearing to strangers. Numerous
> magazines, well filled with corn, oil, wine, cheese, olives,
> and rakee (brandy), sufficient to supply hundreds of men
> for twenty years, occupied the recesses of the cave. Besides
> military stores, there were four mountain guns, brought by
> Trelawny from Missolonghi. Water was supplied by a small
> stream that issued from the rock in winter, and which
> dropped from the roof into large vessels, prepared for it
> during one or two months of the summer; and Mr Gill was
> now constructing a large cistern. The fortress, therefore, was
> as secure against a blockade, as, from its inaccessible pos-
> ition, it was against attack. Cranes, with ropes and pullies,
> conveyed up or pulled down everything required, with facil-
> ity. Trelawny was also building a house, as his chieftain's
> sister was now his destined bride. Two half-brothers of
> Ulysses were in the cave; but so high was the state Ulysses
> preserved in his household, that they were not admitted to

Byron (left) and Shelley (below), the 'revolutionary Dioscuri of English poetry' who formed Trelawny's youthful imagination. It was the romantic Byron of Phillips's portrait that Trelawny had expected to meet in Italy, and not the worldly realist he found. His first meeting with Shelley, seen here in Amelia Curran's portrait, was equally surprising: 'Was it possible' he wrote, 'this mild-looking beardless boy could be the veritable monster at war with all the world? – excommunicated by the Fathers of the Church . . . denounced by the rival sages of our literature as the founder of a Satanic school?'

The Casa Magni, Shelley's final home, with the *Don Juan* – 'the treacherous bark which proved his coffin' – after a drawing by Daniel Roberts. It was at the Casa Magni that Trelawny broke the news of Shelley's and Williams's deaths to their widows.

The cremation of Shelley's body, from Trelawny's *Records*. Fifty years later Trelawny was still peddling Shelley relics to devoted disciples.

Edward Trelawny (above right) by the
American painter W. E. West. Here is the
'giovane stravagante' who charmed
a younger and more impressionable Mary
Shelley than is shown in Rothwell's
portrait (above) when he first arrived in
Pisa in 1822. According to Claire
Clairmont (right, by Amelia Curran)
West's portrait was 'too smooth and sleek
though resembling'.

The Philhellene Monument, Nauplia, the most balefully impressive memorial to the men who fought and died in the cause of Greek independence. Byron (Lord) is listed as number 10 under Missolonghi, eight places above General Normann, who died broken-hearted after the disaster of Peta.

The Evvenus river. It was here that Trelawny heard the news of Byron's death at Missolonghi in April 1824.

Missolonghi. 'The pestilential fever of these torpid waters seems to have infected everything,' Trelawny wrote in the wake of Byron's death; 'imbecile councils – intriguing people – greedy soldiers, and factious captains, are the beings I have to deal with in this Ionian sand (or rather slime) isthmus.'

Tithorea as Trelawny would have
known it, from an engraving after
Edward Dodwell. The ruins in the
foreground are still standing.

The Mavre Troupa in 1824, showing
the ladders, parapet and houses
Trelawny constructed in his bid to
make 'this cave the most beautiful as
well as the strongest fortress in the
world'.

Inside the Mavre Troupa,
the upper grotto.
'Numerous magazines,
well filled with corn, oil,
wine, cheese, olives and
rakee (brandy), sufficient
to supply hundreds of
men for twenty years,
occupied the recesses of
the cave.'

The ladders up to the
cave. The guardhouse at
the bottom has gone, and
only remnants of
Trelawny's parapet still
survive.

Alexander Mavrocordato (left), the most westernized of the Greek leaders, and Odysseus Adroutses (right) the brutal and unscrupulous bandit chief Trelawny hailed as a second 'Washington'.

A view of the Acropolis showing the old Frankish tower. It was at the base of this tower that the corpse of 'the worthless and assassin Odysseus' was found in June 1825.

his table . . . Our fare in the cave was sumptuous: flesh of all kinds, fresh and salt water fish, game, and poultry.[3]

Trelawny had been in his cave for a little over two months. He had come here straight from Missolonghi at the end of May, at the head of a 'splendid suit', as he told Finlay with an engagingly transparent excitement – '55 horses,'

> loaded with stores for Odysseus – a small brigade of mountain guns – 300 of Flannel cartridges and grapeshot, and 20 picked artillery men . . .
>
> Tell O I will get lots of powder, and otherwise attend to his proper interest with Gordon – Blackquire, as by that means I am best serving Greece, (so I think). Is he not a noble fellow – a Bolivar? let's make a Washington out of him; there are elements in him to form one. I am thirsting to be with you, and only await till the return of my courier I forwarded to him eighteen days back. I want to complete some plans for rendering this cave the most beautiful as well as strongest fortress in the world – tell him to send me a white litter. I have Gilo with me and all the tools and necessary things to do everything.
>
> My particular events – since we separated – must be told, not written. Stanhope was ordered home by the King through influence of the Legitimate ambassadors. Gordon was hourly expected when I left Zante; I left, as did Stanhope, letters to enlighten him as to who is who in Greece . . .
>
> Mavro leads the life of a dog at Missolonghi; the soldiers would all have come off with me, and fired the city had I set them on; he is impotent. Millingen has been at Death's door, but – Death would not let him in. He is out of great danger and sends his love – cannot write.[4]

It is a dangerous illusion to imagine one can finally 'know' a man like Trelawny, and yet if he is revealed anywhere, if there is one place in which one can at least come close to some understanding, it is surely in this new world he was conjuring into being for himself on Parnassus.

It is only here on Parnassus, too, that a simple but easily forgotten fact of his earlier life fully sinks in. With the subjects of most biographies it is possible to construct some picture of their interior lives from 'without,' but Trelawny would seem to have grown up devoid of all the baggage and props which usually help define a life, a wandering, rootless being without home or possessions, moving from house to house, from ship to ship and inn to inn, untouched by his surroundings, uncluttered by belongings.

'Pity the poor creature,' George Eliot wrote in *Daniel Deronda*, who has nowhere to call '"home", no one spot sanctified by early associations and affections', but Trelawny is probably one of those rare humans who had no need of her sympathy. During his first lonely nights at school or sea he might have repined the home and family he never had, but the truth is that like a soldier with his field marshal's baton, Trelawny had always carried around with him an ideal of where he belonged that on Parnassus finally became reality.

It is this as much as anything else which gives this fortress cave so central a part in his story. There could be no temptation for instance to think that if one knew what the family house in Soho Square or Bristol looked like we would be any nearer the man, but here in his mountain cavern, in the 'Mavre Troupa' – the Black Hole – an empty space which he could deck out in his own image, his interior world takes on a palpable form we can at last grasp.

In all its mystery and theatrical irrelevance, in its physical and metaphorical aloofness, the Velitza Gorge was everything Trelawny had searched for. On the shores of the Gulf of Corinth a dozen miles away, women and children were starving to death in 1824, refugees from the north heading south while Moreots headed north in their hopeless migratory dance. In Corinth itself nothing except the howls of jackals disturbed the silence, its streets so choked with skeletons that when Millingen passed through it was impossible to avoid tripping over the dead. On Psara, eight thousand Greeks lay freshly butchered, their heads piled high in a ghastly pyramid. In

Alexandria preparations continued on the ships that would soon bring the Ottoman Empire's Egyptian army to Greece. Here, though, in the cave they had everything, not just the luxuries that seduced Humphreys, their own water, their own honey, plans for their own billiard table – but their own climate even, mild in winter and cool in summer, a world complete in itself, impregnable and useless, connected with reality by its iron ladders and an interminable view across the charnel house of Greece that only served to reinforce its sense of isolation.

This rather than the existential freedom of the Missolonghi dead was what Trelawny had come to Greece to find and almost alone among the volunteers he saw no need to dissemble the raw egotism of his ambitions. For softer romantics like the young Humphreys this was something that always had to be kept at bay, a vanity which needed sublimating into a 'nobility' derived from the soil itself, from the heady thought among failure and betrayal that he was fighting 'on the same ground of action, and with as fair a chance of renown, as the heroes of antiquity'.[5] For others who died insane or killed themselves even this was not enough to blot out the horrors of rape and impalings, but in the Byronic individualism that flowered in this cave Trelawny had found a surprisingly more robust myth to sustain him.

It is in fact no exaggeration to claim that it is only with Trelawny's arrival on Parnassus that the Byronic hero took on its definitive shape. There is always a temptation to ridicule this side of his personality, to see no further than the external trappings of the pose, and yet it is difficult to think anyone saw the early Byron with the same clarity as Trelawny. Those eastern romances and tales which first made Byron's name enjoyed such an astonishing social *éclat* that their misanthropy was somehow domesticated in the process, their note of crude and dangerous egotism drowned beneath the sound of carriages pulling up outside Murray's in Albemarle Street. Trelawny never made any such mistake about them. What he saw in them – what he unwittingly showed Kirkup – was a glamorized reflection of a brutality which beneath all the uncertainties was the bedrock of his personality.

149

It is this hard self-sufficiency with its accompanying indifference to common morality that equipped Trelawny for survival when other Philhellenes crumpled. He could talk about 'the cause' with the best of them, but on his lips the word takes on all the displaced egotism it has in his favourite *Othello*. He could write to Claire Clairmont of 'honour' but his honour was a more aggressive and Homeric thing than the gentlemanly code that wilted in the fierce heat of Balkan warfare. Trelawny almost alone among the volunteers needed nothing, admitted no claims above those of self, recognised no moral jurisdiction, stood at no bar but that of his own imagination. Greece for him was not a final chance of redemption, not a solemn duty or debt of gratitude. Landscape was not 'inspiration', nor 'moral influence', nor 'theology', nor any other of the consolations it offered the romantic soul: for this most calculating of fantasists, Greece and its landscape were simply 'setting' for the realization of a dream twenty years in the making: 'Dear Mary, Dear Jane,' he wrote to the Pisan widows in the first intoxication of fulfilment: 'turn your thoughts this way. No more a nameless being, I am now a Greek Chieftain.'[6]

The undisguised sense of triumph conjured up by that title captures Trelawny's mood at this time in a way that the more sophisticated egotism of his *Records* never does. Over the next months there are glimpses of him in the memoirs and journals of other Philhellenes, passing himself off as the model for Byron's Lara or playing on the fringes of Nauplia politics with Odysseus, but his hero-worship had taken a familiar turn, his friendship with his Greek 'Washington' serving a private ambition which had shrunk to the confines of his fortress cave.

Through the summer of 1824, as Greece moved to its second civil war, work went on to bring the cave in line with Trelawny's ambitions. When Odysseus had first occupied it the previous year there had been little except remoteness to recommend it, but now with the help of Gill who had come from Missolonghi, a cistern was begun at the back of the cavern, the old larch ladders replaced, rooms built and construction started on a long parapet to shield the guns and turn it into a permanent fortress.

To Odysseus it had never been anything more than a stronghold and a bolt-hole, but to Trelawny, as he plundered the churches of their decorations, filled the cave with rugs and fabrics, and built his house in readiness for his child bride, it was an expression, an extension even, of personality. In his cave on Parnassus he could at last be himself. From the cave he could fire off his letters, as if the mere address – 'Spiglia, Parnassus' – dashed of with an almost illegible flourish, conferred on them an *ex cathedra* authority over a distant and petty world.

Somewhere too in this romantic idyll, completing the dream and erasing finally the memories of Caroline and Captain Coleman, was the twelve or thirteen-year-old child he married here, Odysseus's half-sister, Tersitza. It is perhaps indicative of the way that Trelawny saw his new wife that in all his correspondence she is never once mentioned by name, and yet even if she was essentially the embodiment of a fantasy rather than a figure of any individuality in his life, her presence in the cave – elusive, suggestive, disturbing, erotically charged – is one that must somehow be summoned up.

In Philhellene journals from this time there is the occasional, slightly stiff and awkward reference to this 'pretty' and 'interesting' child, as if no one was quite sure of the respectability of their attraction to a thirteen-year-old girl, but the only description that gives any sense at all of what she may have looked like is from the pen of a naval surgeon, James Forrester. He saw her in Nauplia in August 1825. 'Mrs Trelawney,' he wrote, '(Odysseus's sister),'

> had completed her 13th year a month ago and is at present
> 4 months pregnant; she is a slight little girlish creature, but
> very pretty; – her eyes are full, hazel, or rather a dark grey
> and have exactly what I understand by Byron's simile of the
> gazelle, namely an innocently wild expression.[7]

It is not much, perhaps, but the reference to Byron is pointer enough that the place to be looking for Trelawny's bride is not in the Anglo-Saxon attitudes of surgeons, parsons and army officers but in the literature which spawned the ideal she embodied. In tale after tale of Byron's there is the kind of heroine of whom Forrester might have been thinking when he looked at Tersitza, yet there are two other sources which can give us an even more immediate picture of the role Trelawny envisaged for this girl, his own *Adventures*, and that improbable and tedious work of Walter Savage Landor's, the *Imaginary Conversation between Odysseus, Tersitza, Arete and Trelawny*.

Trelawny met Landor in Florence shortly after leaving Greece and co-operated with him on this imaginary dialogue, supplying an historical footnote on Odysseus and much, one imagines, of its heroic colouring. For the most part it is not a collaboration that does credit to either man, but in amongst its political posturing and specious theorizing there are two aspects which give it a biographical interest, the subtle tampering with ages that turns the relationship of Trelawny and Odysseus into that of father and son, and the insight it provides into how Trelawny must have thought and spoken of Tersitza.

In direct descent from the heroines of Byron's Eastern Tales, the Tersitza of Landor's dialogue is a shy and artless faun, her lovely face expressive of her confused emotions, her tender heart alarmed at every imagined ill that might touch this strange and unsettling foreigner. 'I would ask something,' she nervously says to her brother. 'Speak at once: I grant it,' he replies. 'Grant what?' 'What you would ask.'

TERSITZA: Do you really now command that noble youth?
ODYSSEUS: Is that all?
TERSITZA: Tell me, tell me! do tell me!
ODYSSEUS: Yes, my love! He has declared his resolution to obey my orders.
TERSITZA: Oh! do command him the never more to ride between me and the edge of a precipice . . . so terribly high a brook seems only a long vine-tendril from it, and a fountain a glossy leaf: where the path is not level enough for any but the flattest stones to lie upon it (rounder would roll off) nor

broad enough for the surest-footed beast to walk safely, tho quite alone.

ODYSSEUS: Thoughtless young man! why did he ride there?

TERSITZA: I asked him myself the same question: he said he rode there to admire the magnificence of the view.

Surely to look down on the peaks of rocks and the summits of pines, is not so pleasant as to lie back and see them one above another, from a tufted knoll of solid sirpolet, where the lavender under it does not prick one's legs, because the roe has lain down and slept on it, and broken its brittle stalks.

Tell him this: remind him the very first time you ride or walk together . . . and before you have gone far. He is seven years older than I am, or six at the least, and is not half so considerate and wise in many things.[8]

'I could kiss the eyes of that brave and just young man', Tersitza murmurs for no very obvious reason, but if the imaginary Zela in Trelawny's *Adventures* is anything to go by he would have expected nothing less of his future bride. She, too, comes of the same Byronic lineage.

I sat down on a projecting crag, above a deep chasm, with my eyes rivetted on the light and winged movements of Zela, who was flitting about, like a bee or a bird, from tree to flower, examining nicely into each scent and quality . . . A child of the desert is like a vine in the wilderness, spreading its leafy tendrils in profusion . . . The richest fruits, the sweetest flowers, the balmiest air, the brightest and purest water, are found amidst rock and sands, nursed in solitude and liberty; and there man communes with God and nature till, in love and worship, his feelings are almost divine. There too I have seen her virgins, and Zela was one of these, untaught as her wildest children, whose exquisite loveliness shamed the Grecian sculptor's art, his measured lines and

153

cold proportions, by beauties such as inspiration, with the perfection of science, could never dream to trace . . .

She had just turned her fourteenth year; and though certainly not considered, even in the east, as matured, yet, forced like a flower, fanned by the sultry west wind, into early development, her form, like its petals bursting through the bud, gave promise of the rarest beauty and sweetness. Nurtured in the shade, her hue was pale, but contrasted with the date-coloured women about her, the soft and transparent clearness of her complexion was striking; and it was heightened by clouds of the darkest hair. She looked like a solitary star unveiled in the night. The breadth and depth of her clear and smooth forehead were partly hidden by the even silky line from which the hair arose, fell over in rich profusion, and added to its brightness; as did the glossy, well-defined eye brows, boldly crossing the forehead, slightly waved at the outer extremities, but not arched. Her eyes were full, even for an orientalist, but neither sparkling nor prominent, soft as the thrush's. It was only when moved by joy, surprise, or sorrow, that the star-like iris dilated and glistened, and then its effect was most eloquent and magical. The distinct ebon-lashes which curtained them were singularly long and beautiful; and when she slept they pressed against her pale cheeks, and were arched upwards.

That portion of the eye, generally of a pearly whiteness, in hers was tinted with a light shade of blue, like the bloom on a purple grape, or the sky seen through the morning mist. Her mouth was harmony and love; her face was small and oval, with a wavy outline of ineffable grace descending to her smooth and unruffled neck, thence swelling at her bosom, which was high, and just developing into form. Her limbs were long, full, and rounded, her motion was quick, but not springy, light as a zephyr.[9]

After all this it seems only fair to Trelawny's intelligence if not his morals to point out that at the same time as he was marrying his gazelle-like bride he was declaring his undying love to Claire, and yet the old world and friendships of Italy were losing their hold on him. In a letter to Jane Williams written a month after occupying the cave he spoke with fond regret of their Pisan Circle, but at the same time made it clear that his life from now on belonged to Greece.

In letters to Mary, to Claire and to the Hunts the same point is made time after time, and at the heart of his new life was the cave. At the end of August he was writing again to Kentish Town of his new role, and for all the cryptic hints of political manoeuvrings it is the cave that dominates every line, its romance and scale which have become the mirror and index of his new stature. Three thousand of Odysseus's palikars had taken refuge in it; twenty-five thousand Turks besieged it for twenty-five days without success. It was the 'strongest and most important in Greece,'[10] he told Mary, and in a description aimed at the wider audience of Hunt's *Examiner*, set it high above 'the most gigantic and precipitous ravine in the world . . . to the north and south [!] of the mountain Delphi.'[11] 'I will come to England,' he threatened Mary and Jane Williams, 'take you both from what holds you there, and transport you to Parnassus Fortress. I can assure you, you will not want society there.'[12]

Even now something of the enchantment conjured up by that invitation seems to hang about his valley. The time to see it is in late spring or early summer as Trelawny himself first did, when every step throws up the heavy scent of herbs and the whole hillside is a mass of euphorbia and mophead sage, of campanula, scabious and wild aubretia, of deep blue tassel hyacinth, vetch and giant mullein.

It would take a hardened soul to resist the spell of the place at a time like this, but it is not in any spurious sense of identification, nor even in the frisson of danger of the final assault on the ladders, that you feel the sway of Trelawny's fantasy, but in an air of unreality that stills clings to this private world. 'Time we have nothing to do with, as to date and days,'[13] he wrote to George Finlay of his life in the cave, and it is the same still. Only the clack of goat bells, the universal sound of the Greek countryside, ever disturbs the peace. From the massive limestone overhang above the cave drops of water fall in slow motion to the rocks beneath. In its inner chambers footprints lie undisturbed in the dust from one year's end to the next. Look at a watch, and it is four in the afternoon. Glance at it again in what seems no more than minutes and it is six and as impossible to explain away the hours as it is those long months in 1824.

The cave is at once empty and full of Trelawny, timeless and fixed by every detail, disappointing and supremely evocative. The parapet built as one last bastion against reality has almost entirely gone, along with the houses they built and the guns dragged over the mountains from Missolonghi. A whitened rock face draws the eye, though, and beneath its natural vaulting the crumbling remains of a tiny apse reveals the chapel in which Trelawny married Tersitza. Next to it is the blackened evidence of a brick kiln. High up at the rear of the cave, half-buried in a sunless tangle of dead and twisted undergrowth, are the beginnings of Gill's cistern. Roof tiles and house timbers scatter the floor. Scratch in the soft, fine dust and there still are the ashes of their cooking fires, bones and skulls of goats, painted shards of pottery, the last relics of Trelawny's determination to make this 'the most beautiful fortress in the world'.[14]

Only the sense of security has gone beyond imaginative recall. It can be a disturbing place now, the ladders precarious, the sloping floor unstable beneath the feet, the crumbling terrace dropping away vertiginously to the gorge eight hundred feet below. High above the cave entrance a single sapling has taken root in the rock, growing bizarrely and threateningly downwards. Where Humphreys sat and smoked that August in 1824, and watched the distant camp fires of the Turkish army and re-read Scott's *St Ronan's Well*, or listened to the strange hybrid Italian of Odysseus and Trelawny, only the roots of a tree hold the loosened earth together. Disturb a stone as you scramble down to the top rungs of the ladder, and seconds later the crash of falling rock echoes warningly across the valley, smashing among the ruins of the guardhouse seventy feet below before it rolls and bounces on down the steep mountain slope towards the bottom of the gorge.

Perhaps, however, this sense of unease, of physical danger, is not far off the mark. The impregnability of the cave, the security of Trelawny's new role, were as illusory as everything else. 'I am no changeling, I must rise and fall with Ulysses,' he had told Mary Shelley,[15] but as early as August it is clear he had little idea of what that might mean. Elsewhere in Greece the great events of 1824 took the country step by step towards the tragedies of the coming year, but in Trelawny's life they seem no more than footnotes. In June, the first £40,000 of the loan was handed over to the government. In its wake Odysseus was at Nauplia, in a last attempt to profit out of the power struggles of the Morea, and lay his own claim to a share of the English gold. That, though, failed. His influence was on the wane, the world of the private fiefdom a thing of the past. From now on no soldier in his pay could be relied on to stay loyal. Ahead of him lay only two alternatives: submission to a Government that hated him, or, the old resort of Ali Pasha's henchman, an uneasy treaty with the Turks.

'Our chief is in the mountains,' Trelawny wrote vaguely to Humphreys, 'checking the advance of the enemy . . . We have no news.'[16] There was nothing that he could do but wait. Events had long outstripped his limited understanding of the war. From the useless safety of his cave all he could do was watch Greece tear itself apart, fortified by the lonely knowledge of his own physical and moral superiority to the rabble below. 'I am left alone here as security that the English are interested in the fate of Greece,' he told Stanhope in a lofty apologia,

> is it not a shame and disgrace that a nameless & all powerless individual should be left to support (even for a moment) the name that England is – shame on the great the rich and the talented.[17]

He was, he said, 'to be christened afresh'. His 'Romily' soldiers had given him a new name, and constituted him a 'Romily'.[18] 'I am governed by my destiny,' he wrote again to Stanhope, 'and who can controul his fate – mine binds me to Odysseus. I am bound to him by the ties of brother and must play a part I little thought of.'[19]

This is an oddly Byronic surrender to fate for a man who had 'soared above' his former patron. As Greece hastened towards civil war, and Trelawny's life its greatest crisis, a curious inertia seems to have gripped him, an almost collaborative blindness to danger, a near-fatal disjunction of reality and fantasy at that precise moment when for the poet and romantic in him they had at last seemed to fuse. On 27 May, when he had written to Finlay with the news of his arrival, he had added this encomium on one of the men who had accompanied him,

> a Capt'n Fenton, an approved good artillery officer . . . a Scotchman of the right good sort – independent – will do anything, and wants nothing in payment but lice – of which we have enough.[20]

It was Trelawny's most dangerous misjudgement. With an unconscious irony, he suggests himself the nature of his error. 'I have pretty well finished the Prince,' he wrote of Mary Shelley's 'wooden God', Mavrocordato. 'I have "scotched him" not killed.'[21] His quotation comes from *Macbeth*.

> We have scotch'd the snake, not kill'd it:
> She'll close, and be herself; whilst our poor malice
> remains in danger of her former tooth.

With the arrival of Fenton – Mavrocordato's spy and 'bosom friend'[22] of the man of whom Trelawny had unwittingly made an implacable enemy in Missolonghi, George Jarvis – the serpent lay unnoticed in his new paradise from the start.

7

THE PLOT

'He is a man I am proud to own as a countryman.'

Howe on Jarvis[1]

'A blacker villain as ever bore human form.'

Howe on Fenton[2]

IT IS TYPICAL OF Trelawny's euphoria in the weeks after Byron's death that he seems to have remained completely unconscious of the threat George Jarvis posed. They must have first met – and met often – at Missolonghi at the end of April, where Jarvis like so many other Philhellenes had been drawn by the prospect of fighting at last in a properly equipped and paid force.

Of all the foreigners in western Greece in the spring of 1824, Jarvis was one of the few who might have been some use to Byron. The son of an American consul and businessman in Europe, he had been living in the Danish town of Altona when Ypsilanti raised his standard, and accompanied by a young Hanoverian sailor called Heise, set out one moonlit night in the November of 1821 on the seven-hundred-mile walk south to Marseilles and a ship for Greece.

There is something of the innocence of the Children's Crusade about their journey which captures the spirit of early Philhellenism, and yet even at the age of twenty-three George Jarvis had a toughness and stamina that set him apart. In the three years that had elapsed since he said farewell to his parents for the last time he had probably seen more action in the war than any other volunteer, fighting on both land and sea for his adopted country with a dedication and single-mindedness that no disappointment could deflect. 'Mr Gervase' – Jarvis, that is – a chaplain of an English man-of-war who met him at Nauplia in 1825 wrote,

> is a modest, unassuming, man, with a perseverance and a devotion to the cause in which he has embarked, as singular as it is surprising. The glow of youthful enthusiasm must now have abated; the selfish, ill-according, and paltry views of some of the principal chiefs must have produced disgust; the hardships and privations which he has endured, and still endures, must (one would conceive) have alienated the most fixed attachment to the cause which, if it triumph cannot as yet – and still he is the same to them as he was four years ago, ready to sacrifice his life, as he has expended his property, without reaping either fame or profit.[3]

From November 1821 to November 1824 this superficially quiet and modest man kept one of the fullest diaries that survives among Philhellene records. Written in an ugly and only semi-literate mix of French, German and English, it is scarcely a document that anyone would read for pleasure, but even across a distance of almost two centuries the personality that emerges from its pages provokes a sense of uneasy recognition that one feels with virtually no other volunteer in this war.

It is only too easy to lose sight of historical difference in a spurious sense of familiarity and yet there is a chilling modernity about the author of these journals that is difficult to resist. Over his years in Greece Jarvis developed an air of certainty that carries with it ominous signals, a burning conviction all the more frightening for the unassuming modesty behind which it lurked – the conviction of the modern terrorist, the humourlessness of the convert, the inner strength which belongs to the man who has made over not just his life but his whole moral being to a cause that has become his own. There would be no surprise in finding Jarvis in the Paris of 1793, in the pages of a Conrad novel or a semi-detached IRA bomb factory in south London, but he is so unusual a type among Philhellene ranks that it is little wonder Trelawny never saw him for what he was. In the last days of April Trelawny was probably too caught up in the excitement of Missolonghi politics to notice this reserved and cautious American, but the simple fact is that Jarvis was everything he could never understand. He was an idealist where Trelawny was an adventurer, austere where Trelawny was luxuriantly imaginative, hard where Trelawny was no more than indifferent – as remote from Trelawny as Trelawny was in his turn from the soft-bellied romanticism of a volunteer like Humphreys.

It is certainly true that the American was as much Mavrocordato's man as the Englishman was Odysseus's, but the difference here again is that there was no trace of egotism in his loyalties, no confusion of personal ambition with national interests. In his early days in Greece he had been as vainglorious as any other young Philhellene, and yet whereas in other volunteers disappointment led to disillusion, with Jarvis it was as if the vanity of the individual ego was subsumed into something bigger, his whole identity subordinated to a title he embraced with a passion nothing could cool.* 'I have been honoured by an Englishman yesterday with the title of a Greek,' he wrote in a letter to Parry after Byron's death; 'they meant to hurt my feelings by thinking me too much of a Greek. I have no other desire here than to pass for one.'[4]

This was an ambition he realized with a success no Philhellene in the whole course of the war ever matched. With other volunteers there is a constant sense that Greece was at most a staging post in their lives, a rehabilitation centre maybe, or a launching pad to a wider and more public fame. For Jarvis, it was home. 'Never has an object interested me more,' he wrote before the heroic Battle of the Mills near Argos, 'never did I feel more sincerely for my own family, than I did and do for the poor Greeks.'[5]

And with his three piastres a day, subsisting often on a diet of grubs and wasps, a Greek soldier was precisely what Jarvis became. Trelawny might pose for Kirkup in a Florence studio in full chieftain's regalia, but Jarvis talked and looked like the meanest palikar, kept the same festivals and church feasts as his men, and adopted the same calendar for his journal. He had fought with their army at

the Mills and the siege of Athens, where the Turk and Greek pos-
itions were in places no more than twenty-five feet apart. He had
commanded their guns at Nauplia and sailed with their fleet on the
Themistokles while Trelawny was still hunting game and poets in
Italy. It was as a 'Greek' that Jarvis looked on at the antics of
Missolonghi's 'foreigners' in the weeks after Byron's death. It was
as a 'Greek' that this son of an American consul set out to inject
some steel into the soul of the Europeanized, frock-coated 'poltroon'
Mavrocordato. It was finally – and in all the rich suggestiveness of
the word – as a 'Greek' that he watched his 'bosom-friend' Fenton
accompany Trelawny through the gates of Missolonghi for the cave
on Parnassus.

J. W. Fenton – 'Thomas was, I think, his Christian name' Trelawny seems unilaterally to have decided in later years[6] – had arrived
in Greece in the immediate aftermath of Byron's death with the
intention of joining his brigade. He had first introduced himself to
Trelawny when the two men were in Missolonghi at the beginning
of May, 'a tall, bony man, with prominent eyes and features, dark
hair, and long face,' Trelawny recalled him later, copies of Shakespeare and Burns in his knapsack, 'in the prime of life, thirty-one
or thirty-two years of age ... restless, energetic, enterprising ...
sensual'[7] – a veteran of the Spanish wars, recklessly and profligately
brave by every reckoning, and as much at home among the crags
of Parnassus as Trelawny was in his cave.

There seems something so vividly alive about Fenton, something
so pungently animal-like about his presence, that it is easy to forget
how little we really know of him. In the aftermath of his death there
was no villainy or crime of which his enemies did not accuse him,
but the difficulty of getting beyond these victors' judgements to any
fuller sense of what Fenton might have been like is that of all
Philhellene history – a lack of hard evidence, the violently partisan
nature of surviving records and the problem in the end of deciding
between lie and lie in a war where truth was not so much a casualty
as a quaint irrelevance.

According to the different accounts that circulated in the Philhellene community in 1824–5, J. W. Fenton came of a respectable and

even 'gentlemanly' Scottish family who had property in Lanarkshire. Among the directories and land registers for the period there is nothing to substantiate this claim, but one baptismal entry does exist that might possibly fit a more humble profile for him, the record of a John Fenton, a 'lawful' son born in Glasgow on 3 February 1794 to William Fenton, a soldier in the 37th Regiment, and a Mary McMaster.

We have no way of telling for sure, but this entry feels right for Trelawny's Fenton, chimes in nicely with the Burns and the Shakespeare, with the social ambiguity and the real but shadowy military career that preceded Greece. In one version of this career passed on by Humphreys, Fenton claimed to have learned his sol-diering with the guerrilla leader, Mina – Spain's answer to Coloco-trones or Odysseus – and as an ensign in the 23rd of Foot, with whom he was wounded at the age of twelve, at the storming of Badajos alongside a brother who was killed.

There is no record of any Fenton in the 23rd of Foot, no Fenton on the casualty roll from the Peninsula, no J. W. Fenton anywhere in the Army Lists, no mention in General Mina's memoirs of his 'chief engineer', but there is something imaginatively stilted in this kind of determination to unpick the fictions with which so many Philhellenes like Fenton heralded their arrival in Greece. What this historical literalism ignores is not just the extent to which men and women constantly reinvent themselves, but the way in which these fictions become imaginative realities, enabling and self-fulfilling in a way for which Trelawny's whole life provides the classic model. There was almost nobody who arrived in Greece without something to hide, some blemish on their lives, some failure to atone or dis-appointment to erase; hardly a Philhellene who did not need Greece more than Greece needed him. That was as true of Byron as it was of General Normann. Hastings would never have been there if he had not been struck off the Navy List. Humphreys was only in Greece because there was no commission for him in the British Army, and – sliding inexorably down into the comic world of 'Don Juan' – it was a chance for many to be what luck, birth, poverty or peace had denied them in their pasts; a chance for sergeants to masquerade as captains, captains as generals, Washingtons as *Washingtons*, parvenus and tricksters as marquises and counts.*

Fenton's lies put him in the mainstream and not on the fringe of the Philhellene adventure and if it seems strange then that there should be any contact between a single-minded idealist of Jarvis's stamp and the unscrupulous charlatan of myth it should perhaps be a warning against accepting the verdict history has handed down on him. It is clear from Jarvis's letters that he took Fenton's Peninsular credentials at their face value, but in the factional in-fighting that followed Byron's death that in itself could scarcely have been enough. Only the present and not the past could have brought the two men together. It was a sense of common purpose which forged their formidable alliance against Trelawny's party. 'I have only two friends in Greece,' Jarvis wrote in his dour, awkward way to Byron's unlikely friend, Parry, on 10 May 1824,

> but those are friends; I do not associate with any other Englishman but when forced to do so; these are Mr. Hastings, R.N., a man of great honour, the friend of truth, and of a very consistent character; the other, Mr. Fenton of Scotland, who, a gallant young officer in the Spanish wars, gave up his half pay to embrace this noble cause, is the noblest-minded Englishman I remember to have seen; he is my bosom friend, and please God, our power, united by friendship and harmony, may be sufficient to produce some good for the country.[8]

There can be no certainty now as to when Jarvis and Fenton determined to seize Trelawny's cave but a tentative answer is to be found in Jarvis's journal for 1824. It is a sobering exercise to compare the entries for this period with those of 1822, to chart in them the impact of endless months of warfare on Jarvis's character, the contraction of personality and growing intolerance, the emotional and psychological damage done to the youthful *ingenu* who crossed the Elbe that moonlit night almost three years before.

The feeling of openness and wonder of the early entries gives them a poignant charm, but it is in the aridity of the journal for 1824 that one comes face to face with the lonely truth of the Philhellene experience. For other volunteers drawn into the web of Greek politics the lack of emotional support this journal illustrates, of any external point of reference or stable moral framework, was to have devastating consequences: for Jarvis, alone for weeks on end with his palikars, unsure from day to day of their loyalties, under a constant strain of paying and provisioning them, frustrated by the indecision and illness of Mavrocordato, its impact showed itself in a ruthless and obsessional conviction that the end would justify any means.

The journal ends abruptly at precisely that moment when one most wants it, but in the terse and secret entries for the autumn of 1824 it is just possible to trace the dangerous opening moves in Fenton's and Jarvis's bid for the cave. From the evidence of these entries it seems inconceivable that Fenton was not a spy from the start, but the initial proof of any contact with Jarvis only comes in an entry for 17 September 1824 (O.S.), almost exactly four months after Trelawny first took possession of the cavern. 'This afternoon, returned the three soldiers from Missolonghi,' Jarvis wrote from Mavrocordato's mountain base at Ligovitza, a day's ride away, 'and brought me a letter from J. W. Fenton, who had arrived from the Cave.'[9] A week later on the 24th there was a second letter from Fenton, still in Missolonghi. That same evening Jarvis noted: 'Dined with the Prince . . . Left, two hours after sunset, with ten men for Missolonghi on a special mission.'[10]

There is no way of knowing for sure if the initiative was Jarvis's or Mavrocordato's, but over the next days the purpose of his mission begins to assume some sort of shape in his journal entries. On the 26th of the month he had the first of what he stiffly calls 'Interviews' with 'J. W. Fenton, wherein he acquainted me with several matters of great importance.'[11] On the next two days there are these further entries in the diary:

Saturday 27th: Went to the Epitrope [the local governing committee] ... They all wished to find out the mission I had been sent for. All day rain. Stayed with Fenton.

Sunday 28th: Sunday interviews with F. Dispatched early in the morning the decarch Yanni Lampon, with nine others, to the camp with a letter to the Prince.[12]

A copy of Jarvis's letter survives, pasted into the back of his journal. It is a warning of a plot of Odysseus's against Mavrocordato, and an urgent request for a secret meeting between the Prince and his unnamed informer and friend – '*comme mon ami ne doit pas être vu, ni connu.*' The whole business, he stresses, must be conducted in the most complete secrecy as – even leaving aside Mavrocordato's own safety – '*nous avons deux autres têtes á perdre dans l'affaire.*' 'Come, my Prince,' he finishes, 'and the traitor's blow will fall on his own head. The Turk has never been a more formidable enemy.'[13]

Mavrocordato was too ill to make their rendezvous, but the following day he wrote back from his sickbed with alternative instructions. By the time, however, his messenger arrived at Missolonghi, Jarvis and Fenton were already on their way to his camp. On the 29th they had – interestingly in the light of future developments – seen Humphreys off for the Morea. The next day the two men set out on the journey to Ligovitza, and on the morning of 1 October were on the plain below Mavrocordato's headquarters. Jarvis's journal continues the story.

Wednesday 1st October: Left Captn. F. at the foot of the mountain. Prince very ill. Had an interview but was unable to talk very much. Went down to the plain and begged F. to return to Mesolonghi. Sent three horses and two of my soldiers along with him.

Thursday 2nd October: Was called to the Prince and after having taken his word mentioning nothing, acquainted him of everything concerning U., T., & & & [Ulysses – as foreigners often called Odysseus, and Trelawny.][14]

For all its brevity that diary entry reveals the peculiar difficulty in which Jarvis and Fenton now found themselves. As their plotting hardened into a definite plan to deliver up Odysseus's stronghold to the government party, it was inevitable that the original secrecy would have to be sacrificed. For Fenton in particular, however, a spy in a hostile world, the dangers of this were acute. From the beginning he had only been able to communicate when he was used for missions in western Greece or the Ionian Islands, but with every meeting the likelihood of detection increased. He would not, either, have had to have fought with the guerrillas in Spain to know what exposure would mean. The Greek countryside, littered with mutilated and decapitated corpses, with the evidence of roastings or impalings, provided all the grim reminders anyone could want that death was unlikely to be swift.* '*A word to the wise,*' he had written at the top of a scrap of paper addressed to Jarvis at the end of September, underscoring the words for emphasis:

> Dear Kiria – you know much depends upon silence and secrecy in our matter – you also know my life is in question – let me entreat you therefore not even to hint to the prince in Misolonghis the slightest – the most distant word of what we have in hand–[15]

Under these circumstances, it is not surprising that the strain took its toll in a plethora of missed meetings, mutual suspicions and recriminations. By 18 October relations between the two men had almost reached breaking point. The previous night Jarvis had ridden to keep a dawn rendezvous with Fenton, firing off two muskets in a prearranged signal from one side of the river bank at Boudelavitza to announce his arrival. Answering shots were heard from the far bank but there was no sign of Fenton. Instead, soldiers appeared with a letter. As Jarvis turned back for Mavrocordato's camp, another messenger overtook him with a second letter from Fenton. Neither of those have survived but that evening Jarvis replied with an obscure and uncharacteristic burst of self-pity that shows how frayed his nerves had become.

My dear Sir!

There was a time in Greece when I was free, and a free man I always glorified in being – but this time no more!

I here hold all the disadvantages without receiving any benefits generally attending such stations – and believe me when I tell you that this lot is far more unhappy than may appear.

Do you accuse me of faithlessness, or is it want of friendship you attribute to me? Honour has always been my guide; to assist and help the needful, my motive. But often, very often, appearance is against a man, when even the most pure motives instigate his actions; and in Greece, this incomprehensible country, where man is intricated in a thousand labyrinths – should it be otherwise?

'T is a word to the wise.

I have in silence borne my misfortune and God knows no small share has fallen to my lot, nor can anyone say I have ever complained of my fate. The severest blow, however, is given when a friend whom you honour and love suspects your fidelity and attachment.[16]

This is a bizarre letter from someone of Jarvis's self-restraint, the letter of a man at the end of his tether. The cave, however, judging from the pressure Jarvis brought to bear on Mavrocordato, was becoming an obsession. On arriving back at the Prince's headquarters after his missed rendezvous, he delivered his report and Fenton's letters to his chief. The following day he wrote again to Fenton, adding a Byzantine postscript to his previous day's outburst. 'I have at last settled the affair with the Prince,' he told him

The Prince does NOT intend to enter into your plans, as far as regards his taking it upon himself and your executing it for him; he APPROVES of your plans, however, but being call'd to the seat of Government, he wishes you to go the Cave to hold yourself ready; and the Prince, as an instrument of Government, shall send us word as soon after his health be restored, he arrives at Napoli. By the same time money must be here, and as you yourself say, without this nothing

can be done . . . I hope soon to hear from you and with all
my heart subscribe myself.
    Continually yours,
    G.J.[17]

It is interesting that Jarvis writes of 'your plans', but it seems unlikely
that this means what it would seem to suggest. The evidence surrounding all these manoeuvres is too fragmentary to be sure about
this, and yet Fenton seems too much the opportunist to have taken
a sustaining role in a scheme that bears all the marks of Jarvis's
obsessive character.

    More important than this, however, is Mavcrocordato's attitude,
because the longer he allowed his natural scruples to stand in the
way of action, the more he took refuge in the classic fudge of decent
men, the greater was Fenton's danger. As the year drifted towards
its close, and Fenton returned to the wintery solitude of the cave,
conscious that Odysseus had his spies in the government camp,
the anxieties on his behalf grew. On 10 November (OS), Jarvis's
frustration, his sense of the danger of Fenton's position, pushed him
to one final bid to commit the Prince to some decisive action.

    Mon Prince!
        Here is an extract of the news which reached me by my
    friend's courier:
        Odysseus is gathering the soldiers. His name as a great
    captain makes them flock to his banner. He has in view the
    total destruction of the Government. His friends in the Morea
    are numerous. They are powerful. With the soldiers he
    attracts and as he gathers all the Moreots, he is in a position
    thus aided to carry it out. If not – ten thousand Turks are
    at his disposal. Remember, my Prince, that with a garrison
    of a hundred men the Cave is a serious obstacle to the Turks.
    On this account and to save the Morea from civil war and
    to guard Roumelie against an unexpected attack, you (or the
    Government) must take possession of the Cave and the head
    of the traitor must fall. This is how:
        Dispatch a courier straight away to the Government to

send us two or three trusted men to Salona, under some pretext. I can be found there in the Department of Venetico where I am in winter quarters with my soldiers, and I will immediately send those of my men who are in on the affair to my friend in the Cave.

The Government commissioners must bring about two thousand dollars in gold, since such a sum will be necessary to win over around fifty soldiers, of whom there are about two hundred at Rachova. In the Cave itself there are the soldiers of my friend, to whom the command will be given as soon as Trelawny leaves for England. There is not a moment to lose.

Trelawny, although set on helping Ulysses in all his wicked enterprises, up until now nevertheless has prevented him bringing Turks into the Cave.

Judge, my Prince, the importance of the affair, and what the decisive measures should be. The Government cannot deny the importance, the necessity, of taking some decisive measures; or claim that the sum of 2000 dollars is such a big amount, when I, alone as I am, me, I say, have already advanced and spent around four hundred dollars on this affair which has been on the go now for more than seven months, as is known to Your Excellency . . . The peace of the Country and the possession of the Cave with so much wealth, will make up for everything.

Mon Prince,
Ayant etc.
G.J.[18]

With this was enclosed a letter from Fenton, written from the top of a tower at the Monastery of Osios Loukas, less than a dozen miles south-east of the cave.

My dear Jarvis,

You are my friend, my only friend. Yes, my life is in danger, I know that perfectly well! But O. surely would never dare, without evidence, to go to extremes? And then, I have a strong following among the soldiers here, and it is certain that I will go to the cave; but I will wait until the time that we are ready to act. Mark well that each moment is precious. Come in any case to Salona with the Government agents. I tremble for Greece and for Liberty. At this very moment the crisis approaches. O. is united with all the important chiefs of the Morea, and soon – even in a short time – all will be over. I am always optimistic, but what will the Government be able to do? Certainly, so formidable an enemy, having so many means to harm us, and without ties, it is essential to confound him. I will not surrender the glory I expect for my part in this great enterprise, not for all the riches that England possesses. Greece, that name is enough! If you had not taken the precaution of sending two letters, I would be dead. O. demanded to see it. One of his companions read it to him. He intended to visit your soldier, but the poor devil seemed to be so mad that I have nothing to fear from him. Had you sent a man of spirit, I would have communicated some secrets to him – but perhaps it is better as things have turned out. I beg you, for the love of God, don't send me any more men before you get to Salona. My dear friend, why is it that you don't go to Napoli yourself, so that things go well. It is a horrible uncertainty in which I find myself and Trelawny constantly calls me to the Cave so that he can leave for England. He proposes to do great things for O. in London and he will take money for a warship. I am sorry to hear that the prince is still ill, but I hope to God that he will be spared for Greece. Tell S.A. that I hope soon to have the honour to congratulate him on the destruction of one of his most formidable enemies. But my heart tells me that the Government will delay, that they will put the affair aside. Speak to the Prince, tell him of the advantage of going to Napoli – go – I'm not able to write to you any more. I have been writing this letter on the top of a tower and I have pulled up the ladder, but I see that your soldiers are looking for me.

Adieu, my very dear friend,

Your sincere friend,

J.W.F.[19]

In the light of future events these two tense and nervous letters provide the most intriguing glimpse we have of Fenton's and Jarvis's plans. There is no way of knowing how serious Trelawny was in his talk of England and certainly nothing ever came of it, but what is interesting to note here is that even as late as November when these letters were written the Mavre Troupa and not his life was plainly the plotters' target.

With his decision to remain in Greece, however, his fate and that of the cave became one. Through the long summer months of 1824 he had striven to create a fortress palace that would be a physical expression of his inner world, and the irony now was that the very success of his dreams, his genius for sweeping others along in the wake of his fantasies, was about to bring his life into danger.

It was irrelevant whether those fantasies had any base in fact, irrelevant whether in its defensive fastness the Mavre Troupa had any strategic importance, irrelevant whether there was gold, as was believed, it was the perception of these things that mattered.* On 13 November Jarvis received Mavrocordato's reply. The Prince had already written to the government at Nauplia. All necessary steps would be taken. '*Soyez persuadé qu'il ne negligera rien,*' his secretary added, '*mais*' – the cry of every Greek politician through the war – '*croyez moi qu'il y a grande penurie d'argent.*'[20]

The 'affair' had entered a new phase, the secrecy Fenton and Jarvis had both enjoined now imposssible. On the same day Jarvis committed the consequences to his journal: the authorities in Missolonghi, he noted, had been drawn into the plot.

> We all had a consultation on the subject and came to the resolution of dispatching immediately a courier to Fenton to leave U., for fear of U. being acquainted on receiving news from the Morea, the affair no doubt spreading by the friends that U. has in Government Party.[21]

This is one of the last entries in Jarvis's journal. Just over a fortnight later, on 3 December, the journal comes to an exhausted end. 'Things . . . bearing a very bad prospect,' he wrote from western Greece.

No bread – no money – for the soldiers. The Peloponnesus in anarchy. The poor defenders of the country and the frontier, without bread, and no notice taken of them.[22]

Worn out, destitute, ill-equipped and ill-fed as he was, Jarvis's pessimism was premature. As its fame spread and the scale of Odysseus's fortress increased with every telling – a hundred foot high in Humphreys's account, a hundred and fifty said Green, the British consul at Patras – it was as if the 'black hole' in its remote Parnassan gorge had taken on a metaphorical life of its own. It had become an unattainable answer to every prayer, a symbol of power or wealth, of sexual or romantic fulfilment, a space to deck out in the image of a dozen different fantasies – the hiding place for Odysseus's fabled treasure, the strategic key to eastern Greece, the incarnation of Byronic adventure, the hidden retreat of Trelawny's beautiful child bride.

It is easy to lose sight of the larger picture in the details of the cave, but if this was a dangerous enough set of delusions and half-truths for Trelawny to have helped spawn, beyond the confines of the Velitza Gorge events outside his control were moving in a direction that would fatally compound his difficulties.

For five months after the first instalment of the English loan there had been an uneasy peace between the Greek factions, but by the November of 1824 the government was ready again for war, determined this time to crush its enemies in the Morea and eastern Greece and with the money and men at last to do it.

Through the autumn and winter of 1824–5 the great Captains of Roumeli and the Peloponnese, lured by the promise of English gold, went over to the government side, leaving Colocotrones and Odysseus isolated in their private fiefdoms. Devastated by the death of his son in a skirmish near Tripolis, Colocotrones was the first to fall, surrendering himself to haughty imprisonment in a monastery on Hydra.

Next it was Odysseus's turn. The power, the influence that Jarvis and Fenton feared, were again no match for gold. One by one, his old supporters deserted him. In the New Year, his former pipe bearer and trusted lieutenant, Ghouras, joined the defectors and with that desertion Athens was lost to Odysseus. To a man devoid of patriotism or principle, a pupil to the last of Ali Pasha, there could now be only one recourse. If there was no place for him within the new Greece, there remained his old Turkish masters, and sometime at the beginning of 1825 he concluded a treaty with Omer Pasha of Negroponte.

In the Mavre Troupa Trelawny heard the news. That same evening he left the cave in a snowstorm, riding through the night to the ruined town of Livadia, twenty-odd miles to the east of the Velitza Gorge. On the plain he could see the immense caps of Turkish cavalry, and on meeting Odysseus was told that a three months truce had been concluded with Omer Pasha. 'It is the only way in which I could save the people from being massacred,' he assured Trelawny,

> I have written to the Athenians to say that, as the government
> have not only refused to give me rations for my troops, but
> are doing their utmost to induce them to desert, I cannot
> longer defend the passes which lead to Athens.[23]

Behind this bland formulation of treachery lay a campaign of cattle-rustling and sheep-stealing with which Odysseus took his revenge on Ghouras and Athens but Trelawny's devotion remained absolute. It is plain from what he later wrote that he did all he could to dissuade his chief from his new alliance, yet when it came to a choice between Greece and personal loyalties there could only be one conclusion and within days he was himself sitting down with the Turkish enemy he had come to fight.

This event – the betrayal of everything to which he had aspired when he sailed with Byron – occurred one stormy night among the ruins of Charoneia, midway between Livadia and the cave. An English traveller, a Major Bacon, who had blundered into the war zone and been brought in by Odysseus's soldiers, has left a vivid account.

The camp had been expecting an attack from Ghouras's troops all day, and at the door of the hovel which had become their campaign headquarters, Trelawny's and Odysseus's horses stood already saddled in the torrential rain. If Ghouras, however, appeared the main danger, Odysseus was taking no chances with his new allies. When at the end of a rough meal the Turkish Aga was announced, Odysseus placed himself in one corner of the room, his back to the wall, his weapons at hand. Next to him was his Italian secretary, Antonio. In front of him, hand on pistol, right foot advanced, still as a statue, stood Trelawny's deputy in the cave, a Hungarian hussar called Komarone. Trelawny himself, Bacon admiringly recalled, his hair worn long in the Suliote style, his face and neck bronzed by wind and sun, as wild-looking as any of his men,

was in an adjoining corner engaged in writing a letter to his friends in England, with which I was to be entrusted it having been arranged that I should leave the camp soon after midnight. I had seated myself on a stone to the left of Trelawny: the Aga, accompanied by five or six Albanian chiefs entered and the whole party placed themselves, after their manner, cross legged on the ground opposite to but some distance from the fire, completing a semi-circle of guests. The Turkish attendants intermingled with the followers of Odysseus crowded around, this armed group in varied and rude attire had a most imposing effect: mutual distrust and apprehension was depicted in their fierce sunburnt countenances. In this group was a youthful Albanian Turk pleasing and comely in the costume of his country, of a lively and kind disposition and much attached to Odysseus, having been intimate with him at the court of the Vizier Ali Pacha of Yanina. From time to time at midnight, unobserved by the Turks, this youth had visited the quarters of Odysseus, and appraised him of their evil intentions towards his person and on the occasion of this visit had warned him to be on his guard. Coffee and pipes were as usual in requisition. Odysseus received his visitors in his accustomed courteous manner, the penetrative glance of his eye embracing the minutest object or movement, and therewith held communion with his own party. Close upon my left squatted a black Egyptian Turk, whose intent and malignant gaze was often directed towards me. This man had served in the war on the Danube against the Russians and insisted that I was of that race of Giaours; in truth my sandy coloured moustache and Cossack costume were calculated to occasion such an impression. I could not help expressing to Trelawny, who continued writing, my conviction that some catastrophe was at hand. By way of soothing my apprehension he privately placed a pistol in my hand, desiring me upon the slightest aggressive movement on the part of my Ethiopian neighbour, that instant to shoot him dead.[24*]

Neither the Major nor Trelawny has left any precise record of Odysseus's dealings here, but the meeting eventually broke up without further alarm. As soon as the Turks were gone, Trelawny laid down his head upon a stone in a state of perfect ease. Around the room the palikars lay asleep, their bodies stretched out across the mud floor on all sides, oblivious for the moment to the proximity of danger. Odysseus alone never rested. Throughout the night he remained on the alert, as messengers appeared, whispered in his ear and disappeared into the darkness again. In between he sat at the blazing fire, smoking and talking with Bacon, partly in French, partly English, 'his quick apprehension and expressive delivery' sustaining the conversation and whiling away the anxious night.[25] Odysseus talked of England and Byron, and speculated what might have happened had he and Byron met. 'It was not the Turks,' he told Bacon,

neither was it the treachery of Lieut: Gouras or the fanariots that had driven him to the present difficulties, but the interference of Englishmen and English gold.[26]

The appearance of Bacon at this juncture would later have vital consequences for Trelawny, but his main interest here is as a witness to the last occasion on which Trelawny was to see Odysseus. There is a certain credulity about the Major's account which smacks of the old Philhellene weakness for the klepht, yet even when allowances are made for that there is something touching in his portrait of both Odysseus and the wonderful sangfroid of Trelawny in their last moments together that survives the knowledge of their treachery.

Bacon, certainly, never seems to have had any doubts about them. In the nervous hours before the Aga's arrival he had agreed to carry a letter to the senior British Naval officer in the Aegean requesting a passage to the Ionian Isles for Odysseus, but when he left the next morning he was determined to go further. Slipping out of the camp towards noon with two palikars as guides, he made his way by a circuitous mountain route to where the merchant vessel he had arrived on was waiting for him, and persuaded its captain to stand as close in to the shore as he dared in the hope of picking up Odysseus.

It was a rendezvous Odysseus never kept. The memory of his father's betrayal by the Venetians, the incident on the *Hind* perhaps, but above all his whole character and training, prevented him trusting himself now to a stranger's help. While the *Maitland* stood off the rocks near Iolanda, waiting as long as it could, Odysseus frittered away his last opportunity to escape in empty negotiations with Ghouras. One by one his last followers fell away, bought off by the promise of three months' salary. Within days his secretary Antonio, even his brother, were gone, leaving Trelawny almost alone in his loyalty. That, though, never wavered. At their final parting, Trelawny recalled in *Records*,

> he called some of his principal followers, and said, 'I call you to witness, I give this Englishman the cavern and every-thing of mine in it.' Then turning to me he said, 'Do what you think best without referring to me. As we sat on the turf by a broken fountain, he placed his rough hairy hand on my bosom, saying, 'You have a strong heart in a strong body: you find fault with me for distrusting my countrymen, – I never doubted you. I trusted you from the first day as I do now on the last we may ever be together.[27]

On 19 April 1825, caught between his new allies and his old, distrustful of and distrusted by both, Odysseus gave himself up to the improbable mercies of his former henchman, Ghouras, and imprisonment in the Venetian tower on the Acropolis at Athens.

'When a great tree falls,' someone has written in a nineteenth-century hand across the margin of a document about the cave in Greece's National Archives, 'small men fight over the branches.'[28] Within days of Odysseus's surrender Ghouras's troops were encamped in the Velitza Gorge beneath the Mavre Troupa, waiting their chance to get their hands on the wealth that was believed to be in the cave. Trelawny, literally as well as metaphorically, had become a prisoner of his dreams. Ambition, greed, lust and necessity had all conspired to make his private idyll the next battleground in the struggle between the old Greece and the new.

And from as far away as Persia and America, from England and Hungary, lives as yet unconscious of each other's existence were converging on the cave, drawn into the world of Trelawny's imagination. Fenton, ignoring Jarvis's warnings for his safety, was already in place. 'Foul plots,' as Trelawny histrionically put it, had been devised. Now 'fit instruments' had to be found.[29]

8

WHITCOMBE

'What was I? – A being of mere instinct; a child over which
the cravings of the sense still reigned uncontrolled – only at
ease among those who defy convention.'

Thomas Hope: Anastasius[1]

'I should by no means be surprised if you, Sir, who I know
to be of family – rank, and of vast acquirements, by keeping
yourself always aloof from these barbarians, whom I have mentioned; and being biased by no other hints than my own, may
eventually lead a career not less than I have done. Our names
will then of course be mingled in the reminiscences of some
masterly pen – and think of the luxury of being known and
quoted as the heroes of a romance fraught with incident; the
inspiration with which the young beauties of our realm will
lisp our names upon every occasion, and fondly hope that their
lovers may be such.'

Sketches of Modern Greece . . .
by a Young Volunteer in the Greek Service[2]

IN MARCH 1825 A small company of Greek irregulars paused on
their way south from Nauplia to Navarino to rest in the middle of
the day. Among them was an American doctor of twenty-three who
was later to make his name as one of the great reformers and
philanthropists of the century, Samuel Gridley Howe. As he woke
from his afternoon doze, his head propped up against the root
of a fig tree, he drowsily took in the scene that surrounded
him.

The little blue banner of the cross was planted in the ground; the baggage mules, relieved of their burdens, but tied each one with its head to his fore-leg, were nibbling the short grass; the soldiers, with their picturesque costume, 'with their snowy chemise, and their shaggy capotes', were scattered around on the ground in every attitude; there were some, whose heads thrown back, and lips apart, and deep heaving chest, proclaimed the soundest sleep; while others, with languid, half-open eyes, were lying between sleeping and waking; here was a group smoking their pipe in silence, and there a soldier combing out the long curly locks, that reached below his shoulders. The object, however, which most interested me, was the slender but elegant figure of a stripling lad of nineteen, who lay at my feet with his head half raised, and resting on one hand, while in the other he held a morocco case, which I took to be a miniature, and his eyes were fixed upon an open letter on the grass before him. My companion always looked interesting, but now more so than ever; his graceful figure, just budding into manhood, had the suppleness and ease peculiar to his age, which make every posture graceful; his features were regular and beautiful, though strongly marked; and his complexion, dark by nature was still more darkened by exposure; yet was his soft skin clear, and you might see the rich blood mantling beneath it; and his eye, his large black eye, ever restless and full of fire, gave life and animation to his whole countenance. Then his costume, the rich and picturesque costume of the Albanian Greeks; the blue-lapelled red cap; the neck and bosom bare; the gilt and embroidered jacket and sash with slashed sleeves thrown back, and the right arm bare to the shoulder; the tight sash of blue encircling his slender waist; the white flowing kilt, embroidered gaiters, and net sandals; the whole relieved by the large shaggy capote, or over-cloak, on which he was lying, gave a perfect picture of a young Greek, in the person of an Englishman of family and fortune.[3]

180

The object of this innocent and wholly period eroticism was a volunteer recently arrived from England called William Guise Whitcombe. There is as little known about his early life as there is about most Philhellenes, but he had been born on 3 March 1806 at the family home at Blackheath, the youngest of eight surviving children of a Sir Samuel and Lady Whitcombe.

The boy's father was a successful and earnestly conventional lawyer, but when Sir Samuel died after a fall it was left to William's mother to bring up her large and young family. There is almost nothing to go on for these years beyond a vague family tradition of William's 'wildness', and yet if there is any truth in that it was soon clear that he had inherited nothing of the solid respectability of the sprawling Whitcombe clan. Whether or not William followed his brother Thomas to school in Greenwich is unknown, but if his nephew is right the mother's favourite and black sheep of the family was packed off at an early age into the East India Company's Navy, remaining there until his behaviour made 'the service too hot for himself' and forced his return to England.[4]

From surviving records it would seem that Whitcombe in fact made only one journey out to China on the *Warren Hastings*, sailing from England in 1823 and returning in the June of 1824 when he was paid off with the sum of £20-8-4, his midshipman's pay for thirteen months and twenty-six days at 35/- a month. During the long voyage out to China there had been a serious mutiny on the ship, but while discipline among even the officers seems to have been dangerously lax there is nothing in the ship's log to suggest that Whitcombe lived up to family legend. Back in England, however, and unemployed, he was clearly restless, and in November 1824 offered his services to the London Greek Committee in a letter that is typical in its vacuous conceit of a hundred others that fill its archives. 'To the Gentlemen Composing the Committee of the Greek affairs,' it is addressed,

> We your Petitioners Robt James and William Whitcombe late Midshipmen on board the H.C.S. *Warren Hastings* most respectfully offer our Services to enter either the Greek

Army or Navy. Being a cause for which we have early evinced and still maintain a strong enthusiasm. For our character as Gentlemen, or for our rank in Society the most respectable and undeniable references can be given. Were you by your assistance to further our views, you would confirm an eternal obligation on Gentlemen your most humble petitioners
    W. G. Whitcombe
    Robt. James
    John's Coffee house in Cornhill[5]*

There is no reliable record of how Whitcombe travelled to Greece, but in spite of his enthusiasm he was clearly in no hurry, and it was not until the early spring of 1825 that he finally reached the Morea, landing at Gastoumi on the western coast before crossing to the capital of Nauplia on its eastern seaboard.

Like so many Philhellenes who made this identical journey, Whitcombe's first view across the blue waters of the Argolic Gulf to Nauplia and the distant Palamidi seemed confirmation that he was at last in the 'real' Greece. From high above Lerna on the western side of the gulf the plain of Argos stretched back from the water's edge a thousand feet below him, ringed to the north by mountains and chequered and dotted with orchards and white villas, an intoxicating blend of physical beauty and mythological appeal, of expectation and association, the haunt at once of Helen and Agamemnon and the heart of independent Greece.

Fifty years later Heinrich Schliemann, the great archaeologist of Mycenae and Troy, described this as the most beautiful view in the world and yet in the early spring of 1825 it was a beauty that only masked the horrors of a war which was entering a new phase. After the relative calm of 1823 when it seemed that the Ottoman Empire had no more to threaten, its soldiers had returned to their task of subjugating Greece with a renewed and terrifying frenzy, flooding Nauplia with refugees from Psara and the southern Morea, where in the previous February an Egytian army had been landed to destroy Greek resistance once and for all.

As Whitcombe made his way down the interminable zig-zag to the shore of the Argolic Gulf, it was a journey from one mental and physical extreme to the other, a descent from a landscape of the fancy into a Greece that was as much a hell of the imagination as it had been the idyll of his dreams. Down at the sea's edge war had turned the bay itself into another Styx[6] as emaciated refugees waited to be ferried over to the necropolis that Nauplia had become. Outside the walls of the town on the eastern side of the gulf, starving refugees from the nightmare of Psara, where seven thousand islanders had been butchered the previous summer, huddled among the rocks waiting to die, or stood watch over their dead, jealously guarding their shallow graves.

To any newcomer unused to the extremes of revolutionary Greece the town itself provided a scene of bewildering and repellent contrasts. In its narrow and disease-ridden streets squalor and extravagance went hand in hand. Gaudily dressed *capitani*, the beneficiaries of English gold and government bribes, strutted among the dying with their bands of palikars, equally oblivious to the misery surrounding them or the threat which grew with every day that the Egyptians consolidated their position in the south. 'Every man of any consideration in his own imagination wanted to place himself at the head of a band of armed men,' the Philhellene historian George Finlay recalled,

> and hundreds of civilians paraded the streets of Nauplia with trains of kilted followers, like Scottish chieftains. Phanariots and doctors in medicine, who in the month of April 1824, were clad in ragged coats, and who lived on scanty rations, threw off that patriotic chrysalis before summer was past, and emerged in all the splendour of brigand life, fluttering about in rich Albanian habiliments, refulgent with brilliant and unused arms, and followed by diminutive pipe-bearers and tall henchmen.[7]

It must have been some time in the early part of March that Whitcombe made his way through the emaciated bodies that crowded against the town's wall, past the distracted mourners at the funeral of a young girl, and plunged into the moral sink of Nauplia for the first time.

The only independent record of his arrival comes with a passing mention in a letter of the Italian Philhellene, Giacinto Collegno, but three years after this, an account of Greece in 1825 was anonymously published in England which enables us to follow his movements and development over the next months with a fullness that is perhaps unique among Philhellene volunteers.

The book was an autobiographical 'novel' called *Sketches of the War in Greece* by a Young English Volunteer that from all internal and external evidence can only be the work of William Guise Whitcombe. Its story opens with the arrival of a young Philhellene at Gastoumi in the early spring of 1825, and follows his journey eastwards along the course of the Alpheius to Tripolis and Nauplia where he joins up with an American doctor for the march south to face the Egyptian army at Navarino.

Within these early chapters of the novel there are enough points of comparison with Howe and other sources to confirm the author's identity beyond any reasonable doubt, but it is not so much for its external framework that it is of value but for the pathology of the man who wrote it, for its revelation of a personality formed as consciously and dangerously on a romantic model as was Trelawny's own.

The inspiration behind *Sketches*, the inspiration behind Whitcombe's whole journey to Greece was a Byronic novel called *Anastasius* written in 1819 by the designer and decorator, Thomas Hope. Both the book and its author are now very largely forgotten, and yet in 1825 the name of Anastasius enjoyed the same sort of cachet and celebrity as Frankenstein, Melmoth or Byron's own Lara, a universally recognized point of reference, a type of dazzling and romantic antinomianism and emotional desolation of which Trelawny was perhaps the most famous imitator.

Callous, charming, attractive, ruthless and brave, the hero of Hope's novel is an amoral and brilliant young Greek from Chios who schemes and philanders his way through a series of wild and exotic adventures before falling victim to his own nature and dying in bitter and lonely isolation.

When three years earlier Trelawny had first arrived at Pisa, Mary Shelley had described him in her journal as a new Anastasius, and from the moment that Whitcombe reached Nauplia he loudly and publicly put down his claims to this same character, immersing himself in his adopted role with a flamboyant and narcissistic absorption that was symbolized by a new name and dress. In his *Sketches* he recorded this moment of transformation, his passage from English gentleman to Greek adventurer, from 'Whitcombe' to 'Nastuli', the diminutive and reincarnation of his fictional hero Anastasius. 'He was so perfectly a Greek,' he wrote of this alter ego,

> with his Turban gracefully, nay dandily, wrapped over him; his waist was so small, and his pistols sat so negligent thereon; his eye too was so bold, and his complexion dark, that he eluded the suspicion of all, as to his origin having been a foreign one.[8]

If any sense is to be made of Whitcombe's actions over the next months, it has to be remembered that it is this 'Nastuli' rather than a young English boy of nineteen that one is following. There was of course nothing unusual in Philhellenes dressing in the way he did, but with Whitcombe it was not simply a matter of clothes. When a young romantic of Humphreys's stamp put on Greek costume he remained no more than an Englishman in fancy dress, with all the moral and emotional lumber that entailed. For Whitcombe, however, as Trelawny, or even in a different idiom Jarvis, the clothes were symbolic of a much more radical and ominous change. With the new clothes and the new name – sometimes 'Nastuli', sometimes, it seems, 'Vasili' – came a whole new identity, a fresh and exultant sense of freedom and licence, a determination to answer to nothing but the imperatives of his own reckless egotism. The old self, and with it all the moral restraints of civilization, were rejected. 'The meanness of those who had crossed his path, in the shape of Franks,' he wrote of his fellow Philhellenes, 'formed the subject of his meditations.'

The ridiculous conceit, the spirit of detraction, the narrow prejudices – everything, in short, which distinguished them, combined to disgust him, and he determined finally to shun their tribe – to assume the feelings and habits adapted to the dress he wore, and the plans he had formed for himself; striving to forget, meanwhile, amid the congeniality and sameness of Greek manners, all the boasted polish he once had learnt to pride in – to study nature, and adore her – to frame his works by the influence she inspired – nay, to verge even into barbarism, in following her precepts, rather than forget her by studying fashion.[9]

There seems something vaguely uncanonical about the thought of Whitcombe and Trelawny linked together, as if the creations of two separate fictions had blundered into the same drama, and yet from the moment that this alter-ego, 'Nastuli', was born it is impossible to think that his destiny in Greece lay anywhere other than in Trelawny's Parnassan cave.

It is highly improbable that Whitcombe can have been in Nauplia long and not heard of the Mavre Troupa and its fabled treasure, and for a boy addicted to the spurious and unprincipled glamour of Byronic romance, the rumours of the cave would have represented everything that the Morea was not. To Whitcombe himself it certainly seemed in retrospect that the hand of an inexorable fate had led him to find Trelawny, and if that seems a fanciful abdication of responsibility then it is only too true that there was little in his character or morals to bind him to the grim duties that lay further south.

After the slaughter and brutalities of 1821 it seemed impossible that the war could have anything worse in store, and yet nothing in the early years of the conflict had prepared mainland Greece for the misery that the Egyptian army were about to bring. At the beginning of 1824, while the Greek factions were busy with the first of their civil wars, Sultan Mahmoud had come to terms with the most ambitious of his vassals, Mehemet Ali of Egypt and, in return for granting the Pashalik of Morea to Mehemet's son Ibrahim, had secured himself an army which combined the training of a western force with the innate ferocity of Ottoman troops.

On 23 and 24 of February 1825 – 'days pregnant with sorrow to Peloponnesus' as Gordon put it[10] – this army of invasion landed at the port of Modon in the south-west of the Morea to begin a two-year campaign of terror which would only end with the inter-vention of the Great Powers.

For the last six months before the Egyptians arrived the Greeks had known more or less when and where they would come, but not even the horrors inflicted on Psara the previous summer had been able to shake a complacency founded on all the wrong lessons learned in victory and defeat at Peta and Dervenakia. 'At the begin-ning of 1825,' George Finlay indignantly wrote,

> no words were strong enough to express their contempt for the regular troops of the Egyptian pasha. They said that the Arabs would run away at the sight of the *armatoli*, who had always been victorious over the bravest Mussulmanns in the sultan's empire. This self-confidence had prevented them taking any precautions against an enemy they despised. For more than six months the Greek government had known that Navarin would be the first fortress attacked, but no defences had been adopted for putting it in a state of defence.[11]

It was among the rag-bag of Roumeliot captains and Moreot troops, of destitute Italian counts and preening Phanariots, belatedly and blindly heading south to the relief of Navarino, that the American doctor, Samuel Gridley Howe, sat during a halt in their march, and observed Whitcombe. There was clearly something about the young Englishman that appealed to the generous romanticism in Howe's character, but behind the graceful elegance of Whitcombe's pose there was already a disillusioned Anastasius plotting his escape. As he lay beneath the fig tree brooding, the pent-up frustration and ambition of his first weeks broke out in a sudden fit of petulance. He had come out to fight, he complained, to make a name for himself, and had not seen so much as 'the tail of a pasha'.[12] He was damned if he was going to stay in the Morea, he told Howe, when there was more excitement to be had in a week with Ulysses than they would get if they stayed where they were till doomsday.

The spell of the afternoon was broken, their small encampment alive with sudden activity. The column prepared to resume the march. As the mules were caught and loaded with the soldiers' capotes and earthenware cooking pots, pistol belts tightened, primings and locks checked, and muskets slung across shoulders, Samuel Gridley Howe dropped back through the line in an attempt to humour his new companion.

It was a thankless task. The march ahead took them through some of the loveliest country in the Morea, and yet for Whitcombe everything was refracted through the medium of his frustration. Their soldiers were all cheats and liars, the ruins of antiquity 'humbugging piles of marble', the scenery nothing to Scotland.

It was only Howe's promise of action, that Whitcombe would soon enough feel a 'scimitar's edge'[13] across his neck, that kept him with the column at all, but it was several more days before he had his first taste of the excitement he craved. Their march had brought them on a south-western route across the Morea into Messenia, when a distant rumble of gunfire told them they were closing on Navarino and the enemy. A vote among the men had taken their company by a direct route out onto a plain rather than the safer but circuitous paths among the hills, and late afternoon found them in a village occupied only by other bands of irregulars. Towards the end of the afternoon, as Howe sat smoking his pipe, the whole camp wrapped in stillness, he heard 'a low, rumbling, sound, like the roaring of a distant beach'.[14] With a foot, he awoke his manservant Francesco. Francesco put his ear to the ground. In another second he was on his feet again, running towards the edge of the village. The next moment Howe could hear his shrill warning, 'The Turks! The Turks!'[15]

A cloud of dust, seeming to extend in all directions, was advancing on them across the plain. The camp was a sudden frenzy of activity. Mules and baggage trains were driven into the church, barrels and huge oil jars rolled into the streets as barricades, loopholes driven into the walls of the cottages for rifles, earth thrown up in front of hastily started trenches. Only Whitcombe was oblivious to the panic.

His spirits seemed to rise, and his eyes to flash fire, as he stood impatient on a bank, with his hand on the trigger of his cocked gun, the muzzle resting on his left arm, his body bent forward, and watching the coming host. I stood beside him, and though I mastered my feelings and showed the same front and bearing that he did, I think it was not the same within. I glanced at the space between our station and the mountains – there was no hope of escape there; I looked at the dense mass of horses and riders, now for an instant at a stand. I saw the plungings and curvettings of the impatient steeds, the glitter of their trappings, the flowing, gilded dresses of their scimitars, and I could distinguish, dashing here and there, among the mass, the high-cap of the furious Delhi; and as I thought of the feeble barrier on which I stood, and over which they could dash their steeds at a single leap, I half shuddered, and my thoughts flew back to my home, to my mother, and to the nursery; I felt all that man must feel when first in danger, but which we are too cowardly to betray by look or words.

But there was no time for thought; there was a sudden movement of the foe – their horses dashed forwards towards us at a gallop, the riders waved their scimitars, and raised a tremendous yell of 'Hu! Hu! Allah! Hu!' – when I felt myself pulled into the ditch by Francesco – where, putting out my gun through a hole made for the purpose, I lay and waited till they should be within shot. There was a deadly, breathless silence among us; there was moving of lips in prayer, but no sound; there was making of a sudden crosses, but no eye ceased to glance along the gun-barrel towards the foe, who, advancing like lightning, now began to raise

189

their carbines. I saw them bend their bodies, and try to crouch behind their horses' necks; I saw the very glare of their eyes, – when, in an instant, a flash of fire ran along their line – their balls whizzed over our heads – our muskets instantly rattled in reply; the smoke arose, and after that, I saw nothing, and thought of nothing, but to load and fire; and fire we did so fast and furiously into the cloud of smoke, out of which flashed the enemy's guns, and where they seemed to be a moment checked; but as the smoke arose I saw a troop of a dozen, dash within a few yards of us, fire their pistols, receive our shots, wheel, and away; and, when the smoke again cleared up, they were half a mile distant.

Then there was shouting, and congratulation, and exultation, in our hitherto breathless band; W. leaped over the barrier, and yatagan in hand, would have advanced – but no one followed the foolhardy boy. In a few moments more the enemy were moving off at a full trot, and we saw no more of them.[16]

There is a peculiarly American sentimentality about this passage that would seem more familiar in the letters and songs of the Civil War a generation later, and yet in its gaudy romanticsm Howe probably takes us as close to the core of a certain type of Philhellenism as we are likely to get. Even the excitement of an action like this, however, was not enough to hold Whitcombe for long. On 28 April, on the eve of their attempt to relieve the besieged fortress of Navarino, a more sober Howe recorded in his journal his companion's departure with another Philhellene, a sternly religious veteran of America's war with Britain. 'Miller and Whitcombe left the camp,' he wrote,

the first for Miss., the second for Gastouni; I hope to see again their faces in ten or twelve days. Miller, I am certain, will return, if alive; but Whitcomb is such a fickle-minded, harebrained boy that it would puzzle Solomon to calculate his course. That he is brave there is no doubt, but he has not one spark of generous or philanthropic feeling towards Greece, and his only motive in coming was the hope of distinguishing himself. Rather than sacrifice this hope he would have poor Greece struggle on years more, in a contest which is racking her to her vitals. How opposite in every respect, how inferior in worth to the noble and generous, though stern, enthusiast, Miller. Ambition in every man I applaud; without it he is not, cannot be, great; but let it not control everything else, let it not stifle humanity and philanthropy.[17]

It is easy to forget in a feeling of impatience at Whitcombe's egotism just how very young he was in 1825. The irritation in Howe's journal can be only too contagious, and yet as one follows Whitcombe now on the edge of a drama beyond his understanding, this sense of extreme youth returns with an involuntary sympathy for a life about to be destroyed almost before it had begun.

There is no question, however, that Howe was justified in his criticism. The early successes of 1822 might have fatally blinded the Greek captains to the threat of foreign soldiers, but Whitcombe himself knew as well as any Philhellene that if Navarino with its deep harbour fell, the rest of the Peloponnese and Greece itself was at the mercy of Ibrahim Pasha's Egyptian army.

In spite of this, though, it would seem that he had always intended to abandon the army before it reached Navarino, because at Gastoumi on the western coast he took his farewell of Miller and struck out alone for Patras, where that other young romantic, Humphreys, whom he had met at Nauplia in March, was waiting for him.

Together the two men set off for Corinth and a boat across to Roumeli, marching eastwards with a band of Suliote irregulars along the same route that Dramali's retreating army had taken in 1822. After three years of Turk and Greek brutalities the landscape of the Morea was little better than a desert, but keeping them company on their left the great mass of the Parnassan range loomed above the northern shore of the gulf, a distant and almost spectral presence in the morning light, close enough to touch in the evenings, drawing them onwards with its illusory promise of the Greece that both men craved.

It was late in May 1825, however, before Humphreys and

Whitcombe finally left Corinth and the whitening bones of Dramali's soldiers behind them, took a boat for Aspra Spitia and landed on the northern shore of the gulf. Their first intention had been to join the Greek army at Salona, but even before they had left the Morea the troops had retreated eastwards onto the great monastery of Osios Loukas with its ancient double church perched high above one of the loveliest valleys in the whole country, a patchwork of blossom and corn spread out like a piece of Italy gone astray, a fragment of a Lorenzetti fresco, civilized among the bleak sweep of the surrounding mountains in a way that the Greek landscape seldom is.

From Aspra Spitia it was a long hard climb up to the monastery, and it was late on the same day on which they landed before Whitcombe and Humphreys finally reached their destination. For almost every Philhellene there was a timelessness about Greek camp life that never lost its attraction, and after the miasma of disease and misery which hung like a pall over the ruins of Corinth there was a genuine exhilaration for Whitcombe in being at last in a world that measured up to his expectations.

For all its picturesque charms, however, with its clusters of soldiers lying on branches strewn on the ground, their weapons hung from the boughs above them, it was not the rhythms of camp life which had brought either man to Parnassus. The same night that they arrived at the monastery Humphreys slipped out of the camp alone, met up with Yanakis, the brother of the imprisoned Odysseus, and marching silently and rapidly through the night, made contact with the beleaguered Trelawny at the Mavre Troupa. It is not known why, and nothing Humphreys says of this journey makes any sense. It is not known whether he carried with him any message of compromise or treaty from the government party. It is not known whether Ghouras, in command of the army, knew of it. All that is known is that when he left the next evening he was carrying with him an invitation to the cave for Whitcombe.

It was not long either before Whitcombe, soon tiring of his new life, was ready to take up the offer. On 28 May the army had advanced west from Osios Loukas into the plain beneath Delphi, but finding the Turks already in possession of Desfina retreated again on their defences at Dystomo. After this only the occasional alarm or savage brutality punctuated the monotony of campaign life. On one occasion five prisoners were taken, captured setting fire to a church. Four of them were impaled, and the fifth slowly roasted alive. As the man expired over the fire, never begging mercy, defiantly certain of his martyr's crown to the end, Whitcombe was moved by his courage to prayer. 'You have not, like us, had your sisters debauched,' he was told by a Greek soldier, 'your parents crucified, and your little brothers or children tost on the point of the scimitar.'[18]

On 7 June 1825, the nineteen-year-old Whitcombe left the Greek camp and made his way towards a destiny – 'indefinable in its nature, but not less darkening'[19] – that had been beckoning since he first wrote to the Greek Committee offering his services. Ahead of him rose 'the far-famed hill of Parnassus', its eagles 'skimming at times the air, then dashing down as though hurled with impetus by some power who resisted their approach so high'.[20]

It is an apt image of Whitcombe's own ambition, and only fitting, too, that as he moves at last within the gravitational pull of Trelawny's world, from the realm of history into that of romance as Howe put it, his journey can only be followed in the person of his fictional alter ego, 'Nastuli'.

In reality it was a day's hard march for Whitcombe, across the barren crossroads where tradition has it that Oedipus killed his father, and through the low pass over the eastern foothills of Parnassus that leads to Daulis and the plain below Tithorea.

In Whitcombe's *Sketches*, however, our solitary source, this same journey has a dreamlike, almost surreal quality. Facts, character, structure, plot, dissolve into a chaos of incoherent memories, fantasies, distortions, betrayals and self-deceptions. Tricked by a Suliote who has won his confidence, 'Nastuli' is lured towards an unknown destination high on the northern slopes of Parnassus, and led in the dark through 'paths and windings,' until he comes to a steep cliff,

> where stood a ladder curiously constructed and another
> placed over it, leading to a cave, which formed by nature,

stood in the rock above them. Here they mounted by means of these steps, and arrived in the interior, illuminated by torches, which gleamed fitfully over numerous implements of war ... He laid down in his capote and slept, while visions of hope and happiness hovered over his repose. But the morrow was destined to change these to disgust, and in dissipating their illusions, destroy his lightheartedness for ever. A mistaken zeal, an attachment to a traitor, while it led him to participate in crimes, – unconscious, till too late, of their being so – sunk his ardent and susceptible nature under the weight of miseries which itself had created; dimmed his eye from the lustre it before possessed; and gave to his cheek that sunken hue which defies aught to restore it to its bloom.[21]

9

ASSASSINATION

'Not so my own conscience! Loud and ceaseless were its unbraidings. 'Thy dagger,' it said, 'has been lifted on thy friend; it has killed thy brother. To the last day of thy life, the wound inflicted by thee ... shall continue to fester in thine own distracted bosom ... it shall follow thee beyond the grave.' To my wine it gave the taste of blood, and to my bread the rank flavour of death!'

Anastasius[1]

IN THE JUNE OF 1825 the Mavre Troupa was a very different place from the fortress Humphreys had visited the previous summer. From the day in April when Odysseus had given himself up to his former henchman, the cavern had been under government siege, making the helpless rump of its garrison virtual prisoners in their own stronghold, the gorge below abandoned to Ghouras' troops, the troglodytic world of the Mavre Troupa shrunk to a hole in the rock face twenty yards deep and a narrow ledge thirty yards long.

Trelawny is seldom a man one need feel sorry for but there is a poignancy in the picture of him in his Parnassan stronghold in the weeks after Odysseus's capture that is difficult to resist. It is hard to remember in the dreary melancholy of his fortunes that it was barely a year since he and Fenton had first arrived with the guns from Missolonghi, and yet in that time he had seen his ambitions of a chieftain's role in the war collapse around him, the man he had modelled himself on imprisoned for treachery and his own name impugned in letters and papers across Europe as a traitor to the Greek cause.

'We hear of very great preparations in Albania by the Turks,' the Ionian banker Samuel Barff wrote to Edward Blaquiere at the end of March,

> and what is worse the strange fact of Odysseus having positively gone over to the Turks – they say also Trelawny will accompany him . . . [2]

Through the summer the rumours and counter rumours gathered momentum, until even on her employers' estate in Russia, where she was working as a governess, the garbled news of Odysseus's defection reached Claire Clairmont. 'I read in the newspapers that Odysseus has been defeated four times near Atalandi by Gura,' she wrote in her diary on 24 June, two months after his surrender,

> that he has given himself up prisoner and has been conveyed to Napoli. What this means I cannot make out – I cannot believe that the chief Edward has chosen is one capable of betraying his country; but I am naturally extremely low spirited at the news tho' I do my best to believe it false.[3]

Her faith in Trelawny reflects well on both of them but Claire's despondency was justified. To the end of his life Trelawny would always see Odysseus as a victim of petty jealousies and factionalism, yet as both his own *Records* and Bacon's account make clear there is no escaping the bleak fact that he was culpably aware of what Odysseus was doing.

Loyalty and courage, even when misplaced, remain however among the most attractive of human virtues and in Odysseus's moment of disaster Trelawny now showed that he had both. It could be argued that he was too deeply compromised by Odysseus's treachery to follow any other course, but a more pertinent truth is that he could no more have abandoned Odysseus in disaster than he could have given up his own dearly-won sense of self. There could be no room now for doubt, or for the even more corrosive self-doubt that he had been wrong in the man he had dubbed the new 'Washington'. A Philhellene at war with Greece, a 'chieftain' without an army, all that was left to him was the ennobling consciousness of his own loyalty and bravery. If he could not live the life of the klephtic warrior, he could at least die like one, and play out the last moves with a style that would not betray his Byronic self-image. 'What could I do but cling to De Ruyter,' he demanded in *Adventures* in a scene that echoes his last parting from Odysseus

> Like one suspended over a cliff by a single rope, I held him; and the feelings that overcame me at parting were as seeing that rope giving away, or as, with more appalling agony, a sailor fallen into the sea at midnight, catching the last glimpse of his ship, his limbs paralysed, his swelling heart bursts. I am one whose faith is that love and friendship, with ardent natures, are like those trees of the torrid zone which yield fruit but once, and then die.[4]*

And yet among all the wreckage of his dreams, if death in the high romantic style was what he was after, that old genius of his for drawing others into his imaginative world had one last service to render. As far back as November 1824 Jarvis had tried to persuade Fenton to get out of the cave while he still could, but whatever communication between them followed, Fenton obviously decided to brave out the dangers, as if the Mavre Troupa and all its imaginary romance had seized hold of his mind too, keeping him, like Trelawny, a willing prisoner at his desolate post while the world and the war passed it by.

It is hard to think of any other reason that can have kept him in the Gorge through the early summer of 1825 when he must have seen how pointless his vigil had become. There seems no way that he can have spent so long in the cave without knowing that its fabled treasures had either gone or never existed, and as the summer months wore on the grim stalemate in the valley must have brought home too the military and strategic limitations of the cave.

If there was no way in to the Mavre Troupa, there was equally no way out, as two incidents in April had made obvious. Throughout the winter months Trelawny had been in the habit of riding out each day for news, but sometime around the date of Odysseus's surrender he had been surprised in the gorge by Ghouras's men and almost killed before he could make it back to the safety of the ladders and the covering fire from the cave above. Shortly after this a large body of Ghouras's soldiers arrived at the village of Tithorea an hour's ride from the cave, bringing with them a 'message' from Odysseus. A detachment approached the Mavre Troupa, Trelawny remembered,

> on coming near, one of them advanced, holding a green bough as a flag of truce: he said Odysseus was with the troops below, and that he had brought a letter from him to me. It was to this effect, that he – Odysseus – was now with his friend Ghouras; he entreated me to come to him to confer on matters of great importance; saying that hostages would be given for my safe return, &.
>
> I merely answered, 'If what you say is true, why don't you come here? You may bring Ghouras or half- a-dozen others with you.
>
> Several notes of this sort were exchanged. In the last, our chief urged me to capitulate as the only means of saving his life; telling me that I might now do so on my own terms, for those with him were Roumeliotes favourably disposed to him and to me; and that if I lost the opportunity, I should be blockaded by his enemies the Moreotes, who would give us no quarter. Of course I declined, for I knew the chief was writing under compulsion.[5]

With the failure of Ghouras's bid to take the cave Fenton was effectively alone, but by this time it is probably no longer tenable anyway to think of him as a simple instrument of government policy. There can be no question that through the previous autumn Mavrocordato had listened with sympathy to his plans, and yet whether he had finally gone along with them is another matter. The evidence is too fragmentary to be conclusive, but every instinct about Mavrocordato, about his weaknesses as much as his strengths, his vacillations as much as his central decency, militate against his approval of a plot that from the moment Trelawny abandoned thoughts of England could only succeed with his murder.*

After Trelawny's behaviour at Missolonghi Mavrocordato certainly had every reason to dislike him, but if nothing else was going to temper his resentment, it is hard to see him murdering the friend of his old pupil Mary Shelley. Certainly as late as the February of 1825 – three months after Fenton had demanded two thousand dollars in gold to 'buy' fifty soldiers to take the cave – Jarvis was still pressing for an answer, still irritably trying to edge him and the government from passive acquiescence into active collaboration. Jarvis had, he told the Prince, two (?) of his own men within the cave itself, and knew of everything that passed there. '*J'ai mes yeux sur lui*,' he wrote of Trelawny,

> I await your orders on this subject; the prevarication of the government exasperates me a little. To take possession of the cave now would be more difficult than any moment since I proposed it; but the cave is in my hands as soon as the Ulysses affair is decided.[6]

It would seem, however, from a letter of Fenton's that whatever money and offers were made by the government must have stopped short of the final commitment the two men sought. There is no date to the letter – one of only two in Fenton's hand that survives – but it must have been written at about this same time, on his return from a journey he had made to Nauplia in January.

> My Lord. I have the honour of writing to your Highness. I shall not trouble you with a long letter. Captain Jarvis knows my last determination if that it does not meet your appro-bation. I have only one thing more to most earnestly request of you, namely that all that has passed betwixt me and your Highness may be kept secret. It is not surely presuming too far to request this – my life is in your hands – the slightest hint and I am lost. I know whom I have to do with and knowing that I may tremble, but as for you my Lord I do not doubt your honour, and now write more to put you on

your guard of any lapses of speech, than from supposing you could be base enough to ruin one who would have served you. Wishing your Highness success over all your enemies and good fortune in all your undertakings.[7]

It is not on the basis of Mavrocordato's personality that any doubts of involvement finally rest however, because since the February of 1825 events throughout Greece had moved in a direction that had long outdistanced Fenton's and Jarvis's plots. When they first launched their scheme a year earlier Odysseus had been in a position to make eastern Greece his own, but with the dramatic collapse of his power over the winter and the arrival of Ibrahim's Egyptians the whole focus of political and military interest had shifted from Roumeli to the southern Peloponnese, relegating the cave and all its concerns to a forgotten limbo.

Through the winter of 1824–5 a supine government had done nothing to prepare against invasion, but when on 28 March the Greek army including Howe and Whitcombe finally marched out of Nauplia to meet the Egyptians at Navarino, both Mavrocordato and Jarvis were with it. The brief campaign that followed was a disaster. Since Peta and Dervenakia the Greeks had despised western methods of warfare and they were now about to learn their lesson. On 19 April more than seven thousand of their irregulars, fighting a defensive battle on ground of their own choosing, were put to ignominious flight by the disciplined bayonet charge of a force little more than half their strength. On 8 May, the key island of Sphacteria, guarding the entrance to Navarino Bay, was also stormed and taken, Mavrocordato only just escaping by boat with his life. On the 11th, the fortress of Pylos surrendered, and ten days later Navarino itself followed suit, its garrison, including Jarvis, marching out under an amnesty, allowed to go unarmed but unharmed by an Egyptian commander eager at this early stage to try the effects of clemency as an instrument of policy.

The dates of these defeats are important, because it was against the background of Navarino, and the subsequent campaign in the Morea as Ibrahim abandoned mercy for more traditional Ottoman methods, that events now unfolded in a cave that the course of warfare and history had passed by. After all the months of danger and exposure it must have been a bitter experience for Fenton to find himself marooned in this way, to have become a forgotten part of a forgotten garrison that had shrunk to no more than a dozen men and women – one Greek, an Albanian Turk, a Hungarian and an Italian, all deliberately chosen for this Parnassan Babel to prevent treachery, an old priest and a couple of servant boys, Tersitza, Odysseus's son, wife and mother, two other women, and Trelawny himself.

It was to this isolated and besieged fortress, literally and emotionally primed to explode, that Whitcombe made his way on 7 June 1825. In his *Sketches* the whole drama that followed is contracted to one nightmarish and unexplained night, but in fact it spread over four days. There is no coherent record of how this time was spent but, in that uncanny way that the cave has of existing outside the normal rhythms of time, these days can seem to stretch out with an agonizing slowness and pass with a rapidity that baffles belief. Images take on all the ghastly permanence of tableaux, the participants frozen in symbolic action: Fenton, his long, gaunt face unshaven in the tra-ditional sign of grief for Odysseus's capture, beside the kiln at the front of the cave, patiently filing down an iron ball to fit Whitcombe's carbine; night, and Fenton again, at Whitcombe's ear in the bunker at the foot of the ladders, working away on his credulous, impulsive nature with stories of betrayal and promises of wealth and power; the thirteen-year-old Tersitza, two months pregnant and 'beautiful as an angel'; the great Thessalian hound, padding the terrace during the day, keeping watch on the guard-house at night; Trelawny, supercilious, arrogant, oblivious to the hatred that threatened him; and all the time the Hungarian, Komerone, watching, silent and wary, grimly prepared at a moment's notice to put a light to the magazine and blow the whole cave to pieces.

For the first time, too, an almost palpable sense of evil imposes itself. When Fenton embarked on his schemes in April 1824 politics and principles had unquestionably played their part, but with the successive disappointments of his expectations all that was left to him was a raw enmity that had nothing to do with either. 'I will not surrender the glory I expect for my part in this great enterprise,' he had written to Jarvis in November, 'not for all the riches that England possesses. Greece, that name is enough!'[8]

Now, however, it had nothing to do with Greece, or riches, or power, or anything other than the dislike that months of close confinement together had matured into a deep hatred. When Humphreys had visited the cave a fortnight earlier Fenton had been barely willing even to sit down at the same table with Trelawny, but with Whitcombe's arrival he was more circumspect, subordinating open antipathy to policy with a chilling deliberateness. Cynically, corruptly, he set out to infect the impressionable nineteen-year-old boy with his own savage contempt. 'In one single day,' Howe wrote of this drama, stretching the four days out to six with an almost biblical cadence:

> Whitcombe became the admirer of Fenton; thought him the noblest, the most romantic, the bravest of men; in one day more he thought him injured and abused by Trelawny, learned to hate Trelawny, believed that Trelawny despised him and meditated injuring him; and on the third day he swore eternal friendship to Fenton, and that he would stand by him at all hazards, in any attempt to regain what he believed his right. Still Fenton did not dare propose his horrid plan; he had wound his coil about his victim, but feared that the spring of virtue might not yet be poisoned. Two days more were passed in riot and drinking, and Whitcombe was excited by wild plans of power, and of becoming prince of the surrounding province, if Fenton would become master of the cavern, and there was only Trelawny in the way.[9]

The climax came on 11 June, a Saturday. The day was intensely hot, Trelawny remembered, and the men and women of the garrison had retreated into the upper grotto for their siesta. He had eaten his midday meal with Fenton and Whitcombe, and the three of them were sitting on the veranda of his house at the front of the cave, smoking and drinking.

A deterministic streak of self-destructiveness lies at the heart of all misanthropic individualism and there seems an inevitability about the following moments that has as much to do with Trelawny's character as Fenton's plottings. In Trelawny's version of events Fenton asked if he would umpire a shooting match between him and Whitcombe, adding that Trelawny could easily beat them both. In Whitcombe's account it is the other way around, Trelawny sneeringly dismissing their skills, boasting that even with a pistol he could outshoot their carbines. It is a small difference, but symbolic. In the gap between these two versions, in that moment of arrogance, a moment of almost collaborative self-destruction, Trelawny's fate was perhaps decided: a different man then, a different response, and Whitcombe's resolution might yet have failed.

As the three men got up to settle their wager, Trelawny sent his Italian servant Everett to put up a target at the far end of the terrace. It was Trelawny who shot first, Whitcombe later told Howe,

> and after hitting the mark, he bent a little forward, and in his usual cold, unsocial way, stood with his back to them; Fenton raised his carbine, (which was not loaded), and pointing it at Trelawny, snapped – he looked with pretended dismay at Whitcomb, as begging him to second him, cocked and snapped again: 'he turned on me such a look – I know not what I did – I raised my gun, pulled the trigger, and fell from my own emotions'; these were the words of the mad boy, who had become all but an assassin.[10]

Whitcombe's carbine was loaded with two balls, and as they smashed into Trelawny's back, he staggered without falling towards the wall, crying out that he had been shot. Fenton rushed forward to support him, apparently full of concern. As Whitcombe lay almost paralyzed by what he had done, he heard Fenton calling across to Komerone and the Turk Achmet who had rushed out from inside the cave: 'There is the young traitor; shoot him, cut him down, do not let him speak.'[11] A shot was fired by someone, but no one was hit.

Then Whitcombe watched Fenton turn, look up, and see Komerone levelling his musket. The Hungarian, 'a dead shot', was aiming at Fenton.[12] Without the least sign of emotion Fenton straightened to face his executioner, a hand on his chest: 'Fire again, I am ready,' he called out.[13] A second shot rang out, striking him in the heart. He fell, rolled over on his face, and died without a groan. 'Round he spun, and down he fell,' as Humphreys exultingly put it, 'To the last an infidel.'[14]

In the confusion which followed, while Trelawny's soldiers were carrying him inside, Whitcombe staggered to the safety of Odysseus's house perched above the trap door to the ladders. With a courage born of terror he undid his sash, lashed one end to the casement bars and, suspended seventy feet above the ground, lowered himself down until he could reach the second ladder and scramble to the bottom.

At the foot of the cliff he began to run, scarcely knowing what he was doing or where he was going, stumbling and scrambling through scrub and thorn down the precipitous hillside to the grove of oaks that surrounds the chapel of St George. There he was overhauled by Trelawny's men, and brought back without resistance. Back in the cave, he was dragged before Trelawny. A noose was thrown around his neck, a gun pressed to his heart, and a confession demanded. Whitcombe, beside himself with fear, denied any involvement, said the plot was Fenton's – Humphreys's – the Greek captain, Kariaskaki's. As he was hauled out onto the terrace again, he saw Fenton's body lying where it had fallen, threw himself down on it and wept.

It is perhaps predictable that no two accounts of this shooting agree in every detail, and yet what is more interesting is that it would have been as impossible within a week of the incident to be certain of what happened as it is now. By the time that Humphreys made his way to the cave on the 16th the embellishments and colouring had already started, and when Trelawny came to it in his *Records* the events had long since firmed into the dubious shape that is now romantic lore. It is worth following what happened next, however, in his words.

Achmet, the Turk, seized [Whitcombe], bound his arms, dragged him to a crane used for hoisting things from below, put a slip-knot in the rope, and placed it round his ankles to hang him. His convulsive shrieks and the frantic struggles he made as his executioners were hoisting him over the precipice, calling to God to witness that he was innocent, thrilled through my shattered nerves; he besought me to let him live till the morning, or for one hour, that he might write home, or even for five minutes until he had told me everything. Everett informed me what they were at; I sent him to the Hungarian, desiring him to defer what he was doing until I had ascertained from Whitcombe the facts which constitute my present narrative. I could not conceive it possible that an English gentleman, my guest, on the most cordial terms with me, should after four days acquaintance, conspire with Fenton to assassinate me – there had been no provocation, and I could see no motive for the act. Fenton had never seen Whitcombe before, nor had I. If there was foul play, Fenton must have been the traitor: I had very great difficulty in staying the execution, everyone in the cave clamouring for vengeance. His life now hung on mine, and everybody thought that I was mortally wounded. They all swore, if I died, they would roast him by a slow fire: this was no idle threat, for it had been done on more than one occasion during that sanguinary war.

When I was shot, I sat down on the rock I had been standing on; bending down my head to let the blood flow from my mouth, a musket ball and several teeth came with it – the socket of the teeth was broken, and my right arm paralysed. I walked without assistance into the small grotto I had boarded up and floored and called my house; it was divided into two small rooms, and there was a broad veranda in front. Squatting in a corner, my servant cut open my dress behind, and told me I had been shot with two balls between my shoulders, near together, on the right side of my spine, and one of them close to it. One of the balls, as

I have said, its force expended on my bones, dropped from my mouth without wounding my face; the other broke my collar bone, and remained in my breast – it is still there. No blood issued from the places they had entered at. We had no surgeon or medicines in the cave; the air was so dry and pure, our living so simple, that this was the first visit sickness or sorrow paid us. Nature makes no mistakes, doctors do; probably I owe my life to a sound constitution and having had no doctor.[15]

There are discrepancies between this account and an earlier version Trelawny gave Humphreys that can be laid at the door of time and memory, but more important here is that it shows how he would eventually come to handle the attempt on his life. In a letter Hastings wrote to Finlay, he acutely observed that the real humiliation for Trelawny would be to find that he had been Fenton's dupe, and yet in Trelawny's memory even that is skilfully metamorphosed, his credulity and lack of judgement seen as part of a heroic and self-sufficient simplicity only the nobler for its vulnerability to an intrigue beneath its understanding.

Trelawny's description of this incident has all the wonderful poise and control of his mature prose but what is perhaps more telling from the author of *Adventures* is his almost suburban astonishment that 'an English gentleman and guest' could have behaved in this way. It is of course true that when he wrote this he was addressing a mid-Victorian age, and yet it is as if at this crisis of his whole existence, at that moment when he finally had to pick up the tab for a lifetime's Byronic posturing, his faith in a world of violence and self-assertion failed him, punctured along with his shattered body by Whitcombe's bullets.

It is a curious discovery to find this, an anti-climax not untinged with disbelief, particularly if one has come this far with Trelawny. There had seemed nowhere that the romanticism of both Trelawny and Whitcombe could not take them, but one of the fascinations of this whole incident is that for neither man was it enough to sustain him through the reality of attempted murder and death. For Trelawny, it was as though the phantom victims of his imagination had risen up in revenge, as ruthless and indifferent to the social laws as he saw himself, their violence as beyond comprehension in fact as it had seemed accessible in his eastern dreams; for Whitcombe, crazed with fear, guilt, and shame, chained to the rock in the deep recess of the cave, there was a similar, crushing disbelief at what he had done. At nineteen years old he was like his hero Anastasius, 'a being whose sin has placed between him and society a gulf fitter to be removed by any hands but his'.[16] 'But I cannot, cannot bear so sudden a transition into exquisite misery and shame,' he later, despairingly wrote to a friend, 'without a line which may give palliatives to my offence.

> Scan it with a dispassionate eye; my only motive for begging this last favour of you is, that you may rather hold me the weak, unsuspecting tool, than the practised, unprincipled villain. Others played that part; others saw my easy nature, and thought me a fit instrument for the furthering of their grand speculations and enterprises. They discerned rightly . . .
>
> On my arrival I was beset by Fenton's utmost talents of duplicity (in which never mortal man has excelled him). Touched by his mournful tales of wrongs, rejection, deprivation of right, viewing him only as the romantic, the injured, the generous hero he had been represented by Humphreys, I swore to stand by him on his resolution to recover his rights or die. He worshipped me for it, and being too good a discerner of character to disclose further the nature of his designs, at the idea of which he knew I would revolt, he nailed me to the spot and moment of action, and by not giving a minute's time to recover from my infatuation, he precipitated me into that hell of guilt and shame which had long yawned for the wretched adventurer as his need, but which, without arraigning Providence, might still, methinks, have been withheld from me. But where misfortune ever exists, there am I sure to get acquainted with it. And because

such a villain survived in the same land, I, without holding with him a shadow of previous connection . . . am nevertheless doomed, solely because such a one exists, to connect myself, and all my happiness and honour, irretrievably with his fate. I am now a wandering outcast, a being whose very claim on society is departed, and would not now wish to renew those claims, from the recollections of dependence which would necessarily hang on that renewal.

But it is not for myself that I am wretched. No: I can roam to far distant regions, and amidst other scenes and other inhabitants, commence a new career, unembittered by the past. It is for my family who had boasted that, through all their branches and connections, it had never had a spot to sully it. That that family should, through my faults, be disgraced, is more than I can bear.[17]

He was right. It was more than he could bear. That night Trelawny lay on his pallet, hovering between life and death. In the darkness of the cave, mad with terror, screaming and shrieking if anyone approached him, Whitcombe struggled with his new identity. The 'barbarism' that 'Nastuli' had embraced had brought him to a crime for which the son of Sir Samuel and Lady Whitcombe would have to pay the price. Somehow, though, in a moment of lucidity, he managed to get a message to Trelawny. 'For God's sake let me explain myself,' he pleaded,

and do not let me be murdered without a word of explanation. Oh God! my misery is already too great; they care not for what you tell them; they want to tie me up by irons to the beam of the room, and cut my head off.[18]

10

HUMPHREYS

'Trelawny had said I was like his vampyre. I had indeed brought him nothing but trouble.'

W. H. Humphreys[1]

'It remains, however, in some degree a mystery. Fenton, who might have solved it, lies buried beneath the battlements of the cave – his crimes his monumental stone.'

W.H. Humphreys[2]

NEWS HAS ALWAYS travelled quickly in Greece. When the great topographer Colonel Leake visited the battlefield of Plateia in 1804, he calculated that it would have taken only eight fires to carry tidings of the expected Persian victory from Attica to mainland Asia, the first on Mt Helicon, the second on Zia, and then across the chain of Aegean island stations to Mt Gellesus, Mt Tmolus and Sardes.

The Persian fires were premature, but rumour has traditionally travelled faster still. Within days of the attempt on Trelawny's life, word of it had reached government and Philhellene circles in Athens and Nauplia, then the British consuls in Patras, Zante and Corfu until finally – shrouded in doubts and uncertainty, conjecture and contradictions – his family and friends, the newspapers, the British Government, and, again, even Claire Clairmont in Russia. 'I do not know how I have the courage to trace the remembrance of this unhappy day in my Journal,' she wrote on 13 August.

After dinner I take up the Newspaper by accident and read there an account of a duel between Trelawny and another Englishman. In a moment my whole peace is destroyed . . . They say he is dangerously wounded, but I must hope – what else have I left to choose, but to despair or hope, and hope I must, but I know despair will come.[3]

Claire's fears are a touching reminder at this juncture of the deep and lasting affection Trelawny was capable of inspiring. She might have fled from his extravagant courtship in Italy but she never lost sight of what he meant to her in the months after Shelley's death, never stopped asking for news of him, never stopped wondering to what extremes his character – and her rejection – might drive him. 'It is a year I received no letter from Trelawny, which makes me very anxious about him,' she had written to Jane Williams the previous autumn:

Pray, dear Jane, let me know what kind of life he leads there, and if he is actively employed in the cause, or only a spectator – If he is associated with other Englishmen, or walked off alone by himself, in search of death, in those regions of trouble and danger – For nothing in the world would I have anything happen to him there; for it would be very melancholy – so pray say something cheerful to me about him –[4]

It would be months before the fears of Claire and his friends in England were allayed, but in Greece itself the confusion surrounding the shooting seemed to clear when a second and even more dramatic event occurred in Athens. On the morning of 17 June, less than a week after the assassination bid, the battered corpse of Odysseus Androutses was found on the rocks at the foot of the Venetian tower which then stood at the south-west corner of the Acropolis. He had, the authorities quickly announced, fallen while trying to escape. 'As in duty bound,' the Chief Secretary of Athens reported back to the governing body of the city,

I relate, that on the morning of this day, about half past nine, I was invited by the noble Vice President, Mr J Mamouris, to the Acropolis, where I saw the body of Ulysses Andretzos, broken on the right thigh, and on the right side of the head, lying below the tower of the Acropolis, distant from the base four or five paces, bound by a pretty long cord round the waist, and another coiled up and tied also to the waist . . .

From the fortification of the tower hung a rope sundered at about one third of its height from the summit to the base. The height of the tower is about eighteen perches, and the rope was broken at the length of six perches eighteen feet.

I enquired of the Vice President; and he answered, that about the fifth hour of the night, a sentinel, who was not far from the tower, informed him, that he heard a crash near its base, and a groan. The gentleman ran immediately to the place, and discovered the body lying in the manner above mentioned, as it was also at the moment when I went; it had been left designedly untouched. I inquired of the soldiers of his guard, and they told me that one of them slept behind the gates, and the other in the same part with the dead man; and that they did not know when he arose and fastened himself to the rope, in order to escape. I asked them, if they knew anything about the rope; and they answered me with an oath, 'NO'.[5]

There are various and conflicting accounts of the weeks leading up to Odysseus's death, but there is no real doubt that after torturing him in a vain attempt to find out where he had hidden his treasures, his captors had strangled and then thrown him from the tower to make his murder seem an accident. In line with the secretary's report a post-mortem was held to confirm the official version, however, and that same morning, with the permission of the Eparch and full sacred rites – 'for "the dead is justified from offences"' as the official bulletin confidently announced – five priests celebrated the funeral of 'the worthless and assassin Odysseus.'[6]

There seems a perfect symmetry in the fact that Odysseus should have died at the hands of Ghouras, a killer he had promoted from pipe-bearer to lieutenant for his ruthless treachery. In the memoirs of the great Greek captain Makriyannis, it is recorded that Odysseus's murder was the single crime for which Ghouras ever expressed regret, and yet it should have been some comfort for him to know that his sacrifice of feeling to policy, of sentiment to greed, was a calculation that his own mentor and – in apostolic succession beyond him – Ali Pasha himself would have recognized as the only practical course.

And it is in the end as a pupil of Ali Pasha, unscrupulous, pragmatic, shameless and unrepentant, that Odysseus lived and died. It could be argued with some justice that only his talent distinguished him from a dozen other unscrupulous captains who dealt with the Turks, but it was precisely those abilities which might have won him a position within a new Greece that made it impossible for the government to ignore or forgive him in opposition.

It is a graphic illustration of the fear that the name of Odysseus could inspire even in death that the authorities should take so much trouble to dissemble their part in his murder, but they can have had no real hope of being believed. Within forty-eight hours gossip in Nauplia was pointing the finger at his old enemy Mavrocordato, and when in the next days letters were found among Fenton's papers implicating the Prince, cave and tower fell into place as parts of a single Phanariot plot to seize eastern Greece and Odysseus's mythical treasures.

With the racism endemic to Philhellenism, no foreigner seemed very surprised at the involvement of Mavrocordato, but it was suddenly and hysterically open season on Fenton, a declaration of war on a man who had made that unforgivable transition from 'Philhellene' to 'Greek'. If Trelawny had been killed by of one of Ghouras's henchmen there would have been nothing more than a sense that he had got what he deserved, and yet with Fenton's action it was as though the whole ethical superiority of the Philhellene world lay in tatters, as if in a moment of collective panic they glimpsed in his crime not just the moral ambiguity at the heart of their own lives but the sordid logic of all their conceited pieties.

From all the surviving evidence Fenton had actually been a sociable and popular figure before the assassination attempt but now there was nothing that could not be said of him – and believed – as the Philhellene community recoiled in moral revulsion from the posthumous contagion of his memory. In one version he had been in collusion with Ghouras or Kariaskaki, in a second, Mavrocordato, in a third about to desert to the Turks the very day Humphreys had visited the cave on 24 May. No one asked how he could have been in league with the Turks and Mavrocordato at the same time. No one wanted to know what had happened to the money the government was alleged to have paid to the soldiers it would have bought, or why the execution of so finely tuned a plot should have been left to Whitcombe.

No one wanted to look or think further than the demonized scapegoat who was now mercifully dead. Humphreys was almost physically sick at the thought that he had once shaken the assassin's bloody hand. Fenton was 'a young man endowed with great personal advantages, but a cold blooded deliberate ruffian,' wrote Howe, who never met him.[7] 'Among the inmates of the cavern was one Mr Fenton,' James Emerson wrote for *The Times*:

a native of Scotland, who had arrived a mere adventurer in Greece, last winter, when during intercourse with the European residents in the Morea, he had proved himself totally divested of every principle or feeling of a gentleman. He had even stooped so low as to offer himself to a person in power as the assassin of Ulysses, for a remuneration of a few dollars – I believe not more than 60. The proposal had been accepted, but a disagreement in terms, or some other circumstances, had prevented its execution. The publicity which Fenton had given to the depravity of his character among his countrymen rendering his residence with the Europeans impossible, an order from the Government to leave Napoli di Romania determined him on joining the party of the very man whom he had offered to assassinate, and to whom his quarrel with the government was a sufficient recommendation. He was accordingly received among the inmates of the cave, where Mr. Trelawny, almost totally separated from

intercourse with his countrymen, was not aware of his des-
picable character.[8]

If the desire to bury Fenton's crimes with his bones was almost
universal, there were two Philhellenes, however, for whom his death
had a sharper relevance, the Englishman, Humphreys, who had
introduced Whitcombe to the cave in the first place, and the figure
behind the original plot, George Jarvis.

There is so little known of Jarvis's movements in the early part
of 1825 that it is difficult to be sure what if any role he played in
the last, drawn-out rites of the Mavre Troupa. Through the autumn
of the previous year it was his energy that had kept the plot alive,
but a single surviving letter to Mavrocordato written in February
suggests that by the time that Whitcombe arrived in Greece the
government's vacillations were wearing away even his enthusiasm
for the cause.

With the invasion of Ibrahim's Egyptians that same month, however, there can have been little time anyway for Fenton or the cave,
and after this there is no evidence of any communication between
the two men at all. It is of course possible that he went on pressing
Mavrocordato in Nauplia, but from at least 28 March, when Jarvis
and the Prince both left with the Greek army for the south, it seems
safe to assume that Fenton was on his own.

The campaign for the relief of Navarino was one of the great
turning points of the war, proof even to the Greeks that irregular
soldiers were no match for trained troops, and for Jarvis himself it
seems to have been a watershed. On his release from captivity in
Ibrahim's first and last act of clemency, he made his way back to
Nauplia ostensibly the same man he had been before, and yet behind
the mask it would seem that something had altered, that the old
intimacy with Mavrocordato had weakened, and that Fenton, Trelawny, the cave and everything to do with it belonged to a past
which calmly and ruthlessly he put behind him as if it had never
happened, silencing with his cool, quiet version of events the doubts
of men like Howe who did know of his involvement.

'The account given of Fenton's character is of the worst description,' the Rev Charles Swan, the chaplain of the *Cambrian* eagerly reported.

> What he did was solely for money; and it appears, from good authority, that he associated both with Ulysses and Trelawny for the express purpose of selling them. This assertion is made upon the authority of Mr Gervase [Jarvis], the American formerly mentioned, who introduced him to Mavrocordato, and discontinued his acquaintance on Fenton's intimating a design to murder his friend, the man upon whom he was dependent, and with whom he lived in the strictest terms of intimacy!! Such is the statement of Gervase, who regrets, as he well may, having had the least acquaintance with him.[9]

Elusive, frustrating and finally unknowable as Jarvis remains, the real mystery of the cave surrounds the role of another foreigner who has drifted almost unnoticed through Trelawny's story, the young W.H. Humphreys.

There is typically little that can be said with any confidence of Humphreys's part in this drama, but if there is one undisputed fact it is that it was he who brought the invitation to Whitcombe to visit the cave in the first place. It is quite possible that this was as innocent and uninformative as he later claimed, although if that is the case certain problems arising from his own visit to the Mavre Troupa only days before the assassination attempt remain unresolved.

As an officer in the government's pay and an admirer of Odysseus, Humphreys might well have seen a broker's role for himself at the cave, but the real sticking point lies in his friendship with Fenton. In his own account of this he understandably establishes all the distance he can between himself and a hated assassin, but Whitcombe's version of these same events puts a different and darker gloss on things. 'Charmed by Mr Humphreys's account of the excessive intrepidity, honour, romantic situation & & of his friend Fenton,' Whitcombe wrote,

> I was induced by the repeated, by the urgent entreaties of that Mr. Humphreys, added to a letter (expressing the most

pressing invitation from Fenton addressed to Humphreys, with many dark mystic expressions, known only I presume, to himself) – I was induced, I say, to pay that visit to the cave. On my arrival I was beset by Fenton's utmost talents of duplicity (in which no mortal man excelled him). Touched by his mournful tales of wrongs, rejection, deprivation of right, viewing him only as the romantic, the injured, the generous hero he had been represented by Humphreys, I swore to stand by him on his resolution to recover his rights or die.[10]

There can be no reason why Whitcombe should lie here, and Humphreys's own apprehensions about seeing Trelawny lend a certain weight to his claims, and yet it is hard to believe his involvement was anything but accidental. There was something too priggishly and self-consciously high-minded about Humphreys ever to have allowed him to sink to murder, and what seems more likely is that in the complex bartering and dealings that surrounded the cave he unwittingly played into Fenton's hands in a way he later tried to hide.

Historical characters, at any rate, are entitled to the same benefit of the doubt as anyone else, and when the first word of the assassination reached Humphreys at Ghouras's camp on 15 June he reacted with a speed that probably reflects more on his good nature than his guilt.

That same night he set off to find out whether Trelawny was still alive, marching this time under the watchful escort of Yanakis and ten of Ghouras's soldiers. Their route took them over the same desolate schist Whitcombe had crossed only eight days before, and past the near deserted Jerusalem Monastery on the eastern slopes of Parnassus. There was torrential rain, thunder and lightning and it was late into the night by the time they crossed the Kakoreme at the bottom of the gorge.

After the events of the last Saturday Humphreys would never have got near the cave with Ghouras's men, and under the cover of darkness he darted into a thick tangle of scrub near the chapel of St George to evade his escort. Going on alone, he reached the base of the cliff as dawn broke, and sheltered there in a small cave until it seemed safe to see Trelawny.

Humphreys's caution is interesting, because even if he later tried to laugh it off, it underlines just how aware he was of the look of things, of the kind of accusations that Whitcombe might have brought against him. 'I was amused at Cameron's [Komerone] perplexity at the supposition I could have been concerned,' he wrote,

> my unexpected appearance at the cave, my being now a government captain, and my correspondence with Fenton while with Kariaskaki, all tended to make Whitcombe's assertion very plausible, and the men naturally suspected me.[11]

Whatever the doubts of Komerone, however, it would seem that Trelawny at least was convinced of his innocence. When Humphreys was finally allowed up the ladders he found him lying where he had been carried five days earlier, propped up on a couch with Tersitza and her mother at his side. His lungs were obviously affected, but his voice was still strong and he spoke without great difficulty, tracing out for Humphreys the story of the previous Saturday.

It must have been a strange and tense encounter under Komerone's watchful gaze, suspicions on one side, protestations on the other, and only yards away the assassin himself, his life hanging from the same tenuous thread as Trelawny's own. There were details in Trelawny's story that differ from other accounts, but in its main lines it was essentially the same. Right to the end he had had no suspicions of Fenton, though Komerone had. Asked why he had not informed Trelawny, Komerone's answer had a simple but authentic ring: Trelawny would have blown his brains out if he had said anything.

In spite of Humphreys's account, however, we know little of Trelawny's state of mind in these weeks after the shooting. In his *Recollections* he gave a wonderfully spare and vivid description of his physical sufferings, but if he ever secretly wondered at the hatred he had inspired in two fellow-Philhellenes or the ease with which Fenton had seduced Whitcombe he was silent about it.

He wrote nothing either about facing up to the prospect of his own death. Throughout his later years he would speak of it with an indifference that seems perfectly genuine, but even for a man who regarded old age with an almost visceral disgust, the intense loneliness of his plight must have brought despair perilously close.

But with his ambitions in ruins, nursed by a child-bride and her mother who spoke no English, immured in a cavern that had become a prison, Trelawny was still able to put up a front for Humphreys that remains impenetrable. Before he left that evening, however, Humphreys was allowed to see the prisoner, who was more eloquent about his sufferings. Fenton had poisoned his mind with promises of treasure and women, Whitcombe told him, and with claims that Trelawny had betrayed Odysseus, and that he, Fenton, was in touch with Odysseus and only waiting 'authority from him to shoot Trelawny as a traitor'.[12]

It was only his immense strength that had kept Trelawny alive this far, and after talking with Whitcombe Humphreys found himself a mule in Tithorea and set off for Nauplia and help. The weather was even worse than the previous night, the driving rain and intense blackness making the narrow mountain paths almost impassable. It had been Humphreys's plan to slip past Ghouras's camp as quickly as possible, but mid way through the night the weather defeated him and he was forced to take shelter in a ruined church. The next morning, after only an hour's sleep, and a fraught night shared with a company of deserters going over to the Turks, he continued on through Dystomo and the last few miles down to Aspra Spitia.

The only vessels now that sailed between here and Corinth were ferrying corn or troops across to Ghouras's army from the Morea, and it was the evening of the next day before he was able to secure a passage. It was a perilous journey. There was room only to stand on the crowded deck, and the caique sat so low that it barely cleared the water. Halfway across the gulf a sudden squall threatened to sink them, but then just as suddenly the wind dropped and with the help of oars they were able to make Corinth, where the first news which greeted him was of Odysseus's death.

It was again late before Humphreys could find himself a horse, but riding all night he reached Nauplia on the morning of the 20th having slept no more than a few hours in the last five days. The first person he met in the town was Jarvis, and knowing that anything he said would find its way to Mavrocordato told him that he was on his way to Gastoumi on the western coast of the Morea. He then went to find a Dr Tyndall, and arranged to travel back to the cave with him the next day. The following morning, however, as they were riding through the gate of the town, Humphreys was seen from the battlements by the Minister for War, and as an officer in the government army detained for leaving camp without permission. 'Leave a Greek camp without leave!' Humphreys wrote of it indignantly,

> There was not a shadow of excuse in such a here unheard of proceeding. I cocked and drew a pistol from my belt. Had there been a gesture made to attack me, I should have used it; but the minister of police coming up to me, implored me to surrender. I really saw no use in taking the lives of the wretches who surrounded me, or of losing my own without any reason, and I threw the pistol down; and then, for very vexation, burst into tears.[13]

Whatever Humphreys's unwitting part in Fenton's plot, he had done everything he could to make amends and his tears are those of an exhausted man. That night he spent in a Nauplia gaol with a deserter, a robber and a murderer, and the next day gave his parole on the condition that Mavrocordato would do nothing to prevent Tyndall treating Trelawny's wounds. How natural, Mavrocordato had told the doctor, that he should wish to go *'pour servir son compatriote'*. 'He professed, instead of wishing to impede his progress,' Humphreys scornfully recorded, 'to be willing to render him every facility, and assured him the government would afford an escort for his journey.'[14]

Humphreys's sarcasm, though, was a luxury he could ill afford, because he was now immured in a town under threat of siege. After the fall of Navarino Ibrahim's troops had advanced eastwards across the Morea, sacking and burning the re-built Tripolis and swelling Nauplia with a new wave of terrified refugees.

It seemed only a matter of time before the capital itself was invested, but on 24 June the Egyptian army was at last held in the heroic Battle of the Mills on the western side of the bay. From his confinement a frustrated Humphreys listened to the sound of fighting. 'St George and Merry England!' he wrote. 'I was as badly off as Ivanhoe, and had no lovely Rebecca to answer my question, "How speeds the fight?"'[15]

There was time, however, for one last Philhellene extravagance before he was done, one final piece of romance to help him forget what he was doing in Nauplia. Two days after the Battle of the Mills, a squadron of Turkish cavalry foraging for livestock appeared outside the walls of the town. Riding out with a band thirty strong to attack them, Humphreys took the lead, driving his horse straight at a party of fifty mamelukes. 'My horse was a fine Arab, but very unmanageable,' he wrote.

> Charging alone, and presenting my pistol, which missed fire, and wheeling á la Turque, he turned restive, which being perceived, the Turks singled me out, and their shots whizzed right and left . . . It was pretty sight enough, and the whole town was on the ramparts looking on.[16]

Even for Humphreys, however, drawn back again and again to Greece in spite of himself, medieval pageantry was in the end not enough. As he rode back into the town, he was forced to watch helplessly as a Turkish prisoner was hacked to pieces in front of him. His resilience, his energy were almost at an end. 'Oh for an English vessel,'[17] was all he could think, and the next morning, as Captain Hamilton, the senior officer in the area, arrived with the *Cambrian*, his prayers were answered. That same day, 29 June, Humphreys wrote to him.

Sir,

It appears that the Greek Government have already mentioned to you the affair of the cave of Ulysses. How they have
stated the affair I know not; but Captain Hamilton, who has
been so long on the Mediterranean station, must be well
aware, not every word from a Greek merits belief. I am now
under arrest on that account. The plea they state is ground-
less. They arrest me because I left the camp without leave.
I did not do so. I had the permission of my general to go to
the cave, when I was first informed of the atrocious attempt
to assassinate Trelawney. I found him in imminent danger,
from want of medical assistance. I came instantly to Napoli
to procure it, without returning to the camp it is true, as
going and returning would have occupied two days. I ask
you, as a military man, whether, in our service, I should not
have been perfectly justified in so doing: and here, where
military regulations and discipline have not an existence, is
absurd to a degree, and in the case of a native captain,
would never have been thought of. (The villain Fenton, the
perpetrator of the act, was, some months ago, engaged by
Mavrocordato to murder both Ulysses and Trelawney. I was
then with Ulysses, before he joined the Turks, and Fenton
at that time carried on the intrigue, under the pretence, to
us (true or false) of entrapping Mavrocordato. A Mr Jarvis,
an American now here, was Mavrocordato's chief agent in
that affair: it passed over: but the other day, Trelawney was
attempted to be assassinated by this same Fenton, and
immediately after, Ulysses was killed (how, heaven knows) at
Athens.) I am arrested and imprisoned, among thieves and
assassins, because I came for a surgeon for Trelawney. What
I now demand, is to be set at liberty, or, if they have any
charge against me, to be tried. I am vexed to find myself
obliged to occupy your attention on affairs, but I should feel
obliged if you would exercise your influence in my favour.[18]

The next day, the 30th, Humphreys heard a rumour that Dr Tyndall
had been held by the government's orders at Corinth. Considering
himself absolved from his parole, he followed up his letter to Hamil-

ton in person, and secured from him a promise that if necessary he would send the ship's surgeon to Trelawny.

Humphreys had done all that he could, mentally and physically. On 1 July, twenty days after the assassination attempt, a note arrived from Tyndall saying that he had been delayed by nothing more treacherous than adverse winds. Humphreys however had reached the end of his tether. With Mavrocordato's assent – keen simply to rid himself of a man publicly slandering him – he boarded the *Rose* under the command of Captain Abbot and, on 2 July, sailed for Zante. The sight of so many English faces was enough to reduce him almost to tears. That night he slept, the first night in months, in 'snow white sheets'[19] in a hammock prepared for him, mercifully unconscious of the judgement his fellow countrymen were passing on him. 'His conduct, by his own shewing, has been most injudicious and improper,' the Chaplain of the *Cambrian* wrote, before sweeping into a general prayer for Greece and Greeks to be spared from Philhellenism:

> He left the army without permission, and being a known and acknowledged partizan of Ulysses, corresponded with Trelawny, and forsook his duty to succour his friend . . . Besides which, he has written a virulent letter to Mavrocordato, accusing him of bribery and assassination, in the instance of Trelawny, as well as of a design to carry him off in the same manner! These facts warrant a harsher proceeding than an arrest on parole . . .
>
> But above all, keep from them that Quixotic class of interlopers who run about the country peeping into this corner, and bouncing out of that; meddling with affairs above their comprehension, and disturbing the national councils with a crude train of school-boy dreams and maudlin fancies.[20]

It goes against the grain to agree with the navy's answer to Mr Collins, but on this occasion Swan was right. It is unlikely that Humphreys ever knew what he had blundered into, and could never allow himself to recognize the part he had played in Fenton's plans.

He had also failed, in spite of all his efforts, to rescue Trelawny, whose fate now lay out of his hands. He described the wounds to the surgeon on the *Rose*, and was told that by now Trelawny was either dead, 'or had he survived to the present time, he would no longer be in such imminent danger . . . The die then was cast, or there was no immediate fear for his life.'[21]

On the 9th the *Rose* docked at Cephalonia, and Humphreys went into the lazaretto to serve out his quarantine. From there he wrote to Sir Frederick Adam, Maitland's successor in Corfu, to Colonel Napier and to John Cam Hobhouse back in England, to try and whip up official support for Trelawny. On the 12th a reply arrived from Adam, stating that he 'could not officially interfere, though he had no objection to any vessel that happened to be near the spot, extricating them'.[22]

The official response in England, when Humphreys's letter reached Hobhouse with news of the cave, was even more cautious. A letter from George Canning survives, written at Welbeck in answer to a plea from Trelawny's uncle Sir Christopher Hawkins for help. 'I had the honour to receive yesterday evening your two letters of the 12th inst.' Canning wrote:

> To the first I can only reply by expressing my satisfaction in your good opinion, & my obligation for your tender of support.
>
> To the second, after the fullest consideration of its evidence, I am really at a loss how to reply – for I do not see what it is possible for me to do in the case to which it refers, even if it were proper [?] to do anything. British subjects in defiance of an act of Parlt engage in the war between the Turks and the Greeks.
>
> It is hardly possible to persuade the Turkish Gov't that this is done without the consent, if without the direct instigation of the British Government. Hundreds of British subjects are scattered through the Turkish Dominions, with their families, & their fortunes – all of which are put in jeopardy by the irregular zeal of their compatriots – and

then, when one of these warriors (who is thus risking the lives of his countrymen, & acting in defiance of the law) gets into difficulty, his Govt is called upon to get him out of it.

Surely it must be plain that an application to the Turkish Power in favour of a British subject taken in arms with the Greeks would be construed into an avowal that the British Govt did allow of such service – for otherwise why interfere for a breaker of the laws? So the Turks would reason – not unfairly – and if the consequence of such reasoning should be the pillage or imprisonment of British merchants at Constantinople, or at Smyrna, who would be to blame?

But the case of your nephew is more difficult even than the one that I have supposed. For he is in danger from Greeks as well as Turks: having sided, it appears, with a beaten party among the many conflicting parties into which Greece is divided.

I beg you to look over again the picture which your correspondent draws of their distractions, and then ask yourself how it would be possible for the British Govt (which has studiously avoided mixing in any of them) to change its conduct – from abstinence to interference – for the chance of helping – but how I protest I do not know – an individual who has thought fit against the warning of the law to plunge himself into such a quarrel.

I trust the particularity with which I have considered your request will satisfy you of my willingness to pay a proper attention to it – but I really & truly do not see how I can, consistently with [public] duty, or (if I could overlook that consideration) how I could with any reasonable chance of benefit, interfere in behalf of Mr Trelawny.[23]

Canning's argument was unanswerable, but even if he had wished to help it would long have been too late. As Humphreys prepared to return to England in a bid to interest the British government in the Greek cause, events were already outpacing his information on the cave. Assistance was coming from much closer at hand. At the beginning of August the word reached Cephalonia that the *Sparrowhawk* and a Major Bacon had sailed from Nauplia in a bid to rescue Trelawny. 'When British tars put their hands to a work,' Humphreys wrote in his diary on 3 August, Englishman to the very end, 'one is sure that what men can do will be done.'[24] With Francis D'Arcy Bacon aboard – the same Bacon who had wandered into Odysseus's camp at Charoneia – his confidence was justified.

11

ENTER THE MAJOR

'The major is one of your odd sort of fishes, who has been wandering about in Russia, Turkey and Persia, the devil knows where or what for.'

Journal of Samuel Gridley Howe[1]

AT THE EDGE OF the path that leads to the door of the church of St James Friern Barnet a dozen miles north of London, stands a small stone tomb. A sycamore has begun to envelop it from one side, while a small yew hides it from sight on the other. An inscription records that it is the resting place of

John Bacon Esq., of Friern House,
Departed this life Feb 26th 1816, Aged 78.

There is something peculiarly baleful in the nineteenth century's penchant for commemorating lives in terms of property, and yet with 'Friar' Bacon, as he was known to his friends, and Friern House, this was not wholly out of place. The house was a comforting blend of Georgian elegance and medieval romance for which Bacon had paid 10,000 guineas, a gentleman's seat which, in the manner of Jane Austen's Northanger Abbey, simultaneously declared the improving ambitions of its owner without suggesting the taint of new money.

Behind the house, with its eighteenth-century facade and older core, its wrought-iron gates and medieval cloisters, the park dropped away steeply to a small brook before rising again towards the lands in Finchley which the canny Bacon acquired when the common was enclosed. From the front the view stretched out eastwards across the Lea Valley to Essex; to the south, lay London and the family town house in Grafton Street; and to the north an avenue connected the house with the churchyard where John Bacon now lies buried.

The tomb is the Bacons' only monument and, except for a hatchment high above the chancel arch in the church, the solitary link between the family and a part of London they once briefly owned. Just across the road from St James's a public park still preserves part of the old estate, but John Bacon's manor has long since gone, his Roubiliac Handel and Bacon portraits – Lord Keeper, Chancellor, Roger – dispersed, his land broken up and built over, the family name and all their ambitions and energy buried with an even-handed irony beneath the site of the nineteenth century's most famous lunatic asylum, Colney Hatch, and the North Middlesex Golf Club.*

John Bacon himself lies alone, without antecedents or descendants to dignify his dynastic ambitions. On his tomb, however, there is a second inscription. It is of a later date than that commemorating the 'Friar' himself, but it is virtually illegible now, its incised lettering obscured beneath the vein-like tracery of ivy and the grey mottling of lichen, decipherable only when the sun's rays catch it at an angle. 'In Memory Of Major Francis D'Arcy Bacon,' it once read,

> Second son of the above John Bacon Esq.
> and of Mary his wife daughter of John Linnell, Esq.
> who departed this life Dec 2nd 1842 Aged 64 and whose remains
> are interred at St Mary's Lambeth.

Nothing could seem more apt than the obscurity that has enclosed the life of a man known to literature only as 'the Major', but behind the apparent respectability of that title has lain buried for 150 years one of Philhellenism's most engaging and improbable characters.

The difficulty of recovering a story like Bacon's at this distance, too, the very faintness of the trail which leads back to him, provides a perfect metaphor for the obscurity so many Philhellenes sought in Greece. For every volunteer who wanted fame there must have been a dozen who were only there in search of an oblivion as deep as the grave, and the determined anonymity of these men is sometimes the best clue to their identities that we have, the first and often only indication that, as with Bacon, there is a reason why they did not wish to be known.*

Francis D'Arcy Bacon was born in London on 27 May 1778, the second son of Mary Linnell and John Bacon, a man widely regarded in his lifetime as an illegitimate child of Frederick, Prince of Wales.† Little is known of John Bacon's childhood or family but at an early age he entered the 'civil service' of the Church of England, rising in a long and distinguished career to be Receiver of the First Fruits and the prestigious Secretary to the Sons of the Clergy.

With the help of a £20,000 fortune brought by his wife, a daughter of the great Linnell furniture-making family, and an entrepreneurial sharpness which would now be called insider-dealing, John Bacon made the smooth transition from professional to landowner, becoming a well-known and respected figure in London society and a Justice of the Peace at Friern Barnet.

For a man of this position and social aspirations at the end of the eighteenth century, the army would have been a logical career for his second son, and in 1798, after four years at Harrow and a brief flirtation with the First Fruits Office, D'Arcy Bacon was commissioned into the infantry with a lieutenancy in the 5th of Foot.**

It is one of the galling ironies of military life that during a period of national crisis it is possible to see as little action as during a time of profound peace, and Bacon's career was not a distinguished one. He joined his regiment when it was stationed in Lincolnshire, recruiting a second battalion to meet the growing threat posed by the rise of Napoleon, and for the next fourteen years this was very much the pattern of his army life – soldiering of the desultory sort that forms the background to so many nineteenth-century novels, with balls in Boston and the thanks of the civic authorities in Chichester, recruitment in Northampton and garrison duty in Clonmel – a career of blameless boredom punctuated only by two brief campaigns in the Low Countries and South America which rank among the most spectacular displays of British military incompetence.*

In 1812, a brevet major by purchase in the 19th Light Dragoons, Bacon resigned his commission to begin a life that is best followed now in the long trail of debts which he left behind. His father's death in 1816 was followed by a series of complex financial disputes and litigation which, at this distance, it is almost impossible to disentangle, but wherever the responsibility ultimately lies for the collapse of the family's fortunes most of the land the sons inherited was already gone when, seven years later, his elder brother, John William, was imprisoned for his share of debts amounting, in modern terms, to millions.

A list of these debts survives from the time of his arrest in 1823, preserved in the London Record Office, and they give a wonderfully colourful picture of the brothers' lives over the previous decade. From an early draft of their father's will it is clear that there had been financial extravagances as early as 1802, but it is only in the years either side of John Bacon's death that D'Arcy in particular seems to have finally cut loose to attack his financial difficulties with that creative zest which is the hallmark of Regency England.

There was nothing that they would not try to raise money on, no bill too large or petty to be left unpaid. There are unpaid bills for school fees and clothes, for livery, tithes, wood, hairdresser, even for their father's funerary hatchment in Friern Barnet church. There are dubious land deals and constant mortgagings and remortgagings, life assurances on friends and family guaranteed and the annuities never paid. There are Bills of Exchange unhonoured, capital debts and lawyers's bills left to accumulate interest, every conceivable ruse for raising credit in early nineteenth-century England explored and finally exhausted. At the beginning of the document the alleged grandson of 'Poor Fred' and heir to all John Bacon's dynastic ambitions has put his signature to a list of the possessions allowed him in gaol: '1 coat, 3 waistcoats,' for instance, valued at 30/-; 1 pair trousers, 7/-; 2 shirts, 2 pairs of stockings 12/6; 6 kerchiefs, 1 hat, 1 pair of shoes. And for his wife, still at Friern Barnet: '3 gowns, 4 peticoats, 2 stockings, 1 pair of stays,' clothes for their infant child, a couple of mattresses, a bed, a bolster, two pairs of sheets,

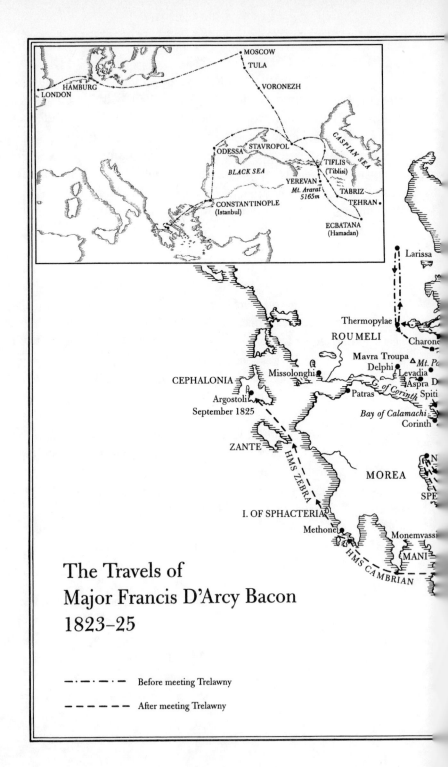

MOSCOW
TULA
VORONEZH
HAMBURG
LONDON
STAVROPOL
ODESSA
CASPIAN SEA
BLACK SEA
TIFLIS
(Tiblisi)
YEREVAN
Mt. Ararat
5165m
TABRIZ
TEHRAN
CONSTANTINOPLE
(Istanbul)
ECBATANA
(Hamadan)

Larissa

Thermopylae
ROUMELI
Charone
Mavra Troupa △ Mt. Pa
Delphi
Levadia
Missolonghi
Aspra D
CEPHALONIA
G. of Corinth Spiti
Patras
Argostoli
September 1825
Bay of Calamachi
Corinth

ZANTE
MOREA
N
SPE
HMS ZEBRA

I. OF SPHACTERIA
Methone
Monemvassi
MANI
HMS CAMBRIAN

The Travels of
Major Francis D'Arcy Bacon
1823–25

—·—·—·—   Before meeting Trelawny

— — — — —   After meeting Trelawny

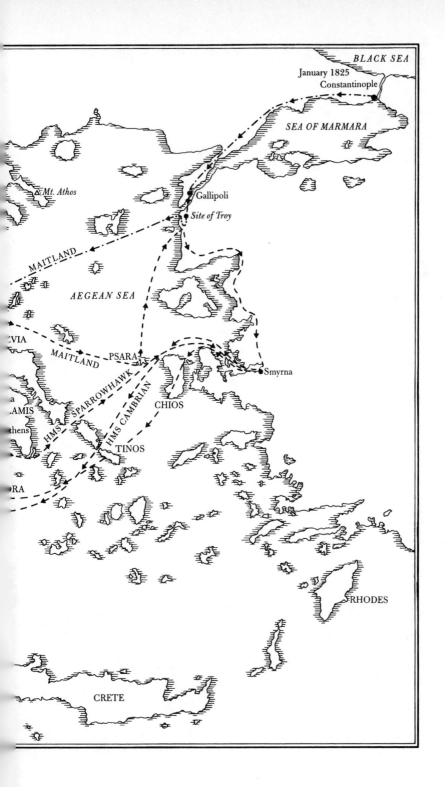

BLACK SEA

January 1825
Constantinople

SEA OF MARMARA

△ Mt. Athos

Gallipoli

Site of Troy

MAITLAND

AEGEAN SEA

MAITLAND   PSARA

Smyrna

SPARROWHAWK

HMS CAMBRIAN

HMS

CHIOS

TINOS

VIA

AMIS

thens

RA

RHODES

CRETE

a blanket, a table, two chairs – the whole list coming to £17–16–0, £2–4–0 inside the £20 allowed to debtors. Following on this is a total list of debts amounting in all to £67,923. Finally, there is a note. 'Causes of Insolvency,' it begins: 'I attribute my insolvency to having entered into securities for my brother Francis D'Arcy Bacon.'[2]

By the time he signed this however, however, his brother D'Arcy, with debts to John William alone of £4,613, had left the country on a journey of almost eight thousand miles that would keep him safely out of England for the next three years. He had sailed from London for Hamburg by steam packet three months before John William's arrest, and travelled eastwards through Lübeck, Trasemunde, Riga, and Novigorod to Moscow – 'of all cities the most interesting to the traveller'[3] – before heading south by sledge and then horse into the Caucasus and the Persian Empire.

A change of scale, a widening of vision, a breath of air that is perhaps no more than the inevitable corollary of Russian travel enters into Trelawny's story with this journey of Francis D'Arcy Bacon. It is as if the imaginative yearnings of the romantic mind were suddenly given their head, as the cold and empty wildernesses that touched writers as diverse as Mary Shelley and Charlotte Brönte stretched out in an endless vista ahead of him. Leaving Moscow in the intense cold of January 1824, Bacon headed almost due south across a landscape of unbroken steppe towards Stavropol, his sledge gliding effortlessly across the frozen surface under a sky of constant blue, the air calm, the atmosphere dry, temperatures of 20 to 30° below zero nothing to a man for whom the immediate alternative was the King's Bench prison.

South of Varonez this exhilarating sense of liberty, of emptiness only increased. Nothing, now, marked his progress except the occasional desolate station post, an ancient burial mound, or the 'rude carved figures'[4] that littered his route. Beyond Stavropol he turned east towards the headquarters of Russia's Circassian Army at Georgievsk, and then from Mosdoc south again through Kasbek at 14,000 feet above the Caspian Sea before descending through the Kobi pass to what is now the modern Tbilisi.

The story of Bacon's involvement with Trelawny only properly begins with the major's appearance at Livadia but this journey south across the vast land mass of Russia illuminates an aspect of the Greek war that the narrow focus of factional politics can easily obscure. There is of its very nature a tendency to see Philhellene history in terms of individuals and personalities, yet Bacon's travels are a reminder that, in the language of another war, their involvement was no more than a 'sideshow of a sideshow' to European governments for whom the revolt was less a matter of ideals than of the strategic and political consequences of Ottoman decline and growing Russian might.

The golden age of Russophobia still lay in the future but that infatuation with the Russian 'soul' which periodically grips the British public was already giving way in 1824 to an alarm for which Bacon's journal provides interestingly early evidence.* Throughout his travels the tastes and observations of this accidental Philhellene remain those of the gentleman dilettante, interested in everything from Nestorian Churches to trout fishing and the quality of game. As he moves south, however, towards the Persian border, the trained eye of a soldier focuses with increasing alarm on Russia's military might, noting the strengths and weaknesses of border posts, the conditions of roads and communications, or the state and size at Niclieff of the Russian fleet threatening Constantinople and the Eastern Mediterranean.

In January 1824 Bacon had recorded the Muscovite belief that their generation would see the cross supplant the crescent over Constantinople and as he crossed into the Ottoman Empire almost a year later there seemed little to suggest their confidence was misplaced. While in 'the City' he watched with admiration the progress of Sultan Mahmoud to Friday prayer, and yet there was no sign that the superb spectacle of Ottoman rule was anything more than pageant, or that Mahmoud's attempts at modernizing his empire were bearing fruit.

Leaving the city by the same gate that had seen the first breach in 1453 Bacon headed south. His original plan after Constantinople had been to travel down the Asian coast as far as Smyrna, but after a few days shooting game and rehearsing his Homeric geography in the Troad, he 'fell in' with an English captain shipping Turkish grain to Greek rebels and accepted instead the offer of a passage to 'the seat of the present war'.[5]

The exact chronology of Bacon's travels at this point is uncertain, but it was probably sometime in February 1825 or even later, after wandering as far north as Reshid Pasha's headquarters at Larissa, that Bacon was woken from an exhausted sleep among the ruins of Livadia and brought in as a prisoner to Odysseus's camp. We have already seen his own account of the night he spent there during the meeting with the Turkish Aga, but it is perhaps worth picking up the thread of the narrative with Trelawny's own version of their first meeting because, different as it is in every detail from the description in Bacon's journal, different in its numbers, geography and tone, it provides our most vivid and engaging portrait of this curious and endearing traveller who was to play such a vital role in his story.

> It was early in February we stopped at Talanta on a wet stormy night: in selecting his quarters, our chief with his usual sagacity fixed upon the ruins of a Greek church, situated, as the Greek churches, chapels, and monasteries usually are, on an elevated and defensible site – the town was abandoned and in ruins. After we had supped and were smoking our pipes, some of the Greek patrols came in, saying they had captured two Franks. They were ordered to bring them in. I told the chief to make no allusion to me, but to question them through his secretary.
>
> As they entered, one of them observed to his comrade in English, 'What a set of cut-throats! Are they Greeks or Turks?'
>
> 'Mind what you say.'
>
> 'Oh! they only want our money,' answered the other. 'I hope they will give us something to eat before they cut our throats. I am famished.'
>
> Certainly appearances were against us. At one end of the building, Odysseus, the Greek chief, the Turkish Bey, and I sat smoking our pipes. At the other end, within the church,

stood our horses saddled, ready for mounting, the soldiers lying down in clusters along the sides, with all their gear on, for neither Greeks nor Turks divest themselves of a single article of dress or arms during the night. Their hands still grasped the weapons, and they slept so lightly that if in talking a voice was raised their eager wolfish eyes were instantly on the speaker. On the strangers entering, some of the soldiers sprang up, others leant on their elbows to listen or rather to look on, for they could not understand a word. The travellers told their story, – stating that they were last from Smyrna, and had landed that morning from an English brig, at a small port in the Gulf of Euboea, with no other object than to see the country. Neither of the chiefs believed them, nor did I; nevertheless, they were treated hospitably, had supper, coffee, and pipes, and their baggage placed beside them. They sat together in a spare corner close to us, with no arms but fowling-pieces. One of them was very ill at his ease, the other, who I learnt from their discourse was a Major, took things as coolly as if he had been at an inn, said the cold lamb (it was goat) was the best he had ever tasted, and asked the Greek attendant if he had no rackie (spirit), the only Romaic word he had learnt. Odysseus, understanding what he wanted, told the boy to give him wine.

'If they are robbers,' exclaimed the Major, 'they are damned good fellows, so I drink success to their next foray.' Soon after one of them lay down in a dark corner. Turks, Greeks, and all orientals consider it the greatest possible insult, as well as an outrage to decency, for anyone in public to change his garments or expose any part of his person below the waist. The major was a remarkably tall, gaunt, bony man: after finishing his wine, he set to work to make up a comfortable bed with horse-cloths, slips of carpet, a bag for a pillow, &c.; when he had done this to his satisfaction, we supposed he would lie down, as his companion had done. On the contrary, he deliberately, as if in his own barrack room, utterly regardless of our presence, took off his boots, socks, coat, waistcoat, trousers, and shirt, folding each article carefully up and placing it by his bedside. Thus exhibiting himself in all possible attitudes stark naked, he leisurely filled the bowl of his Turkish pipe, and advanced towards us to light it at the fire.

The two chiefs at first looked on the Major's novel proceedings with curiosity, as visitors in the Zoological Gardens do at the hippopotamus; but as the process of stripping advanced, they looked serious; the shirt scene took away their breath; their pipes went out when the major advanced towards them. The Turk started up in horror with his hand on his sword. The major, supposing he was making way for him from civility, and unconscious of giving any offence, made a very polite bow to us generally; and, in a gentle and conciliatory tone, said, in his own language, 'Pray, gentlemen, keep your seats, don't let me disturb you;' he then bent his body into a sharp angle, so as to draw a light from the burning embers. The position he stood in was so ludicrous, that Odysseus and I could not resist laughing. The Major, considering this a token of good fellowship, insisted on shaking hands with us, saying, 'I am sure you are both good fellows – Good night!'

I now saw by the light of the fire that he was not absolutely naked, for he had a leather waistcoat and drawers on, but they fitted as tight as his skin, and were exactly of the same colour.[6]

One of the consequences of prolonged exposure to Trelawny is a natural temptation to prefer almost any alternative source but with the account of this same incident in *The Journal of the Travels and Wanderings by Major D'Arcy Bacon of the 19th Light Dragoons* this creates certain problems. There would usually be no reason to doubt a journal that was never intended for publication, and yet by the time that Bacon came to write it he was already a long way down that road which took him from the wealth of Friern Barnet to a

single room in a Battersea boarding house, and in the heroic glow
with which he covers these events we can probably glimpse their
importance to him in a life increasingly bereft of dignity or colour.

But even when every adjustment is made for time and distance,
there are few things in the career of Trelawny and Odysseus that
better illustrate the allure of their lives than the enthusiasm with
which Bacon threw himself into their affairs. There is nothing surprising in young romantics of the stamp of Humphreys or even the
young Finlay falling under their sway, but Bacon was a man of
forty-six at the time, a veteran of two of the most disillusioning
campaigns in British military history and not some vainglorious
Philhellene, an urbane and educated traveller with the resources and
style to have run up debts of thousands in Regency England and
the panache to have chosen the Caucasus in preference to the King's
Bench as the solution.

There was, however, nothing now that he was not prepared to
do to help Trelawny and Odysseus. When he slipped out of the
camp the morning after his first meeting with Trelawny, he was
carrying with him a request for help to Captain Hamilton of the
Cambrian. As he and his guides made their way through a glen of
dwarf myrtle among the hills above Charoneia they saw birds so
gorged with food that they could scarcely struggle off the ground
at their approach. A few yards further on the headless corpse of a
Roumeliot soldier lay where he had been recently killed. The eagles
already sated on his flesh, a fox had taken possession, and was so
intent on its prey that for all Bacon's shouting he could do no more
than drive it off a few paces.

The next day, after a night spent in a monastery still friendly to
Odysseus, Bacon made the coast and found a boat that would
take him to where the *Maitland* was moored off Thermopylae. He
discovered later that Odysseus had seen and fatally ignored the
vessel, but after Captain Emsworth had taken his ship as close in
to the rocky shore as he dared there was nothing left to them but
to head north for the Dardanelles and Constantinople.

It was the beginning of a mission for Bacon that would only end
five months later on the island of Zante, of a physical journey that

would take him on foot and ship from Smyrna to Parnassus, and of a mental odyssey that would take him from traveller to partisan and then, in the face of Turkish horrors, to full-blown Philhellene.

It was not long, either, before Bacon had his first graphic evidence of what Ottoman brutality could do. As the *Maitland* sailed along the coast of Euboea, a sudden squall got up, driving the ship eastwards and forcing Captain Emsworth to take refuge in a sheltered cove on the small and barren island of Psara, the most northerly and exposed of Greece's three maritime powers.

Not even the desolation of Roumeli, with its burned and ruined villages, had prepared Bacon for what he found. In the previous July the Turkish Capitan Pasha with a force of two hundred sail and fourteen thousand Janissaries, Arnauts and Anatolians had attacked an island population swollen by irregulars and refugees from mainland Asia. Caught by surprise, the defenders' losses were appalling. Over three and a half thousand islanders alone died, and probably as many again from Roumeli and mainland Asia, their heads piled high in a massive victory pyramid. Many of those who might have lived preferred death to the miseries of slavery, the women drowning themselves and their children rather than be taken prisoners. Even so, two hundred were despatched in triumph to Constantinople by the Capitan Pasha, along with another five hundred heads and twelve hundred ears which were displayed at the Seraglio gates in an act of belated revenge on the courage of the Psarian navy.*

Ten months later, when Bacon went ashore, the evidence of the massacre was still everywhere. 'The immolated corpses,' he recalled,

> unburied, lay bleaching by wind and sun, intermingled with the ruins of the fortress. There appeared to be no living thing on the island, except an aged monk, who came forth from some hiding place and thankfully received a donation of biscuit and a small bag of flour.[7]

Bacon was to see worse than this before he could redeem his promise to Trelawny but it is noticeable that after Psara the language of his journal changes. He would always remain in a sense a 'made' rather than a 'natural' Philhellene, closer in spirit to a later generation of 'Great Gamers' than the typical volunteer, but with Psara the iron of war entered into his soul and from now on the Turks are 'barbarians', their armies 'hordes' and 'fiends'. their religion 'perverted'.

As he began his great sweep of the Eastern Aegean in his search for Captain Hamilton, there was confirmation too at every stage, of the undisciplined fanaticism of Ottoman soldiery and the regulated ferocity of Imperial rule. When the *Maitland* finally reached the Dardanelles Bacon engaged a Janissary to accompany him down the Asian coast as far as Smyrna, and on the second day of their journey south he received his first authentic demonstration of the arbitrariness of life under the sultan. They had been joined on horseback by a Tartar Janissary from Constantinople on a 'special mission' to the Pasha of Pergamus. When they reached Andrimetti the party halted for two days while he conducted his business with the local authorities. On the third morning, as Bacon watched the Tartar ride out at daybreak, followed now by a precautionary escort of twenty cavalry, he learned what that entailed. The Janissary had a *schatti sherrif* to deliver, an imperial demand for the Pasha of Pergamus. 'Where thou deservest to die,' the command ran,

> it is our pleasure that after performing the *abdest* (washing of the head, hands & feet) and repeating the accustomed *Nomad* (prayer) thou deliver thy head to this our messenger.[8]

'Neither innocence of crime nor personal merit,' as Bacon wryly noted, were any insurance against imperial vengeance, and as they passed though Pergamus the next day they learned that for all the Pasha's popularity 'the affair' had gone off 'in the usual way'.[9]

It was on the Island of Scio or Chios, however, that Bacon finally caught up with the full terror that Asian Turks could inflict. Landing from a small boat on the eastern side of the island, he was met by a scene that was a repetition of Psara. Only now the natural beauty and fertility of the island, the sense of what it had once been, with its reputation for charm and ease, for the grace of its women and the almost effeminate softness of its culture, combined to give its present state an air of crowning desolation.

Over the first four years of the revolution the ships of Psara had done all they could to excite the revenge of the Porte but Chios had come only late and reluctantly into the war. Under Turkish rule its thriving and almost exclusively Orthodox population had enjoyed virtual independence, but when a force of insurgents under a Samian adventurer landed on the island and besieged the small Turkish garrison the population was drawn into a war that it could not possibly hope to survive.

At its closest Chios is no more than two miles from mainland Asia and when retribution came, it came with a savagery that seemed designed to make up for the previous lenience. The island was helpless to resist. It seems gratuitous to rehearse the details of the massacre that followed, the horrors of Chios are only too familiar from Tripolis, Navarino, Athens or Psara. What, though, cannot be ignored is the sheer scale of what happened here. Numbers for any battle or massacre during the war are notoriously inaccurate, but in their nicely rounded proximity the figures in Finlay's or Gordon's accounts are a poignant reminder of the cheapness of individual life. In the monastery of Aghios Minas alone, according to Finlay, five thousand were killed. In the eleventh-century monastery of Nea Mone another two thousand were slaughtered or burned alive; across the island twenty-five thousand in all, Gordon reckoned, the inmates of the hospital, madhouse and deaf and dumb institution not excluded, with another forty thousand women and children shipped off into captivity to glut the slave markets of Constantinople, Smyrna, Egypt and the Barbary Coast.

Delacroix's painting is only the most famous reminder that no single event in the whole course of the war did more to excite the indignation or sympathy of Christian Europe. In the spring of 1821 there had been 100,000 Greeks living on the island, with a thriving city, sixty-eight villages, three hundred convents and seven hundred churches. When Bacon landed three years later it was a graveyard, with only the occasional figure of a child, hiding naked among the ruins, reduced to a state little removed from that of a wild animal, disturbing the solitude that reigned on all sides. The plantations of mastic which had once supplied gum to the harems of the empire lay useless, the orchards of lemons, fig and mulberry untended and out of control. The whole island seemed to Bacon a wilderness of destruction. 'Not a house', he wrote of the main town,

> had escaped the visitation of the fiends who laid waste this terrestrial paradise: no inhabitants survived save some decrepit old women and some young children, whose parents had either been killed or carried into captivity, their helpless and useless infancy having been the sole reason for their preservation.[10]

The journal of Bacon's travels down the Asian coast and through the islands is a grim reminder that Ottoman brutality more than matched the Greek atrocities of the war. For every Tripolis there was a Chios, for every Navarino or Athens a Psara or Kosof, for every Turkish woman mutilated a twelve-year-old child like the girl the American Philhellene Miller found, her lips and nose sliced off by Ibrahim's Egyptians.

The sense of disgust Bacon felt at the horrors of Chios is an important reminder, too, of the bleak truth that Greek freedom would ultimately owe more to her defeats than her victories. For the first bloody years of the war Britain and the other powers had maintained an official coldness to the claims of the Greek insurgents, but as one massacre followed another the moral indignation of those who witnessed them crystallized into a sense of public shame that no Christian government could in the end bury under the claims of neutrality or self-interest. 'Can it be believed that there is no danger in neglecting or despising [public opinion] . . . ?' one Philhellene apocalyptically demanded in the *New Monthly Magazine*,

> they [the common people] will learn that all the Govern-ments of Europe in concert, propose to accomplish an object the most contrary possible to the wishes of the people of Europe . . . these details [of Ottoman atrocities] will con-

stantly augment the hatred of the people against all existing governments, and that hatred will at length produce a terrible explosion, which will wrap them in its blaze and avenge their crimes.

The preservation of the social order in Europe requires the independence of Greece.[11]

The process by which Britain, France and even Russia would move from official hostility to armed intervention on the side of Greece was a long and slow one, but in Chios, Psara and the terrors which Ibrahim was inflicting in the Morea we can trace its origins. It is typical of Bacon's whole personality, too, that these wider implications of the war always find a place in his journal, yet his immediate concerns were less with thoughts of national shame or of French influence in the Aegean than with tracking down Captain Hamilton.

His energy, his determination were unflagging and after three days on Chios he set off again on his hunt for the *Cambrian*, sailing first to Tino and, hiring a boat there, for the Greek naval centre of Hydra.

And with his arrival sometime towards the end of June on Hydra, at one of the great outposts of revolutionary activity, Bacon's eccentric orbit of the Philhellene world intersects for the first time since Charoneia with more familiar and regular paths. One of the problems with the journal he kept of these travels is the lack of any corroboration or firm chronology, but from this point on it is at last possible to chart and date his progress with some confidence, testing his account against a body of surviving independent evidence.

After a single night on Hydra, spent at a house given over to 'struggling philhellenes,'[12] Bacon set off the next morning for Nauplia, sailing in a crowded caique that included the exotic figure of William Washington, brandishing constitutions and denouncing Britain in the plumed and cocked hat and uniform of a French Republican general. Also with them was the Miller who had been with Whitcombe, and a third and quieter American, just returned from humiliating defeat and capture at Navarino, George Jarvis.

It is an intriguing image to think of Bacon and Jarvis crammed into the same overladen boat, their characters and backgrounds so diametrically opposed, their lives already unconsciously but indissolubly linked. If there was anyone, too, in that vessel who could have understood Jarvis's humiliation as a soldier at Navarino it would have been Bacon, but if they spoke of it or of Trelawny and the cave no record survives.

It was the following day before their caique made it to Nauplia and Bacon had his first ravishing view of the citadel at Argos and the great fortifications of the Palamidi. Like so many Philhellenes before him, however, his excitement survived no longer than it took to land. The conditions in the town were, if anything, even worse than they had been three months earlier when Whitcombe was there. Policy had dictated Ibrahim's clemency to his Greek prisoners at Navarino but that had soon given way to a campaign of horrifying brutality which had swamped Nauplia in a tide of refugees. At every street corner fugitives lay at the point of death. Under the shadow of its walls, and in the crevices of the rocks, men, women and children hid from the burning sun, without water or medical help, dying daily of want and the putrescent fever which gripped the town.

For Bacon, sick himself, sleeping rough on the quay, but more determined than ever after learning of the attack on Trelawny, the wait was increasingly irksome. He had discovered on landing that his caique had crossed with the *Cambrian* during the night, and when news came that Hamilton's frigate was expected at Hydra he decided to retrace his journey. On 14 July he was back on the island, staying again in the same Philhellene house with the Scot Masson – 'one of the few Philhellenes who are not entirely Phil-themselves,' as Howe said of him.[13]

Five days later, on 19 July, Bacon's determination was finally rewarded when the *Cambrian* dropped anchor. For countless Greeks and Turks the sight or news of the *Cambrian* during the war had meant nothing short of life itself, and if there was one man more than any other who preserved Britain's tattered reputation during this time it was its captain, Gawen Hamilton.

The son of a leading United Irishman and friend of Mary

Wollstonecraft, the son-in-law of one of the eight men to have attended Shelley's funeral in Rome, Gawen Hamilton combined all the liberal and humanitarian principles consistent with such a rich and unlikely pedigree with a long and distinguished record as a serving officer. For any naval officer of Philhellene sympathies at this time there was an inevitable struggle between instinct and national policy, but it was to Hamilton's supreme credit that through all his years in the Eastern Mediterranean he managed to reconcile the demands of both, combining a warm sympathy for Greece and close working friendship with Mavrocordato, with an impartial humanity that won the absolute trust and gratitude of Turk and Greek alike.

Even Odysseus, who trusted almost no one, trusted Hamilton and he was right to do so. There was nobody that Bacon could have approached now with more confidence. On 22 July he went on board the 48-gun frigate to plead Trelawny's case. The great Greek sailor, Miaulis, was also present, and Conduriottes, Mavrocordato and other members of the Greek government. Almost a month later – too late for anything to be done to prevent his initiative – Hamilton reported back to Admiral Sir Harry Neale, the commanding officer in the Eastern Mediterranean.

> Sir,
> I have the honour to inform you that being off Hydra on the 22nd ultimo, a Major Bacon (a Traveller) came on board to inform me that Mr Trelawney had not been killed by the infamous attempt made to assassinate him by two Englishmen, but was still in possession of the cave, but without however the medical advice that was necessary for his desperate wounds, and that it was supposed my influence might procure his release.
> It was difficult to determine how far you might approve of my interfering for a person in the situation of Trelawney, against whom there were so many reports and serious accusations; but on the other hand, some of these reports were known to be false, others to be exaggerated, and it was painful for me to think the life of an individual depended on my

determination, and I decided on demanding permission for his embarkation as a British subject, stating at the same time that I did not consider Mr Trelawney entitled to the full protection that that character would have given him in other circumstances, but that I wished it to be extended to him from motives of humanity. Prince Mavrocordato met my views, and agreed to his release with reasonable sums of money belonging to himself; and as it was supposed that he would not quit the cave without the persons who had been entrusted to his care by Odysseus, it was arranged that the whole, whether Turks or Greeks, should accompany him in safety if they pleased, but without carrying off the treasure, if treasure there was.[14]

Hamilton was not in a position to send any of his officers to the cave but offered Bacon his support if he would undertake the rescue. Despite the obvious risks from both Turk and Greek, Bacon 'readily acceded' to the suggestion.[15] He was provided with a letter from Mavrocordato for the Commander of the Acropolis in Athens, requesting an escort of twenty-five palikars for the journey to Ghouras's camp near Salona. A letter, too, was sent from the Executive to Ghouras himself. It required his co-operation, and a guarantee of safety. 'Mr Hamilton has written to Trelawny to leave the cave and it is likely that he will wish to come and meet him', Odysseus's assassin was instructed.

> Given this fact, you should be very careful that nothing adverse happens to Mr Trelawny and that he is safe in every way. In this matter you will take the appropriate measures.[16]

The next day Bacon boarded the sloop *Sparrowhawk* under the command of Captain Stewart for Piraeus. The arrangement with Hamilton was that after landing Bacon, the *Sparrowhawk* should sail to a rendezvous in the Bay of Calamachi on the eastern side of the isthmus of Corinth and wait there for him to return with Trelawny.

On 25 July – six weeks after the assassination attempt in the cave – Bacon was put ashore at the Piraeus, and made his way inland along the line of the ancient double wall that had once linked city and port. 'Suddenly,' he wrote in his journal, 'Athens with its noble Acropolis and lofty Venetian Tower, together with a full front view of the Parthenon, burst upon the expectant imagination.'[17] With that view, though, came a reminder of a more recent history which made fewer demands on the imagination. From a window of the tower – decoy and *memento mori* – the broken rope with which Ghouras had hoped to disguise the murder of Odysseus still hung.

The town of Athens itself was almost deserted, its natives fled in time-honoured ritual to the islands of Salamis and Aegina. Bacon had a letter of introduction to the Italian Doctor Vitelli who had performed the autopsy on Odysseus, and after first visiting him he presented himself with Mavrocordato's orders to the military commander of the Acropolis. There was, unsurprisingly, little enthusiasm for an operation that would take palikars through Turkish-occupied country, but rumour of the riches inside the cave 'overcame all scruple'[18] and on the second or third day Bacon was ready to move.

A round journey of some two hundred miles lay ahead of him before he could make his rendezvous with the *Sparrowhawk* off Corinth. His initial plan was to cross via Salamis to the isthmus and then from Corinth follow the same route Humphreys and Whitcombe had taken in the late spring, sailing over to Aspra Spitia on the northern coast of the Gulf before making the long climb up to Parnassus and the cave.

Their party, however, had got no further than Megara, some thirty miles west of Athens, before he was forced to rethink. Rumours of Turkish cavalry in the vicinity were enough to make a number of his escort desert, and when a Turkish corvette was sighted from the isthmus patrolling the gulf, all hope of a ferry was gone.

As things turned out, Bacon was lucky to lose his deserters because at Megara their places were filled by six Suliotes under the leadership of a Vasili Dangly who had served in the Greek battalion in the Ionian isles and knew Trelawny from Missolonghi. Bacon was now ill, though, suffering, as he puts it, from 'the diseases common in this country'.[19] The heat, too, was fierce. The path ahead, however, with the sea-route blocked, left him no alternative but to abandon his donkey and travel on foot. With the spectacular mass of Acro-Corinth visible on their left, the party cut up into the mountains, bivouacking that night in an olive grove before making their way down again the next morning to a small inlet on the north-eastern shore of the gulf, where they pitched camp in the hope that the Turkish corvette might yet disappear.

Bacon's party was two days in the cove, while their supplies ran down and the heat took its toll. A group of emaciated refugees from the north was already in hiding there, women with their children hoping to escape across to the relative safety of the other shore. The indifference of the Greeks to the suffering of these countrymen appalled Bacon. A small boat was moored in the creek with provisions, but it was only at an exorbitant price that he could buy coffee and flour to help them. He did what he could for a woman of thirty who lay dying, while her children – a girl of eight with black eyes, and a boy of five – played with shells and pebbles on the beach, unconscious of the unfolding tragedy. Only days later, Bacon subsequently learned, Albanian Moslems had reached the cove to add these refugees to the countless casualties of the war.

After two days on the shore of the gulf, the growing shortage of provisions and the presence of the corvette forced Bacon's party back into the mountains. Ahead of them was a thirty-mile journey through a landscape that taxed even his Suliotes, brought up among the rugged peaks of Epirus as they were. It took them three days of hard travel, in the middle of the summer heat, to reach Dystomo near the monastery of Osios Loukas. There, at Dystomo, they found in charge the eldest son of the old klepht Panuria, whose family treasures were rumoured to be in the cave. From him they learned that Ghouras with his army headquarters was at Castri, the village on the site of ancient Delphi.

It is a far easier journey along the low eastern pass across Parnassus to the cave from Dystomo than it is from Delphi, but there was nothing Bacon could do about Trelawny until he had first seen

Ghouras. Leaving Dystomo he marched that same day as far as the desolate Jerusalem Monastery on the eastern slopes, spending the night sheltering in its crypt, looked after by an old monk who was the sole survivor of the pre-war community.

The ease with which Bacon could adjust himself to any world, his total lack of prejudice, his warm sense of the kindness of this old calloyer are rare enough qualities in Greece at this time to deserve more than a passing mention. A generation earlier the traveller Edward Clarke had crossed over Parnassus to this monastery in the middle of winter, and his Gibbonian disgust at what he found strikes a note that is only too typical among Philhellenes. There was no sign of a book in the monastery, Clarke recalled, nor of a monk so much as able to read. 'It was', he wrote, 'entirely heathen . . .

> Nor is it possible that a Cree Indian, capering before his idol in the wilds of North America, exhibits a more abject debasement of human intellect, than a calloyer in the exercise of his . . . bowys.[20]

Where Clarke saw nothing but ignorance Bacon saw only kindness, and after a night as a guest of the last of this community he was ready for his journey on to Ghouras's headquarters. At the ruined village of Arachova some five miles east of Delphi, Bacon left his escort to wait for him and went on with only Vasili for company. Their journey took them along the last stretch of the ancient Sacred Way, along the line of the Turkish road above the Pleistos gorge, the great grey mass of Parnassus on one side and Mt Cirphis on the other. Towards dusk a wounded Greek soldier lying beside a fountain gave them their first indication that they were approaching Ghouras's camp. Leaving Bacon there, Vasili went on alone, returning shortly after with Antonio, the former secretary to Odysseus whom Bacon had last seen at his chief's side at Charoneia. With them was a man in his late thirties, taller and more heavily muscled than most Greeks, with a martial bearing, pistols, yataghans and dagger thrust into his belt, and a face blackened with gunpowder from the day's fighting. It was Odysseus's former pipe-bearer, henchman and assassin, Ghouras.

Urbane as ever, as much at ease with murderers as monks, Bacon greeted Ghouras with the ironic comment that British generals limited themselves to the cleaner business of giving orders, leaving the fighting to others. Ghouras's reply was a smile, and the counter-assurance that 'unless he set the example and led the way his soldiers would do nothing.'[21] Pleasantries over, Bacon was then taken to a hovel in the village of Castri by the ruins of Delphi. There the barest of meals was eaten and the two men settled over the obligatory pipes to negotiate the terms of Trelawny's release.

It soon seemed clear to Bacon that Ghouras had not only been involved in Fenton's plot to seize the cave, but from the safety of his own power-base was not going to pay much attention now to his government's instructions. He believed there were still riches and provisions in the cave, and instinctive greed and the shortages of his army drove him towards making his own terms. He told Bacon that Trelawny could only leave on surrender of his stronghold, but this was a guarantee Bacon was unable to give.

It was, however, not only greed that hardened Ghouras's bargaining stance. In a reply to the government's demand for co-operation with Bacon, he wrote back saying that he had 'eagerly' fallen in with their instructions. 'But the Government knows', he went on, 'that this Trelawny is not a friend of Greece, and did not behave like an Englishman, but even worse than a Turk.'

> One man who was inside the cave and now is with me confessed to me that the Turk who was inside the cave was instructed by Trelawny to give him 200 grosia and other promises in order to leave and go and find the Turks and hand them over the cave. This man did not accept this and so the business was prevented.[22]

This is difficult to believe and impossible to disprove, but whatever the motives for Ghouras's intransigence, it was almost dawn before the discussion broke up without agreement. Ghouras had not, however, forbidden Bacon's journey, and it would seem that in the end he had simply decided to wait on events, because the next morning, after a drink at the Castalian Spring mixed with raki in an unsuccessful bid for inspiration, the major and his Suliotes began the long climb towards the peaks of Parnassus with Antonio accompanying them to guard his new master's interests.

With the Turkish army close to Ghouras's camp at Delphi, and their cavalry controlling the plain below Tithorea, Bacon's only route was a path straight over the mountains that is only really passable in high summer. From September to May the top of Parnassus is an inhospitable place and even in summer the snow still clings to its northern slopes, filling its crevices and gullies and giving its bleak highland beauty a remote detachment that is only enhanced by views which grow and change with every step, expanding in space to embrace range after distant range of mountains, and contracting in scale until the Gulf of Corinth beneath seems no more than a lake.

Even to a man who had crossed the Caucasus it was an exhilarating sight. As Bacon and his party climbed beyond the high pastures of Livadi to the bare slopes above the tree line, the whole of Greece opened up before them, with a view that stretched from Pindos and Olympos to the Gulf of Volos, and then, in one great southern sweep, across Helicon to the mountains of the northern Peloponnese and distant Taygetus. 'Passing ravines and over the summit of mountains abrupt,' Bacon wrote, with a nicely bathetic inadequacy,

> precipitous and thickly clothed in many places with pines and lofty cedars, the snow still remaining, notwithstanding the rays of a blazing sun, the party with considerable caution and difficulty approached this most singular domicile.[23]

The march from Delphi to Tithorea is about fifteen hours, and it was evening before Bacon's party finally halted in the steep ravine of the Kakoreme. High above them, and visible for the first time, the black hole of Trelawny's cave stared blindly out from its limestone cliff to the distant plain of Livadia. Leaving his Suliotes and Antonio to wait among the ancient oaks of Apollo, Bacon and Vasili began the climb up the last gruelling slope to the base of the cliff, 'making signals of friendship' as they approached.[24] As they reached the bunker at the foot of the ladders, occupied now only by a few women, Komarone appeared above them. Trelawny was alive, but still too weak from his wounds to come down. In a short time the topmost ladder was lowered into place, and Bacon 'invited', as he put it, 'to make the difficult ascent'.[25]

To Vasili's extreme irritation he was refused entry, but it was not long before Bacon wished that he too had been turned away. Climbing the first of the ladders and turning on to the second, he made the mistake of looking down. Seven hundred feet beneath him yawned 'the vast abyss'[26] of the gorge. 'Feeling somewhat giddy,' he wrote – it is one of those rare moments of empathy which obliterate time, that can make one feel with absolute confidence, however briefly, what it was like to be Francis D'Arcy Bacon,

> I was obliged to descend, when taking off my shoes and
> wetting and rubbing my feet in sand, I was at length enabled
> to ascend the dizzy height.[27]

He found Trelawny lying upon a mat in one of the recesses of the cave, his right arm in a sling, 'much emaciated in appearance and sadly altered since I had last seen him'.[28] Their first words have a charm that could not be improved on.

> To Trelawny, I said, 'Here I am, come to redeem my pledge
> of rendering you a service and to enable you to quit Greece';
> languidly stretching forth his hand he replied, 'You are a
> friend indeed.'[29]

For the next three days Bacon soaked in the magic of the cave, while he brokered terms, allayed suspicions, and added a new piece to the mystery of the assassination attempt that cast Antonio in the role of jealous suitor for Tersitza's hand. Down in the valley Vasili and his Suliotes waited with increasing impatience, but Antonio had dug in against Trelawny leaving without first surrendering the cave. Neither Trelawny, though, nor Helena, Odysseus's widow and the mother of the infant Leonidas – the ten-month old 'future hope of the house of Andritzo' – would accede.[30] 'With a firmness worthy a Spartan mother,' Bacon admiringly wrote, she haughtily said she would rather precipitate herself and infant son from this fearful summit than surrender to the assassin of her husband.[31]

There was nothing in the end that Antonio or anyone else, denied entry and frustrated of any treasure, could do to impose their terms. It seemed to Bacon likely, too, that Antonio saw that his best chance of securing the cave lay with Trelawny's departure. After three long days of arguing, it was eventually agreed that he could leave. Trelawny tried to persuade Helena and Odysseus's mother Acrive to accompany him, but they refused, preferring to hold on to the only legacy left them. 'All matters being arranged and mules provided,' Bacon wrote,

> on the morning of the fourth day Trelawny with difficulty (having lost the use of his right arm) descended the tottering ladders, accompanied by the young brother and sister of Odysseus, and taking with him the Italian domestic.[32]

For all the disappointments and failure that the cave had come to represent, it was an exit fitting a Byronic hero. As they made their way down the valley and past Fenton's shallow grave marked only by a few loose stones, the pregnant Tersitza cross-legged *á la Turque* on her mule and Trelawny so weak he could barely keep his seat, salute after salute rolled down the Velitza gorge from the cave's guns. At the bottom of the gorge, Vasili and his suliotes were waiting for them still, distrustful of Ghouras and – conscious it would almost seem of the history they were witnessing – determined to pay this last service, 'out of respect to the memory of Lord Byron, as they recognized in the person of Trelawny the friend of that lamented nobleman.'[33]

It took their party two more days to reach the coast at Aspra Spitia. On the third morning a small boat ferried them across to the southern side of the gulf, and in a few hours they were landed some three miles from Corinth. On the other side of the narrow isthmus the *Sparrowhawk* lay waiting at their rendezvous in the Bay of Calamachi. It had been there for thirteen days, occupying itself in that mix of drills and diplomatic exchanges with the fortress, in small and large arm practice, in mending clothes and flogging sailors which made up the daily routine of life in the service Trelawny had so hated. The rebel now, though, was turned grateful guest. The young midshipman who gloried in *Adventures* in thrashing his superior was 'a shattered hulk'.[34] 'I have been near going down –', he wrote to Roberts,

> two shots between wind and water – all my timbers carried away – standing and running rigging cut up – two balls entered my back, broke my jaw, breast bone, cut all the nerves of my right arm, and in short, all but did my business. After a two month struggle between my constitution and these severe wounds, by which I suffered daily death, the former triumphed.[35]

The date was Tuesday 9 August, almost two months to the day since the asassination attempt in the cave. The winds were moderate, the weather fine. '10 a.m.,' the Captain's log for the day reads, with a naval economy that does scant justice to the heroic efforts of Major Francis D'Arcy Bacon: 'Came on board Mr Trelawny, family & servant for passage from Greece being British subjects requiring protection.'[36]

12

SHAME

'In a few weeks, days – perhaps hours – will for ever drop over my person, my actions, and my errors, the dark curtain of death; – and then nothing will remain of the once vain and haughty Anastasius, but an empty name, and a heap of noisome ashes.

'O ye who tread their scattered remnants! – ere you execrate that name, the theme of so much obloquy, remember my suffering: be merciful to my memory, – and may Heaven's mercy rest upon yourselves!'

Anastasius[1]

ON THE EVENING OF 7 August, just two days before Trelawny and Bacon boarded the *Sparrowhawk*, the American Samuel Gridley Howe was sitting on the terrace of his house on Hydra when his attention was caught by the slowly approaching figure of a young man. He seemed in a state of extreme weakness and exhaustion, and his finely embroidered dress was torn and filthy, making 'a strange contrast of rags and riches, of splendour and dirt'.[2] He was carrying no weapons, though a silver cartridge box and pistol belt showed that he had been a soldier. 'As he drew near,' Howe later recalled,

I saw that he was sallow and emaciated, and was surprised to find him turning in at our gate; I met him at the door, against which he supported himself with one hand, while he, hesitatingly, held out the other to me, and fixed upon me his ghastly sunken eyes. I took his hand, doubtfully, when he exclaimed in a hollow voice – 'Do you not know me?'[3]

It was Whitcombe. 'Can this be the young, genteel, romantic boy I parted from but two months ago,' Howe asked himself in his journal that night, 'his blooming looks changed to hollow sallowness, his rich dress for the garb of a common soldier?'[4] There had been 'strange tales' circulating for some weeks of events in a cave on Parnassus, of 'dissipation and unnatural crimes; of treason and assassination,'[5] but there had been nothing for Howe to connect these rumours with the feckless but 'generous' boy he had parted from outside Navarino. The exhausted Whitcombe was given food, and cajoled into some sort of explanation. Nothing they could do, however, could shake his mood of heavy reserve:

> or, if he roused himself, and tried to laugh, it was with a hollow, heartless laugh of the distracted. I suspected his mind was affected, and we got him to retire, having made up the best bed we could, with some rags, on the floor of the adjoining room.[6]

Piece by piece over the next days the story of Fenton's plot emerged, but it was the night of the 10th before Whitcombe was forced into a full confession of his own role. The next day Howe described what had happened in his journal.

> Aug 11th: could it be expected that a boy of nineteen, of a rich and honourable family, unconnected with any party, and without any hope of gain, should be drawn into a plot for treason and murder? Yet such is the case with young Whitcomb. The occurences of last night, too well impressed on my memory ever to be forgotten, made him reveal all. Since the affair of the blockade, we have been apprehensive of some attack on our house, and have kept our arms ready. Last night being very hot, I had thrown myself down on the floor in the entryway between two chambers, in one of which slept Masson, and in the other Miller and Whitcomb. In the

dead of the night I was awakened by the most dreadful screechings in the chamber of Miller and Whitcomb. The cries were, 'Oh, Miller, Miller, save me! for God's sake save me! Oh! oh, murder! murder! for Christ's sake save me!' Before I was well awake, I conceived that some ruffians had entered by the chamber window, and seizing my sword and pistol I staved open the door, and entering, found Whitcomb stretched out on the floor beside Miller's bed, groaning in a frightful manner. He stretched out his arms in the direction of a dark corner of the room. 'There! oh, there they are! They have stabbed me to the heart! O God!'

I pointed my pistol in that direction, and strained my eyes to see something to fire at – but saw nobody; and 'There is nobody here!' said I. 'Who has stabbed you?'

Miller now began to awaken. 'It was not me!' says he. 'I have not hurt him!' 'They must have gone out of the window,' says I.

'No! no!' cries Whitcomb, in a voice of horrid, agonizing terror, 'Look! look in that corner!'

I advanced, and felt round with my sword, my heart in my mouth, but no one was there. I then questioned Whitcomb where he was wounded, but he could not answer distinctly. I felt his body: it was cold, and his pulse was almost gone, but I could find no wound, and then began to suspect the truth. He had been dreaming. After a while a light was brought in, and things began to clear up. Whitcomb threw himself on his bed, and lay trembling and weeping. He insisted that he had not been asleep; that he was lying meditating on the horrid proceedings at the Cave, when four horrid figures entered the room, and they seized him, dragged him across the floor, and just as I burst into the room, they plunged their daggers into him and vanished.

During the first minute after I had entered the chamber, the state of my mind can be better conceived than described. At my feet lay Whitcomb groaning and screeching, and as I thought, writhing in the agonies of death; beside me lay

Miller, silent, and, I supposed, stone-dead; my pistol was directed toward a dark corner, from which I expected every instant to see the flash of another, or a ruffian start out upon me, yet the thought of fear did not enter my mind. I held my pistol without its quivering, and grasped my sword with the other hand, intent only on killing the murderer. But in a minute after, when the thing began to be explained, I began to tremble; a sensation of horror came over me, and I was most completely unmanned, and for half an hour after, I could not approach the dark corner of the chamber without a sensation of terror, which I had not felt when I thrust my sword there, in expectation that its point might reach a ruffian.[7]

With the exception of Howe's journal there is no written evidence that can place Whitcombe anywhere between the day Trelawny freed him from the cave and five years later on 25 June 1830 when he was commissioned into the British Army. It is as if for these intervening years Whitcombe's descent into this gothic hell was a literal as well as mental one, as if isolated by his own shame and the growing contempt of his Philhellene comrades, he simply disappeared from the face of the earth. It is not even certain when Trelawny – generous in the superb way of his hero, Lara 'not in pity, not because he ought, But in some strange perversity of thought' – set him free. Howe says that it was after a month. In a letter to Daniel Roberts, Trelawny gave it as five weeks, and in his *Records*, and to Bacon, twenty days. There is no record, either, of how Whitcombe found his way from Parnassus to Hydra, of how he spent those missing weeks; nor of where he went after. Humphreys, writing in the *New Monthly Magazine*, claimed he was 'in high favour' with Ghouras.[8] Howe gives the Greek navy. The Reverend Charles Swan – as free of charity as any man who ever took orders – simply noted with satisfaction in his journal entry for 22 August, that he had left Hydra 'in a dudgeon, the Europeans there having hinted to him that they should decline his acquaintance'.[9]

In a world where literature and life ape each other so insistently, it is again only fitting that it is in the fiction of Whitcombe's anonymously published *Sketches,* rather than any evidence, that we have to look for him. It would almost certainly be a mistake to accept the external events of the novel as an accurate account of his movements in the months after the assassination bid, but as an insight into alienation and shame, as a revelation of what it was like to be an attempted murderer there is nothing in romantic literature that can compare with it.

It is necessary to pick up the thread of its narrative where it was dropped earlier, at that moment when the young 'Nastuli', full of confidence and expectation, his head crowded with 'visions of hope and happiness', climbs the ladders into the cave on Mt Parnassus. 'But the morrow' – it is so strange, so elusive a confession as to bear repeating –

> was destined to change these to disgust, and in dissipating their illusions, destroy his light-heartedness forever. A mistaken zeal, an attachment to a traitor, while it led him to participate in crimes, – unconscious, till too late, of their being so – sunk his ardent and susceptible nature under the weight of miseries which itself had created; dimmed his eye from the lustre it before possessed; and gave to his cheek that sunken hue which defies aught to restore it to its bloom.[10]

The oddity of this revelation cannot be gauged unless it is stressed that this is the first and last time that the cave or any 'crime' is mentioned in the whole book. For all its absurdities the first half of *Sketches* is a fairly coherent account of Whitcombe's early months in Greece, a mixture of romantic fiction and thinly disguised character studies, tedious and repetitive but at its best no worse than the earliest novels of the young Disraeli.

From the moment he enters the cave, however, the whole book changes, structure and plot collapsing under the weight of a shame too crushing even to be named. Because from this point on, even though the whole of Nastuli's life revolves around the memory of the cave, there is no indication among the enveloping chaos of its pages, among its passages of bitter self-recrimination, self-justification and Byronic hauteur of what it was that *happened* to set its hero apart from his fellow men.

The next time we see Nastuli, weeks – and chapters – later, he is entering a Nauplia held in the grip of disease, a figure immediately recognizable from the pages of Howe's journal.

> The day which was cloudy and melancholy, seemed to sympathise with the gloom that the increasing malady had diffused, when a young stranger, followed by two palicari, entered the town. His countenance was pale and sunken, his vestments as mean as his followers, save a tattered gold phermeli which he wore, and the haughtyness only of his brow denoted him to be their commander.[11]

That flash of defiant conceit in the last sentence is authentically 'Whitcombe', but as the figure makes his way through Nauplia's streets every familiar sight is a reminder of the gulf that now separates him from his former self. He goes to the inn where he had stayed only months before, but everything there is different, and the looks of admiration that once followed him changed to suspicion and distrust of a figure who seems scarcely to belong to this world. "'But you are so changed",' he is told,

> you are so melancholy, so wan, that, by the vampyre of the old klephtes, my father, you deserve rather to take his place, and haunt the old ruined mosques, than to retain any share in this life.[12]

No book so assiduously disguises its real subject as Whitcombe's *Sketches* and at the same time reveals so publicly the horror that lies at its heart. It is not just that Nastuli's whole appearance and personality mirror his fallen state, but the crime he is hiding, the sin that is never mentioned, shows like a stigmata to betray his shame. As Nastuli throws off his gold phermeli, the tattered symbol of his previous extravagance and glamour, he notices the Minister of War, Adam Ducas, 'casting a look of keen inquiry on him. His waist, he perceived, had been uncovered, and the mark of heavy iron-ligatures were visible upon them, as well as upon his ancles.'[13]

The marks of the irons in which he had been chained at the back of the cave through Trelawny's long convalescence are the badge of shame that Whitcombe's fictional self can never hide. Their presence on Nastuli's body remains bewilderingly unexplained within the novel, but the degradation they symbolize, the outward expression of an inward disgrace, acts like a corrosive on Nastuli's life, cutting him off alike from kindness and contempt – a vampire of Greek folk tale, the outcast of Byronic romanticism, the reincarnation of the fictional Anastasius on whom the young Whitcombe had modelled himself.

There is almost no resource of legend or literature, of Greek lore or romantic myth, that is not pressed into service to express this alienation. Like a ghost he walks among the living, his crime obvious even to strangers. 'Now everything that came athwart him in his path'

> looked on him with a cold and unkind gaze; the very old women, true to their legendary creed, would mutter curses as his wild look met theirs, and would spit and cross themselves to avoid the evil eye.[14]

It is not, however, just in the eyes of every passer-by that Whitcombe read the proof of his disgrace. In one passage of gothic fantasy he sees himself as a spectral figure haunting the public gallows on the waterfront at Zante, his only companions a murderer hanging in chains upon the gibbet and a hooded vampire figure at his side. But it is the lazaretto, the quarantine centre, at Zante that provides the most potent image of alienation. As Nastuli serves out his plague quarantine, physical disease becomes the metaphor for moral corruption, marking him out as an object of fear and loathing. 'It was in the Lazaretto,' Whitcombe wrote, 'that Nastuli first felt the preciousness of liberty.'

> Even in his solitary rambles he was obliged to submit to the companionship of an extortionate guardian, who, with a large rod, would keep him like a beast at bay from mankind. If he touched a stone, all would run from it; and the terror

of his presence never ceased until the hour arrived for being locked up in his cell.[15]

There could be no more eloquent expression of pain than Whitcombe's *Sketches* but at the same time it is strangely lacking in any commensurate feeling of remorse. There is a quality about it that seems of a curiously alien strain, that betrays a psychology untouched by western, Christian values or restraints – a sense of pride stronger than conscience, a hatred of humiliation independent of any sense of right or wrong, a morbid sense of shame without any obvious feeling of guilt.

It was, however, perhaps not always the case. In his journal entry for 20 August Howe noted Whitcombe's departure from Nauplia for Hydra, to join the Greek fleet. 'I pity him,' he wrote

> and, notwithstanding his crime, I cannot help being attached to him; he feels the most bitter remorse, and cannot be more completely punished than by his present state of mind.[16]

Howe was always generous enough to put the best gloss on any action, but even if he was right about Whitcombe it is interesting that in the three years that elapsed before *Sketches*, remorse had hardened into something less attractive. It would be expecting too much to find in its pages some explanation of a crime that baffled its perpetrator as much as its victim, but there is something chilling in its lack of regret, or comprehension even, that comes out most graphically in its portrait of the man who for all his faults had spared his life. It is worth quoting his description of Trelawny at length. In Whitcombe's *Sketches* he is called Simkins. The encounter is placed in Nauplia, but as the only time the two men met was in the cave it can stand as Whitcombe's portrait of the man he tried to kill. It is Simkins speaking. He complains of the Greeks, their ingratitude, their manners. But for all that, he goes on,

> there is a charm in having sported so long the oriental dress, and in taking a tinge from the languor which the eastern clime inspires, to accompany one home, and excite some interest among the fair sex. My costume, which they assure

me becomes me amazingly, though I am not myself capable to judge the truth, cannot sufficiently have hidden from you, Sir, my fame, as to render you ignorant of who I am.

You will cease to hesitate when I remind you that I am the same dark mysterious being whom Byron has designated in the person of Lara. My family name is Simkins, and it is my intention to send over to Scotland the analysis of many admirable scenes to which I have been witness, which cannot fail to enrol me among the list of heroes of the celebrated author there . . .

But you are not yet aware, my dear Sir, of the beasts you have got amongst. The vulgarity of all the Europeans here is so strikingly base, that any man of refined taste, like myself, creates, I assure you, by being singular, a vast field of interest and adventure. I should by no means be surprised if you, Sir, who I know to be of family – rank, and of vast acquirements, by keeping yourself always aloof from these barbarians, whom I have mentioned; and being biased by no other hints than my own, may eventually lead a career not less than I have done. Our names will then of course be mingled together in the reminiscences of some masterly pen – and think of the luxury of being known and quoted as the heroes of a romance fraught with incident; the inspiration with which the young beauties of our realm will lisp our names upon every occasion, fondly hoping that their lovers may be such.[17]

The price that Trelawny had to pay for his extravagances was the contempt of men inferior to him in every way, but it is less the justice of this portrait that is at issue than the mind of the man who could frame it. There is a certain rough comedy about Whitcombe's description that from another source might seem fair enough, but in the context of their actual relationship, of the ties that bound them together, there is something appalling in the patronizing derision with which Whitcombe repays his debt to Trelawny. It is as if the memory of that obligation, the memory of his own humiliation, when he sobbed and pleaded for his life in the cave, can only be expunged in public ridicule. The creator of Nastuli, morbidly alive to every real and imagined slight, could never forget the shame symbolized by the marks of the irons round his waist and ankles: still less could his pride allow him ever to forgive the man who had not just pardoned him but witnessed his humiliation and pathetic gratitude. 'Much-injured Sir', he had addressed Trelawny, on being given his freedom,

> I cannot express to you what I feel for your unmerited kindness to me for releasing me from an untimely death; other release it is not in the power of man to procure for me, my internal misery and shame being complete. May you never feel the half that I do. May you never be like me, reduced by an acquaintance of four days with a villain from the smiling circles who loved me, and had pleasure in my society, to the solitary wretched outcast I am now become. I have now no home, no family, no friends – and all I regret is that I have still the gnawings of a conscience which makes me prefer life a little longer, with all my former enjoyments cut off, to an ignominious and untimely end. I can say no more, perhaps now I have troubled you too much.
>
> That God may send you a speedy recovery, and turn every curse which falls upon my head into a blessing on yours, is the prayer of the wretched
> W.G.Whitcombe[18]

We can do no more than guess the steps by which Whitcombe moved from this to the gloomy egotism of the novel, but romantic literature again offered a pattern of behaviour that he could seize on as his own. There was, of course, a ready source of misanthropy to draw on in popular Byronism, but Whitcombe's personal allegiance had always and publicly been to Hope's *Anastasius* and now in his disgrace he found in the self-pitying and self-dramatizing misery of Anastasius, a model he could still follow in fiction and life as assiduously as he had done in more prosperous times.

A certain caution is inevitably employed when the relationship between art and life comes under discussion, a self-restraint that has more to do with critical embarrassment than anything else. In Whitcombe's case, though, sophistication and caution are equally misplaced. The relationship is a crude one, shocking in its immediacy, disturbing in its implications, brutal in its stark simplicity. Whitcombe had not just imitated his hero Anastasius, but become him. He took over his morals, adopted his manners, shared in his disgrace, and then dramatised his own life as a way of handling a shame that he was unable to face.

This is not a matter of literary plagiarism, but possession. There is nothing about Whitcombe that he could have called his own, nothing that his alter ego Nastuli suffers that had not been anticipated in Hope's *Anastasius*. If Whitcombe was cut off in fact and fiction from the world around him, then Anastasius was before him; if Adam Ducas sees Nastuli as a Vampire, then Anastasius was 'at best but a vampyre, only permitted to walk among the living, until the last awful summons should fix it for ever among the vaster myriads under ground'.[19] If Nastuli finds an unbridgeable gap between his past and future, then Anastasius has foresuffered all the horrors of the cave himself:

> the golden link which had so gloriously conjoined the past
> and the present had been riven – been snapped asunder.
> The Anastasius of the morrow was no longer the Anastasius
> of the eve. The wide new world which I was going to tread,
> was a world devoid of interest; and the vast new prospects
> unfolding to my view, were prospects without life, animation
> or sunshine. Struck by heaven's vengeful lightning, my soul
> saw nothing in the dark surrounding waste to cheer its
> deathlike sadness, and shrunk from every slightest exertion
> as from an Herculean labour. On every stone I met in my
> way, I could have laid me down to die.[20]

This is not simply a sequence of literary echoes, however uncanny they may be in their similarity. Even Whitcombe's nightmares recorded in Howe's journal, genuine and terrifying as they are, were second-hand. In Whitcombe's dream it is Trelawny's soldiers who are seeking out their revenge for his crime; in *Anastasius* his past too rises again to threaten him, the woman he has wronged turning into a fiend to grapple with him, until he wakes to find himself lying on the floor of his room – in a frightening anticipation of the scene that so unnerved Howe – 'weltering in a stream of red blood, drawn forth from my vitals by my unconscious exertions'.[21]

Literature has been transmuted into life, and reinterpreted again in fiction. Byron, Lady Blessington reported, wept that he had not written *Anastasius*, and wept that Hope had. Those are tears to which Whitcombe can lay a more bitter claim. Romanticism can boast of no more willing nor pathetic a victim. 'Veil'd Melancholy has her sovran shrine', Keats had written in 1819,

> Though seen of none save him whose strenuous tongue
> Can burst Joy's grape against his palate fine;
> His soul shall taste the sadness of her might,
> And be among her cloudy trophies hung.[22]

It is an apt image, though it was at the altar of Byronic Romanticism, rather than Keatsian melancholy that Whitcombe was sacrificed. He had still five years to live before his strange death would end his miseries, but his Greek life was over. There is no record of when or how he left, or whether his last weeks in Greece were in fact spent with Ghouras's army or with the fleet. The only thing that is certain is that he left Nauplia for Hydra on 20 August, our last mentions of him being the note in the Rev. Swan's journal for the 22nd, and one final Christian judgement from him two days later. 'Mr Whitcombe' Swan wrote,

> has returned to Hydra, very little sensible, as it seems, of the heinousness of his conduct. He is said to be an extremely weak young fellow; full of daring and romance, and desirous of aping the extravagant character of Hope's Anastasius.[23]

After that, all we are left with is the bitter misery of *Sketches*. 'Your faith you have broken', Nastuli is told by a former friend, Staunton, modelled on the stern and religious American, Miller, not only to *me*, but to your God; and now that I can no longer serve you, now that nothing can reach your heart, go commune with it as you will – adieu![24]

It was advice Nastuli was ready to take. Wherever he went in Greece, his shame followed him, leaving him nowhere to hide. Even on Zante 'the quill-drivers had arrived breathless from the land, in eager rivalry who first should blast his reputation'.[25] His last sight of the country that had seen his destruction came from on board a ship. 'The golette moved cheerily from port,' he wrote,

> shaping her course towards Genoa, and the fate of the young Capitano, whose hopes had been ruined and heart-blighted from the susceptibility of his nature, became again unknown to all.[26]

13

THE LAST OF GREECE

For the first twenty days after being wounded I remained in
the same place and posture, sitting and leaning against the
rock, determined to leave everything to nature. I did not change
or remove any portion of my dress, nor use any extra covering.
I would not be bandaged, plastered, poulticed, or even washed;
nor would I move or allow anyone to look at my wound. I
was kept alive by yolks of eggs and water for twenty days. It
was forty days before there was any sensible diminution of
pain; I then submitted to have my body sponged with spirit
and water, and my dress partly changed. I was reduced in
weight from thirteen stone to less than ten, and looked like a
galvanized mummy.

Trelawny[1]

IF THERE WAS EVER a time in Trelawny's long life when it might
seem possible to glimpse behind the Byronic mask to the man
beneath, it is during these weeks and months after the shooting.
Nobody who has so much as seen a hospital could question the
intimate connections between personality and health, or doubt that
character becomes most rampantly itself under the pressure of pain,
when strengths and weaknesses that might lie happily dormant take
on a salience that cannot be escaped.

There is a quickening sense of anticipation in following Trelawny
now with this in mind, a realization that not just physically but
mentally his life is at a crisis point, an anxiety – an expectation
almost – that under the acute suffering caused by Whitcombe's

bullets those crippling inadequacies that lay beneath the Byronic swagger would at last be exposed.

It is an ungenerous and conventional thought – the reflex faith that behind every bully is a coward, tucked away inside every Lara a Simkins – and with Trelawny it is a deeply misplaced one. If there was ever any question of his bravery his stoic and uncomplaining strength during this period would answer it. It took an exceptional strength to survive of course, and an unusual constitution. It took, though, a mental stamina as well, a lack of self-pity, an ability to live with pain that in a man of Trelawny's highly imaginative temperament is extraordinary.

A civilized hierarchy of courage places this kind of physical brav- ery some way below its moral equivalent and yet unless its existence is at least recognized the realities not just of Trelawny's experience but that of every volunteer are buried under a smug and unhistorical complacence. It is easy enough to look at a man like Humphreys and dismiss the romantic silliness of his motives, but one only has to follow his movements to realize that he was operating for days and even weeks on end at the very limit of physical and mental endurance, living without sleep or rest or food in a terrain in which every step is an effort, a battle against heat and cold and thorn and rock and illness.

The same is true of Howe and Jarvis, of Whitcombe, Fenton and Bacon – forty-six years old and sick when he marched for three days across the Helicon range in the heat of a Greek August, and then over the eight-thousand-foot peaks of Parnassus to the cave. Even by these standards, however, Trelawny was exceptional. He could do what few others could. He could put up with extremes of discomfort and pain without bending to them. He could, to put it in the terms his whole life demands, live up to the role he had created for himself with a style and conviction that leaves no room for doubt that image and man were one.

Over the next two years, in the privacy of letters, the mental and physical suffering inflicted by Whitcombe's shots are sometimes betrayed but in public Trelawny was never less than himself. From the moment he stepped aboard the *Sparrowhawk* he was defiantly at ease in a world he had once loathed, taking strength from a sense of his apartness, playing to the gallery he knew so well, the exhibitionist in him creating a *succès de scandale* out of illness and failure.*

His new fame guaranteed, too, that his progress would not go unnoticed. Sailing from the isthmus past Aegina and Sounion, where fifteen years earlier Byron had carved his name on a column, Trelawny and his party were taken to the port of Smyrna and there transferred to the *Cambrian* where the Rev. Swan recorded their arrival. 'The *Sparrowhawk*, Captain Stewart, arrived from Athens,' he noted in his journal for 13 September 1825.

> He brought with him Mr Trelawny, his wife, and a quick clever lad, the brother of Odysseus. They were transferred to the *Cambrian*. Trelawny was in Albanian costume, with his arm in a sling. His wounds have been very severe; the carbine with which he was shot, was loaded with two balls. Both entered his back; one of them has not yet been extracted; the other passed along his neck and came out at his jaw, carrying away several teeth ... This affair, [the release of Whitcombe] so far as it is related to us, tells favourably on the part of Trelawny; and in truth, that person requires some palliating circumstances to lighten the huge mass of obloquy which attaches itself to his public and private character. If one half of what is circulated respecting him be true, (of which I pretend not to judge,) his conscience must be callous indeed, if it remain at rest beneath it: his heart must be as black as it is bold, and unfeeling as it is adventurous! His wife is a little girl, certainly of not more than thirteen or fourteen years of age; of pretty features, but impressed with a deep shade of melancholy. What companionship can such a one have with a man of at least five and thirty?[2]

It is a Godsend that of all men it was Swan who was in place to leave this first portrait of Trelawny because no-one could better embody the kind of audience Trelawny so much liked to shock.

Swan's journal in fact provides valuable evidence of the way Trelawny's reputation had already spread by 1825, but more interesting still is the way in which it shows Trelawny playing up to expectations and prejudices, feeding his audience with what it wanted, toying with it in the same way he had Mary and Claire with stories of violence and revenge. 'He flew upon him,' Swan wrote, repeating one of Trelawny's stories of Odysseus's treatment of a rival in love,

> seized him by the throat, and bound him to a tree: he unsheathed his ataghan, and in a few moments literally hacked him to pieces! Such a relation, proceeding from the mouth of one so lately connected with him by the closest ties that can bind humanity, needs not any further comment: it speaks with a louder voice than the strongest reprobation could express. A story equally barbarous is told by the same person of Goura; but it is of too gross a description to be related here. Trelawny speaks well only of such persons as Fenton, Whitcombe and Co; and he is, or, in all human probability, soon will be, one of those unhappy and pitiable beings 'whose hand is against every man, and every man's hand against him'.[3]

These were the sort of tales he had been telling in Pisa but the difference is that they were now rooted in his own life and in these skirmishes with Swan it is perhaps possible to make out not just the first movements of rehabilitation but the foundations of a whole future strategy for living. For the last three years Trelawny had done little more than feed off the pickings of Byron's table, but as he soaked up the attention on the *Cambrian*, he must have recognized that for the first time he enjoyed a notoriety which was authentically his own, a history and personality that he could mould into that definitive shape that future generations would recognize as 'Trelawny'.

Whether it was conscious or not, there is something dazzling, almost heroic, in the speed with which Trelawny seems to have passed from suffering victim to architect of his own reputation. It was still only three months since the shooting that had shaken the myth of Byronic superiority, but it was now again in place and as strong as ever. It was there, though, with this subtle but important difference. For the early part of his life he had lived through his fantasies: from now on, he would live off them. It was as if, in an important sense, with his exit from the cave his life was 'complete', 'lived': now all that was left was to celebrate it.

But behind the mask, behind the bravado and public courage, the refusal to bow down to pain, Trelawny was carrying injuries that would take months and even years to heal fully. On board the *Cambrian* in the harbour at Nauplia, where they had sailed after Smyrna, the surgeon of the *Alacrity* had a look at his wounds. 'One [shot]' he wrote,

> passed over the scapula to the clavicle which it fractured in the middle and then lodged. The other passed also over the scapula; but afterwards took a turn round the neck, and knocking out three of the upper grinder teeth of the right side, passed out of the mouth.[4]

Even if he had the will or strength to resume his old life, though, there was no chance that he would be allowed. Hamilton had only negotiated his release with the Government on the condition of his leaving Greece, and while Bacon was ashore at Nauplia helping Swan barter for a classical relief, Trelawny and his family stayed on board under the cautious gaze of the navy.

On 29 August, the *Cambrian* was ready again to leave. As it made its slow way down the Gulf, its decks crammed with refugees, Nauplia disappeared behind them, until only the outline of the Palamidi was visible beneath a moon of 'unusual splendour'.[5] It was the last time he was to see the town that had played such a large part in his life. He must have felt a genuine sense of release after the cave, but a certain poignancy still hovers about this departure, with Trelawny half guest, half-prisoner of the navy he had hated, the outsider, the great individualist 'cribb'd' and 'cabin'd' by the rhythms of ship life, the supreme fantasist in thrall to the minutiae of the naval log. 'Weighed anchor,' Swan recorded, the quarter deck covered with 'Parthians and Medes and Elamites, and the dwellers in Messapotamia, and in Judea and Cappadocia, in Pontis and Asia' – Jews and Cretes, Arabians and Turks: verily, never quarter deck exhibited such a motley assemblage. Here, on the carriage of a gun, sits a military priest in Albanian costume; there stalks Levi the Jew; and a little further on, a group of Turks in earnest conversation. Mr Trelawny (whose nation I am at a loss to imagine!) is squatted on the taffrel . . . [6]

Making its way down the eastern coast of the Peloponnese under light breezes and clear skies, the *Cambrian* and its strange cargo of humanity rounded the Cape of Matapan on the evening of the 31st. The next day they hove to off Modon, the old Venetian port Trelawny had so cavalierly dismissed from his strategic calculations two years earlier. There they waited for the sloop, *Zebra*. On the 8th she arrived, and the next day Bacon, Trelawny, and his family were welcomed aboard for the final part of their journey to Cephalonia.

The trip was uneventful. On 10 September 1825 they dropped anchor and hoisted their quarantine flag off Zante, and on the morning of the 12th, exactly two years and ten days after Trelawny had entered the same harbour on board the *Hercules* with Byron, he was finally put ashore at Argostoli to begin his twenty days of quarantine.

Isolated in the lazaretto together, Bacon and Trelawny drank from the same silver goblets they had used at their first meeting in Odysseus's camp at Charoneia. At the end of their confinement Bacon prepared for the journey back through Italy and France to England, carrying with him a brief note for Mary Shelley, written with Trelawny's 'left fin' in an evocatively shaky and child-like hand.[7]

Dear Mary,
    I have just escaped from Greece and landed here, in the

hopes of patching up my broken frame and shattered constitution. Two musket balls, fired at the distance of two paces,
struck me and passed through my framework, which damn'd
near finished me; but 'tis a long story, and my writing arm
is rendered unfit for service, and I am yet unpractised with
the left. But a friend of mine here, a Major Bacon, is on his
way to England, and will enlighten you as to me. I shall be
confined here some time. Write to me then at this place. I
need rest and quiet, for I am shook to the foundation. Love
to Jane and Clare, and believe me still your devoted friend,
   Edward Trelawny[8]

As Trelawny sank back into life on Cephalonia and then Zante, the
note struck at the end of this letter – a weariness and with it the
insistent tug of old friendships – recurs time and again in his correspondence. During his months with Odysseus he had enjoyed the
sense of companionship and belonging that he so badly craved, and
now in his despondency he seems to have turned automatically to
the only other group who had ever provided the same emotional
security. In October he wrote to Daniel Roberts, the co-designer of
Shelley's boat, promising 'some good smoking together',[9] and in the
following February, after a silence of two years, to Leigh Hunt.

Dear Hunt,
   There is a tremendous gap in our correspondence – but
none I trust in our friendship – that will hold together proof
against time and accident – at least with me – writing is a
pleasant substitute between friends when debarred talking
together . . .
   So you are in London again. Johnson says no man abuses
London that has lived in it . . . but this I will say, the sun
here is sometimes seen – and the skies are occasionally blue
– which is more than any one has ventured to say of that
Devil's Paradise London . . .
   However, old haunts and old friends are pleasant things
wherever found – Hell would be no Hell with them, or
Heaven Heaven without them! so I give you the joy of your
being in London – nevertheless do not forget the land we

caroused pottle deep – right Etruscan grapes – together. – Did you not visit Rome? – and what's become of our good friends Brown and Severn? – has Mary Ann the Lover of dark beards recovered her strength? I think often of you all and oftener of those of our Pisa circle – Shelley, Byron, Williams! – And where are they?[10]

> In vain – in vain: strike other chords;
> We will not think of themes like these.

But it was not, in fact, to the dead but to Mary Shelley and Claire Clairmont that Trelawny's thoughts most often and indiscriminately turned during these months. 'Dearest Friend,' he wrote to Claire on 22 October 1825, recounting his injuries with a superb flourish that recalls all the Byronic extravagances of his Italian letters and courtship,

> For 18 months it has been utterly out of the question my writing – it was impossible!!
> I am now emancipated; I have descended from my mountain strongholds on Parnassus, where I have been carrying on the war for nearly two years – and was landed here from an English Frigate – had I staid another month my bones had been now whitening there. – I have had a narrow escape Claire – terribly cut up – Death thought me his own – he seized me by the body and limbs – but relented ere his icy paw had clutched my heart – and whether in pity – or hate – or perhaps considering his own interest best served – he let me go . . . [11]

Curiously, though, if Trelawny's letters are to be trusted, it was the thought of Mary, the first person he had told of his injuries, that stirred the deepest emotions. 'An old friend of mine, Capn Watt,' he wrote to her from Zante in May 1826,

> a Lieutenant in the navy – but now turning account in a merchant vessel of his own – sailed on his way to England ten days back – and I desired him to call on you – with

Thomas Hope (left) by Sir William Beechey. Collector, decorator and novelist, Hope was the creator of Anastasius, the fictional romantic outcast who became the role-model for Trelawny's assassin, W. G. Whitcombe. Trelawny himself, shown by Kirkup in the Mavre Troupa (below left), was also described by Mary Shelley as a second Anastasius. Samuel Gridley Howe (below right, by John Elliot), the great American reformer and Philhellene, and the man to whom Whitcombe confessed his crime.

Mt. Parnassus, the saddle between its two highest peaks. This was the route from Delphi to the Mavre Troupa taken by Bacon in 1825.

The Velitza Gorge beneath the cave. As the wounded Trelawny, accompanied by Tersitza and Bacon, made his last exit, the guns of the Mavre Troupa echoed down the valley in one final salute.

17 Sep 1825
Cephalonia

Dear Mary

I have just escaped from
Greece & landed here — in the hopes of patching
up my broken frame & shattered constitution

Two musket balls passed at the distance of
two paces behind me & passed through my frame
work which almost near finished me —

but tis a long story. and my writing arm
is rendered unfit for service — & I am yet unprac-
-tised with the left — But a friend of mine
here a Major Bacon is on his way to England
& will enlighten you — as to me I shall be
confined here some time — write to me then
at this place — I need rest & quiet — for I am

shook to the foundation
Love to Jane & Clare & believe
me your still devoted friend
Edward Trelawny

relawny's first letter to Mary Shelley, written with his 'left fin', after the attempt
his life.

A celebrity at last. Trelawny in four sketches by Duppa (top left), Landseer (top right), Severn (bottom left), and Duppa again (bottom right).

Augusta, Trelawny's third wife, painted by John Linnell in 1827.

Trelawny (second left) and the Philosophical Radicals: almost the only relic of Trelawny's political ambitions before he abandoned London for married life in Usk.

The house on Llanbadoc Rock, high above Usk, that Trelawny built for himself and Augusta. In the background can be seen the cedars planted in the churchyard below from seeds taken from the site of Shelley's grave in Rome.

Even in old age Trelawny had lost nothing of the physical magnetism that had so impressed Claire Clairmont over fifty years earlier. 'His sunken eyes gloomy with reverses,' she had written, 'but indelibly beaming with that intense hardihood and genius which seemed to command the world and even Fate itself.' The portrait by Millais (above) almost provoked Trelawny to a duel with the artist.

Myth in stone: pieta of the dead Shelley
cradled in the arms of Mary (top left) by
Henry Weekes and (top right) Onslow Ford's
memorial at University College, Oxford.

Graves of Shelley and Trelawny in the Protestant cemetery, Rome. 'When I die,'
Trelawny had written in 1823 to Mary Shelley, 'there is only to lift up the coverlet
and roll me into its – you may lie on the other side or I will share my narrow bed
with you if you like.'

letters and commissions &. as he returns here – to Zante –
speedily; two days back he was obliged to return to here;
and so I go on chatting to you – it's the only way we have
of talking, now Mary – the winter ensuing I hope we shall
be together – I often wish you were here – I often think of
inviting you to come here – and when my affairs allow me
to move from here I should like to fix my residence at Naples
or at least in Italy – I do not wish to visit England in my
present state of poverty – England is not a country for the
poor to thrive in – a little time, Mary, and fortune will
relent his persecution of us – I hope – for that is the great
impediment that separates us – and I never was poorer than
now – you say you have formed no new attachments – and
that I hold a place in your affections – you know Mary that
I always loved you impetuously and sincerely – and time
proves its durability – we are both somewhat self-willed and
cross-grained – and choose to love in our own fashions, –
but still where is there a truer friendship than that which
cements together Mary S. and E.T? If I lose you I should
be poor indeed.[12]

Trelawny was always a more ardent friend on paper than in person,
but if his declarations here should be taken as Mary or Claire
regularly would and did take them, it is clear that there was nothing
left to hold him to Greece. Through 1826 and 1827 there was
desultory talk of campaigning alongside Napier, but Trelawny had
lost the will to go back, the will to fight, the will in moments of
genuine depression even to live – 'an old patriarch', as he called
himself in a letter to Mary Shelley, 'who has outlived his generation.'[13]

Even the invincible fortress cavern, the centre of his Byronic
dreams and the focus of so many warring ambitions, now stood as
a desolate symbol of his failure, its parapet torn down, its defenders
dispersed. 'A catalogue of things that Odysseus took from me,' lies
among the papers of the National Archives in Athens. It is a document drawn up by a man called Lambros Alexandrou, and is dated

6 August (O.S.) 1825, twelve days after Trelawny finally left. It lists bedlinen and mattresses, kilims and carpets, bales of cloth and silk, cushions, trumpets, pistols, 'money stolen from my father when Odysseus killed him', pearls, gold and diamond rings, earrings, golden cups, two large round tables, twenty-two pots with lids from Constantinople, and ten items of underwear. It is across this document that the words already quoted were written, 'when a great tree falls, small men cut up the branches.'[14]

As if to prove that true, the different factions had held their ground after Trelawny's exit, mutually distrustful, ready to fight each other rather than concede the cave. In Nauplia the government continued its plans to secure possession. On 24 August 1825 a letter was sent to Odysseus's mother, Acrive.

> You are well aware that your son kept the cave by force and used it as a refuge, and became a dissident. No Greek who is subject to the Laws, has the right to keep under his command a fortress or other fortified place that belongs to the nation, and should be in the possession of the Government. The Government has appointed a Committee consisting of the representatives Anagosti Dedes and Pangiotis Lidorikis, in order to take over the cave, and the things in the cave, except for those things which belong to you.
>
> The Government therefore orders you to come out of the cave, without trusting the deceitful words of people who, either because of malice or for their own profit, are trying to inspire you with unreasonable suspicions and fears.
>
> The Government has no reason to consider you guilty of what your son has done. You will be guaranteed safety and your property as well. The Government will praise you and will take care of you as a child of theirs. But if you disobey this order and insist on staying in the cave, all the expenses that follow will be debited to you, and you will experience the consequences of a thoughtless disobedience to the orders of the Government.[15]

By 15 September an agreement had been reached. From the cave their representatives reported back to the Government. The cave was to be handed over; the family might stay there until a European ship could convey them to safety; all the state property and that of the other persons should be returned; Odysseus's family would receive a pension from the government; the surviving two soldiers in the cave would come under government control.

This is a sadly bureaucratic end to a dream, and to Trelawny's hopes of influencing the course of the war. Broken, impoverished, and disappointed, there was nothing to do now but watch impotently as, across the narrow channel that separated him from the Morea and his old life, Greece slid friendless to her apparent destruction. 'Alas poor Greece,' he wrote to Hunt,

> after its long and bloody struggle to rend its chains asunder
> – it has come to this – their only chance of freedom seems
> at present the sharp edge of a Turkish scimitar – and there
> is no lack of such bloody emancipation – Ibrahim Pasha
> with his Arabs are as deadly as the simoon of their own
> deserts – he says he will exterminate the name of Christian
> in the land – and transplant his Arabs there – and if Europe
> continues her apathy – then he will accomplish his vow –
> three parts of the Peloponnesus are now in his hands, with
> the five best fortresses – the Greeks have only Napoli –
> Corinth and the Acropolis in Attica – Ibrahim is now at
> Patras – preparing military engines to storm Missolonghi –
> under the direction of his French officers – and tis probable
> he will succeed in taking it – all the other parts of Western
> and great part of Eastern Greece is already in his hands –
> and on the fall of Missolonghi – the Acropolis of Athens
> will be bombarded.[16]

In letter after letter back to England, the course of the war across the water forms this grim counterpoint to his own unhappiness. Two months later in April 1826 his worst fears were realised, and Zante, as he told Hunt's brother, 'sunk into gloom and despair' by the news of Missolonghi's fall. 'I always said Greece could not liberate herself', he wrote to Mary Shelley,

> it seems Europe leaves her to her fate – and that fate is not far distant – which will verify my predictions. Missolonghi, reduced by famine – strictly blockaded by Ibrahim Pasha – by sea and land – unaided by the Greeks – has fallen a prey to the Arabs – the sword and bayonet have made clean work there – and of its ten thousand inhabitants – I doubt that ten are living to tell the tragic story of their fate – fire and powder has completed the destruction of what was Missolonghi –
>
> > And many a time ye there might pass
> > Nor dream that e'er that fortress was:
>
> The next slaughter will I think be at Hydra. – The Greeks will then no longer stay in Napoli – and yet surrounded by ruin and death the Greeks were never so far from being united as they are at this instant – the Greeks seem indifferent to the fate of their country – so that they can glut their private hatred; revenge with them is a virtue – their jealousy and hatred of each other seems to fill every bosom – and the sacred cause they armed in is forgot – thus then a revolution commenced by a million of slaves against their masters in 1821 ends in 1826 with the loss of more than half their numbers – and the survivors are ceded from their slavery to the free and not cruel Turk – to be bondsmen to their Arab slaves – to be slaves of slaves – and sunk into abject, hopeless, and eternal slavery . . . [17]

It would seem from Trelawny's letters at this time that he was a more genuine and disinterested Philhellene than he had ever been, but with Odysseus dead, as he confessed in another letter to Mary, he 'felt no private interest for any individual in this country'.[18]

On Zante, too, there was little enough for him to do and for such an inveterate and gifted storyteller, it is perhaps strange that he never at this period seems to have thought of capitalizing on his Greek adventures with the kind of book that so many Philhellenes were producing. It is clear from Swan's accounts of the *Cambrian* that he was only too ready to live up to his new-found notoriety, but for the time at least the memory of the Mavre Troupa and the assassination attempt – the raw material of so much of his future fame – were too painfully tied up with failure to dwell on.

There is the testimony of the British consul for Trelawny's reluctance to hear it mentioned, but a more graphic illustration came in 1826 with a strange codicil to the affair in the cave, a small incident so full of combustible promise and such a damp squib in the end, that it shows more vividly than anything else Trelawny's mood at this time.

Sometime in the previous autumn the first news of William Guise Whitcombe's disgrace had filtered back to his family in England, and two of his brothers, Samuel, on half-pay from the navy, and Thomas, the closest in age to William and a lieutenant in the East India Company artillery, set out in December for Greece to find out what had happened.

In February 1826 they arrived in the Ionian Isles in search of Trelawny. On the 13th Sir Frederick Adam's military secretary, Major Rudsell, wrote to Colonel Napier on Cephalonia, warning him of their arrival, and anxious to ensure that Napier should 'make the most effectual measures to prevent any breach of the Peace occurring between the Parties concerned'.[19]

The next day Rudsell wrote again to Napier, more concerned this time, after a promise from Thomas that there would be no duel, with Trelawny's possible behaviour than that of the Whitcombes. 'The Gentlemen', he told him,

> declare that they seek an interview with Mr Trelawny for the sole purpose of ascertaining from him the real state of their Brother's proceeding and to obtain from Mr Trelawny any assurance if he have it in his power fairly and conscientiously to give it that their Brother's conduct has not been of so dark a kind as has been set forth.[20]

It is easy enough to imagine a time when Trelawny would have taken umbrage at far less – and Thomas later fought a duel that was almost certainly over William – but while there is no record of their meeting it obviously passed off without incident.

In these sombre and muted months after the assassination attempt he seems in fact a more human and honest figure than at any other time in his life, but if with weakness and injury had come a surprising integrity, with recovery the old Trelawny was ready to re-emerge. As early as the May of 1826 a puzzled Claire Clairmont had written to Mary Shelley, putting her finger on a side of his life on Cephalonia and Zante that never featured in his letters. 'I hope Trelawny will come to England,' she wrote,

> as the repose and the visit will likely do him good. It is very strange that he should not mention his wife and it is strange that he should feel solitary. I do not understand what he wants.[21]

It is probable that Trelawny himself did not know at this time either, but whatever it was it was certainly not Tersitza. Swan had been right when he said that there was nothing to tie a fourteen- or fifteen-year-old girl to a man now in his mid-thirties. It was a relationship that belonged to a world that Trelawny had left behind. On Zante, too, as she grew older, Tersitza was less prepared to be a mere chattel, a Byronic accessory. A daughter, Zella, conceived in the cave and named after Trelawny's mythical eastern bride, had been born at the end of 1825, but by the time Tersitza had a second child, she had already left Trelawny and was living in a convent.

In the protracted lawsuit that followed their separation the reason she gave was that Trelawny 'had failed to treat me with that consideration and nobility which distinguished the men of his nation'.* A story current at the time, that Trelawny had hacked off her hair in public when she defied his injunction against western dress, gives a certain colour to this, but it was another incident in their married life which echoed scurrilously down the nineteenth century, adding a macabre note to Trelawny's reputation. The story was told in an oddly garbled form to Joseph Severn's son in 1878 by John Cooke, who had heard it over forty years earlier when he was a midshipman in the Mediterranean. 'It is a curious and rather ghastly story,' Cooke wrote to him,

> Your father well remembers that when Trelawny was in Greece he lived *maritalement* with the daughter of the Greek chief, Odysseus, in the Morea and she had a child with him. Months afterwards the Odysseus family was made aware of the certainty of not seeing their respected son-in-law again and wrote to him begging that the child might be sent back. A long time passed, and at last a letter to say that if the Chief Odysseus or his representative would come across on a certain day to Zante the child would be forthcoming. A scampavia was dispatched and away went some of the Odysseus family to Zante. The Custom House authorities could give no account of any child, but they stated that a box had arrived via Corfu which it was much wished should be removed by the Greeks, as it smelt offensively. Whereupon the box was delivered and opened, and a child's dead body, dead some weeks appeared; whether any invoice or remarks by Trelawny accompanied it I never heard. The child had died and he took this grim and savage way of ridding himself of all connection with the Odysseus circle.[22]

The truth was rather different but scarcely an improvement. 'The stories you have heard are doubtless exaggerated,' the Deputy Collector of Customs in Corfu was assured by an Englishman on Zante. 'I will tell you the real one.'

> While his wife was at a convent a daughter was born which she sent to Mr Trelawny. He put it out to nurse; it died and he as a punishment sent the dead body to the Castle monastery.[23]

With this piece of Jacobean melodrama behind him Trelawny was ready for England, or desperate at least to quit Greece. 'You err most egregiously,' he irritably told Mary Shelley, if you think I am occupied with women or intrigues, or that my time passes pleasantly. The reverse of all this is the case; neither women nor amusements of any sort occupy my time, and a sadder or more accursed kind of existence I never in all my experience of life endured, or, I think, fell to the lot of human being. I have been detained here for these last ten months by a villainous law-suit, [his divorce] which may yet endure some months longer, and then I shall return to you as the same unconnected, lone, and wandering vagabond you first knew me.[24]

This is the last letter from Greece in the collected edition of his letters, and if it seems a bitter end to four years of excitement, danger and fulfilment, it is all the more so when one thinks of the date it was written – 24 October 1827, just four days after the combined British, French and Russian squadrons under the command of Admiral Codrington had sailed into the great bay at Navarino, and dropped anchor opposite the Ottoman and Egyptian fleets.

What followed next at Navarino was an accident, but an accident that most of Europe had been more or less willing to happen for six long years. For the first years of the war the governments of the Great Powers had stood out against popular Philhellenism, but from the summer of 1825 a gradual shift of policy had brought Britain and Russia, and then France, to the verge of co-ordinated intervention to halt the miseries of Greece.

In 1826 the first protocol was signed, and in July 1827, at the Treaty of London, the three powers committed themselves to military force, if necessary, to keep the belligerents apart and prevent the absolute destruction of Greece.

The fleet that was sent to the Eastern Mediterranean to enforce this policy was officially neutral, but acting under only the vaguest of orders and the strongest of Philhellene sympathies, an eventual conflict with Ibrahim's fleet was inevitable.

The bay at Navarino is about three miles long and two wide, closed in on the west by the island of Sphacteria, and open to ships only from a channel to the south-west. The Turkish and Ottoman vessels were already riding at anchor when, at about mid-day on 20 October, the allied fleet of twenty-seven ships, with Codrington's flag ship, the *Asia*, in the van, sailed under the shore guns of Navarino and Sphacteria, and one by one came to rest within the enveloping crescent of Ibrahim's fleet.

The allies' ostensible purpose was merely to prevent the Egyptian and Turkish ships from leaving, but in the face of this nautical *haka*, tensions in Ibrahim's fleet ran high. A boat was despatched from the *Dartmouth* to warn off an Egyptian fire-ship, but when a sharp-shooter shot and killed an allied officer on board, and a second rescue boat was in its turn fired on, an exchange of musket fire escalated rapidly into a full-scale engagement.

It was the last great battle fought by sailing ships, and the strangest, a static battle begun by accident, slugged out for over four hours at point-blank range without tactics or strategy, decided only by the discipline, courage and gunnery of the allied fleets. Not a single French, Russian or British ship was lost, and only 176 men killed, including just one from the *Cambrian*. Fifty-five of Ibrahim's ships were destroyed completely, the rest disabled, and over six thousand men killed.*

Out of the blue, the war was won. Without a navy to subdue Hydra and reinforce his army, Ibrahim was impotent, cut off from his supply-line in a land gripped by a famine that his savagery had done so much to cause. In the north, and on Chios, the fighting dragged on purposelessly into the next year, and at sea the most brilliant of the foreign volunteers, Frank Abney Hastings, was killed in a skirmish, but the only questions after Navarino concerned not the existence but the boundaries of the new Greece.

After six years of folly, heroism, selflessness and greed, the day of the Philhellene was gone. It was time for the adventurers and idealists to go home. From now on the future of Greece belonged to the Great Powers, to conference tables, diplomacy, armies, finances, and the Bavarian House of Wittelsbach. On Zante Trelawny heard the news of Navarino, and saw instantly what it meant. His 'crusade', as he liked to call it, was over. At the end of that same dispirited letter to Mary Shelley he relayed the news of victory, adding it almost as an afterthought, thrown off with a dying fall that sounds the melancholy epitaph on all his Greek ambitions. 'The Egyptian fleet,' he told her,

> and part of the Turkish, amounting to some hundred sail, including transports, have been totally destroyed by the united squadron of England, France and Russia in the harbour of Navarino; so we soon expect to see a portion of Greece wrested from the Turks, and something definitely arranged for the benefit of the Greeks. – Dearest Mary, I am ever your
>   Edward Trelawny.
>   To Jane and Clare say all that is affectionate from me, and forget not Leigh Hunt and his Mary Ann. I would write them all, but I am sick at heart.[25]

14

GOING PUBLIC

'It is enough for you to be here in Greece for me to say to
you: write down either the events which have already occurred
to you in life or those that shall occur to you in future, and
you will find on examination that few romances contain so
many romantic incidents as your own life.'

Byron to George Finlay[1]

'Call me Turk – savage – pirate, robber, any thing – but not
a hireling – a paid menial of a Lord.'

Trelawny to Mary Shelley[2]

THERE ARE MOMENTS IN Trelawny's life when there is nothing
to do but stand back and admire the swagger of the man, and for
sheer effrontery and daring his return to England in the early summer
of 1828 stands comparison with even the great imposture of his
Pisan debut.

Trelawny was always such a success as a fabulist and self-publicist
that it is easy to forget that for the last fifty years of his life he was
never more than an innuendo or sneer away from exposure and
disaster. For seven years he had been able to re-shape his own past
in the relative anonymity of Italy and Greece, but an England and
an English family that knew his early history was another matter,
an unknown and unpredictable quantity that took nerves of steel to
silence in the way he did.

For a man so outwardly contemptuous of popular opinion, however, Trelawny was always a shrewd and cynical judge of his public,

and he seems to have recognized with an instinct stronger than caution or self-doubt that, in the violent and murky history of his Odysseus years, lay both an amnesty for his youth and the raw material of his future fame. During the months in the Ionian Isles, plagued by ill-health, law-suits and the consciousness of failure, uncertainty and depression had never been far off, and yet as soon as he set foot on English soil it was as if his time in Greece had been one long and seamless triumph. At last, at the age of thirty-six, he was what he had always said he was – the Byronic romantic with the scars and the history to outface all doubters, the blood-brother of Greece's most notorious klepht, the master of a Parnassan lair, the husband of an eastern child bride, the victim of Phanariot plotting, a name at last, as he would proudly tell Mary Shelley, to 'raise a spirit'.[3]

If there was any lingering apprehension on his part as he made his way back across Europe, any uncertainty over his reception, the unexpected warmth of his family would soon have stilled it. Seventeen years earlier his mother had declared that she had 'no son' but now, apparently indifferent to the nature of his fame, she and her relatives were ready to welcome home the prodigal. 'You have been very kind in your attentions to my son,' she wrote with a quaintly misplaced optimism and Trelawnyesque spelling to her brother Sir Christopher Hawkins.

> and I make no doubt but that this created some interest. He has acquired much knowledge & having a large share of sence makes him universally liked. Few individuals have made themselves more known in the world.
>
> I some time mentioned to you that he would be a useful person to our government . . . [4]

Although Trelawny was happy to parade as a 'savage' and a 'pirate,' he was also by instinct, tastes and upbringing a member of his class and there was a growing confidence as he recognized that after his early failures he had a place in the world into which he had been born. The weeks after landing in England were spent in a dutiful round of family visits that helped cement this, seeing his mother and uncle in the West Country, holding forth on Greek politics and picking up again with the two daughters of his first marriage – their mother, Caroline had died a year earlier – whom he had not seen since 1820.

It was not only his family who were impressed with him, as artists and writers responded to his presence and personality with an uncritical willingness to take him at his own evaluation. On his journey back home Seymour Kirkup had painted him against the Parnassan background of the Mavre Troupa, and it must have been in Florence at this same time that Trelawny inspired the poet Landor to the ludicrous tribute of his *Imaginary Conversations*.

There was a natural if dangerous affinity with the turbulent Landor that perhaps makes his admiration understandable, but a more surprising endorsement of Trelawny's new status was soon to come from a man of very different stamp. Shortly after his return to England Trelawny paid the first of several visits to the ageing William Godwin, Mary Shelley's father and a survivor from an earlier age of radicalism. In the fictional character of Borromeo in his novel *Cloudesley* Godwin has left a portrait of the fiercely independent and truth-loving figure Trelawny so successfully projected.

The English yeoman had lately formed an intimacy with an Italian of an extraordinary character, whose name was Borromeo. His first destination had been the sea, and he had made several voyages in the employment of the merchant-men of Livorno. In one of these voyages he had been taken prisoner by the Algerines, and sold for a slave. There was in him a remarkable independence and stubborness of temper, very ill adapted to the condition in which he had fallen ... Yet his bluntness, his soul that nothing could bend, or subject to the influence of enticement or menace, and his fearlessness of danger, had in a thousand instances proved his preservation ...

Few things can be more dissimilar, than is frequently the outside of a man from what passes within him. The slave-drivers of the African coast could find in Borromeo no symptoms expressive of pain or injury; no muscle flinched, no feature altered, for all that they could do to him. It was their observation, that you might as well fight with the intrenched air, or lay your lashes on the sea, as expect severities to produce an effect upon Borromeo. But though his muscles did not alter, and he did not gratify the malice of his tyrants by uttering a groan or sigh, it was all laid up in the inner-most core of his heart, and generated in him a creed of a peculiar nature. He never lied: for, as he feared nothing, and encountered both menaces and inflictions with unalterable firmness, he had no motive to deceive. It was not out of consideration for others, but respect for himself, that he always bluntly uttered the truth . . . Utterly regardless of the treatment he might receive, he viewed his fellow-mortals with ineffable contempt. They were to him like so many powerless insects, that we do not even give ourselves the trouble to brush away, but suffer them to enact their pleasures without control and without observation. Yet this man was eminently a moral being. He had certain rules of right to which he rigorously adhered, not for the sake of the good to result to others, but, as certain theologians inculcate in their systems, from the simple love of justice, and without care for the consequences to result.[5]

Among all the improbable successes of Trelawny's homecoming, however, the bustle of his family visits and the admiration of audiences happy to listen to his stories of Greece, there was one unexpected shadow which fell over his relations with the women who bound him closest to his days with Byron and Shelley. During those long months of convalescence and depression in the Ionian Isles it would seem from his letters that only the thought of Mary and Claire had kept him emotionally alive, and yet for some reason the moment now that he had the chance actually to see them again he pulled back. 'Dear Mary,' he wrote from Southampton more than a month after his first arrival in England,

My moving about and having had so much to do must be my excuse for not writing as often as I should do. That it is but an excuse I allow; the truth would be better, but who nowadays ever thinks of speaking truth? The true reason, then, is that I am getting old, and writing has become irksome. You cannot plead either, so write on, dear Mary. I love you sincerely, no one better. Time has not quenched the fire of my nature; my feelings and passions burn fierce as ever, and will till they have consumed me. I wear the burnished livery of the sun . . .

I cannot decidedly say or fix a period of our meeting. It shall be soon, if you stay there, at Hastings; but I have business on hand I wish to conclude, and now that I can see you when I determine to do so, I, as you see, postpone the engagement because it is within my grasp. Such is the perverseness of human nature! Nevertheless, I will write, and I pray you do so likewise. You are my dear and long true friend, and as such I love you. – Yours, dear,

Trelawny[6]

One cannot be sure what lay behind this letter, except that it was something that Trelawny himself would have found difficult to articulate. It is very possible that after five years of anticipation nothing more than natural fear of disappointment held him back, and yet it seems likely that something else is at work here, something that has less to do with Mary or Claire – to whom he wrote in almost identical vein – than with Trelawny's burgeoning sense of his own independence, and with it the growing need to redefine his relationship with those two seminal figures for whom Byron's mistress and Shelley's widow now stood fond but critical proxy.

It is never easy with Trelawny to say where instinct ends and calculation begins, but there seems something deliberate and cold blooded in the way that after years of devotion he now took a pace back from the Pisan women. The crudest explanation was that the years which had only added distinction to his appearance had been less kind to both Claire and Mary, but if there was almost certainly a sexual element in his retreat, there was also a new note of censoriousness, a crueller edge, a coolness behind the stock effusions, an emotional dishonesty even, that spelled out a clear change in the balance of power between them.

He had eventually gone down to see Mary in Hastings where she was recovering from a disfiguring attack of smallpox, and although there is no date for their reunion, he must have met Claire in London sometime in the late autumn after her return from Russia. It was the first time he had seen her since that day on the banks of the Arno in 1822, and when they met it was as two old friends at once familiar and awkward with each other, bound and separated by the past, by their clear-sighted knowledge of each other, but above all by the inexorable circumstances of gender which were opening out fresh opportunities for him as they extinguished hope and life for her.

Their new relationship was clearly uneasy from the start. 'Is it that you find me so very uncommunicative in conversation, that you wish to see if my heart will open itself more freely on paper?' she movingly demanded in January 1829, in response to a letter from him denouncing her as 'horridly prudish', as 'fish-like – bloodless – and insensible', 'the counterpart of Werter – a sort of bread butter and worsted stockings – like Charlotte fit for "suckling fools and chronicling small beer"'.[7]

> You have guessed very rightly. It might have been centuries before I should have been able to express by word what I now shall tell you by paper. I have many times endeavoured to discover the reason why my heart shuts up – at every bodys approach, and the only answer I find is, that in its former days when full to overflowing with kindness to all, it was so misunderstood suspected and slandered, that it has taken refuge in a proud solitude of silence, and there it wears away, in such a deep gloom that its very being becomes doubted.
>
> Do not think the melancholy you see sometimes upon me, is the sign of hopeless wretchedness, I am happy – it is only the shadow of former days, which throws its deep gloom over my mind, which is not yet passed away. How should I not be happy, when I possess so many good friends,

and see you – restored as by a miracle from out of the thousand perils – with which fate had encompassed you. Of all the band which accompanied you in your wild crusade – you return – and return alone. I find you improved, your character has lost much of its original fierceness and wildness. You are softened into something like thoughtfulness – and your passions have died away, and your strong intellect, unclouded by them, lives in wisdom. I wish very much Dear friend to see you married – and I am sure if you were to a beautiful and young woman you would be happy and make her so . . .

What have you done these rainy days dear friend is your mind so occupied with the image of Medora that you are insensible to the elements; I envy the elasticity of your nature that can still cling to a hope, or believe in any thing, a great hurricane has passed o'er my hopes, – and washed away every-thing, and I have no mind to gather together the fragments and begin again – and construct another fortress for my heart – out of the ruins of that devastation? How happy must you be to whom pleasure is pleasure – whilst to me it is only pain – But I have promised not to be gloomy – what must I talk about?[8]

Few things are more poignant than the spectre of a woman of Claire's vitality and generosity crushed by the burden of her past and sex in this way, but it was the very desolation of her letter that repulsed Trelawny. For Claire, as for Mary, the past was a tragedy renewed every day she lived. It was an endless nightmare filled with the ghosts of Shelley and Allegra, and of Mary's dead children. It meant bitterness and remorse, humiliation and rejection, exile, secretiveness, and silence. For Claire in particular it meant Byron and the agony of not even knowing where her child was buried; for Mary the awful sense that she had failed Shelley, the deep depression that had followed his death and the constant fear that their history, in all its daring and vivid unconventionality, would rise again to damage her young son's prospects.

In letter after letter through 1828–9 and 1830, Trelawny tried to tease, bully, reason, charm or cajole Claire out of her unhappiness, but behind his frustration at a misery he was helpless to touch, the real discord lay in the brutal fact that to him this same past was an opportunity and not a secret. It was his 'passport', almost, to a future that we first glimpse in a letter to Mary written only weeks after this exchange. It was sent from Florence on 11 March 1829, two months after he had suddenly quit England again, driven out, he claimed, by the gloom of a London winter sabbath.

> Dear Mary,
> I arrived here some sixteen or seventeen days back. I travelled in a very leisurely way; whilst on the road I used expedition, but I stayed at Lyons, Turin, Genoa, and Leghorn. I have taken up my quarters with Brown . . .
> My principal object in writing to you now is to tell you that I am actually writing my own life. Brown and Landor are spurring me on, and are to review it sheet by sheet, as it is written; moreover, I am commencing as a tribute of my great love for the memory of Shelley his life and moral character. Landor and Brown are in this to have a hand, therefor I am collecting every information regarding him. I always wished you to do this, Mary: if you will not, as of the living I love you and him best, incompetent as I am, I must do my best to show him to the world as I found him. Do you approve of this? Will you aid in it? without which it cannot be done. Will you give documents? Will you write anecdotes?[9]

'I am glad that you are occupying yourself', was Mary's wary reply,

> and I hope that your two friends will not cease urging you till you really put to paper the strange wild adventures you recount so well.
> With regard to the other subject, you may guess, my dear Friend, that I have often thought, often done more than think on the subject. There is nothing I shrink from more fearfully than publicity. I have too much of it, and, what is worse, I am forced by my hard situation to meet it in a thousand ways. Could you write my husband's life without

naming me, it would be something, but even then I should be terrified at rousing the slumbering voice of the public . . .

You know me, or you do not – in which case I will tell you what I am – a silly goose, who, far from wishing to stand forward to assert myself in any way, now that I am alone in the world, have but the time to wrap night and the obscurity of insignificance around me. This is weakness, but I cannot help it; to be in print, the subject of men's observations, of the bitter hard world's commentaries, to be attacked or defended, this ill becomes one who knows how little she possesses worthy to attract attention, and whose chief merit – if it be one – is a love of that privacy which no woman can emerge from without regret.[10]

In the timidity and conventionality of Mary's reply – its 'canting' betrayal, as Trelawny saw it, of her whole radical and feminist inheritance – lies the seed of their future estrangement. Twenty years after her death his festering resentment would break out in a savage and public attack, but even if he could not see it himself at the time, this was a rejection that in the end would serve him and literature well. It would be another thirty years almost before a more mature and stylistically assured Trelawny would write the great memoir of the Pisan circle that Mary blocked here, and yet the truth anyway was that the one subject to which he could have done justice in 1829 was not Shelley or Byron, but Trelawny himself.

That was the theme that engrossed all others, the logical conclusion to his lifelong search for identity, and an ambition that in one form or another had lurked at the back of his mind for almost a decade. As early as April 1821 Edward Williams had credulously noted in his journal that he had talked with Trelawny 'of a play of his singular life',[11] but it was his years in Greece that finally brought things to a head, and the name he had made out there which at the age of nearly forty at last gave him a reputation and history that were bankable.

As he had written to Mary in his first letter to her from Italy, he was living in the house of Keats's friend Charles Armitage Brown, and under the supportive tutelage of Brown and the poet Landor he now set about the task of manufacturing his autobiography. Each day, he told Mary, Brown and Landor would spur him on, reviewing his work sheet by sheet as it was written, and helping select the mottoes from Byron, Shelley, and Keats which headed each chapter. By 7 April 1829, he was telling Claire, seventy printed sheets were already done, and by the beginning of July three hundred and fifty, fairly copied in manuscript and ready for the press.

Not since the weeks after Byron's death had Trelawny shown such energy, or seemed so entirely confident as to who he was. In July 1829 he went to Ancona to collect Zella, his young daughter conceived in the cave, from the Ionian Isles, and on returning with her to Florence installed himself in a villa just outside the town to finish his book. 'I am, now, living in a large Villa two miles from Florence within a stone's throw of where Gallileo once lived,' he told Claire in December,

> it is on top of a mountain – and I am in as perfect solitude as you should wish me. – Oh, that you were here to share it – my little Zella, who is near her fourth year, is my only consolation . . . my occupation is in writing – the second volume of my life is nearly finished; but though I am writing as briefly as perspicuity will admit of – the History of my life will fill five or six Volumes, and that only the marrow of the many events which have happened – three volumes will be ready for publication in a few months – remember Claire I anticipate your assistance in sketching the life of Shelley . . . as to Mary I have thrown the gauntlet down to her – and as she will not contribute – why I'll do without her – or if compelled to speak to her, I shall speak according to her deserts, but not unjustly or in anger.[12]

With 'an excellent woman'[13] to look after Zella, a *contadino* and his wife to see to his own needs, and Brown and Landor those of his manuscript, the fantasies and facts that over the last decade had grafted themselves on to each other in his imagination rapidly took on their definitive shape as his anonymous *Adventures of a Younger Son*. His initial plan had been to narrate the early years under the old family title of 'Treloen' with a second volume on Pisa and Greece published under his own name, but whatever anxieties over its reception or his protestations to the contrary in letters to Mary or Claire, genuine anonymity was never any part of his design when he finally decided that it was time to go public.

From the instructions that flowed out of Italy on the subject of publishers and terms, it is clear that money was one motive for authorship, and yet it was at the most only of secondary importance.* For Trelawny, writing was less an act of finance or even self-expression than of reclamation, of re-possession, a chance at last to become the author of his own experience, the creator of his own personality rather than an inchoate fragment of the romantic imagination.

It was, too, his bid for fame, for parity with the men who had shaped his growth, and there is no more graphic illustration of the compulsion this represented than that he was prepared to stake everything on its success. When the book was finally published in 1831 there were still any number of people in and out of his family who could have exposed the great fraud of his pirate career, but with that audacity that had characterized his whole adult life Trelawny was ready to challenge them all.

His bravado was rewarded too, as his audience, and even his mother who openly boasted of his authorship, responded with a show of selective amnesia and mass credulity that beggars belief. In an important sense, he was lucky with his timing, though as so often with Trelawny, luck turns out on closer inspection to be more a matter of instinct and daring. When she saw the manuscript Mary had objected to the violence of some of its language and scenes, but he seemed to know his readership in a way that the professional woman of letters did not. He knew that the very crudities she protested against, the brutality, the luxuriance, the violence of its central character, were not just its guarantee of commercial success but of the apparent *truthfulness* of its confessions. 'It has been a painful and arduous undertaking narrating my life . . .' he told her.

> My life, though I have sent it to you, as the dearest friend I have, is not written for the amusement of women; it is not a novel. If you begin clipping the wings of my true story, if you begin erasing words, you must then omit sentences, then chapters; it will be pruning an Indian jungle down to a clipped French garden . . . Dear Mary, I love women, and you know it, but my life is not dedicated to them; it is to men I write . . . [14]

Even here, however, he was being disingenuous, dissembling the arrogance which throughout his life lay behind his democratic front. 'To whom am I a neighbour? and near whom?', he had demanded of Mary Shelley on his first return from Greece,

> I dwell amongst the tame and civilised human beings, with somewhat the same feelings as we may guess the Lion feels – when torn from his native wilderness – he is tortured into domestic intercourse with – what Shakespeare calls 'forked animals' – the most abhorrent to his nature![15]

It was for this 'tame' world of 'forked animals' that *Adventures* was written, for a world which stood between Catholic Emancipation and the Great Reform Act of 1832, a world on the brink of a middle-class franchise, of factory reforms and political maturity, of recognizable modernity, of novels like Bulwer's *Pelham* and the ignorant nonsense of the young Disraeli, a world to which the excesses of Trelawny's eastern fantasies were no more nor less alien than the savage realities of the war in Greece. Why should anyone doubt De Ruyter's existence when Odysseus was a fact of history? Or when the paintings of Kirkup and West, and the memoirs of Palma, Swan, Humphreys, Millingen, and Landor's *Imaginary Conversation* had created an image of Trelawny only too coherent with the violence and glamour of his revelations? What reason was there to question the existence of Zela when in a cave on Mount Parnassus Trelawny had married the thirteen-year-old sister of a mountain chief and fathered a daughter named after his dead eastern bride? What were the acts of treachery of *Adventures* to Fenton's and Whitcombe's? What could not be believed of the high priest at the atheist Shelley's cremation?

Trelawny's existence had come full circle. He had lived out his life in Greece sustained by the fantasies of his youth, and now history in its turn had come to validate those very dreams. 'As the hues and forms of nature transcend the painter's art,' the *Military Review* trumpeted to Trelawny's intense pleasure,

> so the incidents of real life equal or surpass the warmest creations of fancy. Romance can go no farther than the actual adventures of the homicidal renegade and corsair the 'Younger Son'.[16]

'Such is the vigour, the freshness and novelty of many parts of the narrative,' the anonymous writer for the liberal *Westminster Review* put it,

> that there can be no doubt that the writer is consulting the deep imprints of experience rather than the brilliant shadows of his imagination. The known European adventures of Mr Trelawny [so much for anonymity!] prepared us not to be surprised that marvels happened to him in the East, the native land of passion and extravagance. His enthusiastic adoption of the Greek cause, his romantic friendship with the chief Odysseus, his inhabitation of that hero's fortress cave, his espousal of his daughter, and his ultimate assassination by a scoundrel Englishman, and the long and painful recovery from his wounds, under the careful nursery, we believe, of his Greek wife, though on board an English brig: these, and other circumstances, more especially the strength and beauty of his form, while it was a youthful one, have for some time marked him out as a likely man to do and dare all those wild things here set down by him.[17]

Trelawny had achieved the equality he was after, had soared out of the shadows of Byron's fame as he had once promised Claire he would do. He was now not just the friend of the late Lord Byron, but 'the person from whom the poet is said to have taken the idea and exploits of his Conrad'.[18] 'We are disposed to think,' the same Westminster reviewer wrote,

> the *Adventures of a Younger Son* the cleverest work of description that has left the press for some years . . . If Lord Byron had written a novel he would not have written a better, but he would have written one very like it.[19]

The model for Byron's corsair, the high priest of Shelleyan atheism, the friend of Keats it was now widely and wrongly believed, all that divided him from the great figures of Romanticism, the review concluded, was that 'he had done more than perhaps all these sons of Apollo put together'.[20]

There were, of course, dissenting voices raised against the 'extreme grossness of the language' and the celebration of a life 'in which there is not a single redeeming point',[21] but a public starved of anything stronger than Disraeli's *The Young Duke* was in no doubt that the *Westminster Review* had got it right.

It is, too, the author of that same long article who put his finger on the reason for the immediate and abiding success of *Adventures*. It is impossible now to imagine how Trelawny could have carried off his imposture for a single moment, and yet even with all the debunking evidence of modern scholarship available it remains just as hard to realize how little fact there is in it. It is just as difficult to resist that 'impress' of truth as it was then, the sense of lived experience that burns off its pages, the compelling probability of 'irrelevant' detail, the fullness and richness of its imagined life – just as hard to remember that these are not proofs of the book's central integrity but the first indications that at the age of forty Trelawny had it in him to become a creative writer of the first rank.

Trelawny had always been a gifted story-teller, but with his *Adventures* he proved that he could make that rarer and more difficult transition from conversation to the page.

There is still a floweriness to much of the prose that is curiously at odds with his character, but even among the excesses of his Zela fantasies one can see a control and sense of pace that already adds up to something more than 'promise', an underlying and independent originality that needs only the confidence of success to show itself in its true colours.

At the height of his powers, however, fully recovered mentally and physically from the cave, buoyed by celebrity and back again, as it were, to his best fighting weight – thirteen stone when he weighed himself in the Burlington Arcade in 1831 – his ambitions went farther than mere literary fame. In the act of writing his *Adventures* Trelawny had discovered what seemed to him a coherent pattern to his life, a logical development that had taken him from childhood rebellion in his father's orchard to Pisa and Greece in a search for justice and fairness. It was this same quest that now craved a larger stage. 'By the bye', he wrote to Mary Shelley on 29 June 1831,

you say justly the MS. ends abruptly; the truth is, as you know, it is only the first part of my life, and to conclude it will fill three more volumes: that it is to be concluded, I thought I had stated in a paragraph annexed to the last chapter of that which is now in the press, which should run thus –

'I am, or rather have, continued this history of my life, and it will prove I have not been a passive instrument of despotism, nor shall I be found consorting with those base, sycophantic, and mercenary wretches who crouch and crawl and fawn on kings, and priests, and lords, and all in authority under them. On my return to Europe, its tyrants had gathered together all their helots and gladiators to restore the cursed dynasty of the Bourbons, and thousands of slaves went forth to extinguish and exterminate liberty, truth, and justice. I went forth, too, my hand ever against them, and when tyranny had triumphed, I wandered an exile in the world and leagued myself with men worthy to be called so, for they, inspired by wisdom, uncoiled the frauds contained in lying legends, which had so long fatally deluded the majority of mankind. Alas! those apostles have not lived to see the tree they planted fructify; would they had tarried a little while to behold this new era of 1830–31, how they would have rejoiced to behold the leagued conspiracy of kings broken, and their bloodhound priests and nobles muzzled, their impious confederacy to enslave and rob the people paralysed by a blow that has shaken their usurpation to the base, and must inevitably be followed by their final over-throw. Yes, the sun of freedom is dawning on the pallid slaves of Europe,' etc . . .

If I thought there was a probability that I could get a seat in the reformed House of Commons, I would go to England, or if there was a probability of revolution . . . Do you think there is any opening among the demagogues for me? It is a bustling world at present, and likely so to continue. I must play a part. Write, Mary mine, speedily.[22]

The tone of this letter is enough in itself to explain why there would be no future in politics for Trelawny, but as in 1828 he was again restless for change. When he had left England for Italy then he had seemed ready to take on the burden of the three daughters of his marriages to Caroline and Tersitza, but Trelawny was predictably no better a father than his own had been and when Eliza, whom he had never known died suddenly in 1829, his interest in his surviving children went little farther than farming Julia and Zella out to be brought up by suitable families in Italy.

The shedding of these ties – 'chains' he called them[23] – was matched by the continued gradual but inexorable estrangement from Mary and Claire. It would be possible to read his letters to both women through the whole of the 1830s and see in them nothing but the old warmth of the Pisan days, but the simple truth was that with the success of *Adventures* he had finally outgrown them, out-grown their advice, outgrown their failures, outgrown what he thought the sad and narrow poverty of their lives, the one wrapped up in her child, Percy, the other in the lonely misery of hired drudgery.

'Dear Clare,' he wrote evasively to her on 4 January 1831, in response to her offer of coming to live with him and Zella, my affection and friendship for you is not nor ever can be diminished. I really know of nothing which could give me such entire satisfaction as realizing the plan you have laid; and I acknowledge with gratitude your considerate kindness in proposing it, that all the benefits which would accrue would fall to my share – your society would be to me a never failing source of comfort; and to my child it would be an inestimable advantage; but as I have often said we are slaves of circumstances. I have struggled all my life to break the chains with which fate has manacled me – but it is in vain – this letter will give you no less pain in reading than it has me in writing. I cannot in the ferment of my mind write clearly or express myself better – I beseech you to think of me as favourably as you can – and to believe me when I say – that my heart bleeds when thinking of all you have endured and the present unhappy state of your mind . . .

   P.S. I am thinking of sending Zella to a friend in England, and resuming my Arab life.[24]

With Claire – pale, thin, and haggard, her spirits broken, still only in her early thirties but looking fifty as he told Mary – there is possibly also a faint sense that he was punishing her for that afternoon in Pisa nearly ten years before, but with Mary it was a different game that was being played. The tasks that she so thanklessly performed over the publication of *Adventures* meant that most of their letters at this time are concerned with business, but from the respective safety of London and Florence they continued warily to circle each others' lives. If they had ever needed proof that their paths were diverging then Mary's squeamishness over *Adventures* must surely have provided it, but it is as if neither could quite relinquish their claim on the other's interest or watch their old friendship cool into indifference without one last stab at an intimacy neither really felt. What would he do if she and Claire either married or died, Mary had asked him in March 1831, leaving him with no one but 'six score new objects for idolatry you may have found among the pretty girls in Florence'.[25] 'I should not wonder if fate, without our choice, united us,' was Trelawny's reply, 'and who can control his fate? I blindly follow his decrees, dear Mary.'[26]

If this was a proposal, it cannot have been one that Mary was expected to take seriously and her sturdy declaration that she would never relinquish the name of Shelley clearly came as a relief. As late as the mid 30s Trelawny would still be dangling the vague idea of a 'union' in front of her, and yet from the very start they were both clear-sighted enough about what they wanted out of life to know that it was only in the safe knowledge that it would be rejected.

'I was more delighted with your resolve not to change your name than with any other portion of your letter,' he wrote to her on 29 June 1831, secure but still piqued enough to press his suit. 'Trelawny, too, is a good name, and sounds as well as Shelley; it fills the mouth as well and will as soon raise a spirit . . .'[27] 'My name will never be Trelawny,' Mary replied,

> I am not so young as I was when you first knew me, but I am as proud. I must have the entire affection, devotion, and, above all, the solicitous protection of any one who would win me. You belong to womenkind in general, and Mary Shelley will never be yours.[28]

With the triumph of *Adventures* opening up a new world, and with two failed marriages behind him, this was at least one vision of his vocation in life that Trelawny and Mary could share. Even at the time of his deepest misery over Claire in 1822–3 Trelawny had been able to console himself in Italy with a very public affair, and judging by a jaundiced remark in a letter of hers to Mary written from Nice in December 1830 little now had changed. 'It must seem to you that I am strangely neglectful of my friends,' she wrote,

> or perhaps you think that I am so near Trelawny that I have been taking a lesson from him in the Art of cultivating one's friendships; but neither of these is the case; my silence is quite on another principle than his: I am not desperately in love nor just risen from my bed at four in the afternoon in

order to write my millionth love letter; nor am I indifferent to those whom Time and the malice of Fortune have yet spared to me, but simply I have been too busy.[29]

Walter Savage Landor, the irascible author of the *Imaginary Conversations*, and midwife to Trelawny's own *Adventures*, was more appreciative.

> It is not every traveller
> Who like Trelawny can aver
> In every State he left behind
> An image the Nine Months may find.
> Considerate, he perceived the need
> Of some improvement in the breed,
> And set as heartily to work
> As when he fought against the Turk.[30]

It would be an exaggeration to say that with the publication of *Adventures* Trelawny woke to find himself famous and yet from the moment that he returned to England in April 1832 its notoriety provided a man of his temperament with only too dangerous an opportunity to indulge the tastes Landor had celebrated. For the next thirteen years London and the nearby village of Putney would provide the backdrop to an inventory of casual and serious affairs, but before he finally and gratefully sank into the role that his autobiography had created for him, there was to be one last adventure that suggests a restlessness and ambition that success had not yet stilled. At the beginning of 1833, at the age of forty and after only six months back in England, he decamped suddenly and without warning for Liverpool, and after a few days wandering its docks and Exchange, set sail on a 'true-blooded Yankee clipper' for what, in a letter to John Murray, he called the '*dis*-united States'.[31]

There is a natural desire to fix a cause to such a radical and unpremeditated move as Trelawny's trip to America but there is nothing in his correspondence to indicate that he knew why he was

going himself. There was certainly talk that the secessionist rum-
blings in South Carolina at this time might provide him with another
war to fight in, but a vague idea that the young democracy and
untouched spaces of America was the only place for a radical of his
kind probably had more to do with the decision than anything else.

In the decade before Trelawny's arrival the Owenite settlements
had popularized and then exploded the ideal of the communal life
in the New World but if Trelawny had ever harboured thoughts of
Nashoba they were soon lost in the suffocating trivialities of a rootless
and aimless existence. There are whole months of his stay in America
when even his whereabouts are unknown, and yet from those few
letters and sightings that have survived a picture of inner crisis
emerges – a crisis of identity and purpose all the more surprising
after the success of *Adventures* – for which his shapeless travels
provide both context and metaphor.

It is from the pen of another English celebrity, the young Fanny
Kemble – touring America with her father on the back of her London
triumphs – that we have our most memorable portrait of Trelawny
as he struggled to find a rationale for life after Greece. On her voyage
over to New York Fanny had immersed herself in both Moore's
Life of Byron and Trelawny's *Adventures,* and in her journal she
recorded her first, fascinated impressions of its author.

> Mr [Trelawny] dined with us: what a savage he is in some
> respects. He's a curious being: a description of him would
> puzzle anyone who had never seen him. A man with the
> proportions of a giant for strength and agility: taller,
> straighter, and broader than most men; yet with the most
> listless, indolent carelessness of gait; and an uncertain, wan-
> dering way of dropping his feet to the ground, as if he didn't
> know where he was going; and didn't much wish to go
> anywhere. His face is as dark as a Moor's with a wild, strange
> look about the eyes and forehead, and a mark like a scar upon
> his cheek; his whole appearance giving one an impression of
> toil, hardship, peril, and wild adventures. The expression
> of his mouth is remarkably mild and sweet; and his voice is

extremely low and gentle. His hands are as brown as a labourer's: he never profanes them with gloves but wears two strange magical-looking rings: one of them he showed me is made of elephant's hair.[32]

It is that 'indolent carelessness of gait', the 'wandering way of dropping his feet to the ground' that offers the most telling insight here, because if it seemed to Fanny Kemble that Trelawny had no idea where he was going, it was no more than the truth. The possibility of a secessionist war had faded away in compromise even before he landed in America, and as he drifted instead through the eastern states in search of a role, moving from city to city and drawing room to drawing room, he was increasingly forced to fall back on the specious celebrity of his *Adventures* and the reflected glory of Byron's friendship – 'no chicken' anymore, as one observer coolly noted, but otherwise the same fantasist who had bluffed his way into the Pisan circle ten years before.

There were compensations in fame, of course – again, flirtations, mainly – and a wonderful vignette survives in the diary of Anna Quincy, the youngest daughter of the Senator and President of Harvard, Josiah Quincy, that catches Trelawny in full, preposterous flight. 'Talked to Mr Campbell, who has just returned from Saratoga,' she wrote.

> Gave me a very amusing account of the various lions of the Springs, the greatest of which at this moment is a Mr. Trelawney, who is said to be the original of Byron's Corsair. It is said that he is the younger son of a Scottish nobleman, who turned first a privateer, met with a variety of adventures, married a beautiful Indian girl, who accompanied him on various of his honourable expeditions, until one day when, as she was bathing, a shark happened unluckily to swallow the unhappy demoiselle. Upon which Mr. Trelawney became so distracted with rage, grief and Sharkanthropy that he turned Pirate forthwith, and after years of adventures too numerous to mention, he returned with a broken heart and a large fortune to England, became acquainted with Byron,

who was so captivated by his story that he forthwith wrote the Corsair upon it, only giving Medora a more picturesque fate than befell the hapless Indian beauty. The marriage and the Shark are the two points that somewhat shake my credulity.[33]

Throughout his life, however, Trelawny never seems to have had any difficulty in making friends, and there was clearly a genuine charm to his performance. 'We are in the habit of seeing Mr Trelawney (Lord Byron's Trelawney, and moreover, your friend Sir William Molesworth's cousin),' Mrs Mathews, the wife of the great comic actor Charles Mathews, reported back from Philadelphia to her son,

> and think him a most agreeable and clever man. He has dined, supped, walked, &c with us; recollects and talks of you; and in fact, is a sparkling jewel in our way, picked up in this huge mine of dullness.[34]

This endless social round was not the whole story, of course, and there was another America beyond the monotony of East Coast society and towns like Philadelphia – formal in plan as a draughtboard and almost as lifeless as Mrs Mathews described it. The vast space, the great rivers and the solitude of the country could genuinely stir Trelawny's imagination too, and yet when he wrote from Charleston to Claire after almost a year's wandering, it is hard not to feel he might just as well have stayed at home. 'I have been in America nearly a twelvemonth – during which period I have circumnavigated the twenty-four states,' he wrote in December 1833 with all his old carelessness for truth or accuracy,

> during the winter I shall keep to the South: the climate of this city as far as I can judge is far better than Florence – perhaps not so good as Naples – the American climate, however bears little resemblance to that of Europe – it is more like the climate of China – with this difference that China is something hotter in summer and colder in winter. The wealthier classes in America attempt to imitate the Eng-

lish in their social institutions – and that is an absurdity – but they are a small sect – with small means and little influence – Democratic institutions are using up to the stump their goose quills – the Sovereign people are bearing down all opposition – they are working out triumphantly their grand experiment – that all men are born free and equal! – the only blot on their charter, slavery, will gradually disappear – it must be spunged out – or cut out soon.[35]

Trelawny was still in Charleston in the New Year, and reappears again in Philadelphia in the following autumn, but the intervening months are largely a mystery. In a letter to a Mrs Stith written in December 1833 he had spoken vaguely of a trip to St. Domingo to 'examine the black republicans',[36] but another letter to her written on 27 October 1834 does nothing to fill in the gap. 'Many things take place on this planet for which no satisfactory reasons can be given,' he wrote

> For instance marriage; and my erratic movements; are not to be accounted for . . . it would be tedious to narrate what I have been doing – 'so let the past be past' my present intentions are to get on board some ship and take a cruze in the Gulf of Mexico – touching at Cuba – so on to the city of the [?] Incas.[37]

It must have been during this period, if at all, that any dreams of a commune were put to the test, but the only relic of more serious intention behind his travels is a strange and unexplained document found among his papers when he died. 'I, Emma Maria,' it read,

> for and in consideration of the sum of one thousand Dollars do bargain, sell and deliver to the said Edward Trelawny my black slave John – to have and to hold the said black slave John for his use at his new settlement in Virginia or elsewhere – Dated at Charlestown on 11th of January, 1834.[38]

There is no way of knowing whether this was anything more than a spontaneous and defiant flash of generosity at the heart of the

slavers' South but nothing in Trelawny's character would suggest
he was ever serious in his plans for a settlement. There had been
endless talk in Pisa with Byron of founding a colony somewhere,
but just as the Greek landscape of Parnassus had been little more
than romantic 'theatre' to him, the reductive truth of his American
experience is that he saw the New World in essentially the same
terms, a mere backcloth for the expression of a romantic individualism that was the very antithesis of the Owenite ideals that had
inspired Nashoba and New Harmony.

It is characteristic of this that the one memory of the American
landscape he ever dwelt on with any pleasure pitted him against it
in its most sublime and awesome mood. The incident occurred in
the high summer of 1833, after a visit to the Niagara Falls with
Fanny Kemble and her party. Their journey up the Hudson had
already seen Trelawny outshine the dull and unpleasant creature
soon to become her husband, declaiming Byron's 'Isles of Greece'
with a passion that reminded her of Keane or goading Fanny ever
closer to the fall's edge with a 'Go on, go on; dont stop!' 'I reached
an open floor of broad, flat rock, over which the water was pouring,'
she recalled,

> [Trelawny] seized me by the arm, and all but carried me to
> the very brink; my feet were in the water and on the edge
> of the precipice, and then I looked down, down, down; each
> mountainous mass of water, as it reached the dreadful brink,
> recoiling, as in horror, from the abyss . . . It was long before
> I could utter, and as I began to draw my breath I could
> only gasp out, "O God! O God!"[39]

The only impression it produced on Trelawny, he claimed, was one
of 'perfect repose', but it was a challenge he could not ignore. On
5 August he returned to Niagara alone, and in a moment of romantic
bravado – more Byron-like than Byron – attempted to swim the
river below the falls. An old Arab sibyl, he told Claire, had predicted
he should die and disappear in the same instant, victim to the mighty
forces of nature he had so often challenged. Never, he wrote, was
she nearer the truth than when he faced the Hudson's foaming

waters 'eddying, whirling, and turbulently boiling in a caldron –'

> Nothing elates me so much – or exercises such power over
> my mind – as witnessing any of the elements at war – instead
> of shrinking at my own insignificance I dilate with high
> thoughts engendered by sublime scenes – therefore I plunged
> into the river of the cataract – I had been told this part of
> the river was dangerous even for a boat – but I remembered
> no European boat could swim in the surf at Madras – yet I
> had swam thro' it often – and my motto is – 'go on till you
> are stopped' – I did so – I crossed with exceeding toil and
> difficulty: in returning I was overpowered by the strength
> of the current and whirled headlong till I observed I was
> drifting towards the rapids – which form a terrific whirlpool
> in which nothing that lives could float an instant – exhausted
> and powerless – I for a moment resigned myself to my fate:
> I thought of the old sorceress's prediction – I was far away
> from all succour, the distant roar of the cataract dinned in
> my ears – my death knell – I was sinking – gasping for
> breath. I then thought of the prediction – to be lost like a
> rain drop in the sand – seeing the land on each side I thought
> it absurd to be drowned in a river – I cannot tell how I
> regained the shore – but this I know, I was so used up I
> could not see things distinctly for nearly an hour.[40]

This was the last throw of an ageing romantic, a piece of empty
heroics, and in his heart Trelawny knew it. He might rail against
the petty conventionality of American social life, but its drawing
rooms had sadly become his proper sphere. He might talk radical
politics with a Shelleyan enthusiasm to Fanny Kemble, but the
sub-Byronic gesture was his only protest against an enclosing sense
of failure that mere celebrity could not hide. He might outshine
with the great, rich glow of his past her American admirers, but it
was the grim Pierce Butler Fanny would marry. 'A thousand thanks
for your kind letter,' he wrote to Charles Mathews from Boston in
December 1834, despondent after a bout of illness that had left him
'ridden like an old crone' and feeling his failure:

Words of kindness are doubly welcome in this cold climate amongst these icy people. The thermometer is now twenty-two degrees below freezing; my hands are freezing, and my faculties are frozen.[41]

It was time for Trelawny to leave. Even American women, the main solace of his visit, were beginning to lose their appeal. 'So you can't read my writing then why should I write', he rounded in exasperation on Mrs Stith,

I said nothing about the Texas, I told you I was going to Mexico . . . damn the Texas – and all that therein is. And then you tell me something or nothing of three hundred boys or three hundred coleges damn them too. In Yankee-land there is nothing that can interest me – but the absurd woman-kind they are well enough – and would be better if they had human voices – teach them music – ye gods – what blasphemy – toades beatles bats – henceforth will be treasured in cages – the shriek owl the screeching jay and obsene raven may now take place of the singing birds. Teach the Yankee girls to knit worsted stocking – herringbone flannel waistcoats – make puddings – anything my dear – teach them – but do not profane – the holy words of divine song.[42]

'If it was not so icy cold,' he complained to her,

I have determined every day for these two months past to take my departure – but cannot and yet I am perishing piecemeal wasting day by day – and now we are bound in with thick ribbed ice alas the pity – I must give over this [?] kind of life. Yet I fear me I should have gone on too far to stop. I should have died ten years ago – I then should have escaped much suffering. Oh it is a dismal world. And after our youth has fled our difficulties deepen – the sunshine which once gladdened my heart no longer warms it. I walk benighted beneath its midday brightness – I long for death and therefore it avoids me.[43]

Trelawny was neither the first nor the last nineteenth-century liberal to be disappointed by America but his problem was that the roots of his discontent lay in his own personality and not in anything he had found. 'My Dear Clare,' he wrote to Claire Clairmont on his return to England in the spring of 1835, as random and purposeless as when he had left two years earlier,

> In whatsoever direction I go forth – however far or rapid my flight – it's all the same – I always find myself here again in London – designedly I go – and have reasons – such as they are – for going – coming back is altogether involuntary – I can assign no motive or reason – any more than the stick of a skyrocket that after its airy flight comes tumbling back again – or the winds – or the tides . . . I that once thought I could put a girdle round about the earth in forty minutes – now feel that I have but existed – as a frog in a swamp: the snail-paced and slug-blooded – that pass vegetable lives – or I that flutter in this our elementary cage and think I am flying over boundless space – lead the same lives – it's all the same – we are in reality but animated sticks and stones.[44]

One of the abiding puzzles of Trelawny's months in the Parnassan cave is the question of what he actually did with his time, and the years after his return from America prompt something of the same incomprehension. There is, of course, a danger here of lapsing into an anachronistic puritanism that ignores the natural parameters of the gentleman's existence, but there is still something baffling in the way that after the triumph of *Adventures* and one last fling at Niagara the great romantic seemed content to fritter away his hours in an existence that could be measured out in coffee spoons.

'But where I say Hours I mean years, mean life,' wrote Hopkins in one of his great sonnets of despair and, in a sadly minor key, the same can be said of Trelawny. There is a downward spiral to many lives that can leave an onlooker with a sense of perplexed disappointment, and yet before the advent of the modern sporting hero there can have been few careers that ended with such a prolonged and dying fall, few men in their early forties who have been ready to live off their past exploits with such an unexpected passivity as Trelawny.

In the hands of an artist like George Eliot or Gissing there might seem something tragic in the shallow emptiness of these years, and yet the central flaw of his character – a preference for appearance over substance – is not the stuff of which genuine tragedy is made. There is always a risk with Trelawny of mistaking those occasional and devastating moments of self-knowledge that punctuate his life for what Roman Catholicism would call a 'firm purpose of amendment', but when it came to the point, celebrity and not achievement was always the real spur to him – fame, however spurious and second-hand, rather than the dull grind of effort.

But to be fair to Trelawny, there can have been few more attractive times or places to enjoy the fruits of a passing celebrity than the London he returned to in the middle of the 1830s. It was the London of Lady Blessington, Caroline Norton and the Kembles, of Sydney Smith and that 'unemployed Hercules' Count D'Orsay, of Melbourne and the young Disraeli, a London that in that brief hiatus between the doomed generation of Byron, Shelley and Keats and the wonderful mid-century flowering of the novel seems to have poured its creative energies with a very un-English lightness into the art of living.

Throughout his life Trelawny had an alchemist's gift for extracting success out of failure, and it is typical of his cool insouciance that on his entry into this world he simply added 'America' to the other battle honours that had made him a celebrity. On 19 December 1835 the artist Benjamin Haydon met him for the first time at Colonel Stanhope's, and that night confided his impressions to his diary – one of the most engagingly indiscriminate and revealing journals of the period from a man who was a far more interesting writer than he ever was a painter. During the evening Trelawny had defended Lady Blessington, putting criticism of her down to female jealousy. He had talked of Virginia and its men – 'a manly race'-

and with rather more dubious authority of South America. 'Trelawny is a fine fellow & I like him much,' Haydon decided.

> I said. 'Did you like Byron?' he replied. 'Do you think I should have remained with him so long if I had not?' I had heard he did not like him.
> Trelawny is making his name in High Life, from the fresh, frank, savage manner of his remarks. He seems astonished at civilized habits. They tell all sorts of stories. I came home with Mr. Cowper & we amused each other in the Cab about him. Mr. Cowper said he had heard he had murdered two wives, & Mrs. Stanhope quizzed him at table by saying he had been making love to some old Dowager with a fortune at Brighton – 'a good thing,' said she, 'for you know so well how to get rid of wives.'[45]

Two days later, Haydon called on Trelawny at the Colonnade. 'Civilized rights seem to bore him,' he wrote, as intrigued as on their first meeting.

> This must be the man who had breathed the air of the Pampas, hunted the Buffalo in the Prairies, fought for Greek liberty amidst the mountains of Greece, & swam torrents in pursuit of a beaten enemy. He is a fine animal. Caroline [Norton] says she feels interest because both her Grandfather & Father were vagabonds, and that she has no pretensions to the beauty she is praised for . . . I like Trelawny exceedingly. I do not wonder Byron liked him.[46]

Haydon's admiration for Trelawny would eventually cool but his first response was typical of the enthusiasm that greeted London's newest lion. 'In a fauteuil by the fire,' the future Mrs Longfellow reported of an evening at the Kembles,

> lolled a beautiful girl, Miss Macdonald, with the Norman blackness of hair picturesquely adjusted, whose dark eyes sought her shoestring neath the piercing gaze of the ferocious Corsair Trelawney at her side. He is a ruffian-looking man, with wild moustache, shaggy eyebrows, and orbs beneath

313

them that have the gimlet property beyond any I ever
encountered. It was droll we should meet him here.[47]

There was one side of Trelawny's London life during the 1830s,
however, that showed a fluttering ambition to make something more
of his celebrity than the conquests of the fauteuil. On the last page
of his *Adventures* he had saluted with his own brand of Shelleyan
rhetoric a new dawn of European freedom, and on his arrival back
in England in 1835 he joined that group of 'Philosophical Radicals'
who bridged the years between the Great Reform Act and Chartism
with a decent and moneyed highmindedness that is now largely but
undeservedly forgotten.

There is no doubting Trelawny's enthusiasm for 'freedom's battle'
in any guise, but in reality there was as little in common between
him and a fellow-radical like the Cambridge Apostle Charles Buller
as there had been in Greece between Odysseus's faction and the
Benthamite Leicester Stanhope. The only political language Trelawny ever genuinely understood was the language of violence and
threat that had filled his *Adventures*, the only enemies he could
envisage were the chimeras of tyranny that stalked the world in his
father's footsteps, and for all the talk of ballots and Colonial reform
at Sir William Molesworth's Pencarrow or among the comforts of
John Temple Leader's house on Putney Hill, there seems to have
been no serious thought of him playing the parliamentary role his
mother had so fondly envisaged ten years earlier.

The solitary reminder of his political ambitions that survives, in
fact, is a group portrait of the political radicals that only serves to
illustrate how far out on a limb he was. Among the group are
men of far greater political and intellectual weight like Buller and
Molesworth, and yet it is the bearded and open-necked Trelawny
who inevitably catches the eye, a swarthy and shameless Elizabethan
throwback among the clean-shaven and primly correct Benthamites
of the nineteenth century, a figure who seems curiously closer in
this domesticated context to his Byronic role-models than he is in
the more theatrical poses of Kirkup's or Severn's portraits.

Whether it was in politics or the drawing room, however, the

theatrical gesture or romantic extravagance were never far away to
scupper expectations of the more solid achievement Mary Shelley
had so long been waiting. He met the young Disraeli and Dickens
– fresh from the success of *Pickwick* and dismissive of Landor's
talents – at Lady Blessington's Gore House. He dined with the actor
Macready, and Mill and Carlyle, who was struck by his appearance
but had no time for his mind. He was sketched by Duppa, Landseer,
Kirkup, D'Orsay and Thackeray, he was courted and lionized, but
ultimately the novelty and the charm of his performance would pall.
'The least agreeable feature of my life is a threatening letter from
Trelawny,' wrote the society hostess Caroline Norton to Lord
Melbourne in the midst of a marriage crisis that would end with
Melbourne cited in the courts.

> I told him in the civilest way possible that he must discon-
> tinue his visits now that I was awkwardly situated and that
> his name had been used by N– among others . . . He went
> into the rage of a savage – so much so that he couldn't speak
> in reply, and wrote his answer in the style of the Arabian
> Nights mixed up with his own novel of 'The Younger Son'
> – mysteriously awful, & vaguely sublime, but very fierce.
> He did not vouchsafe to say what he would do, but great
> things are to be done: and I am to be a skiff
>
> > Day & night and night & day
> > Drifting on its dreary way
>
> without rudder, compass, or pilot '& finally I am to be "a
> *hulk*", an ungraceful end but it is my doom.[48]

The letter is a wonderful reminder of what men saw in the 'never
to be forgotten' Caroline Norton – 'the Beautiful, Artful, Intriguing,
Passionate, Unprincipled Caroline' as a dazzled and embittered
Haydon called her after she and Trelawny had tried to turn his
studio into a secret meeting place.[49] It says a lot too for the style of
Trelawny that he could have interested a woman like Caroline
Norton enough to make her husband's short-list of possible corre-
spondents, and yet it was not in the end the daring and self-

destructive wit of Caroline or Fanny Kemble's eyes that ended this phase of his life but something altogether more secretive and mundane.

On his return from America Trelawny had taken rooms in a house in St James's, and sometime in 1838, seven years after the publication of *Adventures*, began an affair there with an Augusta Goring, a friend of Mary Shelley's and the estranged wife of a Member of Parliament.

As little is known about Augusta as about most of the other women in Trelawny's life, but a miniature of her painted by John Linnell in 1827 does little for the usual view that with this relationship Trelawny had at last outgrown the Byronic child-bride of his fantasies. There is something in the bright, almost doll-like gaze of the blue eyes and the bow of the mouth in Linnell's portrait that seems to contradict this, something in the air of arrested childishness of the face – a kind of wilful silliness of the sort that Dickens portrayed so devastatingly in Dora Spenlow – that conveys the depressing message that the Trelawny who had married the thirteen-year-old Tersitza in his Parnassan cave was in his mid–forties still essentially the same man.

Trelawny belonged not to any one woman but all womankind, Mary Shelley had once famously told him, but Augusta's miniature is a disquieting reminder of the kind of woman who seems to have most permanently attracted him. It would be impossible to read his letters to Claire Clairmont in the wake of Shelley's death and doubt the reality of his feelings for her, but with Claire or Mary there was an equality or superiority of mind that ultimately seems to have precluded the kind of relief that he found in the succession of young girls who would decorate his life – so many incarnations of the imaginary Zela of his *Adventures*, Byronic forerunners of Hardy's elusive and transitory *well-beloved* who have left virtually no trace of their individuality behind.

The miniature of Augusta would be interesting enough as the only portrait of these women we have, but it is doubly so as, after its furtive beginnings, their relationship was to prove the most durable of his life. In its early stages their affair was conducted under the shadow of a landlady in his rooms in Duke Street, but within months Trelawny had moved out to Temple Leader's house on

Putney Hill and taken Augusta with him, installing her first in a cottage on Barnes Common and then in another on the Upper Richmond Road separated from Leader's villa by only three fields. There, in 1839, a son was born, and registered by the local baker, a Mr Hall, under the name of John Granby, the son of Ann and 'John Granby, Merchant'.

It seems a sorry falling off for a man of Trelawny's swagger and dreams, from 'Corsair' to 'Merchant' in little more than ten years, from the Mavre Troupa and its view out over the scene of Alexander the Great's first victory, to Farm Cottage on the Upper Richmond Road, with its crumpled and stained sheets, its drawn blinds, its private access over the fields, its tattling servants and all those other little details of secretive domesticity that emerged in the divorce action which followed.

After all the excitement of Pisa and Greece, and the acclaim which greeted his *Adventures*, it must have felt to Trelawny that he was back in the world of Captain Coleman and Bristol boarding houses. It must, too, have seemed to him that he had outlived his day, a relic among friends to whom he showed less and less tolerance. 'Mary I have not seen,' he had told Claire in 1835, 'her disease grows upon her with years – I mean her pining after distinction and the distinguished of fortune.'[50] 'Old friends are a heavy curse . . .' he wrote in another letter, 'all old things are utterly worthless, aren't they Clare?'[51] 'Clare hollo – do you hear?' he addressed her in 1838 from Leader's house in Eaton Square, which he would seem to have used with the same freedom that he enjoyed at Leader's villa in Putney.

are you alive? or indeed transformed into a tree girdled round by the axe – leafless, lifeless – my dropping gall into your milk was not in wantonness – but to make you into something better than a dish of skimmed stuff . . .

Mary is the blab of blabs – she lives on hogs wash – what utter failures most people are.[52]

Those, at least, who survived still, though there were now few enough of them to remind him of those years in Italy and Greece when it seemed he had really lived. It comes as a surprise, but it was now eighteen years since Shelley and Williams had drowned, sixteen since Byron had died, fifteen years since Odysseus's body had been found at the base of the Acropolis.

Mavrocordato was still alive, in and out of office in a country heading towards its next crisis, Tersitza was married to a Greek and 'distinguished for her beauty,'[53] but almost everyone else involved in the Greek life that had launched him to fame was long since dead. Jarvis had not long outlived Fenton. He had died in August 1827 of fever, and was buried in Argos with the full military honours Greece had denied him in life. By then, too, Humphreys, back in Greece for the third and last time, was also dead from disease. Komarone was killed in a skirmish, Ghouras shot through the head while patrolling the ramparts of the Acropolis.

Even Whitcombe, only nineteen when he had tried to kill Trelawny, had been dead eight years. Five years after his return from Greece, and after writing his anonymously published *Sketches*, his embarrassed family bought him a commission in the army. The Duke of Beaufort, writing to Lord Fitzroy Somerset, described him as 'a young man of respectable family in the county of Gloucester who are very anxious to procure him a commission and would I believe [favour] his going upon Foreign Service'.[54] The coded meaning of that last remark needed no spelling out. On 25 June 1830 Whitcombe was gazetted Ensign in the 2nd West Indian Regiment. The commission was tantamount to a death sentence, the West Indies claiming more lives through disease than the Napoleonic Wars ever managed in battle. Two years later he was back in England. On 30 June 1832 he wrote himself to Somerset, in search of preferment – one of only three letters that preserve his rounded, elegant, surprisingly neat handwriting. He reminded Somerset that the Duke of Beaufort had interceded for him earlier, and that he had since been with his regiment at New Providence, 'until a few weeks ago when I returned home on sick leave.'[55]

He had only three months to live. At the beginning of August he was in the West Country, staying with his brother Charles, the vicar of Magna Sherston near Corsham. While there he seems to have fallen violently in love with a local girl. There was a quarrel, and he stayed at the inn while he tried to make it up. The attempt was a failure. That night people at the inn heard him pacing his room above, 'stamping, exclaiming, and seemingly tearing up papers'.[56] There was a heavy thump, and when they rushed in he was lying dead on the floor, in the middle of a sea of torn papers.

As in life, so in death there was something second-hand and literary about Whitcombe. On 24 August 1770, the seventeen-years-old Thomas Chatterton – the 'marvellous boy' of romantic myth – had killed himself with arsenic. When his body was found, it too was surrounded by tiny pieces of torn paper.

There seems to have been no suggestion, however, that Whitcombe had killed himself, and apparently no autopsy was held. Even in the local newspaper it received no more than a single obituary line, and elsewhere appears to have passed unnoticed. Whitcombe was just twenty-six. He was buried in his brother's church, in the south aisle, eventually to be followed there by his brother Charles, his sister Julia, and his long-suffering mother, 'Dame Mary, Widow of Sir Samuel Whitcombe Knt.' A memorial inscription, placed high on the wall, reads with a touching if misleading generosity:

> Sacred to the memory of William Guise Whitcombe, Lieut in His Majesty's 2nd West India Regt and youngest son of the late Sir Samuel Whitcombe Knt who died at Corsham in this county the 6th Day of October 1832 aged 26 and lies buried in the South aisle of this church. This tablet is erected as a tribute of affection by his surviving brothers.

At the age of forty-eight Trelawny was, as he had told Mary Shelley ten years earlier, an old patriarch who had outlived his generation. In the April of 1841, when Augusta Goring was finally divorced from her husband, D'Arcy Bacon was still alive, but he had only eighteen months left before his decline into the obscurity of a Battersea lodging house would finally end in dropsy and an unmarked grave in St Mary's Lambeth.* Even Captain Hamilton and the *Cam-*

brian, the symbol for so many of all that was best in British inter-
vention in Greek affairs, were gone, the one to his grave in Ireland,
the other to the bottom of the Aegean.* 'I heard the voices of the
dead calling to me', Trelawny had written in the Eagle Hotel, Niagara, after his attempt in 1833 to swim the Hudson,

> I actually thought, as my mind grew darker, that they were
> tugging at my feet. Aston's horrid death by drowning nearly
> paralysed me. I endeavoured in vain to shake off these thick-
> coming fancies, they glowed before me. Thus I lay sus-
> pended between life and death. I was borne fearfully and
> rapidly along, I could barely keep my head above the surface,
> I waxed fainter and fainter, there was no possibility of help
> . . . It had always been my prayer to die in the pride of my
> strength, – age, however it approached, with wealth and
> power, or on crutches and in rags, was to me equally loath-
> some, – better to perish before he had touched me with his
> withering finger, in this wild place, on a foreign shore. Nia-
> gara 'chanting a thunder psalm' as a requiem was a fitting
> end to my wild meteor-like life.[57]

Trelawny's prayer went unheard. An ironic fate had one last card
to deal the arch-romantic: longevity.

15

THE KEEPER
OF THE FLAME

'Alas the dauntless Cornishman who in his youth swept the
seas with De Witt, who in his prime fought with Byron for
the independence of Greece, and who in old age commanded
the sympathy and respect of all true lovers of romance, has
passed away. Never more shall we gather round the old man's
chair, and approach through him the mighty dead.'

Richard Edgcumbe[1]

'I have lived quite long enough and am quite ready to be
extinguished – to avoid dying by inches is all I ask – sudden
death – Shelley and Williams after all were lucky – they were
not more than a minute, and life is not worth much after 30.'

Trelawny to Claire Clairmont, 1870[2]

ON THE SOUTHERN VERGE of the main avenue up to the great
Doric chapel of Kensal Green Cemetery in West London, stands a
forgotten tomb which brings home with a sharp immediacy the
world that Trelawny had outlived.

The monument marks the resting place of John Cam Hobhouse,
one of the moving spirits of the London Greek Committee and
Byron's companion on his first journey to Greece. In among the
trees and undergrowth behind Hobhouse, reachable now only by
clambering over collapsed and yawning graves, is the stone of Lady
Isabella Noel Byron, the wife who drove Byron into exile. Close to

321

her lies Shelley's friend and biographer, Thomas Jefferson Hogg, and with him 'Mrs. Hogg' – Shelley's last muse, Jane Williams – along with the urn containing the ashes of Edward Williams, cremated on the Italian shore in 1822 by Trelawny.

A little further to the south can be found another of the Pisan Circle, Leigh Hunt, true to himself even in death beneath a monument raised 'by public subscription'. Byron's publisher John Murray is here too, and down in the dank gloom of the catacomb, only bays away from the massive dust-covered coffin of the great topographer of Philhellenism, Colonel Leake, the bones of perhaps the only two beings Byron consistently loved, his Harrow schoolfriend Lord Clare and his half-sister, Augusta.

If there is anywhere in England that can underline what longevity would come to mean to Trelawny it is this small patch of earth in West London, the burial ground in a space of no more than a hundred yards square of that incomparable chunk of literary and romantic history with which he had been associated. It used to be said of his father that he would scour the obituary columns in search of dead relatives and the chance of a bequest, but as Trelawny settled into his new life with Augusta Goring and their son, all that he had to do was wait for death and the passing years to leave him in sole possession of the field, the great survivor of the great days and great men of the early century.

In cemeteries such as Kensal Green one can feel, too, what that title meant to the Victorian generations who lived in the shadow of these names. There is a swagger about the earliest inscriptions in these burial grounds that conjures up a golden age of achievement and heroism, the age of Byron, Shelley and Keats, of Wellington, Nelson and Cochrane, of Copenhagen and Badajoz and the Battle of the Nile, an age when even the plainest 'Smith' who is buried at Kensal Green is the 'Smith of Smiths' himself. One monument will record the last survivor from his Corps at Waterloo, another the surgeon who knelt beside Nelson on the *Victory*. There are men here who cut out Spanish Galleys in the West Indies, and others who were with Sir John Moore at Corunna – men who had lived out the stuff of national nostalgia, while crowding in around them, still jostling for place in a melancholy parody of Victorian social hierarchy, lie all those anonymous cohorts of men and women who never did see 'Shelley plain' – the 'snail-paced and slugblooded', as the great democrat, Trelawny, called them, whose only memorials are enshrined in the information that they had lived and died at 106 Edgware Road or Westbourne Crescent.

In the early 1840s, however, the rehabilitation of Shelley had scarcely begun, and with that sense of timing which had served him so well in the past, Trelawny settled down to wait. After the disappointments of America and his political ambitions it must have seemed to his friends that with *Adventures* he had done all he was ever going to do, and when on Augusta's divorce they married and eventually moved to the small Monmouthshire town of Usk, the break with the old literary life appeared complete.

From the outside, the choice of Usk seems as arbitrary as any of Trelawny's movements, but it ushered in the most prolonged and stable phase of his life. With his new wife and son he first took a town house in Newmarket Street, and from there had himself built a home on the great bluff of Llanbadoc Rock perched high above the river, before finally settling his growing family on the nearby Cefn Ila estate.

The documentary evidence for these Usk years is as sparse as for any period of his career, but even in retirement Trelawny was enough of a celebrity to leave his distinctive trace in the local histories of the town. It would seem from the two surviving accounts that he was a respected if aloof figure in the neighbourhood, as successful at his farming as a gentleman farmer could hope to be in the years after the repeal of the Corn Laws, an assiduous improver and planter and a fair employer with a reputation for honest dealing. 'Although he generally assumed a rough and austere deportment towards the public,' a local man, J.H. Clark, recalled almost fifty years after Trelawny had quit Usk,

> he had many good qualities. A man of frugal and temperate life himself, he despised a drunkard or dishonourable person, and would sometimes be very severe to his farm bailiff . . . if he returned from market or fair the worse for liquor.[3]

There is a sense, too, that the eccentricities that he had embarrassingly cultivated in London found a more congenial soil in the Monmouthshire countryside. There can feel something sadly comic in his attempts to shock the sophisticated world of Caroline Norton or Lady Blessington, and yet translated to the country his eccentric ways take on a more familiar and engaging aspect, the authentic oddities of a staunch individualist rather than the gaucheries of a man struggling for a role in life. On Sundays he could be seen doggedly digging and planting his estate, true still to that hatred of cant and the British Sabbath that had driven him from the country in 1829. A heavy drinker as a young midshipman he was now a virtual teetotaller and vegetarian, faddishly dogmatic on the dangers of socks, underwear and hot foods and the virtues of cold water.

As a father, too, he was no less unusual. A daughter, Laetitia, was born in 1847, followed by a second son Frank, and the three children were brought up with that genuine disdain for convention that defies and, so regularly in this country, seduces public opinion. Supplemented sometimes by the exotic figure of Zella, Tersitza's daughter, married now and living in Italy, they would all bathe naked in the river below Llanbadoc Rock. On one occasion preserved in local lore, when a child from the town complained that her curls were annoying her, Trelawny cut them off. On another, a friend of Laetitia's was given a gun on leaving the Trelawnys, with instructions that she was to fire it as a signal when she was safely home.

There is, however, a more tangible and suggestive testimony to these Usk years than the mere handful of anecdotes that, in the absence of anything of substance, gets passed from account to account of his later life. At the foot of the Llanbadoc Rock on which Trelawny built his first house is a small stone church, and in its graveyard stands a row of massive cedar trees planted by him from cones brought from the site of Shelley's grave in the Protestant Cemetery at Rome.

Something about these trees, something about the strangeness of their provenance, about the oddity of finding them where they are, looming incongruously over the small, quiet church of a Welsh hamlet, conjures up the figure of Trelawny more eloquently even than the house that he built on the rock above. There are so few letters of his that survive from this time that any talk of an 'inner life' at Usk must be largely speculative, but in the silent and inexorable growth of those seeds taken from Shelley's grave it seems possible to glimpse the hidden springs of Trelawny's whole career, to recognize in full those obsessions and passions of his youth that alone gave shape to his rootless existence.

It has been fairly argued that marriage with Augusta was his one mature and stable relationship, but domestic contentment is not the only measure of life and for Trelawny there were always other and more powerful imperatives. From a letter sent to the son of Charles Armitage Brown in 1852 it is clear that he took the business of farming seriously enough, yet beyond the limited horizons of Usk the literary world, and in particular the reputation of Shelley, was beginning to change in ways that would draw Trelawny inevitably back into the limelight he had not known since the publication of *Adventures*.

The Victorians' discovery and transformation of Shelley is one of those literary phenomena that have an inevitability about them in retrospect and could never have been guessed at in advance. One of Trelawny's abiding claims to critical independence is that he was one of the few people to have recognized Shelley's powers while the poet was still alive, but during the 1840s under the careful guardianship of first Mary and then her daughter-in-law, an emasculated, aetherialized and all but unrecognizable Shelley was beginning to take a hold on the sensibilities of the nineteenth century that was never to be relinquished.

The first skirmish in the battle between this Authorized Version of the poet and Trelawny's Radical had come over Mary's edition of the poems in 1839, and her omission of the crucial political notes to 'Queen Mab' and the dedication to Shelley's first wife. It had been some years anyway since Trelawny had looked on Mary with any sympathy or understanding, but this 'betrayal' of Shelley marked the end of a friendship that over the years had shown him at his very best and worst.

As Mary slid quietly and decorously towards the grave, however, her eyes fixed mutely through her last illness on the bureau holding the ashes of Shelley's heart, Trelawny found himself up against a more formidable and less scrupulous opponent in her daughter-in-law, the new Lady Shelley. One of the great mysteries of heredity is how the combined genetic influence of the Shelleys, Godwin and Mary Wollstonecraft could have produced anyone so dull as the young Sir Percy turned out to be, but if Mary's son was as blamelessly stolid as even old Sir Timothy could have wished then his wife more than made up for him. A bizarre mix of steely determination and fluffy silliness, of ruthless pragmatism and spiritualist nonsense, the young Lady Shelley threw herself on her marriage into the business of rescuing the dead poet from himself, cutting and bowdlerizing his letters, keeping vigil in the Casa Magni in the frustrated hope of a vision, turning the family home into a violet-scented shrine and Shelley himself into the 'ineffectual angel' of Victorian myth. 'He was fair, he was beautiful,' she would recall an Italian peasant's words to her, 'he was like Jesus Christ. I carried him in my arms through the water – yes, he was like Jesus Christ.'[4]

As one of the principal survivors of the Pisan Circle, Trelawny was obviously someone who needed squaring if the Authorized Version was to achieve the status of history, and during his Usk years Lady Shelley made a number of overtures to him through Sir Percy to co-operate on the biography Hogg was in the process of writing. In old age she told Maud Rolleston that Trelawny, however, had refused to see her. 'I naturally wanted to meet him,' she remembered with that exquisite selectivity with which she remembered everything,

> but there had been some trouble, and either he associated me too closely with it, or felt that to see me would recall the trouble. Percy met him now and again in Wales and Trelawny liked him.[5]

'To assemble together under your roof three of the poet's old friends to tell their storeys is a pleasant dream,' Trelawny had in fact replied to her suggestion that he should come to Boscombe to meet Hogg and Peacock in February 1857,

It is something similar to the plot of Bocacio's Decameron, but the Italian takes care to have youth and summer wr.

I told Percy when he was here that I was too old and selfish to leave my den. In my youth I railed at age as hard and crabbed and so I find it.

I don't believe that either of the men you have mentioned will do what you wish. Indolence and excessive sensitiveness to public opinion will prevent it – as it has already done.

I am, Dear Lady Shelley

Your very Obliged,

E.J. Trelawny.[6]

It is only too likely that a crotchety indolence was one motive for his refusal but it was at best only part of the truth. For almost thirty years since he had first broached the idea to Mary in 1829, the story of his Pisan friendships had been a book that was simply waiting to be written, and if he had not already begun his own great memoir of Shelley and Byron by this time it was certainly in preparation.

There was nothing, however, in his life at Usk that could have prepared the world for his *Recollections of Shelley and Byron*, nor anything he had written before that remotely foreshadowed the supreme qualities of what is perhaps one of the two finest literary memoirs in the language.

There was every sign in his *Adventures* of an imaginative storyteller of genuine power, but in the laconic style of *Recollections*, the taut rhythms of its prose, its understatement and control of pace, its complete absence of that emotional flaccidity which mars both his *Adventures* and his letters, and its ability, finally, to coerce *belief* in the face of every known fact, Trelawny had at last added substance to appearance.

A modern biographer of Byron or Shelley might well decide to ignore *Recollections* as evidence, but for the historian of Romanticism Trelawny's creations have an integrity and value that is independent

of inconsistencies, errors and invention. It is one of the curious
ironies of his life that the man of action should finally triumph
through the pen in this way, and yet Trelawny's wonderful durability
as a writer lies in the fact that the more he is discredited as chronicler
of his own deeds the more distinctly he is seen as an imaginative
artist of compelling power.

He had already produced, in his 'autobiography', one of the great
adventure stories of the nineteenth century and now in 'his' Byron
and Shelley he created two figures that in their compelling solidity
are fit to stand alongside any literary memoir short of Boswell's
Johnson.

For Claire Clairmont, who had known Shelley better than anyone
still alive, they also bore the stamp of truth. It seems to have taken
her nine years to read *Recollections*, but when she did her response
was a characteristic blend of generosity and bile. 'I did not express
how much I liked your book,' she wrote from Florence in 1869,

> Your portrait of Shelley is full of truth – it is him in all his
> unaffectedness, in his simple tastes so fond of woods, seas,
> lakes, mountains; of birds and of music. There was in his
> manner and way of speaking, a touch of the woman, even
> of the girl, and that appears most vividly in your description
> and is attractive. After Shelley, what interested me most was
> your residence in the cavern of Odysseus – I imagine it
> forms the most romantic episode in that Greek war . . .
> Also it brought to mind the great difference between your
> character and that of Lord Byron. Your jaw was broken,
> your arm wounded and entirely disabled – all by an ungrate-
> ful villain who sought your life: you had to remain forty
> days on the hard rock, no pillow during your sufferings but
> a stone wall, with only savages to assist you, and no decent
> food. You content yourself with simply relating the fact,
> but such is your manly nature, so strong your powers of
> endurance, you do not deign to make one complaint.
> Eschylus says the strongest and noblest man is he, who can
> bear without a murmur the greatest load of injuries. Accord-

ing to this, you are a Hero. If a woman who loved him only scratched Lord Byron by an accident with a pin, he magnified the pin into a dagger, the woman he declared was a wicked assassin; he would not forget or pardon the offence: but went on for the rest of his days complaining of the severity of his lot, writing abusive verses on her and calling on Earth and Heaven to annihilate her. If he had to go through what you went through, he would have written an Epic poem about it.[7]

As Claire suggests, however, it is not in the end either Byron or Shelley who are the greatest inventions of *Recollections* but, as the extended reprint twenty years later under the more honest title of *Records of Byron, Shelley and the Author* also recognizes, Trelawny himself. The book is, before all else, the conclusion to the history of his inner life begun thirty years earlier with *Adventures*. Opening in Switzerland with him, it ends in Greece with him, and in between Byron and Shelley are held within the confines of his imagined world, moving and speaking through their last months as he directs them, as much the puppets of his mind as he once was of theirs.

From the beginning the supreme confidence of the author, the strutting consequence with which he moves through his own narrative, and above all this air of proprietorial authority set *Recollections* apart from every rival memoir. There were criticisms of what one reviewer called 'the worldling's notions of poetry and poets', of the 'gross materialism' of his description of Shelley's cremation, or the coarseness of his account of Byron in his coffin, but in their fey irritation they too do nothing more than recognize the 'insolent' and 'defiant' presence of Trelawny in his story.[8] 'Shelley and Byron were thus a pair of ordinary mortals,' the same reviewer in *The National Magazine* indignantly wrote,

> inferior to him in many natural qualifications and acquired accomplishments, however much his superiors in literary composition . . . he was no idealist, such as they were; and therefore, in his own opinion, had a sounder judgment of the world and mankind than they could possibly acquire.

'Byron,' he gravely tells us, 'formed his opinion of the inhabitants of this planet from books; personally he knew as little about them as if he belonged to some other.' Of Shelley he says, 'He had seen no more of the working-day world than a girl at a boarding-school; and his habit of eternally brooding on his own thoughts in solitude and silence damaged his health in mind and body.'[9]

At the age of sixty-six, and after twenty years out of the public eye, Trelawny was once again a celebrity. It is hard to imagine that the prospect of fame held any fewer attractions for him now than it had in the 1830s, but whether or not the process of writing precipitated the crisis in his personal affairs that now occurred or simply coincided with it, *Recollections* was to mark the last major watershed of his life.

As with the previous upheaval, over the affair with Augusta Goring and the move to Usk, a woman about whom virtually nothing is known was behind it. At some stage during the writing of *Recollections* Trelawny would seem to have taken a young mistress, flaunting their relationship before a scandalized public, sweeping her out of his carriage to carry her up Llanbadoc Rock, before finally installing her at Cefn Ila and driving his dignified but exasperated wife into the sympathetic and partisan bosom of the Usk townsfolk. 'There is a sort of simplicity in these great unconscious egoists of Trelawny's type,' a local historian of the affair wrote forty years later in the *Athenaeum*,

> It was not daring . . . to bring Miss B. to Cefn Ila, and set her up to be worshipped there. But society was justly scandalised by the spectacle of this shaggy Samson carrying the diminutive form of Delilah to and from his carriage at the foot of Shanbadoc Rock – his Delilah was not even pretty, if the memories of my informants are to be trusted.[10]

Another phase of his life was over, and as so often with him there is nothing to do but pick among the debris for some clue to what it might have looked like and admit defeat. It is a dispiriting thought if one is tempted to believe that biography can somehow deliver a 'real' or settled personality sheltering behind the Trelawny myth, and yet for twenty years he had lived with a woman we barely know, run a farm of over four hundred acres, raised three children and left nothing behind but his first temporary house, a few anecdotes, some farm implements and a row of trees. What, in its day to day rhythms, was that married life like? What pattern of accident or design, of disappointment or policy, lay behind the dates of their children's births, the eight year gap between the illegitimate Edgar and Laetitia? Or who, even, was the Miss B. who brought these years to an end?

Whatever the answers to these questions, and whatever their relevance to anything in Trelawny's life that ultimately matters, the end when it came was abrupt. On the front page of the *Usk Observer* of 20 March 1858, an advertisement appeared announcing the 'Important sale' of livestock and farm implements from the Cefn Ila estate, over two hundred ewes and lambs, Herefords, mules, ploughs, wagons and – the vehicles that won Miss B? – 'one excellent light gig' and an 'American racing carriage'. On 22 May a second sale was announced, this time of the house contents – the property, as the notice puts it, of Mr Trelawny, 'late of Cefn Ila'.

Trelawny was gone, and as a rare letter to his old friend Daniel Roberts makes clear, a new sense of freedom, of youthful energy, came with the break. 'I am now and have been for some months driving about in a light trap along the Southern and Western Coast of England,' he told him,

> much in the same way you and I did years ago; and I enjoy it much after having stuck so long in the mud of Monmouthshire. – I am still hard and strong, can swim a mile and walk ten without effort, and live on fruit and trash as of old, no wine or at least very rarely, beer occasionally, tobacco regularly, but no excess – simple living, out-door exercise, &.&., and a cold bath every day winter and summer.[11]

The emphasis on his health, the concentration on his physical being, the harmless and even engaging self-absorption of this letter offers certain useful pointers to the tenor of Trelawny's life as old age slowly and warily crept up on him. In the wake of his last public triumph thirty years before he had at least made an effort to *do* something with his fame, but now, with his third marriage over – 'at single anchor' again, as he put it to Roberts, – it was enough simply to *be*.

It seems to have been enough, too, for the new audience and new admirers that his *Recollections* had brought him. While his writing had inevitably revived the old Pisan friendships with Claire and Roberts, there is an increasing sense from now on that Trelawny belongs to a younger generation, and that like some cossetted and cherished 'National Treasure' in modern Japan, the only thing required of him was to be a living witness to a lost and more extravagant age.

Trelawny claimed to have made no money out of *Recollections*, but from the time he moved to Wales and purchased an estate with the capital left to him in his father's will he was always comfortably off. On the breakdown of his marriage to Augusta and the sale of the Cefn Ila estate, Trelawny was thus able to move back to London, and it was largely in his new house at 7 Pelham Crescent that the long drawn-out end game of his life was played. Built in the 1830s by the architect of Belgrave Square, Pelham Crescent provided the perfect backdrop for his final performance too, an elegant world of middle class and professional prosperity and comfort that set off its nineteenth century Diogenes in stark and admonitory relief, his manners, tone, beliefs and very physical presence a challenge to mid-Victorian conventions.

It is a remarkable tribute, in fact, that while his visitors came for the stories of Shelley and Byron, it was Trelawny himself, with his gimlet stare and a voice that seemed to issue from 'some deep cavern',[12] who held their attention. Perched in his armchair with newspapers for cushions, the Curran portraits of Claire and – surprisingly – Mary staring down from the wall above him, a photograph of the 'American martyr' John Brown close at hand, he would begin and end conversations with equal abruptness, dispensing alike with greetings or farewells, sometimes quitting the room and even the house without warning to leave his stranded visitors to find their own way out.

The performance was not confined to his own territory either. Almost fifty years later Joaquin Miller, the American bohemian and friend of Mark Twain, could still recall the impression made by Trelawny's appearances at the Savage Club. 'On one occasion', he wrote,

> he came while a storm was raging, and he must have been wet all through. But he would not drink with us. His collar was open, after the fashion of Walt Whitman, and he had neither overcoat nor umbrella. He stood with his back to the fire, strong and straight as a mast, looked about over us in quiet disdain for a time, then took off his coat, hung it over the back of a chair by the fire, and sat and watched it drying til the storm abated.[13]

The most memorable pen-portrait of Trelawny at this time, however, the picture that best captures his inimitable blend of bluff, brag and genuine eccentricity, comes from the Pre-Raphaelite painter William Holman Hunt, who in 1863 found himself a fellow house-guest at Burton Park, Sir Thomas Fairbairn's seat near Penshurst. 'He was a man of nearly eighty years of age at the time,' Hunt mis-remembered by almost a decade in his memoirs,

> in stature about five feet nine; his shoulders were of great width and his chest of Herculean girth, his neck was short and bull-like, and his head modelled as if in bronze, with features hammered into grim defiance. His eye was penetrat-ing, and his mouth was shut like an iron chest above a Roman chin; it was no surprise to find his voice full and rough. And yet there was a certain geniality about him which he concealed as though he were ashamed of it at first. When I was painting one morning in the park, I saw him approach-ing. When he was nigh I called out, 'How do you do, Mr

Trelawny?' He walked on without answering, and coming closer threw himself down on the grass behind me. I repeated my salutation. His reply was 'I think that is about the most foolish thing one man can say to another.' . . . 'I'm glad you've come to see me, to give me the opportunity of a quiet chat with you,' I continued, not noticing his tone. 'Besides Byron and Shelley, you knew Keats, tell me what height Keats was' . . . 'he was of reasonable height, about our own,' said Trelawny. 'Tell me how the character of his face inspired you,' I continued. 'He couldn't be called good-looking,' he replied, 'because he was under-hung.' 'You use the word in the opposite sense to that in which it is sometimes applied to Charles the Fifth and Philip the Second of Spain, or to a bulldog?' I said. 'Of course Keats was the very reverse,' he grunted, 'and the defect gave a fragile aspect to him as a man.'

A few days later at dinner Trelawny's place at the table was empty, and a servant was sent to his room, who reported that he was not there and could not be found. This arousing curiosity, the master asked the butler if he knew anything about the guest. 'Yes, Sir Thomas,' he said, 'I saw him going with his valise in his hand on his way to the station in the afternoon, and I think, Sir Thomas, he has left.' Being pressed for further news of Trelawny, he said with the gravity becoming a trained servant, 'He was sitting in the afternoon in the lake up to his neck in water reading a book, and he remained there till dusk, Sir Thomas.' Thus ended the visit of this survivor of a past generation.[14]

Trelawny had never been afraid to take risks and he was now as ready to lay claim to a friendship with Keats whom he had never met as he was to Byron's and Shelley's. There was nothing, it appeared, that he could not recall of his Pisan days, no detail or conversation too trivial or remote to be dredged up. His memory seemed to his visitors astonishing, and his impressively oracular delivery made past events not simply come alive but seem to take on their new life through him. 'Every word is stamped with his personality,' that ardent romantic Mathilde Blind wrote of him, 'a personality so powerful that it overtops everything he can say or do . . . To see Mr Trelawny and to hear him talk'

> is to be transported back, as if by magic, half a century or so, to that thrilling period when Shelley and Byron, those revolutionary Dioscuri of English poetry, passed the last years of their brief lives self-exiled in Italy . . . He will begin speaking quite abruptly, as if continuing some previous train of thought. 'What,' he growled, 'is all that rubbish that Symonds writes about Shelley being too beautiful to paint? Too beautiful to paint, indeed!'[15]

In the London and America of the 1830s it had been the name of Byron that underpinned Trelawny's fame, but now it was increasingly of Shelley that visitors wanted to hear Trelawny speak. To a certain extent he was doing no more than he had always done in tailoring his cloth to the fashion of the day, but it is neither as simple nor as damning as that because in old age Shelley's poetry genuinely seems to have answered the needs of his personality in ways that Byron's once had in his youth. Both as writer and man, Shelley had become the benchmark by which all others were to be judged. It was beside Shelley that Browning and Tennyson were dismissed out of hand; it was as Shelley's spiritual heir that the young Swinburne was welcomed to Pelham Crescent. 'Always energetic,' Swinburne wrote of Trelawny in a burst of reciprocal enthusiasm, 'whenever he speaks of Shelley the especial energy of his affection is really beautiful and admirable to see.'[16] Elsewhere, Swinburne returned to this theme,

> To hear him speak of Shelley is most beautiful and touching; at that name his voice (usually that of an old sea-king as he is) *always* changes and softens unconsciously. 'There' he said to me 'was the very Best of men and he was treated as the Worst.' He professes fierce general misanthropy but is

as ardent a republican (*and* atheist) as Shelley was at twenty;
a magnificent old Viking to look at.[17]

It was the name of Shelley that had first brought Mathilde Blind to
Trelawny, and it was with another ardent Shelleyan, William Michael
Rossetti, that Trelawny now formed what was to prove the last
important friendship of his life. As a young boy Rossetti had once
met Trelawny at the Rossettis' London home, but it was only in
1869 when William Michael's own work on Shelley took him to
Pelham Crescent that the literary collaboration began that would
eventually result in Trelawny's final and most permanent achievement, his *Records of Shelley, Byron and the Author*.

The son of the Italian exile and poet, Gabriele Rossetti, and the
brother of Dante Gabriel and Christina, William Michael brought
to the task an identity of tastes and a polarity of temperament that
made him in many ways the perfect foil. At the time that their
friendship began Rossetti was a clerk at the Inland Revenue Office,
and at the end of his working day he would often make his way to
Pelham Crescent where a Miss Taylor – officially Trelawny's niece
– had taken over the responsibilities from the shadowy 'Miss B' of
Usk. 'Everything in the establishment was extremely well kept by
Miss Taylor,' Rossetti recalled in his memoirs,

> and Trelawny, though his habit of life was simplicity itself,
> had in his surroundings nothing untidy, slovenly, or of
> inferior quality. I usually went round to Pelham Crescent in
> the evening, soon after the close of my office hours. My host
> gave me at once an excellent cup of coffee (a matter about
> which he was rather particular), followed by cigars and talk,
> and before I left by a comfortable tea or supper. He was a
> steady but not excessive smoker. Spite of his anti-
> conventional *brusquerie*, Trelawny was essentially a cour-
> teous, or I would almost say a polite, man . . . He was fond
> of warmth, and there was often a fire in his sitting room
> even in weather that could not be called chilly.[18]

There are perhaps more vivid glimpses of Trelawny than those left by Rossetti, but it is in the pages of his memoirs and diaries that we find the most sustained portrait of him in his last years. There seems to have been a genuine fondness that enabled Rossetti to put up with the less engaging eccentricities of his host, and yet what was perhaps more important for their collaboration was he was also shrewd enough to recognize that Trelawny 'was pre-eminently one of those men one must either take on their terms or not attempt to take at all'.[19]

In the end, however, the rewards of Trelawny's conversation and memories were compensation enough for any little *brusquerie* Rossetti might have to suffer. Under his sympathetic prompting Trelawny blossomed into his last great phase as a storyteller, rising to the challenge of every question with fresh details, dredged up from that 'prodigious memory' Mathilde Blind had so admired or simply invented for the occasion. 'Spent the day with Trelawny, at his invitation,' he recorded on Sunday, 7 January 1872,

> arrived at 2, and remained till 11, Trelawny keeping up, without ever flagging, a conversation about Shelley, Byron, and several other matters . . . Trelawny showed me a bit of Shelley's jawbone which he snatched from the funeral pyre: charred white, with the teeth-sockets showing; his features were almost gone when the burning took place. I described to Trelawny the spot shown to me last summer at Via Reggio as being the site of the cremation: he thinks my information must have been inaccurate, the true spot being farther away from the town, and only 'seven yards' from the sea . . . Byron had a habit of keeping by his bedside a Bible and two pistols. Near his end, he made some remark, in a spirit of resignation, to Fletcher: who being of a 'canting' turn (according to Trelawny), availed himself of the opportunity to open the bible, and began reading from it to Byron; but Byron stopped him, saying: 'Shut it up – that is all weakness, weakness, weakness' – striking his hand hard on his forehead. – Byron had no palate: Trelawny could mix his gin and water as

weak as he chose without Byron taking any notice of it
whatever ... Byron's left leg and foot were much worse
than his right ... Trelawny considers that Shelley would
have joined him and Byron in the Grecian expedition, had
he survived, but would not have made a good soldier ...
Shelley was utterly fearless in every way – standing on the
edge of precipices, etc ... [20]

'Called again by appointment on Trelawny,' Rossetti again recorded
a week later,

who treats me most kindly, and I might almost say with
affection. He is about the most remarkable instance I know
of force of body, character, and mind, in the same person
... Shelley never smoked, but tolerated any amount of smoking in Trelawny, etc. Byron, also, could not smoke. Shelley
may, as Hogg and Peacock intimate, have cared about babies
at one time, but took no interest in children: once stepped
over his own child Percy and his nurse, without recognizing
them, in Trelawny's presence. He was as clever with his
legs as other people are with their arms: these were compara-
tively weak in Shelley.[21]

The scandal of Byron and his half-sister Augusta, 'the real reason
of the separation from Lady Byron,' Shelley's first wife, his courtship
of Mary Godwin, there was no subject on which Trelawny was not
ready to pass down judgement. There were occasions on which in
the privacy of his diary Rossetti might suspect the old man's memory
of playing him false, but the compelling immediacy of Trelawny's
narrative style carried with it a conviction and force of truth that
seems to have been virtually irresistible. 'He referred to it repeatedly,'
Mathilde Blind wrote of the way Trelawny would speak of Shelley's
cremation,

picturing the scene, which apparently increased in vividness
while he described it, till I seemed to see with him the long
sweep of sand, the smoothly rippling waters of the bay, the
long dark line of the pine forest skirting the shore.[22]

There were relics, too, that went with the memories – the faded blue velvet cap Byron wore during his last years, the last couch that Shelley slept on, and, most precious of all, fragments of bone from the cremation. On 27 February, 1872 Rossetti wrote in his diary: 'To my intense satisfaction,

> he gave me a little piece (not before seen by me) of Shelley's skull, taken from the brow: it is wholly blackened – not, like the jawbone, whitened, by the fire. He has two such bits of jawbone, and three (at least) of the skull, including the one now in my possession. I must consider how best to preserve it. I enquired whether he had any of Shelley's hair: answer, no, the scalp having, with the hair, been all eaten off the corpse when recovered: this point, I think has never yet been notified.[23]

Trelawny's selfless kindness to the Pisan widows in the months after the sinking of the *Don Juan* was reaping a rich and bizarre reward. Theodore Watts-Dunton might think him nothing more than 'an opinionated, vain man, who lived on his reputation as the finder of Shelley's body', but he might as well have kept his criticism to himself.[24] Trelawny was now too famous to need to worry. When Mathilde Blind wrote her pen-portrait of him for the *Whitehall Review*, he was No. 27 in a series that included Victor Hugo, Prince Napoleon, the Crown Prince of Germany, the King of the Belgians and the King of Italy.

He was famous, too, in a way that lifted him high above the bourgeois animosity of the man who has made a tragi-comic name as the guardian-gaoler of poor Swinburne out at Putney. The more outrageous Trelawny's behaviour, the more it seemed rooted in the standards of a lost and bigger world, the more outspoken his opinions, the more they seemed to speak of an honesty that could brook no deceit. As Mathilde Blind, who on being shown Rossetti's fragment of Shelley's skull had pressed it to her lips in an act of reverent homage, wrote,

> The fact is, I believe that [Trelawny] loves all that is really loveable, admires all that is truly great, and only feels the

scorn of scorn for the sorry shams, artificialities, and general snobbery with which modern English life is half-choked.[25]

And as Trelawny moved fearlessly towards the place next to Shelley waiting for him in Rome, scornful, sockless and contemptuous alike of Victorian dress and Victorian morals, there was an increasingly urgent sense among his admirers that his memories should not be allowed to die with him. It would appear from Rossetti's diaries that as early as 1872 he had discussed with him the publication of material which had not appeared in his *Recollections*, and over the next six years their first vague plans firmed into the volume that appeared in 1878 as his *Records*.

Without Rossetti to perform the editorial tasks that Mary Shelley, Landor and Brown had carried out nearly fifty years earlier, it would certainly not have come out, and yet of all Trelawny's books it is perhaps the most characteristically *his*. It has been argued that in many ways it is a smaller and meaner book than its predecessor, but it is in fact the cavalier handling of detail, the discrepancies, additions and above all the blatant and vengeful recasting of certain relationships that bring us closest to the Trelawny Rossetti or Mathilde Blind knew – Trelawny the myth-maker, Trelawny the storyteller, dispensing history by edict from his chair in Pelham Crescent.

Most of the changes from *Recollections* are of only minor importance, more interesting for what they tell us of Trelawny's method than anything else – the shifting nature of Byron's deformity, the fate of Shelley's heart, the identity of the book found in his pocket when he drowned (Sophocles or Aeschylus?) – but there was one major addition concerning Mary Shelley that landed Trelawny in the last public controversy of his life.

Trelawny's disenchantment with Mary was decades old, but it was only after her death, and as the figure of Shelley bulked increasingly large in his mental landscape, that his private irritation with her hardened into the public contempt of *Records*. 'Jealousy, frivolity', 'mawkish cant', a craving for admiration, the list of her faults was endless. 'As to Mary Shelley,' he had written to Claire Clairmont seven years earlier in 1871,

> you are welcome to her: she was nothing but the weakest of her sex – she was the Poet's wife and as bad a one as he could have found – her aim and object was fashionable society; she was conventional in everything and tormented him by jealousy and would have made him like Tom Moore if she could – she had not the capacity to comprehend him or his poetry.[26]

For fifty years, sure of his audience, Trelawny had been writing to Claire with this kind of freedom, but it was only in the new appendix to *Records* that a wider public were treated to the same accusations. 'Mrs Shelley was of a soft, lymphatic temperament,' he wrote,

> the exact opposite to Shelley in everything; she was moping and miserable when alone, and yearning for society. Her capacity can be judged by the novels she wrote after Shelley's death, more than ordinarily commonplace and conventional. Whilst overshadowed by Shelley's greatness her faculties expanded; but when she had lost him they shrank into their natural littleness. We never know the value of anything till we have lost it, and can't replace it. The memory of how often she had irritated and vexed him tormented her after existence, and she endeavoured by rhapsodies of panegyric to compensate for the past.[27]

Trelawny is right about the novels – sadly right, in fact, about a lot – but in earlier and affectionate days he had written too many letters to Mary that the Shelley family still owned to go unchallenged on this now. 'The new particulars it imparts are mostly dubious or insignificant,' Richard Garnett, Lady Shelley's literary henchman, wrote of *Records* in the *Fortnightly Review,* in June 1878,

> It would, nevertheless be well for Mr. Trelawny, and for us, if he could be restrained from writing about anybody but

Shelley. So long as he is dwelling upon him, he is, like the visitants to the *Witch of Atlas,* "imparadised". As soon as he leaves him, *his* book and mantle are abruptly laid aside, and he becomes in comparison, quite an ordinary personage . . . If such portions of Mr.Trelawny's work indicate a more genial spirit, others are calculated to pain those who would gladly hold him in honour. I refer particularly to those treating of Mrs. Shelley, which can only be described as unjust to his departed friend, to his readers, and to himself.[28]

In a tone of sorrow rather than anger – that note that Lady Shelley herself hit so well – Garnett went through the discrepancies in Trelawny's different accounts of the Pisan Circle, and above all the way in which his attitude to Mary had so radically changed. 'He will also be gratified to learn that Shelley's heart is not "in an ornamental urn on a mantelshelf",' he concluded with one last, silky stroke,

but in a shrine especially dedicated to it, associated with other relics – the Aeschylus already referred to – portraits, manuscripts, locks of hair, including one of Mr. Trelawny's own. To these, but on a distant day, let us trust, will probably be added the portrait of Mary Shelley in Mr. Trelawny's possession, with which, as he declared on the occasion of her death, the strength of his affections would not suffer him to part, even though it was not his.[29]

But Trelawny was fighting battles of this kind before Garnett was even born, and if the Shelley camp thought that in his eighties he would be any more biddable than he had been during the Usk years they were soon disabused. 'As Mr. Garnett has his brief from a lady, I have no complaint to make against him,' he dismissively began his reply in the *Athenaeum,* before going on to compound the original offence with a public denial that Mary Shelley had ever so much as helped him with his *Adventures.* 'If she read it,' he wrote – lie and ingratitude bedded gracelessly down in one sentence – 'it was to satisfy her natural curiosity, she neither added nor altered a single word of it.'[30]

It is interesting that Trelawny should bother to justify himself in this way, but one of the curious inconsistencies of his character is that throughout his life a contempt for popular opinion would go hand in hand with an indignant determination to have his case publicly heard and recognised. There is not a shred of evidence that he ever repented his intemperance over Mary or the pain it caused her family, but behind the tough public front of his article in the *Athenaeum* there seems to have been a vague unease that he had shown a side of himself that was best kept hidden, and that he had misjudged the temper of his audience in a way that is almost unique in his literary career.

He was right, too, because along with the notorious claim in *Recollections* – significantly watered down in *Records* – that he had uncovered Byron's corpse to examine his feet, this bruising treatment of Mary Shelley did his reputation more harm than all the brutality and violence of *Adventures* ever had. Among those who actually knew him during these last years the sheer force of his personality was invariably enough to overpower minor scruples, but beyond the immediate circle a more hostile legend of Trelawny grew up that was rooted in these twin offences against the canons of Victorian decency and friendship. 'He was certainly a damn'd scoundrel,' the old chartist G. J. Harney wrote to the bookseller Dobell in 1881, only days after Trelawny's death, 'to commit the outrage he did on the lifeless remains of the great Poet of whom he was the "*false friend*".[31]

False to Byron, false to Mary, these were subtler, more insidious charges than desertion or murder, and ones that rankled deep with a man who in old age traded on a reputation for plain speaking honesty. When two months after his reply to Garnett's article he received a visit from Lady Ann Blunt, the daughter of Ada and the granddaughter of Lord Byron, the subject was still obsessively on his mind. She, naturally, wanted to talk only of Byron; Trelawny of Mary Shelley. 'She was of an utterly *commonplace* mind,' he told her, insisting that he was justified in turning on her because while she was alive he 'would never have deserted her', but now that she was dead the only thing that mattered was the TRUTH. And 'when excited', his visitor recorded in her diary that night,

> he wd rise from his chair & at that moment suddenly feeling his infirmity wd throw himself back with passionate violence. Mr Trelawny as he spoke brought his fist down with such a bang on the table that I thought he must have bruised himself – However that gesture is his favourite one & whenever he becomes emphatic he uses it.[32]

Only weeks short of his eighty-sixth birthday Trelawny's mental vigour was still there, but the body at last was beginning to fail. Perched in his high chair near the fire, with Godwin's *Political Justice* at his side, his eyes sunken, his cheek bones prominent, surrounded by his 'treasures' – 'various dried heads of pirates and others . . . swords and daggers stained with the blood of enemies' – he seemed to Edward Carpenter like 'some semi-extinct volcano'.

> 'You are interested in Shelley,' [Trelawny] said. And then without waiting for a reply: 'He was our greatest poet since Shakespeare.' And then: 'He couldn't have been the poet he was if he had not been an Atheist.' . . . he rolled out the 'Atheist' with evident satisfaction. He went on to express his contempt for the contemporary poets, like Tennyson and Browning, then returned to Shelley: 'I am not sure he wasn't the greatest man we have ever had: all those others just tinker with the surface; Shelley goes down to the roots' . . . Indeed there was something astonishing in this old man's intensity of rebelliousness, which extreme age had apparently done nothing to reduce.[33]

This meeting with Carpenter took place at Pelham Crescent, but after 1870 Trelawny would spend most of the year down on the south coast, where he had bought himself the house in which he was finally to die. According to tradition Rossetti had once taken him some particularly good figs, and on discovering that they had come from a garden in Sompting Trelawny decided to buy the tree and, of necessity, the house that went with it.

For a few months in the spring and early summer he could be found in London, but as with age he became more reclusive and wary of strangers, the house in Sompting – still known as Trelawny's Cottage – turned into his home. As at Pelham Crescent he would preside over the occasional visit from his chair in the sitting room, a bright 'ship's cabin' of a den according to Mathilde Blind, plainly furnished, with a sky-blue ceiling and gaily coloured wallpaper patterned like a child's picture book with small designs showing the world's different nations engaged in whatever it is that the world's different nations do.

It was a simple and regular existence Trelawny led at Sompting, lived out with that same dogged and engagingly pedantic faith in his systems that had grown through the Usk years. 'At upwards of eighty years of age,' Rossetti fondly remembered, 'he would stand upright [on the principle that after lying in bed one should not sit down] as he disposed in two or three minutes of his breakfast, consisting perhaps of a few fruits and a glass of water.'[34]

He still enjoyed wine, but no spirits, and no hot food or drink. He still went without socks or underwear in all seasons, chopped his own wood, drew his own water from the pump and, whatever the month, swam in the sea. And the man who had once shot the heads off caged chickens on the *Hercules*, now scattered crumbs on his window-sill for the birds and fed the ducks on the village pond.

With Trelawny, however, a life of austerity and a sense of theatre were never mutually exclusive and his eccentricities found their way into local lore as they had already done at Cefn Ila. A familiar though somewhat 'awesome' figure in his Inverness coat and soft felt wide-awake, he would be recalled by locals dispensing sweets to children in the village or his own boots or coat to tramps when the occasion took him, walking back home coatless and barefoot, as unconfined by convention as ever.

These few final tales of Trelawny's oddities have their place in his life, of course, and yet as with London and Monmouthshire it is impossible to review them without an acute awareness of what is missing. There is an inevitable feeling of disappointment the moment one begins to take stock of the little we do in fact know of these years, a nagging feeling that behind the practised gestures of old age the man who had mixed with Byron and Shelley in his youth must have nursed some inner life that is now lost to us.

He was a voracious reader still but almost nothing either in his correspondence or the reports of visitors gives any hint of a more complex figure imprisoned within the well-honed public personality. In his memoirs Rossetti coloured Trelawny's last years with a tinge of remote but habitual melancholy, and yet even that insight takes us no nearer the old man, no closer knowing whether his sadness was the simple exhaustion of a man who has outlived his day or the ultimate and unsharable loneliness of the systematic liar.

What is certain, however, is that the more he spoke of the past, the more he embroidered it for Rossetti, the more entrenched his public persona became, the lonelier he must have been in the sole knowledge of the truth that lay behind it. Throughout his life he had always been ready to sacrifice reality to image, but now in old age when his public image was all he had or was, there was no alternative open to him, no other route to security but in a ferocious allegiance to his own mythology.

No one, not even Claire, the model for Henry James's Miss Borderau, could have guarded his identity, or watched over his reputation more carefully. Like Byron before him Trelawny was always at his happiest in letters slandering one friend to another, but if his asperities are sometimes no more than bluster, age brought with it a narrowing of sympathies, a withering of feeling, and above all a grim determination to bear, like the Turk, no brother near the throne. All his life he was generous with money and things, from his financial kindness to Mary Shelley or to Medwin's abandoned wife in 1832, to the bed that Shelley slept in that he gave Rossetti. He could be generous too in his encouragement of the young, of Rossetti again or Swinburne, and as alert in old age to genius as he was when he went in search of Shelley. He would recite Blake, whom he only discovered in his last years, with the same booming passion with which he had once declaimed 'The Isles of Greece' for Fanny Kemble on the way to the Niagara Falls. George Eliot – 'Eliott' – was Britain's best writer, he told Claire.

They were, though, not rivals. With his own generation, with anyone who could compete with him, dispute his versions of Pisan or Greek history, or challenge his identity, he was ruthless. Swan, the parson of the *Cambrian*, was 'a most ridiculous dandy';[35] Millingen, Byron's doctor, who had satirized Trelawny in his memoirs, 'a traitor, a renegade, the *"caro ragazzino"* of the Jew Mavrocordato'.[36] Medwin and Moore were 'literary vagabonds'.[37] Godwin was 'a grossly selfish man, selfish mercenary and unprincipled'.[38] 'You are the first writer on Shelley that has done justice to him or his writings,' he told Rossetti, 'all the previous writers are incompetent. Peacock had fancy and learning, Hogg the same; Leigh Hunt did not understand Shelley's poetry; Medwin, superficial.'[39] 'Godwin, Peacock, Medwin, Hunt and many others . . .' he wrote to Claire, 'I had antipathy to them all and they knew it!' – they were 'devil strokes sucking [Shelley's] blood.'[40]

Only for Claire Clairmont, living out her last years in Italy, religious in her old age but as implacable in her hatred of Byron as ever, did Trelawny preserve anything like his earlier feelings. Over the fifty-five years of their friendship there were long gaps in their correspondence, but Trelawny was a better friend at a distance than in daily intercourse and his letters to her in the 1860s and '70s have the same fond, hectoring familiarity as those he had written after his return from Greece.

In its odd, unsatisfactory, bruising way it was probably the most honest relationship of his life. It was the one friendship where there was nowhere for either of them to hide. They knew each other too well, saw each other with too pitiless an eye, recognized in each other, for all the differences of temperament, the same demons. Only to her would he admit his regrets, his vanities and follies: only from her did he bother to exact the same self-knowledge, holding up her faults to them both as a mirror to his own.

It was, in fact, only Claire, haunted still by the past, obsessed with fears that her daughter Allegra had never died but been cruelly hidden away from her, who could make Trelawny pause in his relentless persecution of Byron's memory. As early as 1831 he had summoned their joint energies to the life's task of promoting Shelley's name above that of his 'rival' poet, and yet while Byron would always be the 'club-footed Poet' to Trelawny – 'the incarnation of rank selfishness'[41] – Claire's hatred could shock even him. 'Your relentless vindictiveness against Byron is not tolerated by any religion that I know of,' he told her in one letter,[42] and in another,

> I took the rope off a man's neck – as my men were about to hang him for assassinating me – so you may leave Byron alone: he lived an unhappy life and died a miserable death – bad and selfish as he was, there are millions worse.[43]

With Claire's obsession that Allegra was still alive he was even more brutal.

> You may be well in body; but you have a bee in your bonnet – an insane idea has got into your brain regarding Allegra . . . What possible object could he have in feigning her death or wishing it? . . . If I was in Italy I would cure you of your wild fancy regarding Allegra: I would go to the Convent – and select some plausible cranky old dried-up hanger-on of the convent about the age your child would now be, fifty-two, with [a] story and documents properly drawn up, and bring her to you – she should follow you about like a feminine Frankenstein – I cannot conceive a greater horror than an old man or woman that I had never seen for forty-three years claiming me as Father – do you see any of that age or indeed any age that you should like to have as son or daughter? I have not.[44]

Trelawny was not exaggerating his cold disenchantment at the thought of children. In his eighties Laetitia lived with him at Sompting, and in his will he would leave the residue of his estate to her after bequeathing the house to Miss Taylor. His eldest daughter Julia had disappeared from his life early, and her sister Eliza – 'the only creature, the only being, the only tie – from which I expected nothing but sweet remembrances'[45] – had died before he could ever know her. Both the sons of his marriage to Augusta had also died, the younger Frank to Trelawny's mortification a soldier in the Prussian army, and Edgar – born 'John Granby' in Farm Cottage on the Upper Richmond Road, and a 'monster' according to Trelawny – hated by his father and hating him in turn, in 1872.

Edgar's hatred – a hatred that ran to denying their relationship – has an all too familiar ring to it, and it would seem that Trelawny perpetuated more of himself in his children than was comfortable for family harmony. Laetitia would be a formidable woman, and Zella too, Tersitza's daughter, had a spirit that matched her pedigree. The story of her last parting with her father has a grim comedy that throws a rare sidelight on Trelawny's domestic life. Calling on her at her London house in Hinde Street, he turned down a glass of wine with a contemptuous dismissal of her husband's cellar. Zella simply rang the bell for a servant, and ordered him to show her father out. It was the last time they met.

There is a portrait of Trelawny in his last years by Millais that captures perhaps better than any written memoir the dogged and lonely figure he had become. Trelawny had first met Millais at the funeral of the cartoonist John Leech in Kensal Green Cemetery almost twenty years before, but when in 1874 Millais approached him to sit for his portrait Trelawny refused, 'hating, as he did, all the works and ways of modern society'.[46] Millais was still keen to paint him, but in spite of his wife's promptings, was reluctant to risk another rebuff. 'At last, in desperation,' their son recalled,

> she went off unknown to her husband, and boldly tackled the picture-hater, who, after many refusals, turned round suddenly and said in his bluff way, 'But I tell you what I'll do. I am greatly interested in a company for the promotion of Turkish baths in London. Now, if you will go with my niece and take six Turkish baths and pay for them yourself, I will sit six times to your husband.'[47]

Trelawny was already eighty-two when he finally sat to Millais, the splenetic and turbulent old man so many visitors described, as violent in his opinions and prejudices as in his youth – pagan, republican, fiercely independent. All that side of him is there in Millais's likeness, in the hook of the nose, the hooded eyes, the twist of the mouth, the implacable stare that fixed on men like a vice. He is sitting against an open window, with a sailing boat visible in the distance. At his feet a young girl sits – a model not a grandchild – one hand closed over the old man's, the other holding open an atlas. A portrait of Nelson hangs from the wall. On the table is spread a map of the North West Passage. The title – jingoistic, British, Imperial, high Victorian, all those things Trelawny had spent a lifetime hating – reads: 'It might be done and England should do it'.

It is a fine likeness of Trelawny, and one of Millais's best portraits, but it is not that which makes it so rich a document. 'That fellow Millais has insulted me and I'll have his blood,' Trelawny ranted when he saw it at the Royal Academy, threatening a duel. 'He has handed me down to posterity with a glass of rum and water in one hand and a lemon in the other.'[48]

Here is a moment to treasure in the long life of Trelawny, a moment when perhaps something intruded on his consciousness, a realization that the future and his reputation were in some way out of his control. 'But who can controul his fate?' he had asked Mary Shelley in 1826.[49] For almost sixty years, however, he had managed to do just that, directing and milking it to recreate his life in the way he wanted it seen, his name indissolubly linked with Byron's, his grave next to that of Shelley already dug and waiting for him.

Now, though, as he looked at the portrait, and saw the republican turned jingoist, teetotaller turned drinker, freethinker sunk in senti-mentalized Victorian domesticity, something of his certainty of suc-cess must have wavered. There would have been no sense of pity for all those from Mary Shelley to Byron whom he had traduced and exploited over the years, there is nothing of pity in that face: but what of Swinburne or Rossetti, who had sat at his feet, fed on lies and relics, or all those from Edgcumbe onwards who were guilty of nothing worse than good faith – did he see them waiting for him, in the way that Swinburne in his ludicrous tribute would imagine

Shelley standing ready to welcome him, when the great lie he had made of his life folded, and their credulity lay exposed?

It is a tantalizing if unlikely thought, because to the very last he left nothing to chance. His regime was unchanged, he remained as impervious to illness as ever, but his eyes were firmly on his exit. Of his old world, Jane Williams – Shelley's lady with the guitar – was still clinging desperately to life as Trelawny put it, hearing and mind both gone, a pitiful figure occasionally glimpsed in public, rouged on one side of her face only, her hairpiece slipping.[50] On 19 March 1879 Claire had died in Florence, and been buried with a shawl Shelley had given her sixty years before. 'She passed her life in sufferings,' the inscription on her tombstone that she herself wrote recorded, 'expiating not only her faults but also her virtues.'[51]

By this time Trelawny had already said farewell to an even older friend, the Augusta White who had consoled him on Caroline's desertion in 1817 and had since been living in Canada. In 1876, back in England, she had gone down to see him at Sompting. 'I reached the cottage where my old and dearest Friend met me at the door with the hearty greetings as in days gone by,' she wrote,

> 60 years of uninterrupted friendship – tho' long absence intervened has not abated the feeling – we enjoyed our great talk of former friends and great reminiscences of what was of mutual interest – both of us had changed in the course of the years; but not in our perfect understanding of one another ... his cottage has no great attraction but that of perfect seclusion – it is shut out by tall quaint trees cut and trained to prevent their quite shutting out the view – he had planted them all and delighted to stand and have his pipe beneath their shadow. – he never joins the family table but sits in his sanctum, lights his own fire & makes his own coffee as usual – his republican principles seem stronger than ever tho' I could not but ask him why with his spirit of freedom he had cut down so sparingly the trees around his grounds that surely had a right to grow as they liked.[52]

In February 1881, only weeks before Trelawny's death, one last visitor, Sir Sidney Colvin, the Keeper of Prints and Drawings at the British Museum, went down to Sompting to see him. For Colvin, as for Edgcumbe, Rossetti and Blind who made the same journey, it was a pilgrimage to see a legend. Colvin's first reaction, however, was one of disappointment. He had expected vitality and saw only decrepitude, but the disillusionment was momentary. Trelawny had scarcely moved on his entrance,

> but sat in a shrunken attitude, with his hands on his knees, speaking little, and as if he could only fix his attention by an effort ... nevertheless in the ashen colour of the face, the rough grey hair and beard and firmly modelled mouth set slightly awry, in the hard, clear, handsome aquiline profile (for the nose, though not long, was a marked aquiline shape), and in the masterful, scowling grey eye, there were traces of something more distinguished and formidable than is seen in Sir John Millais's well-known likeness of him as an old seaman in 'The North-West Passage'.[53]

But it was the voice that fixed Colvin's attention, the voice of a born actor.

> From time to time he would rise, almost bound up in his chair, with his eyes fastened on yours like a vice, and in tones of incredible power would roar what he had to say in your face. I never heard a voice so energetic as that which burst from the old man in that explosion.[54]

Celebrity and survivor, these were roles that Trelawny had been playing for fifty years, and even at the end he was not going to sell himself short. He spoke of the war in the Transvaal – '"If I were a younger man," he shouted in a strong crescendo, "I would go and fight for the Boers – fight for the Boers – fight for the Boers."'[55] He showed Colvin the scars on his hands from Shelley's cremation. And he spoke of Greece. Had he ever returned? Colvin asked.

> No, if after leaving Greece he had ever gone back there he would without doubt have been assassinated. Why? For the

sake of the plunder; because he, and he alone, knew the caves and hiding places where the chief Odysseus had deposited his treasures.[56]

There could seem something pathetic in the picture of an old man absorbed in the fantasies of his youth in this way, and yet it is not a failure but a triumph that one is looking at in that figure slumped in his chair like Dickens's Smallweed, a victory of imagination over reality, of creative invention over the dull clay of human existence. For over fifty years Trelawny had worked on the raw material of his own personality, had taken the 'great lout' of a boy his uncle had dismissed and turned him into an icon for a whole generation, 'the last of the giants of the Mediterranean seaboard', as an early biographer hailed him,

> the sole survivor of the race of Theseus, Hercules, Og, Cadmus and the Dioscuri who, rayed with semi-divinity, colonised the metallands of Western Europe . . . Some drops of the of blood of Gog and Magog seem to have been transfused into the veins of Edward Trelawny.[57]

The scars, the voice, the presence, the eyes – the eyes, which Richard Edgcumbe claimed would have 'gazed an eagle blind'[58] – all seemed testament enough to those who knew him in his last years of the man he had been, and yet it was the burning sincerity of his own witness that was his ultimate guarantee. There were reviewers and critics throughout his life who revolted from the crudity and violence of his nature, but no one faced with the blunt ferocity of Trelawny in full flow or the trumpeted hatred of all cant ever doubted the central truthfulness of his stories. When Colvin recalled his visit down to Sompting he wondered what among the mannerisms were genuine and what affectation, but his very presence there in the first place was the collusive proof that the question had no force. It was all affected, and all perfectly genuine, all an act and all there was. At some level, too, even his most sceptical visitors knew this, and it is the same still. There might sometimes be a momentary spasm of guilt as one passes over years and even decades of his life with nothing more than a cavalier sentence or two, but anybody who reads his *Records* knows as well as those who made the pilgrimage to Sompting that it is this Trelawny of his own myth-making and not that of history who is important. 'Shakespeare had a wife, so had Milton,' he wrote to Claire Clairmont in 1871, 'who cares to know anything about them? – we know only they tormented their husbands. I am solely interested about Shelley.'[59]

Whether or not the 'true' Shelley can be extracted from his world in the way this suggests, the 'Trelawny' Colvin went to see certainly can. Colvin was no more interested in the Trelawny who had lived in Pelham Crescent or farmed in Usk than Mary Shelley and Jane Williams would have been in a gauche midshipman almost sixty years earlier. The 'Trelawny' they wanted, that Colvin, Edgcumbe, Rossetti or Swinburne wanted, the 'Trelawny' that still compels attention, was a fact of literature and not of history, an imaginative reality which transcends exposure and question, a creation of the romantic mind as true in its lies as in the truths with which they were so fecklessly mixed.

In control to the last, Trelawny had also taken care of his death. In November 1880 he got Rossetti to translate a letter for him to the Custodian of the English Cemetery at Rome.

> In the year 1822 I purchased a piece of land of the then Custodian – I believe your father – under the Pyramid of Caius Cestius. I deposited the ashes of my Friend Shelley in one Tomb and the other I left for my own Ashes. I planted seven upright Cypresses round it. I now desire at my decease, which cannot be far distant, that my ashes may be placed there.[60]

Early in August 1881, when Trelawny was almost eighty-nine, Rossetti went down to see him at Sompting, and found that he had taken to his bed. There was nothing constitutionally wrong with his patient, the doctor told Rossetti, and that if he would only choose to live, he might do so. It was clear, however, that Trelawny had chosen otherwise. He had often said that he had no desire 'to linger on into the last dregs of existence, but on the contrary upheld suicide as a sovereign and befitting remedy'. True to his word, he now faced the end with calm dignity. Rossetti asked if he might see him in his bedroom, but was refused. 'What would be the use?' Trelawny had asked, 'I can't talk.'[61]

It was their last exchange. On 13 August Rossetti received a telegram from Miss Taylor. Trelawny had died peacefully in his bed. 'Tameless in youth,' Rossetti wrote in his obituary notice, 'Trelawny was also untamed in age.'

> Of iron firmness, at once vehement and stoical, outspoken and often overbearing, despising the conventions and the creeds of society, and restive even to its trivial amenities, he was exceedingly generous, kindly in a large sense, a steady friend, and capable of inspiring strong attachments . . . His body was as strong as his mind. To the end he wore neither overcoat nor under-clothing, and he had scarcely ever had an illness. He died at last without disease, simply from old age: more than a month ago, his strength failing, he took to his bed.[62]

His body was taken to Germany for cremation as he had instructed, and his ashes then deposited beside those of Shelley in the Protestant Cemetery in Rome. 'Heart of hearts,' Swinburne wrote,

> Heart of hearts, are thou moved not, hearing
> Surely, if hearts of the dead may hear,
> Whose true heart it is now draws near?
> Surely the sense of it thrills thee, cheering
> Darkness and death with the news now nearing,
> Shelley, Trelawny rejoins thee here.[63]

And there he is still, his right to be named in the same breath as Shelley confirmed by their eternal intimacy in death, their graves side by side, the myth he had spent a lifetime creating set now in stone.

> *These are Two Friends*
> *Whose Lives were undivided*
> *So let their Memory be,*

Now that they have glided
Under the Grave;
Let not their Bones be parted
For their Two Hearts in Life
Were single hearted

It is no use protesting, there is no escape from the pull of that myth, nothing to put in its place that will disturb its power. Trelawny has won. Stand beside that grave and try to imagine a Shelley without him, or stand again on the site of Byron's house in Missolonghi, on a day in late April, when the withered wreath placed by the British Embassy adds a final note of melancholy to the scene. It is not Millingen's Byron one sees, or Gamba's, or Fletcher's, or Parry's, or anyone else who was actually there through his last days: it is – whether the picture is true or not – Trelawny's.

Or stand, finally, on the crumbling terrace of the Parnassan cave that for just over a year in 1824–5 he set out to recreate in his own image. It is badly eroded now, the edge dangerous, the iron ladders bolted to the cliff-face more precarious from year to year. Soon it will no longer be possible to get up there, but for the time being it remains the place to recapture Trelawny, to feel the sway of an imagination that no revisionist truth can curb.

It is no longer the cave Trelawny inhabited, of course, no longer the cave Humphreys and Bacon described in such lavish detail. Even by the time that Trelawny left Parnassus on 6 August 1825, and the boom of the cannon rolled down the gorge after him in a last salute, it was a place that already stood between the fortress of his dreams and the silent, blind hole it is now.

'I believe that the Committee has informed the Government that the cave has no water,' the patriot Vasileiadis wrote six weeks later, 'because the cistern is damaged and cannot hold water in it. I am requesting Respectable Governing body to send 500 grossia . . . The builder says that this money is needed for the repair of the Cistern; otherwise, if the Government neglects this matter, the cave is worth nothing without water. Also the wall of the cave is unfinished, so we are requesting the Government to give authorisation so this wall can be built as well.'[64]

Nothing could be further from the picture Bacon had drawn only a month earlier, with its pigeons and bees, its limitless stores and fresh water. It is as if without Trelawny's presence, without the transforming power of his *belief*, the cave had already become somehow smaller, more impoverished. Odysseus's property was still there, but after all the hopes and extravagant expectations that did not add up to much: some wheat, corn, flour, barley, dried bread, salt, corn seeds, olive oil, wine, butter.

A list was also sent back to the government at Nauplia of Trelawny's belongings, the remains of the materials he had brought from Missolonghi with Fenton in the May of 1824. There were thirteen barrels of gunpowder, forty-four boxes of cartridges, ammunition and parts; three boxes containing tools, swords, bellows and anvil, two large saws, sixty canon balls, and the mountain guns Komarone had fired in his last salute to Trelawny.

These are dull props on which to hang a dream. Now there are hardly even those. The sparkling stream that visitors spoke of is nothing more than a slow drip from the vaulted ceiling, but high up in the cave, at the very back where roof and floor meet, where even in high summer damp stains the rock face green, a small cemented runnel shows where its course must once have run. It must have been here too, with the constant drip of water playing on his nerves, that Whitcombe was kept chained to the rock.

And then, piece by piece, the cave reveals itself. A rendered wall, the remains of a doorstep, and a lost room takes shape. A course of stone, jutting out at right angles, and another adjoins it. Above the top rung of the ladder, fashioned into the rock, the remains of steps show where Odysseus's own house stood. To the left of that as one looks into the cave was Trelawny's, where he lay those weeks while Whitcombe's screams of terror echoed around the cave. And beyond that, beyond the remains of the chapel, with the brick kiln next to it, the rock face where the mark they shot at that hot Saturday afternoon was fixed.

These props are, however, enough. Among the rubble of Trelawny's chapel, a sloughed-off snake skin lies curled, surprising, perfect and transparent, an almost embarrassingly apt symbol of the

cave. As one turns back to find again the top of the ladders and
stretches down for the iron cable that leads to the top rung, the
empty shell of Trelawny's dreams disappears instantly from sight,
returning it in all its colour and glamour and violence and hatreds
to the realm of fantasy.

The picture is irresistible, the potency of his dream as strong as
ever, dissolving protest and objections. There can never have been
two thousand men up there. There were never stores to last for
twenty years. There was never a billiard table. There are no stalac-
tites or stalagmites as Trelawny claimed. As one climbs down the
ladders, though, and negotiates the move from one to another that
proved too much for poor Bacon, Trelawny's last public words,
muttered as Sidney Colvin took his leave, echo tauntingly around
the mind: 'Lies, lies, lies.'[65] He never spoke a truer word, but it
does not matter. Soon the ladders will be gone, and his Parnassan
fortress will be inaccessible. Then Trelawny can again take full
possession of his cave, and it can become what it always was: a
palace of the imagination.

NOTES TO THE TEXT

NAUPLIA

p. 5 There is the occasional 'Philhellene Street' to record their memory, including one in Athens and another in the village of Peta near Arta, where so many of the early Philhellenes fought and died in the disastrous battle of 16 July 1822. There are also a number of monuments alongside the statue to Byron in the Garden of Heroes at Missolonghi, raised by various nationalities in memory of their volunteers, at Tripolis and on the site of the Battles of Navarino and Sphacteria.

p. 6 Frank Abney Hastings deserves a biography and not a footnote. After Byron, he is the greatest of all British Philhellenes, and yet his career is one more illustration of the role chance played in the history of foreign volunteers. At the age of eleven Hastings had served as a boy volunteer at the Battle of Trafalgar. In the ten years that followed he saw action almost constantly, and was a rising commander when in the January of 1819 he brought the HMS *Kangaroo* under a reckless press of sail into the crowded harbour at Port Royal. Warnings were shouted from endangered ships, insults traded, the word 'lubber' hurled at him across the bay. The following morning Hastings presented himself in a plain blue greatcoat on the quarterdeck of the flagship. In front of the assembled officers he delivered these half dozen lines, written in a rather childish hand, to the *Iphigenia*'s captain. 'Sir, you appear about

to sail – time is precious tomorrow morning I must have that satisfaction your conduct on the 18th rendered so indispensible. I am not provided with a friend so that I am myself the bearer of this. Frank Hastings late commander of the *Kangaroo*.'[1] Naval regulations on duelling were fierce. The note was forwarded to Admiral Popham with a sustained attack on Hastings's 'unofficerlike' and 'lubberly' behaviour.[2] An enquiry was inevitable, and so too, given Hastings's bravura insolence before the board, the result. 'Your lordship may perhaps find officers who will submit to such language,' he told Lord Melville, 'but I do not envy them their dearly purchased rank.'[3] At the age of 25 his career was over. As with Thomas Cochrane, his intelligence, his courage and his imagination as a seaman and tactician were lost to the service. Britain's loss was Greece's gain. Among the earliest volunteers to sail to Greece, he was on his arrival suspected of espionage. His letter to Mavrocordato perfectly captures the spirit of this man. 'If the English Government required a spy in Greece it would not address itself to a person in my condition. I am the younger son of Charles Hastings, Baronet, a General in the Army, who was educated with the Marquis of Hastings, Governor-General of India; so that I could surely find a more lucrative, less dangerous and more respectable employment in India than that of a spy in Greece.'[4] Imperious, brave, headstrong, insubordinate, talented, chivalrous, it is tempting to see in one combination or another here the essential traits of the Philhellene volunteer. To these, however, Hastings added a physical and moral courage, an ingenuity and perseverance that distinguished his conduct throughout the war. After serving bravely with the Greek navy and army, he commanded with brilliant success its first steamship. He died of wounds received in a pointless naval skirmish with the independence he had fought six years to win already in sight. His heart is set into the wall of the English church in Athens. His grave is on the island of Poros, out of bounds now and forgotten in a Greek naval establishment, a sad resting place for 'the only foreigner in whose character and deeds were the elements of true glory'.[5]

p. 7 Even this was not the end of Bonaparte's posthumous travels. In 1820 his grave was ransacked by shepherds in search of treasure, and his bones scattered. These were collected again, and after six years in a closet in Pylos, sent to the Ethnological Museum at Athens, where they are stored in a reliquary urn bearing the inscription: 'Relics of Paul Marie Bonaparte, Lucien's son, who was killed on board the big frigate *Hellas* in 1827.'

p. 7 For obvious reasons it is difficult to be certain about philhellene numbers or even on occasion names. The most rigorous guide comes in William St Clair's *That Greece Might Still Be Free*. For the earliest phase of the war until the end of 1822, he estimates that 265 German volunteers went out to Greece to fight, 71 French, 62 Italian, 24 Polish, 19 Swiss and only then 12 British. The real figures, too, are even less impressive than this suggests. Many of the British volunteers who came to Greece were products of European rather than British

Philhellenism. Hastings, Gordon, Finlay, Byron, Trelawny, Fenton, Hamilton Browne and Humphreys, for instance, were all on the Continent at or just after the outbreak of war and are hardly evidence of effective domestic enthusiasm. It was only with the founding of the London Greek Committee in March 1823 that Britain became the focal point of both European and American Philhellenism. From 1823 until the end of the war another 77 British volunteers made the journey to Greece, bringing the figure to 99 out of a Philhellene total of 940. A more tragic irony involves the role of Germans in Modern Greek history. The place to feel this is in the town of Kalavrita in the northern Peloponnese. It was 7km south-west of here at the Monastery of Ayia Lavra that Bishop Germanos first raised the standard of revolt in March 1821, one of the great symbolic moments which inspired European but above all German volunteers to fight for Greece in such numbers. It is, though, a very different German contribution to Greek history that intrudes its memories here. On 13 December 1943, 1436 males over the age of fifteen were executed in Kalavrita by the occupying German forces, and the next day the monastery of Ayia Lavra burned and its monks killed. The clock on the Metropolitan Church in Kalavrita still stands at 2.34, the time of the massacre.

CHAPTER ONE
p. 18 Trelawny's ships were first listed in 'Trelawny's Family Background and Naval Career,' the article by Lady Anne Hill which finally exposed Trelawny's *Adventures* by the simple expedient of examining naval records for the period Trelawny claimed to have been a pirate. Between 1805 when he first went to sea and 1812, Trelawny served on the following ships: *Superb, Pickle, Temeraire,*

Colossus, Puissant, Woolwich, Resistance, Royal William, Cornelia, Hecate, Cornwallis, Akbar, Piedmontaise, Armide. The chronology of this career can be traced through Admiralty Musters and Logs, but there is also corroborative evidence for these early years in the collection of Hawkins and Trelawny Papers in the County Record Office at Truro.

p. 29 In the only biography of Trelawny written since Lady Anne Hill's article, William St Clair made the persuasive suggestion that the figure of De Ruyter was based on the French privateer Surcouff – Napoleonic France's answer to Cochrane – who created such havoc among the convoys of the East India Company. There can be no doubt that Trelawny would have heard of his exploits in his years out in the East, but even if St Clair is right the De Ruyter of *Adventures* is ultimately a composite figure, an amalgam of all Trelawny's early heroes, an idealized blend of Shelleyan moral authority (De Ruyter and Shelley are interestingly the same age when Trelawny first meets them), Byronic mystery and the physical prowess of the Greek bandit chief, Odysseus Androutsos.

CHAPTER TWO

p. 36 Among the works listed in Trelawny's notebook at the time of his father's death, is Shelley's 'Rosalind and Helen', but there is no mention of 'Queen Mab'. An edition of 250 had been privately printed by Shelley in 1813, but the pirate edition did not appear until the year after this incident, casting certain doubts over the literal accuracy of Trelawny's story. His enthusiasm, however, was as immediate and genuine as he suggests. In 1880, he wrote to Harry Buxton Forman, the future editor of his *Letters*, describing his earliest purchase of Shelley's works in London on his brief visit in 1820-1. 'A year before

Shelley's death, fifty-eight years ago, I went into a small bookseller's in Vere Street, Oxford Street, kept by a man named Ollier; He was the only one of the tribe of bibliophiles who would publish Shelley's writings. After I had satisfied his mind that I was a friend of the Poet's, he let me have all the poems of Shelley's then published.'[6]

p. 47 Trelawny spent a lifetime distancing himself from the responsiblity for the *Don Juan*, not stopping short either of tampering with the documentary evidence when it served his purpose in *Recollections* and *Records*. For obvious reasons he wanted, and even needed, to believe rumours that the ship had been rammed and not simply sunk because of faulty design, and as late as 1875 was still disingenuously asserting his claims in the pages of *The Times*. A letter from Roberts, written at the time, had made it clear that the gunwhale had been holed in many places, but in Trelawny's version this is changed to fit the ramming theory. 'When I recieved the news from Rome of an old sailor at Spezia having confessed he was one of the crew of the *felucca* who ran down Shelley's boat, I believed it, and do so still, as it exactly corresponded with the event ... After a course of dredging, she was found in ten fathoms water, about two miles off the coast of Viareggio. The cause of her loss was then evident – her starboard quarter was stove in, evidently by a blow from the sharp bows of a *felucca*; and as I have said, being undecked, and having three tons and a half of iron ballast, she would have sunk in two minutes.'[7]

CHAPTER THREE

p. 72 There can be few groups so universally reviled in or out of Greece as the Phanariots, a name in romantic Philhellene lore synonymous with duplicity. A description from the Philhellene turned Turcophile David

Urquhart is typical of the hatred they provoked. They made up, he wrote in *The Spirit of the East*, 'that class of Greeks who . . . coiled themselves round the heart of the Ottoman empire; who corrupted the simplicity of the Turkish system by their political doctrines, the primitiveness of the Turkish pastoral habits by the servility of their own bearing and conduct; and who, after dismembering the empire by their intrigues, now stand forth to glory in their treachery towards those whom they served.[8]

p. 75 The horrors on both sides, so similar in most respects, were different in one important sense, in that whereas to the Greeks cruelty was a matter of pleasure, to the Turks it was essentially an instrument of policy. The execution of the patriarch was an illustration of this. It was axiomatic of Ottoman justice, that as their spiritual head Patriarch Gregorius should bear responsibility for the rebellion of Greek subjects. His own innocence was no defence, and no account was taken either of his great age. On the evening of 22 April 1821, Easter Sunday, he was arrested and hanged at the gate of his own palace in Constantinople with a *fetva* pinned to his chest. His body was left there three days, before being cut down and handed to Jews to drag through the city and throw into the Bosphorus. His corpse was rescued and carried to Odessa, where it was enshrined with great ceremony as that of a martyr. The horrors that the Greeks inflicted on the Jewish population of Tripolis were in part ascribed to revenge for the role played by Constantinople's Jews in Gregorius's death.

p. 81 This was pointed out by the late Mrs Susan Mavrocordato. The most extravagant monument to Colocotrones, a rearing equestrian statue, is that in Tripolis, scene of one of the most disgusting massacres of the war. A more impressive equestrian figure can be found in Nauplia.

p. 83 George Finlay is one of the most interesting of all the Philhellenes who fought in Greece. Born in 1799 and educated in law at Glasgow and then Göttingen, he arrived at Cephalonia in December 1823. 'I thought,' said Byron when he first saw him, 'that you were Shelley's ghost.'[9] (A bust of Finlay in old age, at the British School of Archaeology in Athens, suggests a rather saddening image of what Shelley might have looked like had he lived.) An ardent Byronist as a young man, Finlay's romantic enthusiasm for the Greek cause weathered into the critical harshness which colours his great *History of the Greek Revolution*. Remorseless against the captains and politicians of the war, ruthless in its judgement of every leader and sentimental in its championship of the Greek peasantry, Finlay's account remains for all its imbalances one of the key sources. He stayed on in the newly liberated Greece, an ensnared critic and exasperated Philhellene to the end, and is buried in the First Cemetery in Athens, where he died in 1875.

p. 85 Edward Williams's journal entry for the day he and Jane left England throws a poignant sidelight on this. 'We seemed as it were to be flying from ourselves,' he wrote ' – from a life which promised nothing in the perspective but misery, to one of peace and the enjoyment of our days.'[10]

p. 100 Another and infinitely more reliable Philhellene, Frank Abney Hastings, has left his judgements on the Greek leaders at this time. It is interesting to note that they are scarcely less dismissive than Trelawny's. Only Miaulis, Kanaris, Botsaris and the Tombazzi brothers escape with any real credit. George Conduriottes is 'an ignorant weak man'; Demetrius Ypsilanti, the brother of Alexander, 'bald & feeble . . . he does not so much want talent as ferocity'; Ghouras on the other hand 'possesses courage and extreme ferocity – but is exceedingly ignorant'. Mavrocordato 'has quickness and intelligence but I doubt if he has any solid genius and he wants courage'. Londo is 'a drunkard and a man of no consideration but for his wealth'; Notara 'is said to be a very great coward'; Petro Bey Mavromichaelis – the hero of the Mani – 'a fat, stupid, worthy man'; and Colocotrones an able guerrilla but 'entirely ignorant of war & is not sufficiently civilized to look forward to any other advantage to himself or Greece than that of possessing the mountains and keeping the Turks at bay.'[11]

CHAPTER FIVE

p. 122 History has always been grateful to William Parry for the amusement he brought to Byron's final days. A former supervisor of the Woolwich Arsenal, Parry came out to Missolonghi in charge of the munitions sent by the London Greek Committee in November 1823. Long anticipated – Byron ironically wondered if it was the Parry of the North-West Passage they had been awaiting so long – there was never any chance when he finally reached Missolonghi that he would meet expectations. Byron, proof against the particular brand of snobbery rife in the town's Philhellene circles, enjoyed his company and stories against Bentham to the end. Blaquiere, more typically, called him 'one of the greatest rascals unhung, and as great an impostor . . . as a sot and a drunkard Mr P is unrivalled.'[12] On his return to England he wrote with Thomas Hodgskin's help *The Last Days of Lord Byron*, the best and most moving account to come out of Missolonghi. In the front of the London Library's copy is an inscription recording that it was a gift from Parry to the Superintendent of Hanwell Lunatic Asylum, where Parry had been an inmate. Among the

substantial surviving records from Hanwell – one of the most clinically enlightened asylums at the time – there is no record of Parry's death, so his fate remains to some extent obscure.

p. 135 This has been endlessly debated, but remains unresolved. The crux of the argument lies with the date on which Byron's coffin was sealed, but there is a confusion over even that. Gamba and Millingen both say that Trelawny arrived in time to see Byron's corpse, but that in itself is no proof of the incident Trelawny describes here. As David Wright points out in his edition of Trelawny's *Records*, it is odd that if Trelawny did see the body, he should have passed over the effects of a brutal postmortem. Nobody's testimony, however, seems reliable. Millingen, his doctor, ascribed his lameness to the wrong foot for instance, and when Canon Barber opened Byron's coffin in 1938, his description of what he saw is almost exactly the opposite of Hobhouse's. When Hobhouse saw Byron's face on the arrival of the corpse in London, it seemed to him to bear no resemblance to his friend, the mouth distorted and half open, the teeth on which he had prided himself discoloured, the red mustachios on his upper lip giving a totally new character to his face. Barber, on the other hand, saw perhaps what he wanted to see. 'Within the case was another coffin of wood – the lid had never been fastened. What was beneath it? If I raised it, what should I discover? Dare I look within? . . . Reverently, very reverently, I raised the lid, and before my eyes there lay the embalmed body of Byron in as perfect a condition as when it was placed in the coffin one hundred and fourteen years ago. His features and hair easily recognisable from the portraits with which I was so familiar. The serene, almost happy expression on his face made a profound impression upon me. The feet and ankles were uncovered, and I was able to establish the fact that his lameness had been that of his right foot.'[13] Trelawny's account used here is from his *Recollections*, and differs from the later *Records* in certain details and phrases.

CHAPTER SIX

p. 144 The traveller Edward Clarke recorded that the Kakoreme had received its name because in local belief the village at the bottom of the Velitza Gorge was associated with the site of ancient Thebes. According to legend, the city had been destroyed by the river, and even at the beginning of the nineteenth century, the present village of Velitza was known locally as 'Thebes'. This opens up interesting possibilities on the whereabouts of Odysseus's buried treasure.

p. 145 The landscapes by Edward Dodwell show Tithorea in 1806, which must be more or less the same village Trelawny knew eighteen years later. Only a few houses stand on the site of the larger modern village, scattered among the ruins of the ancient city on the great bluff above the Kakoreme. There is also an oil by Edward Lear painted in 1862, a view across Lake Copais on the plain beneath that shows the Velitza Gorge under snow. In the summer of 1824, when Trelawny was in the cave, the lake was particularly low, revealing features which were usually hidden. It was not until 1931 that the lake was finally drained, and reclamation completed. This is the only substantial change from the scene Trelawny would have known.

CHAPTER SEVEN

p. 161 There are passages in Frank Abney Hastings's journal that throw an interesting light on the callow figure Jarvis cut when he first arrived in Greece. The two men had met in France, and Hastings had paid for Jarvis's passage on the *Trondheim* from Marseilles in March

1822. They had been put ashore together on the island of Hydra, but after Jarvis had interceded with Mavrocordato on Hasting's part, Hastings – as an Englishman – was suspected of spying and relations between them rapidly deteriorated. On 6 May Hastings wrote: 'Jarvis who on several occasions had taken on himself the air of my superior ventured to reform as he said what I had done which obliged me to give him a strong reprimand; this he did not appear to consider me authorised to do. I was therefore obliged to become the Spadassic & offer him his satisfaction on shore – this succeeded & I found myself rid of a meddling kind of charlatan.' Three days later Hastings, who had fought as a boy at Trafalgar, returned to the attack. 'Our men called to us to get into the boat – we did so – all except Jarvis who always pretended to know better than his superiors & those who had seen service . . . No doubt when Jarvis has seen some service he will learn that the duty of an officer is to provide for the protection of his own men as well as the destruction of the enemy.'[14]

It is worth comparing these images of Jarvis with a portrait of him three years later. It comes in the anonymous *Sketches of Modern Greece . . . by a Young English Volunteer*. Jarvis is thinly disguised under the name of 'Baltimore'. 'It was a person of vestments the coarsest and most impaired that could possibly be worn by the merest follower. He was, withal, evidently a *capitano*, for in his suite were some fifteen Palikars, who seemed to have a particular attachment for him, prompted no doubt by a similarity of taste as well as habits, for he had little ostentation . . . Curious as were the manners of this individual, something of dignity was attached to him; for whenever he tarried by any throng, the most distinguished who composed it would approach and converse with him . . . This was Baltimore [he is told] the American General, by title, of the Greeks – the inseparable of Mavrocordato, and one who had no more conscience than the latter; a man who had become more of a Barbarian than the most barbarous of any who strove to inculcate to him the precepts fit for attaining to that enviable state.'[15]

p. 164 The Archives of the London Greek Committee held in the National Library in Athens give an extraordinarily varied picture of the men who became involved at every phase in the Philhellene movement. Perhaps the most elusive is the 'Count de Witsch' referred to in a warning letter addressed to the Committee by 'a friend'. He has, it says, 'been well known at Vienna, Berlin, Hamburgh, Copenhagen, Amsterdam and Paris for the last 20 years and upwards under various names and titles, such as Count de Witych, de Mietz, de Witsch, de Witz, de Winty, Mr Fitzroy, the King of Illyria etc.'[16]

p. 167 With a surgeon's cool detachment – not to mention stomach – the American Samuel Gridley Howe added a note on impalement to his history of the war. 'Impalement is perhaps the most dreadful punishment to which man can be subjected; for the driving of the stake through the body, does not always (as would be supposed) put an instant period to life. If the stake (which is as large as the wrist) is carefully directed along the inside of the spine, it sometimes escapes the vital organs, and the sufferer may live for twenty-four hours, or more. The raising him erect, and planting one end of the stake in the ground, seems a refinement of cruelty, practised in some particular cases; for generally, after being spitted, the victim is left upon the ground to writhe and die. Impalement is a legally authorised punishment in Turkey. In Candia, several Greek priests, thus spitted alive, were slowly roasted by the Turks. This is rarely the case, however.'[17]

p. 176 Out in the darkness, an ancient Greek theatre, its seats carved into the living rock, stared out across the battleground where Thebes' Sacred Band had fought to the last man against Philip's Macedonians, but inside the hovel the irony seems to have been lost on Bacon. This is all the more surprising, as he clearly knew where he was. The superb Lion of Charoneia, over eight metres high on its plinth, which now stands guard over the burial place of the Theban Sacred Band killed in the battle between the Greek City States and Philip's Macedonians in 338 BC., had only just been rediscovered.

Philip's triumph signalled the end of Greek independence 'that dishonest victory . . . fatal to liberty', as Milton called it – and Bacon, allowed to roam freely through the camp during the day, must have been one of the first travellers to see the recently uncovered Lion. In his *Autobiography of an Octogenarian Architect,* G. L. Taylor described its accidental discovery in 1818 when his horse tripped over a protruding stone in the road. Suspecting that it might be the monument described by Pausanias, he and his companions began to dig and uncovered the head and part of the right hind leg. Its immediate fate after this discovery is a matter of controversy. Found as it was on Odysseus's territory, one version has it that he had it blown up in the belief it contained treasure. Bacon's account is rather different. 'I will here notice,' he wrote in his *Journal,* 'a curious piece of sculpture, probably the identical Theban Lion of Charonea, so much sought by antiquarian travellers, and which had remained for such a length of time buried under ground; but which has been very lately brought to light on the plain of Livadia about two miles from the given site of Charoneia, and may have been commemorative of this celebrated battle field. This curious specimen has not been alluded to by the various travellers who have ransacked Greece in search of Antiquities. It was discovered a few years ago by O. then governor of the province of Livadia; he caused the earth to be removed around it between six & eight feet deep; when first seen the figure was entire and represented a lioness.'[18]

Odysseus seems to have told Bacon that rumour then reached the Turks of treasure within it. 'Nothing would satisfy the Turks, by way of discovering the concealed treasure, but blowing to pieces this Lioness, which had remained for years in its perfect state: when I saw the statue it was broken into nearly three equal parts and the earth was again about to cover this curious but now mutilated relic.'[19]

Bacon is, as ever in his *Journal*, generous to Odysseus but it is difficult to imagine the klepht having any scruples about blowing up the monument himself. It seems a defining irony that Trelawny's patriot champion should be the man responsible for destroying this symbol of Greek freedom.

Taylor later tried to persuade the Admiralty to bring the Lion to Britain. It stands, though, where it belongs, above the excavated graves of the Sacred Band, the inspiration for Ypsilanti's volunteers who fought under the same name. A couple of miles across the cotton fields to the north-east, near the railway line, a melancholy clump of cypresses marks the tumulus of the Macedonians killed in the battle.

p. 172 The fabled treasure of the cave, which Trelawny was still talking about to Sidney Colvin only weeks before his death almost sixty years later, remains a mystery. The traditional story that St Clair tells is that it was made up of antiquities pillaged by Odysseus and £15,000 in Austrian double florins kept in gunpowder tins. This was buried one night among the ruins of Thebes, with a

layer of earth, a layer of stones, and then more earth piled on top to prevent any hollow sound from betraying its whereabouts.

It seems extremely improbable that Odysseus and Trelawny would have transported that amount of wealth almost fifty miles across disputed territory from the cave on Parnassus to Thebes. If the story is true, however, it seems much more likely that the 'Thebes' in question is the village at the foot of the Velitza Gorge known to locals by that name in the early nineteenth century. This would have involved a journey of little more than an hour.

CHAPTER EIGHT
p. 182 Among Lord Liverpool's correspondence in the British Library there are letters from the widowed Lady Whitcombe asking for preferment for her children. Whitcombe's own letter to the Committee was supported by a reference from the Countess of Tankerville. It is significant, though, that Lady Tankerville did not know Whitcombe personally, but was willing 'to do you any kindness in my power from the true affection I bear your mother, and also thro' the regard I have for Sir John Aubrey your, as my near connexion.'[20]

It was William St Clair who first identified Whitcombe as the author of *Sketches*. The argument from the internal evidence of the book alone seems absolutely watertight, but since St Clair's *Trelawny*, C. W. J. Eliot has also established that Whitcombe's nephew, Charles Douglas, had confirmed his uncle's authorship.

CHAPTER NINE
p. 197 If there were any doubt that it was Odysseus Trelawny had in mind here, then his imagery provides unconscious corroboration. As a seaman Trelawny would hardly have needed the

hint, but the image of the sailor is possibly remembered from Cowper's fine poem 'The Castaway' which recalls an incident on Anson's voyage around the world – it was certainly a poem Trelawny knew, as it is listed among the works he owned in 1820, and one of the fictional characters who drowns in his *Adventures* is incidentally called Anson. Given the nature of Odysseus's death, the rope here has a poignancy which rescues it from banality.

p. 199 This was certainly the opinion of Mrs Susan Mavrocordato, who spent more time on Mavrocordato's papers than anyone else, and who believed that he could not possibly have condoned Trelawny's murder.

CHAPTER ELEVEN

p. 227 It is an interesting demonstration of the great diaspora brought about by the British Empire, that the families of so many of those involved in the plot to kill Trelawny should end up in Canada, South Africa and New Zealand. The history of the Bacons can largely be followed only through their graves. Mary Bacon, John Bacon's wife, had died nineteen years before her husband at Weymouth, then fashionable by its royal associations. Their eldest son, John William, lies in a lost plot, guarded by the impenetrable jungle and bureacracy of Highgate's Western Cemetery. For another four generations the aspirations of the family were preserved in names that recalled their brief prosperity – William D'Arcy, D'Arcy Johnston, Johnston D'Arcy, but it was the last in this line who died on Vancouver Island. The one daughter of John Bacon fared no better. Maria married a baronet and bankrupt whose ancestor had hung at Tyburn, and within two struggling generations the title had begun the sideways move that would eventually take it to Mobile, Alabama.

p. 228 The evidence that links Trelawny's Bacon with the inscription on the tomb in Friern Barnet, and the history of the Bacon family, illustrates this graphically. On his return from Greece, Bacon wrote an alarmist letter on the subject of Russian expansionism that was published in the *Morning Herald*, and it is from the address appended to the bottom of that letter and on, through an unpaid Poor Rate and the 1841 Census, to a single line in the obituary column of the *Gentleman's Magazine* that it becomes possible to establish the connection.

p. 228 There are problems with D'Arcy Bacon's parentage on both sides. In the edition of the *Gentleman's Magazine* for the month following his father John Bacon's death, mention is made of the widely-held belief that he was the son of Frederick, Prince of Wales. He was entered while still young into the First Fruits Office, but it has proved as yet impossible to establish his origins. It is very likely that the Friern Barnet Bacons were a branch of the Shrubland family. Sir William Johnston, the husband of John Bacon's daughter Maria, had been earlier married to a Mary Bacon of Shrubland Hall, Suffolk.

There is at least a question mark over the identity of John Bacon's wife. In Helena Hayward's and Professor Kirkham's book on the famous Linnell family of furniture makers, she is described as the daughter of William Linnell and Mary Butler, and the sister of John Linnell. Born in 1737, this Mary Linnell first married her father's apprentice William Bond, and then, according to Professor Kirkham, John Bacon.

In Prince Duleep Singh's *Portraits in Norfolk Houses* there are descriptions of paintings of Mary and John Bacon and their three children, John William, Francis D'Arcy, and Maria which were dispersed from Hackford Hall sometime after 1930.

The information given in this catalogue is not completely reliable, but it does seem to bear out this identification.

While this may well be correct, certain problems persist. On John Bacon's tomb, the memorial to Francis D'Arcy describes Mary as the daughter of John Linnell. On the marriage licence of John Bacon and Mary Linnell she is also described as a 'spinster' rather than a widow. There is, too, no evidence of William Bond's death before her marriage in 1773 to John Bacon, while a William Bond, 'carver and gilder', was certainly working and living in Piccadilly as late as 1778.

p. 228 Nobody is commissioned into the army without leaving a trace of their existence, and it is through army records that one can best follow Bacon's movements over the next fifteen years. Bacon moved from the 5th into the 3rd of Foot, and then from the infantry into the cavalry, serving with the 17th Lancers on the River Plate campaign before finally transferring into the 19th Light Dragoons in 1807. He became a brevet major in 1812, the year he left the army.

p. 229 Bacon's two campaigns, which must have done something to shape his vision of life, cannot be allowed to go unnoticed. The first was as part of Prince William of Gloucester's expeditionary force to Northern Holland in the autumn of 1799. The campaign was doomed before it even left England. A march-past of ill-equipped, ill-armed new recruits in front of Pitt and Henry Dundas had to be cancelled when only five hundred men could be found sober enough to remember their drill.

The campaign which followed, from the moment they embarked in their lightest summer kit to the miserable retreat through the driving rain and bottomless mud of a Dutch autumn, has the timeless quality of all military disaster.

For Bacon, however, there was worse to come. He had stayed with his regiment until its second battalion was disbanded at the time of the Peace of Amiens in 1802, and then after a brief period on half-pay and in the 3rd of Foot transferred as a captain into the 17th Lancers.

On 5 October 1806, Bacon embarked from Spithead for South America as part of an expedition aimed at the capture of Buenos Aires. It was a ludicrous mission from the start, ill-conceived, unplanned, bedevilled by faulty communications and intelligence, and chaotically led. 'I have it in command to acquaint you,' William Windham wrote from Downing Street to Sir Samuel Auchmuty in a letter preserved in the P.R.O., 'that the original object of the Expedition, placed under your orders by our instructions dated the 24th of last July, is now resumed, but that you are to consider that and all Instructions subsequent to them, but prior to the present time, as cancelled; and to govern your conduct by the Instructions which I shall now proceed to give to you.'[21]   Those instructions were that Sir Samuel Auchmuty should place himself under the command of General Beresford who, unknown to London, was already a prisoner-of-war. From that point on the expedition unfolded with tragi-comic inevitability. They had embarked from Spithead without enough water to last the journey, but after putting into Rio for fresh supplies eventually arrived at the mouth of the River Plate after 147 days at sea. From there the force moved up river, and attacked Montevideo. Spanish defences were strong, but, as in Holland, the courage of the ordinary soldier made up for the incompetence of their commanders. On 3 February, the town was successfully stormed by the infantry. Ahead of them now, after another journey up river, lay a final, difficult march across hostile country to Buenos Aires. They had to move without cavalry screen, because the 17th had left their horses in

England and the local mounts had proved too small to carry them.

At the end of June, nine months after leaving Spithead, and in spite of swamps and skirmishing, they reached their destination. Inexplicably, the new commander, General Whitelock, ordered his men to advance in columns through the outskirts of the town. As they marched though the streets, under strict orders not to return fire, riflemen on the rooftops picked them off at will. Ignoring casualties, they pressed on, and reached the centre still in good order.

It was now that Whitelock delivered the *coup de grâce* to his baffled army. Having at last reached his object, he decided that it was time to sue for terms. The next day, without being allowed to fire a shot, the humiliated and bewildered expeditionary force began the long retreat back down to the mouth of the River Plate.

It is interesting to note that Trelawny was also off South America at this time surveying the mouth of the River Plate for the Admiralty on board the *Woolwich*.

p. 233 In the years since Peter the Great, Sir James MacNeill warned Britain in the emotive terms of ecologists describing the destruction of rain forests, the Russian borders had moved 700 miles closer to Paris, 500 miles towards Constantinople, 620 miles nearer Stockholm and 1000 towards Teheran. They had absorbed more land in Sweden than remained outside their control. In European Turkey an area larger than Prussia was now in Russian hands. In Asia land of the same extent as the German States, Holland and Belgium combined had been taken. From Persia the equivalent of England had gone, and from Asian Turkey an area the size of Italy, Spain, Greece and all the Ottoman territories in Europe together.

p. 00 There are numerous differences in the two accounts that are probably no more than incidental, but others are more difficult to explain away. In Trelawny's version, Bacon is brought in at night, dressed in European clothes and travelling with another Englishman. In Bacon's version he is alone, dressed like a cossack, and arrives in the early morning. Quite apart from the psychological grounds for questioning Bacon's accuracy there is one other reason that should be mentioned. In his journal he gives a history of Odysseus which he says he had from Trelawny, and while it is only too likely that some exchange of this kind did take place, the account he gives is, word for word, identical with the historical note supplied by Trelawny to Landor for his *Imaginary Conversations*. His conversation with Odysseus, too, clearly shows the influence of Landor.

p. 238 The attack on Psara inspired one of the most courageous defences of the whole war. Surprised by the Turks, the town was put to the torch, until only six hundred Macedonians, with their wives and children, were left in the fortified convent of St Nicholas. Gordon has graphically described the events which followed. 'After plundering and burning the town, the Mohammedans advanced against this post, and were vigorously repulsed in successive assaults until night put an end to the combat. When day dawned, the Capitan Pasha commanded the whole of his troops to renew the attack, which they maintained with incredible fury, in spite of a murderous discharge of grape-shot and musketry from the ramparts. At length the garrison, spent with wounds and fatigue, having lost two-thirds of its number, and hopeless of relief, determined to die, but not without glory and revenge. At four o'clock in the afternoon, a soldier bearing a lighted match was seen to leave the fort, and run on towards the entrance of a great subterraneous powder magazine, situated outside – he fell, pierced with balls, and five of his companions following his example, one after the other shared his fate. Unable to execute their first project, the Greeks resolved to inflame the powder they had within the monastery. They ceased their fire, and the Turks darting on, swords in hand, scaled the walls on every side; when suddenly the Hellenic flag was lowered, a white banner, inscribed with the words 'Liberty or Death' waved in the air, a single gun gave the signal, and a tremendous explosion shaking the isle, and felt far out at sea, buried in the ruins of St Nicholas thousands of the conquerors and conquered.'[22]

CHAPTER THIRTEEN

p. 269 Another sidelight on Trelawny's fame at this time is provided in Howe's journal. In it he reports a meeting with Gamba in Nauplia, who claimed to have just seen Trelawny in Athens. This is impossible. It is difficult to think what Trelawny would have been doing in Ghouras's stronghold anyway, but the log for the *Sparrowhawk* charts a journey between the coasts of Attica and Aegina, round Cape Sounion to the Bay of Marathon, and from there to Smyrna.

p. 280 The full deposition of Tersitza to the Lord High Commissioner reads: 'It is perhaps known to Y E that at about the age of thirteen years I was given in marriage to Signor Trelawny, my family urging that I should live happily with one brought up in the courtesy and good breeding of the country; but, as my experience proved, he failed to treat me with that consideration and nobility of character which distinguished the men of his nation. The nature of the long-continued treatment which I have had to endure at the hands of the said Signor Trelawny is not unknown, and at the last, it is perhaps within Y E's recollection that he brought grief to my very eyes by sending me while in the

Convent, with cunning and brutality, the dead body of my daughter and his.' She was awarded 25 dollars a month alimony.[23]

p. 283 The separate monuments to the Russian, French and British dead are an eloquent reminder that behind the unity of the allied fleet, lay those divisions that would end within thirty years in conflict in the Crimea.

CHAPTER FOURTEEN

p. 295 Trelawny did his bargaining through Mary, who in the end inevitably reaped the rewards of his disappointment with the money *Adventures* made him. He had been hoping at the outset to receive £200 a volume, or £600 in all, though he would have been prepared to settle for five. Colburn's terms were, however, less generous. 'At length, my dear friend,' Mary wrote to him, 'I have received the ultimatum of these great people. They offer you £300, and another £100 on a second edition.'[24] On 26 July 1831 she had to write again, refining the disappointment further. The £300 was to be paid in 'bills of three, six, and eight months, dated from the day of publication, and £100 more on a second edition.'[25] In the same letter Mary goes on to tell Trelawny that his mother 'speaks openly in society of your forthcoming memoirs, so that I should imagine very little real secrecy will attend them. However, you will but gain reputation and admiration through them.'[26]

p. 319 In a letter to Mary Shelley, written with his 'left fin' on 17 September 1825, Trelawny told her that his friend Major Bacon was returning to England and would give her more news of his condition. There is no record of Bacon and Mary Shelley meeting, but as on his return to England he lived in Jeffreys Terrace very close to her in Kentish Town, it seems highly likely. Bacon soon disappears again from sight, but there is one tantalizing and unreadable reference in another letter of Trelawny's to Mary that would suggest that Trelawny and Bacon met again in Calais in January 1829. Given his previous record it is only too probable that Bacon was again out of the country for debt, and an asterisk beside his name in the Camden Poor Rate returns certainly suggests that little had changed. His brother John William continued to live with his family in Kentish Town but the 1841 Census shows Francis D'Arcy Bacon already living in a room in Battersea, obviously in very reduced circumstances. He died in December 1842. The church in which he was buried is now a deconsecrated garden museum.

p. 320 The *Cambrian* went down when she was struck into by the *Isis*, and ran aground on rocks in January 1828. At the court martial held in Malta Hamilton was exonerated of all blame, and the President had it put it on record for its crew that the 'circumstances of having been on the *Cambrian*, would ever operate to their advantage', 'It is with much and sincere pleasure,' he addressed Hamilton, 'that I have to return your sword, and one that has always been used with true credit, and to the good service of your country. I cannot at the same time refrain from expressing to you the regret which the court experiences at the melancholy wind-up of your long and arduous exertions in the Archipelago, performed so ably and with such advantage to the country; and I am sure there is not an officer or man in the squadron who does not join in the feeling.'[27]

REFERENCE NOTES

NAUPLIA

1 S. G. Howe *Letters & Journals of Samuel Gridley Howe during the Greek Revolution*, Boston, 1907–9, p. 333.
2 De Sismondi 'The Extermination of the Greeks,' *New Monthly Magazine*, London, 1826, pp. 90–91.
3 P. B. Shelley Preface to 'Hellas,' *Poems*, 1821.
4 London Greek Committee Archives, Athens.
5 F. A. Hastings Journal, Finlay Papers, British School, Athens.
6 W. Sharp *The Life and Letters of Joseph Severn*, London, 1892, p. 135.
7 R. Edgcumbe *Edward Trelawny: A Biographical Sketch*, Plymouth, 1882, p. 5.
8 Sharp *The Life and Letters of Joseph Severn*, p. 136.

CHAPTER ONE

1 E. J. Trelawny *Adventures of a Younger Son*, Introduction by Edward Garnett, London, 1891, pp. 27–8.
2 Trelawny *Adventures* p. 29.
3 Trelawny *Adventures* p. 29.
4 Trelawny *Adventures* p. 33.
5 Trelawny *Adventures* pp. 32–3.
6 Trelawny *Adventures* pp. 34–5.
7 Trelawny *Adventures* pp. 39–40.
8 Trelawny *Adventures* p. 36.
9 Trelawny *Adventures* p. 36.

10 Trelawny *Adventures* pp. 46–7.
11 Trelawny *Adventures* pp. 61–2.
12 Trelawny *Adventures* pp. 116–17.
13 Hawkins Papers, Chichester.
14 Hawkins Papers, Chichester.
15 Consistory Court of London, Trelawny *v.* Trelawny, 21 April 1818.
16 Consistory Court of London.
17 Consistory Court of London.
18 Consistory Court of London.
19 Donald H. Reiman (ed.) *Shelley and His Circle 1773–1822*, vol. 5, Cambridge, Mass., 1973, p. 79.
20 Reiman (ed.) *Shelley and His Circle*, vol. 5, pp. 90–3.
21 Trelawny *Adventures* p. 81.
22 Trelawny *Adventures* p. 81.
23 Trelawny *Adventures* pp. 85–6.
24 Trelawny *Adventures* p. 75.

CHAPTER TWO

1 I. Origo *The Last Attachment*, London, 1944, p. 298.
2 P. B. Shelley 'England in 1819' *Poems*, vol. 4, p. 6.
3 E. J. Trelawny *Records of Shelley, Byron and the Author*, vol. 1, London, 1878, pp. 2–3.
4 Trelawny *Records*, vol. 1, pp. 7–8.
5 Trelawny *Records*, vol. 1, p. 11.
6 Trelawny *Records*, vol. 1, pp. 12–13.
7 Trelawny *Records*, vol. 1, pp. 15–16.
8 R. Holmes *Shelley: The Pursuit*, London, 1976, pp. 572–3.
9 Trelawny *Records*, vol. 1, pp. 20–1.
10 P. Feldman and D. Scott-Kilvert (eds.) *The Journals of Mary Shelley*

1814–1844, vol. 1, Oxford, 1987, p. 389.

11 *Shelley and Mary*, for Private Circulation only, vol. 3, 1882, p. 742.

12 H. Buxton Forman (ed.) *The Letters of E. J. Trelawny*, London, 1910, pp. 1–2.

13 Holmes *Shelley: The Pursuit*, p. 729.

14 Trelawny *Records*, vol, 1 pp. 191–3.

15 Trelawny *Records*, vol. 1, pp. 210–13.

16. *Shelley and Mary*, vol. 4, p. 947.

17 *Shelley and Mary*, vol. 4, p. 952.

18 M. Kingston Stocking (ed.) *The Clairmont Correspondence*, vol. 1, London, 1968, pp. 24–5.

19 M. Kingston Stocking (ed.) *The Journals of Claire Clairmont*, London, 1968, p. 356.

20 Ashley Papers, British Library, London, 5119.

21 Ashley Papers, 5119.

22 Ashley Papers, 5119.

23 Ashley Papers, 5119.

24 Kingston Stocking (ed.) *The Clairmont Correspondence*, vol. 1, p. 270.

25 Ashley Papers, 5119.

26 Buxton Forman (ed.) *Trelawny Letters*, p. 48.

27 Sharp *The Life and Letters of Joseph Severn*, pp. 135–6.

28 Buxton Forman (ed.) *Trelawny Letters*, pp. 47–8.

29 Buxton Forman (ed.) *Trelawny Letters*, p. 53.

30 *Shelley and Mary*, vol. 4, p. 934.

31 Buxton Forman (ed.) *Trelawny Letters*, pp. 57–9.

32 *Shelley and Mary*, vol. 4, p. 943.

33 Lord Byron 'Childe Harold', Canto I and II, *Poems*, London, 1812.

34 Lord Byron 'Don Juan', Canto III, *Poems*, London, 1821.

35 L. Marchand (ed.) *The Letters and Journals of Lord Byron*, vol. 10, London, 1980, p. 199.

36 Buxton Forman (ed.) *Trelawny Letters*, pp. 62–4.

37 Buxton Forman (ed.) *Trelawny Letters*, pp. 65–6.

38 Marchand (ed.) *The Letters and Journals of Lord Byron*, vol. 10, p. 213.

39 Trelawny *Records*, vol. 2, p. 77.

40 Trelawny *Records*, vol. 2, p. 78.

41 Buxton Forman (ed.) *Trelawny Letters*, p. 20.

42 Marchand (ed.) *The Letters and Journals of Lord Byron*, vol. 10, p. 213.

43 J. H. Browne 'Narrative of a Visit to the Seat of War in Greece', *Blackwood's Magazine*, Edinburgh, 1834, p. 56.

44 Marchand (ed.) *The Letters and Journals of Lord Byron*, vol. 10, pp. 213–4.

45 Trelawny *Records*, vol. 1, p. 26.

46 Trelawny *Adventures*, p. 82.

47 Kingston Stocking (ed.), *The Clairmont Correspondence*, vol. 1, p. 24.

48 Buxton Forman (ed.) *Trelawny Letters*, p. 72.

49 P. Gamba *A Narrative of Lord Byron's Last Journey to Greece*, London, 1825, p. 12.

CHAPTER THREE

1 Buxton Forman (ed.) *Trelawny Letters*, p. 70.

2 Browne 'Narrative of a Visit to the Seat of War in Greece', *Blackwood's Magazine*, p. 393.

3 Trelawny *Records*, vol. 2, p. 122.

4 T. Gordon *History of the Greek Revolution*, vol. 1, London, 1832, p. 222.

5 Trelawny *Records*, vol. 2, pl 108.

6 Finlay Papers, pp. 325–6.

7 Marchand (ed.) *The Letters and Journals of Lord Byron*, vol. 11, pp. 69–70.

8 *Shelley and Mary*, vol. 4, pp. 950–1.
9 *Shelley and Mary*, vol. 4, pp. 964.
10 Buxton Forman (ed.) *Trelawny Letters*, pp. 65–6.
11 *Shelley and Mary*, vol. 4, p. 964.
12. *Shelley and Mary*, vol. 4, p. 967.
13 *Shelley and Mary*, vol. 4, p. 974.
14 Trelawny *Records*, vol. 2, p. 119.
15 Browne *Blackwood's Magazine*, p. 399.
16 H. Lytton Bulwer *An Autumn in Greece*, London, 1826, p. 62.
17 W.M. Leake *Travels in the Morea*, vol. 1, p. 32, London 1830.
18 Bulwer *An Autumn in Greece*, pp. 57–8.
19 Pausanias, vol 2 p. 212.
20 Browne *Blackwood's Magazine*, p. 401.
21 Browne *Blackwood's Magazine*, p. 401.
22 M. Raybaud *Mémoires sur la Grèce, pour servir a l'histoire de la Guerre de l'Independence*, Paris, 1824, p. 466.
23 PRO CO/36/1085.
24 S. Linnér (ed.) *First Journal of the Greek War of Independence* by W. H. Humphreys, Stockholm, 1967, p. 52.
25 *Shelley and Mary*, vol. 4, pp. 974–5.
26 W. Shakespeare *Julius Caesar*, Act IV, Scene 3.
27 Bulwer *An Autumn in Greece*, p. 58.
28 Browne *Blackwood's Magazine*, p. 403.
29 Browne *Blackwood's Magazine*, p. 403.
30 London Greek Committee Archives, Athens.
31 Browne, *Blackwood's Magazine*, p. 403.
32 London Greek Committee Archives, Athens.
33 London Greek Committee Archives, Athens.
34 London Greek Committee Archives, Athens.
35 London Greek Committee Archives, Athens.
36 *Shelley and Mary*, vol. 4, p. 987.
37 *Shelley and Mary*, vol. 4, p. 987.
38 *Shelley and Mary*, vol. 4, p. 983.
39 Finlay Papers, Hastings' Journal.
40 *Shelley and Mary*, vol. 4, p. 989.
41. *Shelley and Mary*, vol. 4, pp. 985–6.

CHAPTER FOUR

1 T. Colocotrones *An Autobiography*, trans. by Mrs Edmonds, London 1892, pp. 4–5.
2 Trelawny *Records*, vol. 2, pp. 121–2.
3 G. Waddington *A Visit to Greece in 1823 and 1824*, London, 1825, p. 78.
4 W. S. L. Landor *Imaginary Conversations*, Second Series, vol. 1, London, 18xx, p. 202.
5 Waddington *A Visit to Greece in 1823 and 1824*, pp. 80–1.
6 M. Shelley *The Letters of Mary Wollstonecraft Shelley*, Baltimore and London, 1983, vol 1, p. 470.
7 J. Millingen *Memoirs of the Affairs of Greece*, London, 1831, p. 152.
8 Trelawny *Adventures*, p. 518.
9 Hastings's Journals, Finlay Papers.
10 T. C. Down 'Pirate Trelawny', *Nineteenth Century and After*, 1907, pp. 800–1.
11 London Greek Committee Archives, Athens.
12 Gordon *History of the Greek Revolution*, vol. 2, p. 108.
13 L. Stanhope *Greece in 1823 and 1824*, New Edition, London, 1825, p. 125.
14 Stanhope *Greece in 1823 and 1824*, p. 126.
15 Trelawny *Records*, vol. 2, p. 117.
16 Mavrocordato Papers, 001, 024, National Archives, Athens.
17 Stanhope *Greece in 1823 and 1824*, p. 126.
18 Stanhope *Greece in 1823 and 1824*, p. 127.
19 Stanhope *Greece in 1823 and 1824*, pp. 140–1.
20 Stanhope *Greece in 1823 and 1824*, p. 299.
21 Stanhope *Greece in 1823 and 1824*, p. 180.

22 London Greek Committee Archives, Athens.
23 Stanhope Papers, K121, National Archives, Athens.

CHAPTER FIVE

1 Lady Blessington *The Conversations of Lord Byron*, London, 1834, p. 391.
2 B. H. Liddell Hart (ed.) *The Letters of Private Wheeler 1809–1828*, London, 1951, p. 236.
3 G. Finlay *History of the Greek Revolution*, London, 1971, p. 325.
4 Marchand (ed.) *The Letters and Journals of Lord Byron*, vol. 11, p. 135.
5 Marchand (ed.) *The Letters and Journals of Lord Byron*, vol. 11, p. 118.
6 Marchand (ed.) *The Letters and Journals of Lord Byron*, vol. 11, pp. 113–14.
7 Lord Byron 'On This Day I Complete My Thirty-Sixth Year,' *Poems*, 1824.
8 Millingen *Memoirs of the Affairs of Greece*, p. 141.
9 *Westminster Review*, July 1824, p. 267.
10 H. Nicolson *Byron: The Last Journey*, London, 1924, p. ix.
11 W. Parry *The Last Days of Lord Byron*, London, 1825, p. 138.
12 London Greek Committee Archives, Athens.
13 Buxton Forman (ed.) *Trelawny Letters*, p. 81.
14 Buxton Forman (ed.) *Trelawny Letters*, p. 82.
15 Buxton Forman (ed.) *Trelawny Letters*, p. 85.
16 Abinger Papers, Bodleian Library, Oxford.
17 Buxton Forman (ed.) *Trelawny Letters*, p. 86.
18 Buxton Forman (ed.) *Trelawny Letters*, p. 89.
19 London Greek Committee Archives, Athens.
20 J. Marshall *The Life and Letters of Mary Wollstonecraft Shelley*, vol. 2, pp. 113–14.
21 T. Carlyle *The Love Letters of Thomas Carlyle and Jane Welsh*, London, 1909, p. 369
22 Carlyle *The Love Letters of Thomas Carlyle and Jane Welsh*, p. 366.
23 Marshal *The Life and Letters of Mary Wollstonecraft Shelley*, vol. 2, pp. 113–14.
24 *The Times*, 17 July 1824.
25 Linnér (ed.) *First Journal of the Greek War of Independence by W. H. Humphreys*, p. 56.
26 Buxton Forman (ed.) *Trelawny Letters*, p. 73.
27 E. J. Trelawny *Recollections of the Last Days of Shelley and Byron*, London, 1858, pp. 222–24.
28 London Greek Committee Archives, Athens.
29 Buxton Forman (ed.) *Trelawny Letters*, p. 81.
30 London Greek Committee Archives, Athens.
31 Stanhope *Greece in 1823 and 1824*, p. 325.
32 Stanhope *Greece in 1823 and 1824*, pp. 339–40.
33 London Greek Committee Archives, Athens.
34 London Greek Committee Archives, Athens.
35 London Greek Committee Archives, Athens.
36 London Greek Committee Archives, Athens.
37 Buxton Forman (ed.) *Trelawny Letters*, pp. 99–100.
38 S. G. Howe *An Historical Sketch of the Great Revolution*, New York, 1828, p. 311.
39 Buxton Forman (ed.) *Trelawny Letters*, p. 100.

CHAPTER SIX

1 Landor *Imaginary Conversations*, p. 160.
2 Trelawny *Records*, vol. 2, p. 210.
3 W. H. Humphreys 'Adventures of an English Officer in Greece,' *New Monthly Magazine*, London 1826, p. 174.
4 Buxton Forman (ed.) *Trelawny Letters*, p. 82.
5 Humphreys *New Monthly Magazine*, p. 173.
6 Buxton Forman (ed.) *Trelawny Letters*, p. 82.
7 Reiman (ed.) *Shelley and His Circle*, vol. 5, pp. 55–6.
8 Landor *Imaginary Conversations*, p. 196–8.
9 Trelawny *Adventures*, pp. 238–9.
10 *Shelley and Mary*, p. 1025.
11 *Shelley and Mary*, p. 1029.
12 *Shelley and Mary*, p. 1027.
13 Finlay Papers.
14 Buxton Forman (ed.) *Trelawny Letters* p. 286.
15 *Shelley and Mary*, p. 1026.
16 Humphreys *New Monthly Magazine*, p. 175.
17 Stanhope Papers, K.121.
18 Stanhope Papers, K. 121.
19 Stanhope Papers, K. 121.
20 Buxton Forman (ed.) *Trelawny Letters*, p. 286.
21 Buxton Forman (ed.) *Trelawny Letters*, p. 286.
22 Parry *The Last Days of Lord Byron*, p. 356.

CHAPTER SEVEN

1 Howe *Letters & Journals,* p. 29.
2 Howe *Letters & Journals*, p. 104.
3 C. Swan *Journal of a Voyage up the Mediterranean*, vol. 2, London, 1826, p. 24.
4 Parry *The Last Days of Lord Byron*, p. 354.

5 G. Jarvis *His Journal and Related Documents*, Thessaloniki, 1964, p. 97.
6 Trelawny *Records*, vol. 2, p. 172.
7 Trelawny *Records*, vol. 2, p. 173.
8 Parry *The Last Days of Lord Byron*, p. 356.
9 Jarvis *His Journal and Related Documents*, p. 194.
10 Jarvis *His Journal and Related Documents*, p. 195.
11 Jarvis *His Journal and Related Documents*, p. 195.
12 Jarvis *His Journal and Related Documents*, p. 196.
13 Jarvis *His Journal and Related Documents*, pp. 240–1.
14 Jarvis *His Journal and Related Documents*, p. 196.
15 Finlay Papers.
16 Jarvis *His Journal and Related Documents*, p. 245.
17 Jarvis *His Journal and Related Documents*, pp. 245–6.
18 Jarvis *His Journal and Related Documents*, pp. 246–7.
19 Jarvis *His Journal and Related Documents*, pp. 248–9.
20 Jarvis *His Journal and Related Documents*, p. 250.
21 Jarvis *His Journal and Related Documents*, p. 210.
22 Jarvis *His Journal and Related Documents*, p. 215.
23 Trelawny *Records,* vol. 2, p. 176.
24 F. D. Bacon *Journal of Travels and Wanderings by Major D'Arcy Bacon of the 19th Light Dragoons*, Bodleian Library, Oxford.
25 Bacon *Journal of Travels and Wanderings*.
26 Bacon *Journal of Travels and Wanderings*.
27 Trelawny *Records*, vol. 2, pp. 183–4.
28 National Archives, Athens.
29 Trelawny *Records*, vol. 2, p. 201.

CHAPTER EIGHT

1 T. Hope *Anastasius: Memoirs of a Greek*, London, 1819, p. 4.
2 W. G. Whitcombe *Sketches of Modern Greece, illustrative of the leading events of the revolution by a Young English Volunteer in the Greek Service*, London, 1828.
3 Howe *Letters & Journals*, p. 290.
4 C. W. J. Eliot *Campaign of the Falieri and Piraeus in the Year 1827*, Princeton, 1992, pp. 30–1.
5 London Greek Committee Archives, Athens.
6 Bulwer *An Autumn in Greece*, p. 82.
7 Finlay Papers, p. 338.
8 Whitcombe *Sketches*, vol. 1, p. 170.
9 Whitcombe *Sketches*, vol. 1, pp. 181–2.
10 Gordon *History of the Greek Revolution*, vol. 2, p. 195.
11 Finlay Papers, p. 357.
12 Howe *Letters & Journals*, p. 291.
13 Howe *Letters & Journals*, p. 291.
14 Howe *Letters & Journals*, p. 385.
15 Howe *Letters & Journals*, p. 385.
16 Howe *Letters & Journals*, pp. 385–6.
17 Howe *Letters & Journals*, p. 42.
18 Whitcombe *Sketches*, vol. 2, p. 82.
19 Whitcombe *Sketches*, vol. 2, p. 64.
20 Whitcombe *Sketches*, vol. 2, p. 95.
21 Whitcombe *Sketches*, vol. 2, p. 108.

CHAPTER NINE

1 Hope *Anastasius*, vol. 1, pp. 211–13.
2 PRO CO 136/502.
3 Kingston Stocking (ed.) *The Journals of Claire Clairmont*, p. 332.
4 Trelawny *Adventures*, p. 511.
5 Trelawny *Records*, vol. 2, pp. 186–7.
6 National Archives, Athens.
7 National Archives, Athens.
8 Jarvis *His Journal and Related Documents*, p. 246.
9 Howe *An Historical Sketch*, p. 253.
10 Howe *An Historical Sketch*, p. 253.
11 Howe *An Historical Sketch*, p. 253.
12 Howe *An Historical Sketch*, p. 254.
13 Howe *An Historical Sketch*, p. 254.
14 Humphreys, *New Monthly Magazine*, p. 202.
15 Trelawny *Records*, vol. 2, pp. 190–3.
16 Trelawny *Records*, vol. 2, p. 196.
17 Trelawny *Records*, vol. 2, pp. 196–9.
18 Trelawny *Records*, vol. 2, p. 194.

CHAPTER TEN

1 Humphreys, *New Monthly Magazine*, p. 201.
2 Humphreys, *New Monthly Magazine*, p. 202.
3 Kingston Stocking (ed.) *The Journals of Claire Clairmont*, p. 353.
4 Kingston Stocking (ed.) *The Clairmont Correspondence*, vol. 1, p. 213.
5 Swan *Journal of a Journey up the Mediterranean*, vol. 2, pp. 95–7.
6 Swan *Journal of a Journey up the Mediterranean*, vol. 2, p. 97.
7 Howe *An Historical Sketch*, p. 253.
8. *The Times*, 14 December 1825.
9 Swan *Journal of a Journey up the Mediterranean*, vol. 2, pp. 101–2.
10 Trelawny *Records*, vol. 2, p. 197.
11 Humphreys, *New Monthly Magazine*, p. 202.
12 Humphreys, *New Monthly Magazine*, p. 202.
13 Humphreys, *New Monthly Magazine*, p. 204.
14 Humphreys, *New Monthly Magazine*, p. 205.
15 Humphreys, *New Monthly Magazine*, p. 206.
16 Humphreys, *New Monthly Magazine*, p. 206.
17 Humphreys, *New Monthly Magazine*, p. 206.
18 W. H. Humphreys *A Picture of Greece in 1825*, London, 1826, p. 332.
19 Humphreys, *New Monthly Magazine*, p. 207.

20 Swan *Journal of a Journey up the Mediterranean*, vol. 2, pp. 100–125.
21 Humphreys, *New Monthly Magazine*, p. 207.
22 Humphreys, *New Monthly Magazine*, pp. 207–8.
23 Hawkins Papers, Chichester.
24 Humphreys, *New Monthly Magazine*, p. 208.

CHAPTER ELEVEN

1 Howe *Letters & Journals*, p. 187.
2 G.L.R.O., Acc/260/1.
3 Bacon *Journal of Travels and Wanderings*.
4 Bacon *Journal of Travels and Wanderings*.
5 Bacon *Journal of Travels and Wanderings*.
6 Trelawny *Records*, vol. 2, pp. 178–82.
7 Bacon *Journal of Travels and Wanderings*.
8 Bacon *Journal of Travels and Wanderings*.
9 Bacon *Journal of Travels and Wanderings*.
10 Bacon *Journal of Travels and Wanderings*.
11 De Sismondi, *New Monthly Magazine*, 1826, p. 90.
12 Bacon *Journal of Travels and Wanderings*.
13 Howe *Letters & Journals*, p. 43.
14 PRO, FO 78/139.
15 Bacon *Journal of Travels and Wanderings*.
16 National Archives, Athens.
17 Bacon *Journal of Travels and Wanderings*.
18 Bacon *Journal of Travels and Wanderings*.
19 Bacon *Journal of Travels and Wanderings*.
20 Clarke, Pt 2, Section 3, p. 213.
21 Bacon *Journal of Travels and Wanderings*.
22 National Archives, Athens.
23 Bacon *Journal of Travels and Wanderings*.
24 Bacon *Journal of Travels and Wanderings*.
25 Bacon *Journal of Travels and Wanderings*.
26 Bacon *Journal of Travels and Wanderings*.
27 Bacon *Journal of Travels and Wanderings*.
28 Bacon *Journal of Travels and Wanderings*.
29 Bacon *Journal of Travels and Wanderings*.
30 Bacon *Journal of Travels and Wanderings*.
31 Bacon *Journal of Travels and Wanderings*.
32 Bacon *Journal of Travels and Wanderings*.
33 Bacon *Journal of Travels and Wanderings*.
34 Buxton Forman (ed.) *Trelawny Letters*, p. 91.
35 Buxton Forman (ed.) *Trelawny Letters*, p. 92.
36 PRO, ADM 53/1251.

CHAPTER TWELVE

1 Hope *Anastasius*, vol. 3, p. 432.
2 S. G. Howe 'From the Memoirs of a Traveller in the East,' *New England Magazine*, 1831, p. 387.
3 Howe *New England Magazine*, p. 387.
4 Howe *Journal*, p. 103.
5 Howe *New England Magazine*, p. 387.
6 Howe *New England Magazine*, p. 387.
7 Howe *Journal*, pp. 106–108.
8 Humphreys *New Monthly Magazine*, p. 208.
9 Swan *Journal of a Journey up the Mediterranean*, vol. 2, p. 185.
10 Whitcombe *Sketches*, vol. 2, p. 108.
11 Whitcombe *Sketches*, vol. 2, pp. 141–2.

12 Whitcombe *Sketches,* vol. 2, pp. 149–50.
13 Whitcombe *Sketches,* vol. 2, p. 150.
14 Whitcombe *Sketches,* vol. 2, p. 333.
15 Whitcombe *Sketches,* vol. 2, p. 296.
16 Howe *Journal,* p. 112.
17 Whitcombe *Sketches,* vol. 1, pp. 109–111.
18 Trelawny *Records,* vol. 2, pp. 195–96.
19 Hope *Anastasius,* vol. 3, p. 423.
20 Hope *Anastasius,* vol. 3, pp. 400–401.
21 Hope *Anastasius,* vol. 3, p. 416.
22 H. W. Garrod (ed.) *The Poetical Works of Keats,* London, 1956, p. 220.
23 Swan *Journal of a Journey up the Mediterranean,* vol. 2, p. 187.
24 Whitcombe *Sketches,* vol. 2, p. 210.
25 Whitcombe *Sketches,* vol. 2, p. 367.
26 Whitcombe *Sketches,* vol. 2, p. 391.

CHAPTER THIRTEEN

1 Trelawny *Records,* vol. 2, pp. 205–6.
2 Swan *Journal of a Journey up the Mediterranean,* vol. 2, pp. 171–3.
3 Swan *Journal of a Journey up the Mediterranean,* vol. 2, pp. 180–81.
4 Reiman (ed.) *Shelley and His Circle,* vol. 5, p. 55.
5 Swan *Journal of a Journey up the Mediterranean,* vol. 2, p. 194.
6 Swan *Journal of a Journey up the Mediterranean,* vol. 2, p. 193.
7 Buxton Forman (ed.) *Trelawny Letters,* p. 94.
8 Buxton Forman (ed.) *Trelawny Letters,* p. 90.
9 Buxton Forman (ed.) *Trelawny Letters,* p. 95.
10 Buxton Forman (ed.) *Trelawny Letters,* pp. 97–8.
11 Buxton Forman (ed.) *Trelawny Letters,* pp. 95–6.
12 Buxton Forman (ed.) *Trelawny Letters,* pp. 102–3.
13 Forman Buxton (ed.) *Trelawny Letters,* p. 110.

14 National Archives, Athens.
15 National Archives, Athens.
16 Buxton Forman (ed.) *Trelawny Letters,* pp. 98–9.
17 Buxton Forman (ed.) *Trelawny Letters,* p. 99.
18 Buxton Forman (ed.) *Trelawny Letters,* p. 103.
19 Down *Nineteenth Century and After,* p. 804.
20 Down *Nineteenth Century and After,* p. 804.
21 Kingston Stocking (ed.) *The Clairmont Correspondence,* vol. 1, p. 236.
22 Sharp *The Life and Letters of Joseph Severn,* pp. 264–5.
23 Down *Nineteenth Century and After,* p. 806.
24 Buxton Forman (ed.) *Trelawny Letters,* pp. 109–10.
25 Buxton Forman (ed.) *Trelawny Letters,* p. 111.

CHAPTER FOURTEEN

1 Finlay *History,* p. 14.
2 Buxton Forman (ed.) *Trelawny Letters,* p. 105.
3 Buxton Forman (ed.) *Trelawny Letters,* p. 166.
4 Hawkins Papers, Truro.
5 Godwin, W. *Cloudesley: A Tale.* Vol. 3, pp. 152–7, London 1838.
6 Buxton Forman (ed.) *Trelawny Letters,* pp. 111–12.
7 Buxton Forman (ed.) *Trelawny Letters,* p. 116.
8 Kingston Stocking (ed.) *The Clairmont Correspondence,* vol. 1, p. 258.
9 Buxton Forman (ed.) *Trelawny Letters,* pp. 116–17.
10 Buxton Forman (ed.) *Trelawny Letters,* p. 118.
11 F. L. Jones (ed.) *Maria Gisborne and Edward E. Williams:Their Journals and Letters,* Norman, Oklahoma, 1951, p. 142.

REFERENCE NOTES

12 Buxton Forman (ed.) *Trelawny Letters*, p. 131.
13 Buxton Forman (ed.) *Trelawny Letters*, p. 131.
14 Buxton Forman (ed.) *Trelawny Letters*, pp. 140–1.
15 Buxton Forman (ed.) *Trelawny Letters*, pp. 111–12.
16 Buxton Forman (ed.) *Trelawny Letters*, pp. 174–5.
17 *Westminster Review*, July 1832, pp. 34–52.
18. *Westminster Review*, July 1832, pp. 34–52.
19 *Westminster Review*, July 1832, pp. 34–52.
20 *Westminster Review*, July 1832, pp. 34–52.
21 Trelawny *Adventures*, p. 12.
22 Forman Dixon (ed.) *Trelawny Letters*, pp. 165–66.
23 Buxton Forman (ed.) *Trelawny Letters*, p. 139.
24 Buxton Forman (ed.) *Trelawny Letters*, pp. 138–9.
25 Marshall *The Life and Letters of Mary Wollstonecraft Shelley*, vol. 2, p. 215.
26 Marshall *The Life and Letters of Mary Wollstonecraft Shelley*, vol. 2, p. 218.
27 Buxton Forman (ed.) *Trelawny Letters*, p. 166.
28 Buxton Forman (ed.) *Trelawny Letters*, pp. 171–2.
29 Kingston Stocking *The Clairmont Correspondence*, vol. 1, p. 279.
30 Quoted in Grylls, p. 167.
31 Quoted in Grylls, p. 240.
32 F. A. Butler *The Journal of Frances Anne Butler* (F. A. Kemble), vol. 2, London, 1835, pp. 237–8.
33 Quoted in Grylls from *The Articulate Sisters*, pp. 240–1.
34 C. Mathews *A Continuation of the Memoirs of Charles Mathews*, vol. 4, London, 1839, p. 311.
35 Buxton Forman (ed.) *Trelawny Letters*, pp. 186–7.
36 Beinecke Rare Book and Manuscript Library. William A. Speck Collection of Goetheana YCGL6/4.
37 Beinecke YCGL 6/4.
38 H. J. Massingham *The Friend of Shelley*, London, 1930, p. 235.
39 Butler *Journal*, vol. 2, p. 287.
40 Buxton Forman (ed.) *Trelawny Letters*, pp. 190–91.
41 Mathews *A Continuation of the Memoirs*, vol. 4, p. 314.
42 Beinecke YCGL 6/4.
43 Beinecke YCGL 6/4.
44 Buxton Forman (ed.) *Trelawny Letters*, pp. 194–5.
45 W. B. Pope IV (ed.) *The Diary of B. R. Haydon*, vol. 4, Harvard, 1963, p. 326.
46 Pope (ed.) *Diary of B. R. Haydon*, vol. 4, p. 329.
47 *Select Letters and Journals of Fanny Appleton Longfellow*, New York, 1956, p. 41.
48 *The Letters of Caroline Norton to Lord Melbourne*, Ohio, 1972, pp. 133–4.
49 Pope (ed.) *Diary of B. R. Haydon*, vol. 4, p. 625.
50 Buxton Forman (ed.) *Trelawny Letters*, p. 194.
51 Buxton Forman (ed.) *Trelawny Letters*, p. 208.
52 Buxton Forman (ed.) *Trelawny Letters*, pp. 208–9.
53 Buxton Forman (ed.) *Trelawny Letters*, p. 196.
54 PRO, WO 31/647.
55 PRO, WO 31/678.
56 Eliot *Campaign of the Falieri and Piraeus in the Year 1827*, p. 37.
57 Buxton Forman (ed.) *Trelawny Letters*, pp. 182–4.

CHAPTER FIFTEEN

1 Edgcumbe *Edward Trelawny: A Biographical Sketch*, p. 5.
2 Buxton Forman (ed.) *Trelawny Letters*, p. 229.
3 J. H. Clark *Reminiscences of*

Monmouthshire, Usk, 1908, pp. 61–2.

4 M. Rolleston *Talks with Lady Shelley*, London, 1925, p. 65.

5 Rolleston *Talks with Lady Shelley*, p. 92.

6 Quoted in Grylls, p. 209.

7 Kingston Stocking (ed.) *The Clairmont Correspondence*, vol. 2, p. 599.

8 *National Magazine*, 1858, IV, pp. 47–51.

9 *National Magazine*, 1858, IV, pp. 47–51.

10 M. B. Byrde 'Trelawny at Usk,' *Athenaeum*, August 1897.

11 Buxton Forman (ed.) *Trelawny Letters*, pp. 216–17.

12 M. Blind 'Mr Trelawny on Byron and Shelley,' *Whitehall Review*, 10 January 1880.

13 J. Miller, Trelawny with Shelley and Byron, New Jersey 1922 p. 24.

14 W. Holman Hunt *Pre-Raphaelistism and the Pre-Raphaelite Brotherhood*, vol. 2, London, 1905, pp. 240–2.

15 Blind *Whitehall Review*, 10 January 1880.

16 C. Y. Lang (ed.) *The Swinburne Letters*, vol. 2, New Haven, 1962, p. 332.

17 Lang *The Swinburne Letters*, vol. 2, p. 16.

18 W. M. Rossetti *Some Reminiscences*, London, 1906, p. 373.

19 Rossetti *Reminiscences*, p. 371.

20 O. Barnard (ed.) *The Diary of W. M. Rossetti 1870–1873*, Oxford, 1977, pp. 145–7.

21 Barnard (ed.) *The Diary of W. M. Rossetti*, pp. 149–50.

22 Blind *Whitehall Review*, 10 January 1880.

23 Barnard (ed.) *The Diary of W. M. Rossetti*, pp. 167–8.

24 T. Hake and A. Compton-Rickett *The Life and Letters of Theodore Watts-Dunton*, vol. 2, London, 1916, p. 16.

25 Blind *Whitehall Review*, 10 January 1880.

26 Buxton Forman (ed.) *Trelawny Letters*, p. 232.

27 Trelawny *Records*, pp. 229–30.

28 R. Garnett *Fortnightly Review*, June 1878, p. 852.

29 Garnett *Fortnightly Review*, June 1878, p. 866.

30 E. J. Trelawny *Athenaeum* 1878, p. 144.

31 G. J. Harney, Dobell Papers, 29 August 1885, Bodleian Library, Oxford.

32 Lady Ann Blunt *Journals*, 20 October 1878, British Library, London.

33 E. Carpenter *My Days and Dreams*, London, 1910, pp. 119–23.

34 Rossetti *Reminiscences*, p. 369.

35 Buxton Forman (ed.) *Trelawny Letters*, p. 106.

36 Buxton Forman (ed.) *Trelawny Letters*, p. 150.

37 Buxton Forman (ed.) *Trelawny Letters*, p. 120.

38 Buxton Forman (ed.) *Trelawny Letters*, pp. 232–235.

39 Buxton Forman (ed.) *Trelawny Letters*, p. 225.

40 Buxton Forman (ed.) *Trelawny Letters*, p. 230.

41 Buxton Forman (ed.) *Trelawny Letters*, p. 230.

42 Buxton Forman (ed.) *Trelawny Letters*, p. 246.

43 Buxton Forman (ed.) *Trelawny Letters*, p. 227.

44 Buxton Forman (ed.) *Trelawny Letters*, pp. 220–222.

45 Buxton Forman (ed.) *Trelawny Letters*, p. 130.

46 J. G. Millais *The Life and Letters of Sir John Everett Millais*, vol. 2, London 1899, p. 51.

47 J. G. Millais *Life and Letters*, vol. 2, p. 51.

48 Quoted in Grylls, p. 226.

49 Stanhope Papers, K121, Athens.

50 R. Gittings and J. Manton *Claire Clairmont and the Shelleys 1789–1879*, London, 1992, p. 223.

51 Gittings and Manton *Claire Clairmont and the Shelleys*, p. 245.

52 *Shelley and His Circle*, vol. 5, pp. 77–8.

53 Sir Sidney Colvin *Memories of Persons and Places*, London, 1921, pp. 243–52.

54 Colvin *Memories of Persons and Places*, pp. 243–52.

55 Colvin *Memories of Persons and Places*, pp. 243–52.

56 Colvin *Memories of Persons and Places*, pp. 243–52.

57 Massingham *The Friend of Shelley*, p. 300.

58 R. Edgcumbe *Talks with Trelawny*, Temple Bar 89, 1890, p. 29. London.

59 Buxton Forman (ed.) *Trelawny Letters*, p. 232.

60 Buxton Forman (ed.) *Trelawny Letters*, p. 273.

61 Rossetti *Reminiscences*, p. 378.

62 Buxton Forman (ed.) *Trelawny Letters*, p. 278.

63 Buxton Forman (ed.) *Trelawny Letters*, p. 283.

64 National Archives, Athens.

65 Colvin *Memories of Persons and Places*, p. 252.

SOURCES TO NOTES

1 PRO, ADM 1/270.

2 PRO, ADM 1/270.

3 Finlay Papers.

4 G. Finlay *History of the Greek Revolution*, London, 1971, p. 344.

5 Quoted in F.D. Ferriman *Some English Philhellenes: Frank Abney Hastings*, London, 1913.

6 Buxton Forman (ed.) *Trelawny Letters*, p. 272.

7 Trelawny, *Letters*, pp. 253–254.

8 D. Urquhart *The Spirit of the East*, London, 1839, pp. 88–9.

9 Finlay *History*, p. xv.

10 F. L. Jones [ed.] *Maria Gisborne and Edward Williams: Their Journals and Letters*, Norman, Oklahoma, 1951, p. 5.

11 Finlay Papers.

12 London Greek Committee Archives, Athens.

13 T. G. Barber *Byron and Where He is Buried*, Hucknall, 1939, pp. 136–7.

14 Finlay Papers.

15 Whitcombe, *Sketches*, vol. 1, pp. 171–3.

16 London Greek Committee Archives, Athens.

17 Howe, *Sketch*, p. 108.

18 Bacon, *Journal*.

19 Bacon, *Journal*.

20 London Greek Committee Archives, Athens.

21 PRO WO1 161.

22 Gordon, *History*, vol. II, pp. 137–8.

23 Down, p. 806.

24 Buxton Forman [ed.] Trelawny, *Letters*, p. 158.

25 Buxton Forman [ed.] Trelawny, *Letters*, p. 171.

26 Buxton Forman [ed.] *Trelawny Letters*, vol. 2, pp. 171–2.

27 J. Marshall, Royal Naval Biography, Or Memoirs of the Services. . . , London, 1823–35, Vol. iv, ii p. 137.

SOURCES AND
SELECT BIBLIOGRAPHY

MANUSCRIPT SOURCES

There is a wealth of Trelawny letters in private hands and libraries in Europe and America, but the principal sources relating to his family are held in two collections:

Papers relating to the Hawkins and Trelawny families (East Sussex Record Office, Chichester)

Papers relating to the Hawkins and Trelawny families (Cornwall Record Office, Truro)

For Trelawny's time in Italy and Greece there are valuable letters and documents among the Abinger Papers (Bodleian Library, Oxford) and in the British Library. In Greece the three collections that throw most light on his activities are:

Finlay and Hastings Papers (British School at Athens)

Stanhope Papers (National Archives, Athens)

Archives of the London Greek Committee (National Library, Athens)

For the Mavre Troupa and the chronology of Trelawny's escape, there are valuable details to be found among papers in the National Archives, Athens, and in Admiralty Log Books at the PRO. The most important unpublished source for this is:

Journal of Travels and Wanderings by Major D'Arcy Bacon of the 19th Light Dragoons (Bodleian Library, Oxford)

For Trelawny's time in America, there is an interesting group of letters in the Beinecke Rare Book and Manuscript Library, Yale University.

PRINTED SOURCES

G. Anakis and E. Demetracopoulou (eds) *G. Jarvis: His Journal and Related Documents*, Thessaloniki, 1964.

M. Armstrong *Trelawny: A Man's Life*, New York, 1940.

B. Bennet *The Letters of Mary Wollstonecraft Shelley*, Baltimore & London, 1983.

G. Biagi *The Last Days of Shelley*, London, 1898.

Lady Blessington *Conversations of Lord Byron*, London 1834.

M. Blind 'Mr Trelawny on Byron and Shelley,' *Whitehall Review*, 10 January 1880.

O. Bornand (ed.) *The Diary of W. M. Rossetti 1870–1873*, Oxford, 1977.

J. H. Browne 'Voyage from Leghorn to Cephalonia and a Narrative of a Visit in 1823 to the Seat of War in Greece,' *Blackwood's Edinburgh Magazine*, 1834.

M. B. Byrde 'Trelawny at Usk,' *Athenaeum*, London, 1897.

E. Clarke *Travels in Various Countries of Europe, Asia and Africa, London, 1810–23*, London, 1839.

J. H. Clark *Reminiscences of Monmouthshire*, Usk, 1908.

T. Colocotrones *An Autobiography*, trans. Mrs Edmonds, London, 1892.

T. C. Down 'Pirate Trelawny', *The Nineteenth Century and After*, London, 1907.

R. Edgcumbe *Edward Trelawny: A Biographical Sketch*, Plymouth, 1882.

C. W. J. Elliot (ed.) *Campaign of the Falieri and Piraeus in the Year 1827*, Princeton, 1992.

P. Feldman and D. Scott-Kilvert *The Journals of Mary Shelley*, Oxford, 1987.

P. Gamba *A Narrative of Lord Byron's Last Journey to Greece*, London, 1825.

R. Gissing & J. M. Gissing *Claire Clairmont and the Shelleys 1798–1879*, Oxford, 1992.

R. Glynn Grylls *Trelawny*, London, 1950.

T. Gordon *History of the Greek Revolution*, London, 1832.

T. Hake and A. C. Rickett *The Life and Letters of Theodore Watts-Dunton*, London, 1916.

R. Holmes *Shelley: The Pursuit*, London 1974.

T. Hope *Anastasius: Memoirs of a Greek*, London, 1819.

S. G. Howe *An Historical Sketch of the Greek Revolution*, New York, 1828.
 – 'From the Mss. of a Traveller in the East,' *New England Magazine*, 1831.

W. H. Humphreys 'Adventures of an English Officer in Greece,' *New Monthly Magazine*, London, 1826.

W. H. Humphreys, J. Emerson and Count Pecchio *A Picture of Greece in 1825*, London, 1826.

F. L. Jones (ed.) *The Journal of Edward Ellerker Williams, 21 October 1821– 4 July 1822*, Norman, 1951.

M. Kingston Stocking (ed.) *The Clairmont Correspondence: The Letters of Claire Clairmont, Charles Clairmont and Fanny Imlay Godwin*, Baltimore & London, 1995.
 – *The Journals of Claire Clairmont*, Cambridge Mass, 1968.

W. S. Landor *Imaginary Conversations of Literary Men and Statesmen*, Second Series, Volume One, London, 1829.

C. Y. Lang *The Swinburne Letters*, New Haven, 1962.

D. Langley Moore *The Late Lord Byron*, London, 1961.

– *Lord Byron: Accounts Rendered*, London, 1974.

S. Linnér (ed.) *W. H. Humphreys: First Journal of the Greek War of Independence*, Stockholm, 1967.

H. Lytton Bulwer *An Autumn in Greece*, London, 1826.

F. A. Kemble *Journal of Frances Anne Butler*, London, 1835.

L. Marchand *Byron: A Biography*, London, 1957.

– (ed.) *Letters and Journals of Lord Byron*, London, 1980.

J. Marshall *The Life and Letters of Mary Wollstonecraft Shelley*, London, 1889.

H. J. Massingham *The Friend of Shelley*, London, 1930.

J. Miller *Trelawny With Shelley and Byron*, New Jersey, 1922.

J. Millingen *Memoirs of the Affairs of Greece*, London, 1831.

H. Nicholson *Byron: The Last Journey*, London 1924.

I. Origo *The Last Attachment*, London, 1949.

W. Parry *The Last Days of Lord Byron*, London, 1825.

M. Raybaud *Memoires sur la Grèce, pour servir a l'histoire de la Guerre de l'Independence*, Paris, 1824.

D. H. Reiman (ed.) *Shelley and His Circle: Documents in the Carl H. Pforzheimer Library*, Cambridge Mass, 1973.

L. E. Richards (ed.) *The Letters and Journals of Samuel Gridley Howe During the Greek Revolution*, Boston, 1907.

M. Rolleston *Talks with Lady Shelley*, London, 1925.

F. B. Sanborne 'Odysseus and Trelawny,' *Scribner's Magazine*, April 1897.

W. Sharp (ed.) *The Life and Letters of Joseph Severn*, London, 1892.

W. St. Clair *Trelawny: The Incurable Romancer*, London, 1977.

– *That Greece Might Still Be Free*, London, 1972.

C. Swan *Journal of a Voyage up the Mediterranean*, London, 1826.

J. Temple-Leader *Rough and Rambling Notes of My Early Life*, Florence, 1899.

E. J. Trelawny *Adventures of a Younger Son*, E. Garnett (ed.), London, 1891.

– *Recollections of the Last Days of Shelley and Bryon*, London, 1858.

– *Records of Shelley, Byron and the Author*, London, 1878.

F-M. Tsigakou *The Rediscovery of Greece*, London, 1981.

D. Urquhart *The Spirit of the East*, London, 1839.

G. Waddington *A Visit to Greece in 1823 and 1824*, London, 1825.

W. G. Whitcombe *Sketches of Modern Greece Illustrative of the Leading Events of the Revolution by a Young English Volunteer in the Greek Service*, London, 1828.

INDEX

Ghouras, General 111, 115, 174, 175,
176, 178, 192, 195, 196, 198,
211–212, 213, 216, 218, 245, 246,
247–250, 252, 257, 265, 270, 318
Gill 136, 146, 147, 150, 156
Gillespie, Colonel Rollo 20
Gissing, George 312
Godwin, William 51, 287–8, 347
Goethe 35, 131
Gordon, Thomas 7, 82, 94–95, 96, 106,
113, 128, 147, 187, 240, 360,
369–370
Gravia 106
Gregorius, Patriarch 94, 362
Guiccioli, Teresa 34, 45, 62, 66, 70, 84
Guilford, Lord 131

Hamilton, Captain Gawen 220–222, 237,
239, 243–245, 271, 319–20, 371
Hardy, Thomas 121, 316
Harney, G.J. 343
Harrington, Lord 140
Hastings, Frank Abney 6, 7, 96, 110,
111, 128, 163, 164, 206, 283,
359–360, 362–363, 364
Hawkins, Sir Christopher 11, 223, 286
Hawkins, John 12, 21
Hawkins, Mary (see Trelawny, Mary)
Haydon, Benjamin 312–313, 315
Heise, J. 5, 159
Helen of Troy 182
Hercules 65–70, 71, 82, 85, 86, 272
Hind, HMS 111, 177
Hobhouse, John Cam 60, 140, 223, 321,
363
Hodges 136, 139
Hogg, Thomas Jefferson 322, 326, 338,
347
Hope, Thomas 179, 184, 263, 264, 265
Hopkins, G.M. 311
Hotel Grand Bretagne 3
Howe, Samuel Gridley 159, 179,
187–191, 202, 203, 213, 214, 226,

254–257, 259, 261, 265, 268, 365,
370
Hucknall 132–133, 134
Humphreys, William 91, 96, 111, 118,
122, 128, 134, 145–146, 149, 156,
157, 161, 166, 191–192, 195, 202,
204, 206, 209–225, 237, 246, 257,
268, 296, 318, 356
Hunt, John 140, 142, 155, 277
Hunt, Leigh 44, 48, 57, 62, 86, 155,
273, 277, 284, 322, 347
Hunt, W. Holman 333–4
Hydra 82, 83, 98, 100, 110, 173, 242,
243, 254, 257, 261, 265

Ibrahim Pasha 187, 191, 200, 214, 220,
241, 242, 243, 277, 278, 282–283
Iolanda 177
Ioannina 105

Jackson, Reverend 66
James, Henry 346
James, Robert 182
Jarvis, George 158, 159–178, 185, 197,
199, 200, 202, 214–215, 219, 221,
242–243, 268, 318, 364–365
Java 19–20
Jerusalem Monastery 216, 248

Kakoreme 145, 216, 250, 364
Kalamata 82
Kalavrita 360
Kariaskaki 204, 213, 217
Keates, Captain 15
Keats, John 7, 8, 47, 56, 58, 62, 265,
294, 298, 312, 322, 334
Keble, John 10
Kemble, Fanny 304–5, 308, 309, 312,
313, 316, 347
Kennedy, Dr James 122
Kensal Green Cemetery 321–3
Kirkup, Seymour 144, 149, 161, 287,
296, 314, 315